Combat Films

For Patrick,

General Hood may have lost Little Round Top but you won a place in our cinematic hearts forever!

All Best,

Steven
8/12

Combat Films

American Realism, 1945–2010

SECOND EDITION

Steven Jay Rubin

McFarland & Company, Inc., Publishers

Jefferson, North Carolina, and London

Photographs are from the author's collection unless noted otherwise.

LIBRARY OF CONGRESS CATALOGUING-IN-PUBLICATION DATA

Rubin, Steven Jay, 1951–
Combat films : American realism, 1945–2010 /
Steven Jay Rubin.— 2d ed.
p.   cm.
Includes bibliographical references and index.

ISBN 978-0-7864-5892-9
softcover : 50# alkaline paper ∞

1. War films — History and criticism.
2. Motion pictures — United States — History — 20th century.
I. Title.
PN1995.9.W3R82 2011   791.43'658 — dc23   2011019217

BRITISH LIBRARY CATALOGUING DATA ARE AVAILABLE

On the cover: Scene from the Normandy landings sequence
from the 1998 film *Saving Private Ryan* (DreamWorks/Photofest)

Manufactured in the United States of America

McFarland & Company, Inc., Publishers
Box 611, Jefferson, North Carolina 28640
www.mcfarlandpub.com

To the men and women of our armed forces,
who jeopardize their lives every day
to keep us safe in our beds.

And to the filmmakers who go the extra mile
to immortalize some of those stories with
a sense of realism and respect.

Table of Contents

Acknowledgments

Forgive me for sounding like my grandfather, but I started writing before there were computers. Back in the 1970s, I looked up filmmakers at the library of the Academy of Motion Picture Arts and Sciences, typed their names on a Remington portable and picked up the phone and called them. I had no idea what other movies they had done. There was no computerized list of their credits.

Today, the job of the researcher is much easier. Most of the time, you don't even have to leave your desk at home. If I'm writing about screenwriter Robert Pirosh (*Battleground, Go for Broke, Hell Is for Heroes, Combat!*) and I want to know what he was writing in 1950, all I have to do is get on the Internet, go to IMDb.com and I'll get a list of all of his credits and the date they were released. As the monk once said in that adorable Xerox commercial after he's received 50 copies of the manuscript that once took him five years to hand copy: "It's a miracle."

And, yet, you still need resources and there is none better than the Academy Library. Now located in a modern facility that was once a substation of the Los Angeles Department of Water and Power on La Cienega Boulevard, the library still has files on every motion picture ever made and you can take your laptop computer in there and type to your heart's content. I salute the Academy and the enormous service they provide to film researchers. I am particularly indebted to their Special Collections department, which provided me with a treasure trove of information from the Gregory Peck special collection, for my new chapter on *Pork Chop Hill.*

I would like to thank Colonel Joseph Clemons, U.S. Army (Ret.), and his lovely wife, Cecil, who provided me with some terrific background on Joe's involvement with the making of *Pork Chop Hill.* I would also like to thank Lt. Colonel Walter Russell, U.S. Army (Ret.), for agreeing to an interview. Russell is Clemons' brother-in-law and he was portrayed by Rip Torn in the film. Stunt maestro Hal Needham and actor William Wellman, Jr., also graciously agreed to be interviewed and supplied additional details on the 1958 filming.

For the chapter on *The Sand Pebbles,* I would like to thank my friends Lee Pfeiffer and Michael Thomas for supplying me with research material and photographs. Michael, in particular, supplied a wonderful interview he did with Richard Attenborough. I also thank former assistant director and cameraman, Robert Liu, who was extremely helpful in describing the logistics involved in wrangling thousands of Chinese for sequences shot on Taiwan in 1965-66.

The *Gettysburg* chapter is a product of an extensive interview I conducted with writer/director Ronald F. Maxwell in early 2010. The latter has almost total recall of the 13 years of effort he put into getting the film made. Consequently, the chapter is a perfect example of the blood, sweat and tears that filmmakers shed when getting their projects — particularly projects about history — greenlit in the modern era.

For *Platoon*, I was fortunate to get an audience with writer/director Oliver Stone, who was wonderfully accommodating in supplying me with key details of his own military service in Vietnam and how that experience influenced what I consider the greatest movie ever made about that war. I would also like to thank actor John C. McGinley who shared his experiences of working on the Philippine location. A special thanks to my friend Michael Singer who gave me access to the *Platoon* chapter he wrote as part of a projected book on Mr. Stone.

Saving Private Ryan is certainly the most successful World War II combat film of all time, and has become a critical part of the new book. I owe a debt to the dean of military technical advisors, Captain Dale Dye, U.S. Marine Corps (Ret.), who provided me with very specific details on the making of that film. I would also like to thank producer Mark Gordon, who carefully presented to me how the movie was originally conceived and sold. And a special nod to actor Tom Sizemore, who provided me with the actor's perspective on the film.

The *Black Hawk Down* chapter features some fascinating behind the scenes information provided by military technical advisor, Colonel Tom Matthews, U.S. Army (Ret.), who not only advised on the film, but actually led the air mission that supported the Battle of Mogadishu in 1991. I also acknowledge the support of production designer Arthur Max who filled me in on the details and challenges of recreating downtown Mogadishu in a poor suburb of Rabat, Morocco. For that chapter, actor Jason Isaacs, who portrayed U.S. Army Ranger Michael Steele in the film, provided me with an actor's perspective. After hating Isaacs for so many years because he had played that despicable British officer in *The Patriot*, I can safely say that I have exorcized that character for good, and I am now an unequivocal Isaacs fan. Philip Strub, the director of entertainment media at the Department of Defense, also contributed to this chapter.

For *The Hurt Locker*, I owe a debt to special effects chief, Richard Stutsman, who graciously sat down with me and explained the enormous logistical problems he faced while supplying director Kathryn Bigelow with the pyrotechnics she needed to create the Best Picture of 2009. He also supplied me with some key behind the scenes photographs. Actor Anthony Mackie, who portrayed Sergeant Sanborn, was kind enough to supply me with his actor's perspective on filming in Morocco.

For information on the support I received from the Hollywood community for the original edition of this book, I have listed the interview sources in the Bibliography, which you will find at the end of the book. Those interviews, which I conducted in Los Angeles, London and Switzerland, between 1973 and 1975, are available at the library of the American Film Institute in Los Angeles.

For additional photographic material, I would like to thank the Academy of Motion Pictures, Arts and Sciences, director Ronald F. Maxwell, Joe and Cecil Clemons, Tom Matthews, Richard Stutzman, Steve Mitchell and Eric Caidin and John Kantas of Hollywood Book and Poster.

Finally, I would like to thank my beautiful wife, Elisa, and my kids, Jaymie and Darren, for putting up with my writer's idiosyncrasies for the last year as we assembled this new edition. And to my mother, who had suggested this update years ago, I can say, "Mom, you were right!"

Introduction

This is not a story of war. Neither is it a comprehensive history of films about war. It is, instead, the story of a group of filmmakers who set out to present stories of warfare without the glory or the manufactured heroics, the very ingredients that had always lured thrill-seeking audiences into the theaters.

Thanks to this new edition of a book that was first published by McFarland & Company in 1981, I can cover the period between the end of World War II and the present. It uncovers those new attitudes, influences and technologies by looking over the shoulders of the men and women who were involved in the production of these films.

Thirty-eight years ago, I was a UCLA history major, struggling through Professor Vryonis' history of the Byzantine Empire class and writing news stories for the *Daily Bruin*. Intent on writing something more than an exposé on term paper factories, I determined to write a book about American war films. Thus, I opened the Beverly Hills phonebook and looked up screenwriter Michael Blankfort, who had written the 1950 Richard Widmark war film, *Halls of Montezuma*. I had made a list of filmmakers I wanted to interview and Blankfort was the first person on my list.

Back in 1973, there was no IMDB.com. Actually, there were no personal computers, either. My only reference source was the library of the Academy of Motion Picture Arts and Sciences, which was located in a small upstairs room above a theater on Melrose. It was there in those hallowed halls of film history that I took my notes with a portable typewriter, which I dragged into the library every day for six months.

They had a file of clippings on most every movie ever made and they also had one reference book called *Who Wrote the Movie?* So that's how I made up my list of screenwriters. Since I had no connections to agents, I simply opened the phonebook and prayed. And, truth be told, there was Michael Blankfort's name.

I called him, introduced myself as the author of a projected book on war films — primarily World War II movies — and he invited me to come over for an interview.

Blankfort was an absolute delight. This was a big thrill for me, because I had never met anyone who had worked in the movies. Actually, that's not quite true. My next-door neighbor's sister worked for MGM, and she had once invited my family and me to come see a preview screening of the Stephen Boyd, Jimmy Durante musical, *Jumbo*, at the movie theater that was located underneath the Motion Picture Academy Library.

However, Blankfort was the real deal, a screenwriter who had written one of my favorite war movies, which I had discovered on NBC's *Saturday Night at the Movies*. More importantly, Blankfort had stories to tell me about the making of that film. He had suggested to actor Richard Boone, a newcomer then, to play the whole movie as if he had a cold. Boone wasn't sure why, but his character stood out because of it. He also explained how sensitive it was that Richard Widmark's character was taking drugs while in command. Every so often in the film, medic Karl Malden would give Widmark some pills. Blankfort explained that Widmark was addicted to these drugs—something that was very atypical for World War II heroes.

Before I left Blankfort, taking with me my reel-to-reel tape recorder, he told me to give his friend Edmund North a call. North had written *Patton*. When I visited Edmund North, he gave me Robert Pirosh's number. Pirosh had written *Battleground*. In turn, Pirosh introduced me to his ex–writing partner George Seaton, who had written and directed *36 Hours*. And so on and so forth.

The result is this book, now an anthology of fifteen stories. Many of the films are well known and some have always appeared on the "Best Picture" lists of all time. However, I have not chosen the films primarily for their greatness. The interesting common denominator is that they each have a unique story to tell. Every filmmaker introduced in this book had a creative vision, but each of them faced enormous challenges to achieve that vision. These are colorful stories of the joy of initial discovery, creative passion and frustration, the genius of collaboration, the magic of performance, of logistical nightmares, location headaches, corporate indifference and interference, followed, in all cases, by a triumph of artistic perseverance.

A passion for war pictures generally stemmed from personal experiences in war or a fascination with the subject.

Producer Darryl F. Zanuck, who personally produced more World War II films than anyone while a producer and studio executive at 20th Century–Fox, was a colonel in the U.S. Army Signal Corps and saw action in North Africa and Western Europe.

Director Oliver Stone, who wrote and directed *Platoon*, which won the Oscar for Best Picture of 1986, was a combat infantryman in Vietnam. The screenplay he wrote was based on his personal experiences "on the line."

Ditto for screenwriter Robert Pirosh, who won as Oscar in 1949 for his script for *Battleground*. He was a sergeant in the 35th Infantry Division, one of the units that helped relieve the "Battered Bastards of Bastogne." The film was a tribute to the combat infantrymen he knew.

Steven Spielberg never served in the military, but he has been fascinated by World War II stories dating back to the time when he was a kid learning about his dad's military service in the Indian/Burma/China theater. That interest has led to some of the seminal war films of all time, including *Saving Private Ryan* and *Empire of the Sun*. Not to mention war elements in films like *Raiders of the Lost Ark, 1941, Schindler's List* and *Indiana Jones and the Last Crusade*.

Prolific director Lewis Milestone, forever tied to the combat film genre, was a veteran of the Signal Corps in World War I, and although he was stationed in Washington D.C., he learned a great deal from the actual combat footage that reeled through his office.

During World War II, many Hollywood artists and craftsmen were assigned stateside to the two major Signal Corps Photographic Centers at Astoria, Long Island, and Culver City, California. Future directors like Richard Goldstone (*No Man Is an Island*), David Miller (*Flying Tigers*) and Carl Foreman (*The Bridge on the River Kwai; The Guns of Navarone; The Victors*) were exposed to massive quantities of combat footage that they incorporated into hundreds of quality government-backed documentary films that covered every subject imaginable, from the art of camouflage to the treatment of sexually transmitted diseases.

Like Pirosh and Stone, there were others who saw war firsthand. Tough, outspoken director Samuel Fuller, who went on to film *The Steel Helmet, Merrill's Marauders* and *The Big Red One*, was a platoon sergeant in the 1st Infantry Division and landed in the first wave on Omaha Beach.

Writers Sy Bartlett and Beirne Lay, Jr., who collaborated on both the novel and screenplay for *Twelve O'Clock High*, served as officers with the U.S. Eighth Air Force in Europe. Bartlett would go on to produce *Pork Chop Hill* with actor Gregory Peck.

Cinematographer William Clotheir, who worked on both *Merrill's Marauders* and *The Devil's Brigade*, had been a Paramount Pictures newsreel cameraman, stationed in Madrid during the Spanish Civil War. Before he was inducted into the 9th Air Force to film documentaries with such directors as William Wyler and John Sturges, Clotheir was filming German Stuka dive-bomber raids on the Spanish capital. Wyler would later use his experience to film the classic Air Force documentary, *The Memphis Belle*, while Sturges went on to create his masterwork, *The Great Escape*, as well as *Never So Few* and *The Eagle Has Landed*.

Director Anatole Litvak spent much of pre–Pearl Harbor World War II being hounded by the German S.S. and Gestapo. He was producing French films up until the invasion of the Low Countries in May 1940 and later in the United States, where he directed the controversial anti–Nazi film, *Confessions of a Nazi Spy*, as well as *Decision Before Dawn*.

The latter film, an engrossing study of the last days of the Third Reich that was filmed in the ruins of postwar Germany was written by Peter Viertel, an American officer attached to the Office of Strategic Services (O.S.S.). While with the headquarters of the U.S. 7th Army, Viertel learned at first hand the espionage story later dramatized in *Decision Before Dawn*.

Authors Irwin Shaw and Harry Brown were both war correspondents, the former using his experiences to wrote one of the great novels of the war, *The Young Lions*, which became a 20th Century–Fox film in 1958. Brown's novel, *A Walk in the Sun*, would become the final combat film produced during the actual war.

Screenwriter James Ruffin Webb, who wrote *Pork Chop Hill* and who later wrote a preliminary draft of *Patton*, was himself an officer with General Lloyd Fredendall's II Corps in North Africa, a unit later commanded by Patton himself.

Aside from being qualified to film accurate war pictures, many of the directors went even further, developing an obsession for minute detail and realism. Kathryn Bigelow was so impressed by screenwriter Mark Boal's unique portrait of Explosive Ordinance Disposal teams operating in Iraq, that, in their movie, *The Hurt Locker,* she eschewed many typical narrative film tools to create an undeniably realistic documentary style for the film. It worked brilliantly and the film won the Oscar for Best Picture of 2009.

While filming *Patton* in Spain in 1969, director Franklin Schaffner and his crew spent days trying to figure out how to simulate the recoil of a tank that was firing dummy ammunition.

On location in France for *The Desert Fox* in 1950, director Henry Hathaway searched so hard for the scene of Rommel's encounter with strafing Spitfires that he actually found pieces of the Field Marshal's staff car alongside a road in Normandy.

Director Ronald F. Maxwell had, perhaps, the most unique experience. He was able to film important segments of his film, *Gettysburg*, on the actual locations where the battle was fought, using thousands of reenactors whose own attention to detail was incredible.

And then there were the technical advisors who brought enormous knowledge and clarity to the war film process. Captain Dale Dye, U.S. Marine Corps (Ret.), a Vietnam veteran, was hired by Oliver Stone to provide technical advising services on *Platoon*. He ended up designing an immersive boot camp that turned a bunch of pampered movie actors into steely-eyed combat soldiers. In the 1990s, he became the "go-to-guy" for war movies, especially on the enormously successful *Saving Private Ryan,* as well as two subsequent mini-series, *Band of Brothers* and *The Pacific.*

Whatever their background or obsession, they all fought the same creative battles with the studio executives, the financial backers, the advertising and promotion departments, and the naysayers who were convinced that what they were considering was sheer folly, let alone, financial disaster.

And no matter how successful the films later became, they still left behind a group of sometimes disillusioned and cynical, sometimes exultant artists, who had given there all for realism.

This book is dedicated to their willpower.

The latest edition of *Combat Films* came about for two reasons. First, McFarland's Robbie Franklin encouraged me to do a new edition and secondly, I felt that there were some truly excellent movies to talk about. After all, the last movie covered in my first edition was *Patton,* which was released more than 40 years ago.

Not only will you find seven new chapters in this book, but I went back and carefully edited the previous eight chapters, sometimes adding information that wasn't available to me back in the late 1970s. For instance, in 1993, I was able to produce a documentary for Showtime on the 30th anniversary of the making of *The Great Escape,* my all-time favorite film. With my producing partner, Deborah Goodwin, I was able to schedule some new interviews with the filmmakers, and some of that information appears here in *The Great Escape* chapter for the first time.

Once again, I believe I have chosen films with terrific stories. I spent nearly four hours with *Gettysburg* writer/director Ronald F. Maxwell who, literally, had an epic thirteen-year story to share on the making of that enormously challenging film. It reinforces the belief today that anyone who can finance, develop, produce and get distribution for a movie deserves our respect. It has become that difficult. I don't care if you're producing a movie for $100,000 or $100 million, you sweat bullets to get anything made, and the obstacles that confront today's filmmakers sometimes appear impossible to overcome. And sometimes they are. But a select few survive the travail to make truly great films and I have provided some new stories that prove that point.

Steven Jay Rubin • Los Angeles, California • 2011

SECTION I

FILMING HISTORY, NOT HEROICS

War films have been with us since the earliest days of the movie business. Even as the first cameras were being hand-cranked, filmmakers were planning battle action for the silver screen. Soon after the Spanish American War in 1898, an innovative producer created what was to be the first combat film — a recreation of the naval battle off Manila. It was filmed entirely in a wash basin with a moving backdrop, paper ships and drifting cigar smoke. The quest for realism had begun.

Nearly a century ago, pioneer filmmaker David Wark ("D.W.") Griffith, at work on the epic Civil War sequences for his controversial masterwork, *The Birth of a Nation* (1915), spoke of his own growing obsession with realism. He strongly felt that such a desire to film the truth would increase the very popularity of films themselves. He predicted that filmmakers of the future would be able to teach history through the film medium, and that when it came to realism, audiences would not settle for less.

Griffith was, of course, correct, especially in the realm of documentary films where multi-segment series like *Victory at Sea, You Are There, The 20th Century, The World at War,* and everything else you find on the History Channel, the Discovery Channel and The Learning Channel, allows contemporary students of history to study the past in moving picture form.

Still, while the movies included many of the realistic elements of the war documentaries, on the whole, Hollywood has strayed from the true portrait predicted by Griffith. In satisfying the public's desire for adventure, romance, action and pathos, the war films, for the most part, have sacrificed realism for commerciality. Only in certain individual cases have they succeeded. Certainly a film like Steven Spielberg's *Saving Private Ryan* (1998) changed that realism paradigm.

During World War II, Hollywood's dream factories created hundreds of motion pictures, many of which were government-financed training films that explained the goals and technicalities of fighting a modern global war. The narrative feature films that were Hollywood's stock-in-trade were divided between combat films and stories that used the war as a backdrop, such as William Wyler's 1942 classic, *Mrs. Miniver,* which was so anti-war, and anti–Nazi that it was rumored that Hitler himself put a price on director William Wyler's head. Wyler probably took this as an honor. Meanwhile, his film symbolized the defiance of the British people in resisting Hitler's devastating air attacks on England — the Blitz.

Many of the early narrative features that focused on the war from the soldier's point of view were outright propaganda films that emphasized a "victory in defeat" philosophy. These interesting productions were usually symbolized by a dirty, sweaty, exhausted American soldier, who (like Robert Taylor in the 1942 film *Bataan*), fought like hell to stop the onrushing hordes of the Japanese army in the Philippines. One cannot forget that final scene in the film in which Taylor, the sole survivor of his patrol, holds off waves of Japanese with a blistering blast of lead from his heavy machine gun, smoke gradually obscuring the scene, his fate tragically sealed.

Similar sequences were repeated in films like *Manila Calling, Wake Island, The Story of Dr. Wassell, Thirty Seconds Over Tokyo, Edge of Darkness* and *Flying Tigers*. The geography might be different, the branch of service or the enemy may vary, but the outcome was always the same: Glory in defeat; or as the narrator says at the conclusion of *Wake Island*, after a Marine garrison on a tiny Pacific Island has been totally wiped out: "This is not the end!"*

But the tide turned, especially after the Battle of Midway, El Alamein and Stalingrad, and motion pictures become much more confident of final victory. The grim, sweat-stained face of Robert Taylor was replaced by the more gutsy visage of Humphrey Bogart in director Zoltan Korda's 1943 film, *Sahara*. It was a movie filled to the brim with confidence.

The story was no different from that of *Bataan*, and yet the film's entire tone and texture was different. Someone had opened a window and the grim foreboding atmosphere that had been so apparent in the foggy Philippine jungles in *Bataan* was gone. Instead, there was the broiling desert landscape of Libya, a solitary tank and ten forgotten men holding off a German mechanized battalion. The difference? Our side wins!

As propaganda and glory were left behind, realism became a prime element in war films. To keep pace, Hollywood, late in the war, returned to the grim and unglamorous themes so present in the late 1930s when *The Grapes of Wrath* and *I Was a Fugitive from a Chain Gang* were telling it like it was.

---

*Wake Island, Paramount Pictures, 1942.

CHAPTER ONE

A Walk in the Sun

Director Lewis Milestone's 1946 film *A Walk in the Sun* was the last of the wartime combat films. It tells a simple story about a platoon of American soldiers who hit the beach at Salerno, in sunny Italy, and who must march six miles to take out a German strongpoint — a lone farmhouse on a strategic crossroads. It's just a little walk in the sun, but in its tense, exciting 117 minutes, director Milestone gives us an extraordinarily intimate portrait of men in war.

Here is the throbbing story of the foot-slogging infantryman who, as medical corpsman McWilliams (Sterling Holloway) points out, "Never sees nothing!" While the generals plan their grand strategy, initiate their careful tactical deployments and prepare for their map and table-oriented warfare, it is the infantryman who must fight for every yard of dirt. This is not a movie about grand strategy and who won the war in Italy. There are no scenes at headquarters, no maps and tactical information. In *A Walk in the Sun*, we are seeing the war over the shoulders of the most vulnerable combatants. As far as they're concerned, the objective is a farmhouse six miles from the beach. That's all they, and the audience, will ever know.

In the film, as an early illustration of the new emphasis on realism, the enemy is seldom seen. When the German Army does make an appearance, it remains hidden behind the machines of war. At the beginning of the film, the platoon's lieutenant is mortally wounded by a shell that appears out of nowhere, slams into the water and scatters shrapnel in all directions.

Later, McWilliams is cut down by a lone enemy fighter plane that appears briefly, killing the medic and wounding two other soldiers, and then flies back into anonymity. When the platoon later destroys an enemy armored car, there are no visible enemy casualties. Milestone's camera simply takes in a smoldering half-track. Even the unit's final objective, the Italian farmhouse, is only a building surrounded by orchards. There is initially no clue as to its occupants and the deadly reception they are preparing.

This was the war film as seen in the waning days of World War II. *A Walk in the Sun* and John Ford's PT-Boat saga, *They Were Expendable* (1945) were a different breed of motion picture — grim, serious and realistic. After six years of global warfare, American audiences had seen a thousand films about World War II and, in the wake of concentration camp photographs and atomic bombs, there was a new expectation for stories that rang true, avoided propaganda and exploitation and told it like it was.

Since the mid–1930s, Hollywood had covered the march of fascism and the alarming events that led to the European war in September 1939 and America's involvement in the war, which began at Pearl Harbor on December 7, 1941. But movie studios were not so much interested in realism, as selling tickets and churning out propaganda and training films for the U.S. Government.

Just as Detroit was converting its assembly lines from producing Fords and Chryslers to churning out M-4 Sherman tanks and Dodge weapons carriers, the Hollywood dream factories started to cover every facet of the war with their full roster of stars and a creative talent pool of writers, directors and producers.

The early movies were either about average middle-class families caught up in the war in Europe (*The Mortal Storm, Mrs. Miniver*), espionage and the rise of the Nazis (*Confessions of a Nazi Spy, Manhunt,* Charlie Chaplin's *The Great Dictator*) and the first battles of the war itself (*Bataan, Wake Island, Guadalcanal Diary, Sahara*). Dana Andrews led Russian partisans against the Nazis in *Armored Attack* (1943), then gritted his teeth as a prisoner of the Japanese in *The Purple Heart* (1944), and later took to the air as a carrier pilot in *Wing and a Prayer* (1944); John Wayne flew the P-40 with the tiger shark emblem in *Flying Tigers* (1942), hit the ground in a Navy construction battalion in *The Fighting Seabees* (1944), then fought his way

Back to Bataan (1945); Gary Cooper, with Ingrid Bergman by his side, fought the fascists in *For Whom the Bell Tolls* (1943), then joined the medical corps in the Philippines in *The Story of Dr. Wassell* (1944); Tough guy Robert Mitchum spent *Thirty Seconds Over Tokyo* (1944) with Spencer Tracy and Van Johnson, then joined Burgess Meredith's Ernie Pyle in *The Story of G.I. Joe* (1945); and Gregory Peck also took up the Russian cause in *Days of Glory* (1944).

Whether they were battling the Axis on the silver screen, or wearing real uniforms and facing real bullets in the far-flung battlefronts of the war, American movie actors and behind-the-scenes personnel contributed enormously to the war effort and helped preserve the emotional feeling of those traumatic days when the outcome of the war was still very much in doubt.

A Walk in the Sun was the product of a U.S. Army staff sergeant named Harry Brown who, in 1942, was sent to London to work on the British edition of *Yank* magazine. Brown, who had served with the Army Corps of Engi-

Harry Brown, author of the novel *A Walk in the Sun*. He would reteam with director Lewis Milestone on the screenplay for *Ocean's 11* (1960).

neers at Fort Belvoir, Virginia, before joining *Yank* in New York, was jubilant about his new assignment. "I wasn't sure what my duties would be," he later remembered, "but I thought for sure that I'd be a field reporter going on commando raids, Wilhelmshaven bombings, and other cloak and dagger operations."[1]

Before Brown left New York, he signed a contract with the publishing firm of McGraw-Hill to write a book, *Sergeant Brown Reporting*. The idea was that for every mission he undertook for *Yank*, he'd write one version for the magazine and one for the book. But much to his chagrin, things didn't work out that way. He found himself trapped as a deskman, rewriting material that the actual correspondents were turning in, and grinding out such lackluster features as *A Week of War*, and *Artie Greengroin, PFC*. This mundane routine lasted throughout 1943, and every once in a while Brown would get a letter from his publisher inquiring, about the progress of the book.

"Towards the end of the year," he recalled, "these letters had built up such a feeling of guilt in me that I felt I had to give them something. Things were going from bad to worse at *Yank*. The tensions between the New York and London offices were unbelievable. Finally, when they wished a new Major on us, the editor of the London edition and I both resigned."[2]

With a great deal of time on his hands, Brown began to nose around London, trying to fit himself into another outfit.

"I was on per diem and did not have to live in the Army barracks," he says. "So, I figured I'd better discharge my debt to McGraw-Hill. I sat down in the top room of the house I'd taken on Brompton Square, and in two weeks, working only in the evenings, I turned out a novel. I called it *A Walk in the Sun*."[3]

How do these men of the 36th "Texas" Division survive their particular brand of hell on Salerno Beach? Sergeant Brown gave them a slogan: "Nobody Dies!" It was a tough, cynical cliché in this platoon of footsore combat veterans. They knew it was a lie. They saw their lieutenant get hit in the face, their sergeant crumple full of machine gun slugs, their last commander go out of his mind. But to come out alive, they had to fight off panic with wisecracks and memories of home and pull their shattered ranks together — and then gamble their final ounce of strength in an all-out assault.

Who were these tired soldiers? Brown created them, remembering many of the letters he had once read while manning the desk at *Yank*. In the film's opening scene, actor Burgess Meredith, who had just portrayed famed war correspondent Ernie Pyle in *The Story of G.I. Joe,* introduced the men.

There was Sergeant Tyne [Dana Andrews], who never had much urge to travel. Providence, Rhode Island may not be much as cities go, but it was all he wanted, a one town man; Rivera [Richard Conte], Italian-American, likes opera and would like a wife and kids, plenty of kids; Friedman [George Tyne], lathe operator and amateur boxing champ, New York City; Windy [John Ireland] minister's son, Canton, Ohio, used to take long walks alone and just think … Sergeant Ward [Lloyd Bridges], a farmer who knows his soil, a good farmer; McWilliams [Sterling Holloway], first aid man, slow, Southern, dependable; Archembeau [Norman Lloyd], platoon scout and prophet, talks a lot but he's all right; Porter, Sergeant Porter [Herbert Rudley], he has a lot on his mind, a lot on his mind; Tranella [Danny Desmond] speaks two languages, Italian and Brooklyn. And a lot of other men."[4]

Brown sent the finished manuscript of *A Walk in the Sun* to McGraw-Hill in September 1943. Back came a letter saying, in effect, "It's a nice job, but you seem to have forgotten that we're a non-fiction house."[5]

Fortunately, McGraw-Hill released Brown from his commitment by offering the novel to Alfred Knopf in return for the $500 advance they had given Brown. The sergeant soon received an enthusiastic letter from Blanche Knopf telling him that they were quite pleased with the book and that it would be published the following June.

A Walk in the Sun was extraordinarily timely as it was published just a week after D-Day in Normandy. Sales were good and the novel quickly gained fourth place on the *New York Times* best-seller list.

While the novel was receiving good critical notices throughout the United States, director Lewis Milestone was recuperating in Los Angeles from a five-week bout with a ruptured appendix.

Of all the Hollywood directors who came to prominence during the thirties and forties, Lewis Milestone was perhaps the most adept at filming realistic combat scenes. Born in Odessa, Russia, on September 30, 1895, he had grown up in the town of Kishinew, the capital of Bessarabia (now Chisinau, Moldova), attended school in Germany and later emigrated to the United States, where he served in the U.S. Army Signal Corps during World War I. Assigned to the Photographic Division (he had previously worked in a theatrical photographer's studio for $7 a week), Milestone was transferred to Washington, D.C., where he worked on training films with directors Victor Fleming and Josef von Sternberg.

Emerging from the Army, Milestone left for Hollywood to work with Jesse Hampton Productions. Hampton, one of Milestone's wartime associates, offered him a position in his cutting room at $20 a week. He soon began editing films for director Henry King, who would later direct *Twelve O'Clock High.*

In 1925, Milestone made his directorial debut at Warner Bros. on *Seven Sinners,* based on his own original idea, which he co-wrote with young screenwriter and future studio mogul, Darryl F. Zanuck.

While Milestone was a very flexible, eclectic director in terms of subject matter, the outstanding success of his 1930 film, *All Quiet on the Western Front,* based on the classic novel by Erich Maria Remarque, frequently tied him to the combat film genre. While his later films were less impressive thematically, they never lost the true humanity that characterized his beloved study of the First World War and its effect on a group of young German soldiers.

Mississippi native Dana Andrews played Sgt. Bill Tyne, who takes over the platoon when his superior, Sgt. Porter, has a nervous breakdown.

All Quiet on the Western Front would affect an entire generation of new directors who were awestruck by the film's impassioned outcry against war and its horrors. Director Don Siegel would never forget the film; his own contribution to the combat film genre, *Hell Is for Heroes* (1962), would explore similar ground.

Following his Academy Award–winning work on *All Quiet on the Western Front,* Milestone, avoided the war drama, as did Hollywood in the pacifist thirties, to concentrate on films like *The Front Page, Paris in the Spring* and *Of Mice and Men.* The attack on Pearl Harbor reawakened Milestone's interest and abilities in the combat film genre.

In 1943, he directed *Edge of Darkness*, an Errol Flynn adventure about the Norwegian resistance against the Nazis, a theme similar to that of his next film, *The North Star,* which told of the Russian resistance against the German invasion of the Soviet Union. Later edited and released under the title of *Armored Attack*, it became a staple on late-night syndicated television in the 1960s. The film was nominated for six Oscars and, ironically, was later labeled as subversive by witnesses who testified in Hollywood for the House Committee on Un-American Activities in 1947.

The year after the original release of *The North Star,* Milestone completed *The Purple Heart*, a gripping drama of American flyers who are captured and tortured by the Japanese for taking part in the Doolittle Raid of 1942.

A chance encounter with producer Samuel Bronston opened the way to *A Walk in the Sun*. Bronston wanted Milestone to get away from the studio system and work on an independent project of his choice that would be released by United Artists. This appealed to the director, who was weary of the major studio bureaucracy.

Bronston invited Milestone to continue his convalescence from the appendectomy in New York, where Bronston was forming a small group of independent film makers, including French exiles Rene Clair and Julian Duvivier.

Recalled Milestone, "They were really living it up at the Waldorf Astoria where everybody had a beautiful suite of his own. Bronston sure knew how to spend money."[6] (Later, the producer would get a reputation for enormous extravagance when he produced a series of epic films in Spain in the 1960s, including *El Cid, 55 Days at Peking, The Fall of the Roman Empire* and *Circus World*.)

The producer's spendthrift approach at first worried Milestone, but the director was in no position to complain. Given a luxurious suite at the Sherry Netherlands, across from Central Park, he mourned the loss of his appendix and began to search for a new film project.

Samuel Bronston was a financial wizard who had recently distinguished himself in Europe, before the war, as a film salesman. Like Milestone, he was a native of Russia who came from a family of nine boys and girls, all reared and educated in France and all distinguished in the fields of law, medicine, art and music. Five of his brothers were doctors, and his sister Carol Bronte became a famous opera singer.

Bronston started out to become a surgeon but fainted at his first autopsy, so he took to music and played the flute with the Paris orchestra to pay for his tuition at the Sorbonne. Later, as a successful film salesman, he gained prominence in Europe and migrated to pre-war Hollywood, where he began his producing career. In 1942, he produced *The Adventures of Martin Eden*, a Jack London story that starred a very young Glenn Ford. This was followed by *Jack London*, which starred Michael O'Shea and Susan Hayward. By 1943, he was an established independent producer, associated with United Artists.

In July 1944, the Zeppo Marx Agency in New York sent Milestone a copy of Harry Brown's *A Walk in the Sun*. Milestone read the little book and the accompanying reviews and told Bronston to buy it. It was as simple as that.

It was only during the bargaining for the novel's rights that Milestone began to keenly suspect Bronston's precarious financial status, as he recalls: "By now, I realized that Bronston owned no oil wells. He was not a wealthy man, and since his mode of living including putting up two other directors besides myself, I wondered how long it could last. The thing to do, I decided, was to move in, get the story done and get out fast. Because it looked as though the sky would soon fall in."[7]

Bronston continued to assure Milestone that everything was in order. He purchased the

Sgt. Tyne (Dana Andrews, left center) confers with Windy (John Ireland) and Sgt. Ward (Lloyd Bridges).

film rights from Knopf and began to make arrangements to secure the $700,000 budget of *A Walk in the Sun.* Two weeks later, Milestone met screenwriter Robert Rossen in the lobby of the Sherry Netherlands, each surprised by the other's presence in New York.

Milestone, who had worked with Rossen on *Edge of Darkness,* immediately offered Rossen the adaptation assignment on *A Walk in the Sun,* as long as the script could be finished quickly.

Rossen, the future writer/director of Paul Newman's *The Hustler,* was fed up with Hollywood politics. He had recently moved back to New York, had enrolled the youngsters in school and decided that he was well rid of the shenanigans typical of front-office movie-making. The idea of making an "independent movie," thus, appealed to him.

Rossen was one of Hollywood's most promising young writers. He was a native New Yorker and a one-time boxer from Manhattan's lower east side. The grandson of a rabbi and the nephew of a Hebrew poet, Rossen's childhood experiences bred in him a rebellious nature which later saw outlet on the screen.

After attending Columbia University, he turned to writing. His theatrical career started, though, when, at the age of 21, he directed future James Bond films writer Richard Maibaum's play, *The Tree,* in 1929. His second directorial effort was another Maibaum play, *Birthright,* and from then on he turned to playwriting. Rossen's first success was *The Body Beautiful,* which was produced in 1934 and which brought him quickly to the attention of Warner Bros. and director Mervyn LeRoy. Two years later, he came west and began writing at Warners.

With Bronston's financial backing, Rossen was quickly put to work on *A Walk in the Sun.* Both Rossen and Milestone were confident that their virtual independence would insulate them from any front-office tampering and help create a unique war story. This was not to be a traditional propaganda film with flag waving; Brown's grim narrative was to be retained, practically verbatim. It was to be a pointedly limited perspective saga of the foot soldier.

Since they had worked together on *Edge of Darkness*, the precedent enabled them to dispense with personality clashes and allow them to adapt the story with a common sense of purpose. Both were excited about returning to work, and their enthusiasm spilled over into a joint project.

Rossen began writing in an office at the Samuel Goldwyn Studios in Hollywood — the virtual haven of independent productions. Producer Bronston had agreed that speed was important, especially since there was talk that the war in Europe would be over in December. Milestone continually relayed the message to Rossen.

In transforming Brown's novel to the screen, Rossen took advantage of the author's lucid style. The 160-page book was straightforward in construction and allowed Rossen to retain the basic narrative in its original form. The screenwriter was also able to transfer whole passages of Brown's own dialogue directly to the screen. In fact, everybody later agreed that Brown's novel was practically a screenplay.

Rossen made only two minor changes in the final draft of *A Walk in the Sun*. He promoted Corporal Tyne to sergeant (he would be portrayed by one of Milestone's favorite actors, Dana Andrews), and he strengthened the part of Private "Windy" Craven (John Ireland), the soldier who composes letters aloud to his sister.

One of the script's outstanding characteristics is its sheer amount of realistic period dialogue. In an early passage of the novel, Brown wrote, "Talking was a form of bravado. If a man said something, no matter what it was, it seemed to him that he was saying, 'Here I am, very calm, very collected. Nothing's going to happen to me. The rest of the company's going to be wiped out, but nothing's going to happen to me. See, I can talk. I can form sentences. Do you think I could make conversations if I knew I was going to die?'"[8]

In a *New York Times* interview in 1945, Lewis Milestone also defended the abnormal amount of dialogue. He told the reporter:

> The big effect was to externalize the thoughts and feelings of men in action. Every soldier talked, and through his dialogue we learned what was going on in his mind. My reaction to the criticism was that you gave articulation to what they would have said, if they could have said it. This was the quality that Harry Brown got into it and that was the quality I wanted to keep in the film.[9]

Rossen, working around the clock, finished the first-draft shooting script in just one week. But Milestone soon noticed that, even with the unifying elements provided by Windy Craven's oral letters, which often served as a practical narration, something was missing, an important factor that could elevate the project.

Milestone, recalling some research he had done on *The North Star*, remembered some scenes in which Russian veterans of various wars were being demobilized without benefit of the brief humanitarian stops at a halfway house, a veteran's hospital, or an institution similar to those that exist in the United States. If the Russian soldier had been crippled by the war, society assumed no responsibility for him. They made no concessions; he could stand on a street corner selling satchels for all they cared.

Milestone remembered that these crippled vagabonds often sang of their experiences while playing a musical instrument like the balalaika. He told Rossen that if they could somehow use that device, then they could dramatize all of Harry's material without a typical narration. In the final film, Milestone's use of the ballad as a unifying element gave the film a poetic quality that was unique and emotional.

The plan was to use the ballads, but only as a narrative device. There would be no singer in the cast. Milestone and Rossen thumbed through the book, marking off scenes they wanted to express in ballad form. They found ten more than they wanted, but both men felt that the ballads represented a truly original filmmaking approach.

Bronston agreed to the idea and immediately hired lyricist Millard Lampell to write the ballads. Lampell, who would later write folk ballads with Woody Guthrie, was blacklisted during the McCarthy era, but he would go on to be a prominent screenwriter in the 1960s. Musician/composer Earl Robinson, whose deep voice was quite distinctive and Western enough to symbolize the Texas Division, joined Lampell, putting the words to music. In the interest of economy, Robinson was also hired to play and sing the finished ballads.

Instead of opening the film with the typical credits sequence, Milestone chose to begin with his first ballad.

After Burgess Meredith introduces the squad, he simply says, "Here's a song about them," a cue that led directly to the deep voice of Earl Robinson.

To this day, Milestone's opening ballad is a powerfully unique introduction to the film. Unlike any other combat film of its time, *A Walk in the Sun* gets under the fingernails of its protagonists, breathing life into soldiers who were often treated like cardboard characters in other films. While it may appear corny today, when this film was released in 1946, after four years of bloody warfare, one can sense the exhaustion and fear in our troops as Earl Robinson sings these ballads.

While Rossen continued to polish the script, Milestone kept a daily eye on the newspapers, scanning the war news for any interesting idea that he could incorporate into the film.

In late December 1944, during the climactic Battle of the Bulge, which extended the war in Western Europe for five months, Milestone discovered an interesting article written by UPI correspondent Collie Small. It was a dispatch from Germany. Small had come across a Brooklyn G.I. talking to a dead German. The kid had just missed the final payoff and was full of the wonder of being alive, while the big blond German lay dead. For the film, Milestone asked actor George Offerman (portraying "Tinker") to recreate the incident. In the scene, Tinker is standing on a burning German armored car talking to a body.

Rivera the machine gunner (Richard Conte, left) chats with his loader Friedman (George Tyne) while Archimbeau (Norman Lloyd, front) catches up on some sleep.

"You know Al," he says, "you there, you got no right to squawk. You made up for one of ours. Look at you. You're deader than a mackerel. Look at me. I still got a whole life to look forward to. Just because of you, I got a tour of Europe that don't cost me a thing, and what did you get? You got shot in a barnyard, that's what." And when another soldier steps over, Tinker just looks at him.

On location in the West San Fernando Valley of Los Angeles, Lewis Milestone (center) confers with Richard Conte (left) and Dana Andrews. (Courtesy of the Academy of Motion Picture Arts and Sciences)

"Just having a little talk with Al here." With one last look at the corpse, he walked away.[10]

In November 1944, Milestone began shooting *A Walk in the Sun* at Agoura Ranch in the western San Fernando Valley, which resembled the hinterland of Italy. Today, you can still see those rolling, grassy dry hills that make up the terrain of the film. Of course, if you look a little bit to your right or left, you'll also see some major housing developments that now dot the land. In those days, it was still the frontier of Hollywood filmmaking. Thirteen years later, Milestone would be back in the same neighborhood, filming *Pork Chop Hill*.

Rivera (Richard Conte, right), who has an opinion on everything, shares one with Rankin (Chris Drake). Drake would go on to play the doomed state trooper who is one of the first victims of *Them!* (1954).

After Milestone had been shooting for a week on location, Bronston phoned from New York with terrible news. The bank that had promised to finance the picture had changed its mind. It was a disastrous blow to Milestone and the whole crew. The production was already $45,000 in debt and was depending on that financing.

Milestone was faced with the choice of losing everything he had done so far or scraping up some money to meet the immediate costs, while Bronston tried to promote a new loan. In desperation, Milestone put some of his own money into the production and managed to borrow enough to keep going, day by day. He soon found himself working all day on the set and then spending most of the night trying to raise money.

Bronston called with the reassurance that he was about to close a deal with a Chicago bank. He called again the next day to announce another, more imminent, arrangement. A group of Chicago financiers were willing to advance $200,000 at six percent interest plus a bonus of 15 percent and 40 percent of the picture's profits. It was a terrible giveaway, and when the Chicago bankers heard about the preposterous deal they withdrew their proffered loan of $300,000. Bankrupt and defeated, Bronston walked away from the picture, leaving Milestone in the middle of the Agoura Hills with a hungry army of cast and crew.

The director immediately flew to Chicago to see David O'Hara, head of the Chicago financiers, who agreed to negotiate a new more reasonable deal for the $750,000. His production bankrolled, Milestone still had some major problems with which to deal.

The finished script had been submitted to Washington for routine approval and the U.S. Army wanted some changes made, particularly in the final scene in which the platoon launches a World War I bayonet charge on the heavily defended farmhouse. The military wondered where the platoon's bazookas were. Milestone explained that there weren't any. If there had been, the infantrymen could have waited out of range and blown the farmhouse to bits.

"And then where would our story be?" asked Milestone.

The Army stood firm, however. "That," they said, "is why we use bazookas. So you had better use them."[11]

Without authorization from the Army, the film could not go into general release, so Milestone had Rossen write bazookas into the story, with a twist that satisfied the Army and saved the last scene in the picture.

Tyne's platoon does have bazookas but, during an engagement with enemy armor (that takes place off camera to save money), all of the bazooka ammunition is used up. When the unit moves against the farmhouse, all they have for support is Rivera's (Richard Conte) light machine gun.

A Walk in the Sun wrapped production on January 5, 1945, with no less than 11 Millard Lampell ballads, each one sung by Earl Robinson. When Milestone showed the finished film to some of his friends, producer Sam Spiegel (who would later produce *The Bridge on the River Kwai* and *Lawrence of Arabia*) was the first to comment. "Milly, you're insane," he said. "You guys have a wonderful war melodrama, and yet you keep interrupting the damned thing with these silly ballads. Every time you have a ballad, the action comes to a dead stop."

The director listened to the criticism but refused to consider cutting any of the ballads. He wanted to hear from movie audiences.

"Thanks for the advice," Milestone told Spiegel. "But the beauty of doing an independent picture is that you don't have to listen to anybody, not even your friends."[12]

At the first sneak preview, Milestone, to his dismay, was aware of a wave of grumbling from the younger members of the audience during the ballad sequences, and he was suddenly afraid that Spiegel had been right. He was still unable to accept the thought that his picture sense had betrayed him. He wandered around the lobby, soliciting opinions from the audience. A group of young people who were leaving the theater caught Milestone's attention.

Milestone ran after them. "Excuse me," he called, "were you by any chance discussing the music in the film you just saw?"

"Yes," they chorused.

"Obviously," Milestone continued, "there was something about it which you didn't like. Would you mind telling me what it was? I produced the film."

"Oh, we loved the picture," said one teenage boy, "but where did you get that hillbilly singer?"[13]

Ah ha! It wasn't the ballads that had bothered them at all. It was squarish Earl Robinson. Relieved, Milestone thanked the young people for their candor, but lamented that Robinson was the best he could find.

Satisfied that the ballads were still a good film device, Milestone nonetheless reduced their number from 11 to 6. He realized that too many might prove intolerable to young filmgoers.

Only a few days after the sneak preview, Milestone was confronted with a new, more complex problem. With Samuel Bronston off the picture, he was told that United Artists had canceled their release agreement. Later, Milestone was told the true story, that UA had already committed themselves to distributing director Lester Cowan's *The Story of G.I. Joe* and didn't want to compete with their own product.

Informing O'Hara that the best idea now was to go to 20th Century–Fox, Milestone contacted his friend Darryl F. Zanuck, who was the head of production for the studio. But Zanuck was a production chief, not a distribution executive; he referred Milestone to the New York office.

Milestone was unstoppable. He knew that a good word from Zanuck would guarantee a screening of the picture for the executives in New York. Zanuck relented, and two days later Milestone sent a print over to Zanuck's home where the production executive had his own private screening room. As luck would have it, the film was scheduled to be shown on April 12, 1945, the day President Franklin Delano Roosevelt died, sending an entire nation into mourning.

Milestone waited in suspense for an hour for Zanuck to push the button on the projector. The President's death had hit him very deeply and he was not in the mood for a war picture. Finally, Zanuck decided to run it.

"We started the thing at last," recalls Milestone, "and when the film was finished, Zanuck was very pleased. He told Milestone that he would recommend the film. 'But you'll have to go to New York personally to run a print for them. And Milly, you have too many ballads. I love them, but you've got to take some out.'"[14]

Milestone wasn't sure he agreed. He had already reduced the number to six.

Zanuck stood firm. "Whatever number you have, cut some more. The first two are marvelous, but after that it becomes an arty trick. Don't give the audience a chance to arrive at the same conclusion."[15]

Because he respected Zanuck's opinion, Milestone grudgingly dropped two more ballads and flew to New York to meet Spyros Skouras, the head of 20th Century–Fox.

But even before he previewed the film for the New York people, Milestone received a long telegram from Zanuck, saying that he liked this picture so much that he had set up a special screening for the directors on the Fox lot. They unanimously agreed it was a marvelous picture, but they didn't like the ballads. In the telegram, Zanuck made a point of mentioning a conversation he had had with director Ernst Lubitsch who had told him, "It's a great picture, but what the hell are the ballads doing in it?"[16] Zanuck's final suggestion was that Milestone eliminate the ballads altogether.

Stalling for time, as he waited for the release agreement to be signed, Milestone pretended not to have received the telegram. After Skouras came through and agreed to release *A Walk in the Sun* under the 20th Century–Fox banner, Milestone sent a wire to Zanuck.

"I appreciate your suggestion in regards to the ballads," he wrote. "Thank all the directors for their opinions and suggestions, but it's too late. I can no longer do anything because there's no more production money. We're just previewed the picture and I'm afraid it's going to go out as it is."[17]

Although the release agreement was signed in late April 1945, just before the German surrender in Europe, *A Walk in the Sun* did not officially premiere in New York until January 11, 1946.

The long delay probably canceled out a great deal of the film's box-office success. The war had been over for four months and military stories were no longer so popular with the public. Still, the picture was a critical triumph.

The reviewer for *Cue Magazine* wrote in his January column that it was "a beautifully acted, superbly photographed and directed record of a day in the life of a soldier, and an age in the life of man."[18]

Six months later, *Los Angeles Times* critic Philip K. Scheuer once more defended the film from those who still criticized its loquacity.

"Okay," Scheuer wrote, "so the real G.I.'s don't talk like that. But the 53 boys of this 'Texan' platoon do talk like that. I read them and I have seen and heard them talking like that, and what they say sounds okay to me. It is both the license and function of the artist to alter nature as much as he wishes, if by doing so he improves on it. And it is the margin of 'unnaturalness' that makes Brown's men, and now Milestone's, seem more real than real."[19]

The *Daily Variety* critic considered the film a "first class job of picture making," but also commented on several of the technical aspects of the film, saying "the ballads used to supplement the narration in atmosphere building have a hillbilly flavor and add little to the effectiveness of the film."[20]

Even 64 years after its 1946 release, *A Walk in the Sun* retains its power as a realistic combat film. It still has that "you are there" quality, particularly when the exhausted and bloodied platoon arrives at the stone wall that borders the farmhouse, and Sgt. Tyne wonders if the building is defended. Having left the binoculars with the dead McWilliams, Tyne and his platoon are hindered.

It's also very much a period piece and a time capsule, with the flavor of 1943 stamped throughout. There's future "Bowery Boy" Huntz Hall talking about Russ Columbo records and the potential for smell-o-vision movies; there's the irrepressible Archambeau, played hypnotically by Norman Lloyd, talking about the Battle of Tibet in 1956 because he's got the facts; and there's Sergeant Porter losing his mind to a strong dose of post-traumatic shock, something that was still being called "combat fatigue" back in those days.

CHAPTER TWO

Battleground

When World War II ended in 1945, so ended the American public's desire to see war films in general, and combat films in particular. A desire to return to normalcy pervaded the country, and realistic motion picture stories of fighting men had no place in the public's collective psyche. For five years, the studios had turned out war pictures. Now it was time to return to a steady peacetime diet of noir thrillers, madcap comedies and adventure films. The combat films had to wait for four years.

One of the first postwar American combat films, MGM's *Battleground* (1949), carried forward the serious attitude and perspective of Lewis Milestone's *A Walk in the Sun*. Even Jarvess, the ex–newspaper man portrayed by John Hodiak, echoes McWilliams, the first-aid man in *A Walk in the Sun*, when he decries the lack of information his infantry squad is given. He doesn't even know what country he's fighting in — is it Belgium or Luxembourg?

Battleground's screenwriter, infantry veteran Robert Pirosh, won an Academy Award for his screenplay, and the success of the film, along with the release of Republic's gutsy *Sands of Iwo Jima* and Fox's *Twelve O'Clock High*, jumpstarted the combat film genre. It would continue almost unabated until the dark era of the Vietnam War.

A seasoned dramatist, Pirosh wrote *Battleground* from a unique perspective. He had known the "Battered Bastards of Bastogne," the nickname given to the members of the 101st Airborne Division who defended a small town in Belgium during the Battle of the Bulge. He had slept in the same mud, picked at the same frozen K-rations, faced the same German soldiers across a stretch of snowy forest.

Pirosh had survived the war and, while many men were shedding all vestiges of war memories and storing souvenirs in the sanctity of their attics, he was prepared to gamble his memories on a successful commercial film that would dramatize the untold story of the infantrymen — the footsloggers.

Battleground was one of Hollywood's best kept postwar secrets. But its story begins a lot earlier, in the freezing cold of the Ardennes forest, in late December 1944.

Master Sergeant Robert Pirosh was leading a patrol near the perimeter of Bastogne. His unit, an element of the 320th Regiment, 35th Infantry Division, had been sent north from General Patton's Third Army to relieve the encircled 101st Airborne Division, fighting for its life in the strategic highway center of Bastogne, Belgium.

Pirosh was a veteran Hollywood screenwriter and, unlike many of his co-workers who donned officer's bars only to edit film in Astoria, New York, or Culver City, California, he had become a combat infantryman. Before the war, he had written comedy films with his partner George Seaton. Such films as *A Day at the Races* (with the Marx Brothers), *Up in Arms* (with Danny Kaye) and *I Married a Witch* (with Veronica Lake) were a far cry from wartime combat, but Pirosh kept a journal anyway, keeping track of his experiences.

In December 1949, on the fifth anniversary of the Battle of the Bulge, he described some of his experiences as a writer on the march:

> Some of the material for *Battleground* came out of notes in my diary. It was not a daily diary, but my mind was always on a possible picture to be written after the war.
>
> For instance, there is an episode involving the Van Johnson character "Holly" and some eggs. That came from an actual incident recorded in my wartime diary. It was my first advance to the front since I joined the outfit. One of the men found 13 eggs. "Find me a frying pan and we'll cook 'em," he said. Well, he never did get that frying pan, as we had to move up right away.
>
> Soon after, an enemy machine gun opened up and we all hit the dirt. I noticed that he went down very slowly trying to protect the eggs. That broke the spell for me. I had to laugh. Remember, he was a seasoned veteran, I was a replacement. I figured that if he could worry about eggs, then we were okay.[1]

As his unit fought alongside the 101st Airborne in the Bulge, Pirosh continued to record his anecdotes on the backs of envelopes, Nazi propaganda leaflets and, sometimes, on soft toilet tissue.

Later, while a screenwriter at MGM, he was able to discuss his film project with Brigadier General Anthony McAuliffe, the general whose reply of "Nuts!" to the German surrender demand at Bastogne became one of the classic retorts in United States military history. McAuliffe enthusiastically approved of the project and Pirosh's plan to show only the G.I. viewpoint of the battle.

The general agreed that it was time the public was shown a new side of war, the reactions of the average man who suddenly found himself in a foxhole. Later, during story conferences, McAuliffe personally annotated and approved every line of dialogue.

"This is the G.I.'s story," he said emphatically, after removing his name from a line of dialogue. "Who cares about generals, except other generals and their families."[2]

Long before it was greenlit at MGM, *Battleground* started out as a project at RKO Pictures. However, in the years shortly after World War II, studios were inclined to release more lighthearted entertainment, so Pirosh's war story sat on the shelf. One morning in early 1947, he was asked to report to the new head of production at RKO, Dore Schary. Schary had known Pirosh before the war and was familiar with his experiences in the 35th Division.

"Bob," Schary began, "we're going to activate your Bulge project. The time has come to make a war picture. People think they won't be made for three or four years, but I think they're wrong. I want to get a shooting script ready. I already have a man in Washington doing research, and I want you to collaborate with him on the script."[3]

Pirosh was surprised by Schary's plan, but he wasn't about to let the moment get the better of him.

"Don't even tell me who this research guy is. If you want me to write about the war, I'll do it. I don't want to collaborate with anyone, and I'll do my own research."

"All right, all right!" Schary yielded. Secretly, he was quite pleased, for he knew Pirosh was uniquely qualified to create the first postwar combat film. Satisfied that he would be the only writer, Pirosh eagerly pounded out his ideas: "I want to write purely from the viewpoint of one squad, because I was in that squad."[4]

When I interviewed Pirosh in January 1974, he confessed, "I avoided at least three clichés

A wrecked U.S. Army tank destroyer, still guarding the road when screenwriter Robert Pirosh came to do his research outside Bastogne, Belgium, in April 1947. (Courtesy Western History Research Center, University of Wyoming)

in writing the script for *Battleground*. There is no character from Brooklyn in the story. Nobody gets a letter from his wife or girl saying she has found a new love, and nobody sweats out the news of the arrival of a new born baby back home."[5]

Given a free hand, he was able to develop the story totally around his "squad idea." Utilizing this distinct perspective, the writer disposed of high-level strategy, in turn, eliminating generals and scenes at rear-echelon headquarters.

"It was just what the guys knew," said Pirosh, "and they knew exactly nothing."[6]

Worried that another studio would beat them to the theaters with a rival war film, Schary kept all pre-production planning secret and gave Pirosh's story a cover title—*Prelude to Love*. With studio authorization, Pirosh and an RKO stills photographer went to Bastogne in April of 1947 to gather research materials for the proposed screenplay.

Pirosh was already in Europe at the time, completing a prologue sequence for a René Clair film, *Le Silence Est d'Or*. Not only was the climate in the Ardennes that spring a far cry from the snowy, freezing weather that Pirosh remembered, but this time he was being chauffeured in a deluxe limousine.

Shuttling between the two-and-one-half-year-old battlefield and the crossroads town of Bastogne, he recorded valuable information which, along with the new stills, would help the studio art department recreate part of the Belgian forest on the backlot.

One afternoon, during a leisurely drive through the countryside, Pirosh shouted the driver to a stop.

"It all looked strangely familiar," Pirosh recalled of a small piece of terrain he had spotted not far from Bastogne:

> I got out of the limousine and took another look across at a farm which sloped down to a dense pine forest in the distance. This was the place all right. There was the stone farmhouse and the demolished barn. Everything had been snow-covered then, but there was no mistaking the scene. This was where I had stood guard, shivering under a blanket with a friend the night before we entered Harlange. And fifty yards away in a patch of woods was where our foxholes were.
>
> The way I ran into that patch of woods, the chauffeur must have thought I was crazy. The foxholes were still there with pine branches tossed over them, just the way we left them. Nobody had bothered to fill them in. In the hole, which I had once called home, I found an empty K-ration box.
>
> It all came rushing back. The taste of K-rations. The sound of the 88's. The fear, the numbing cold, the exhaustion and the terribly, lonely, depression. And I thought of the men who had been in the other foxholes—Besser and Caswell who were captured; Beiss and Levine who were wounded; Gaumer and Gerstenkorn who went back with pneumonia; and Gettings and Butch who were killed. And then I thought of Harlange, Belgium (or was it Luxembourg?), where we went in with two platoons and came out with a couple of squads.[7]

Such a traumatic reunion with the horror of times past reinforced his desire to create the true "G.I." picture. After all, he ruminated, what business did he have writing the epic picture of the war in Europe?

Dore Schary, who had kept a close wrap of secrecy around the project, made an official announcement to the press on May 16, 1948, stating that *Battleground*, an original screenplay by Robert Pirosh, was to be the studio's first production since financier Howard Hughes had acquired the studio. The resulting press release confirmed that *Battleground*, a screen version of the Battle of the Bulge, was to be the biggest production of the 1948-49 year. Schary immediately assigned producers Jesse L. Lasky and Walter MacEwen to the project and signed Robert Mitchum, Robert Ryan and Bill Williams to starring roles.

Although Howard Hughes shared Schary's enthusiasm for a new war film, he did not agree that the infantry should be the focus of a major studio production. Hughes was more interested in doing a film about air power—which was his passion. He also felt that Pirosh's story was too grim and lacked key entertainment values.

Pirosh soon found himself stuck between two stubborn individuals. On the one side stood Schary, soft-spoken, fiercely creative and firmly convinced that *Battleground* was a winner. On the other side stood the egocentric Hughes, new to the studio and ready to gather a new base of power. He was as firmly convinced that an infantry picture would be a disaster.

Neither would budge. Finally, exasperated at Hughes's intransigence, Schary tendered his resignation.

Creative driving force that he was, Schary did not remain idle long. Like a highly touted pro basketball free agent, Schary was immediately signed by Louis B. Mayer to head production at MGM. RKO never recovered from the loss.

With the exodus of Schary, the Pirosh script was quickly shelved. Heartbroken, Pirosh continued to work at RKO on other projects, hoping that *Battleground* could in some way be revived. Three months later, he learned that Schary had purchased two screenplays from RKO. One was a splashy costume drama called *Ivanhoe,* the other, to his everlasting gratitude, was *Battleground.*

That same night, Schary called and asked him to come over to MGM and do a rewrite. "Why get someone else to play Heifetz's fiddle when Heifetz is available," he said.[8]

On October 11, 1948, Schary assigned the project to producer Pandro S. Berman. But Berman left the film for a new project and Schary took over full production chores in March 1949 on the first major studio combat film since 1945.

Although the project proceeded on schedule, there was considerable grumbling among the studio executives. Like Howard Hughes, Louis B. Mayer was skeptical and uneasy about the commercial prospects for *Battleground.* He thought it was too harrowing a story to be made so soon after the war. But to his credit, he did not abort the project.

Nevertheless, the other studio executives continually dogged Schary. They agreed with Mayer about the film's poor box-office potential but, even more importantly, they felt that Schary was starting off on the wrong foot, doing a picture against the wishes of Mayer.

Despite the growing uneasiness about the film, Schary continued with the pre-production planning. Story, not topic, was the deciding factor, he maintained. The basis premise of *Battleground* was honest and sincere, dealing with the average man who, despite fear and a hatred of war, wouldn't quit.

To direct the film, Schary chose William A. Wellman, then in his artistic prime. "Wild Bill" Wellman had directed *The Story of G.I. Joe* for United Artists during the war and he approached *Battleground* with the same forcefulness and characteristic bravura.

An acknowledged expert at directing action sequences — he was, in effect, another Lewis Milestone — Wellman was not known for his grace on the set. He had an intense dislike for ostentation.

A former member of the Lafayette Flying Corps during the First World War, Wellman brought a sensitive directorial touch to *Battleground.* It is surprising that Wellman was able to film two classic studies of the infantry since he always joked that, as an aviator, he was always getting shot at by his own infantry.

It was Ernie Pyle who changed Wellman's view on the infantry and urged him to move mountains to film *The Story of G.I. Joe.* Wellman had become good friends with the famous war correspondent when Pyle was on his way to the Pacific. Together they hobnobbed with W. C. Fields and Gene Fowler, got terribly drunk together and learned a great deal about each other. Pyle came to Wellman's house the night before he shipped out to the Pacific, a voyage from which he never returned. It was the sensitive view of the infantry, seen through

Opposite: Studio head and *Battleground* producer Dore Schary greets members of the 101st Airborne Division who will work on the film in Los Angeles. (Note: Robert Taylor [far left] was still on the project at the time; he would soon be replaced by Van Johnson.) Director William "Wild Bill" Wellman stands behind Schary.

Screenwriter Robert Pirosh (right) poses in the MGM commissary with members of the 101st Airborne Division, the "Screaming Eagles."

Ernie Pyle's eyes, that Wellman brought to *The Story of G.I. Joe*, and four years later, to *Battleground*.

The crucial director/writer relationship between Wellman and Pirosh proved itself during the early story conferences as the script was rewritten and polished for the final production phase.

In April 1949, Schary promoted Pirosh to associate producer, a fact that the writer announced on the set one morning. Wellman grunted and continued to line up a scene. Eager to add new levels of realism to the film, Pirosh began to follow the crew around the studio during pre-production.

As he explained, "Maybe it was an obsession with me, but the uniforms never looked quite right to me. I wanted them to look as if they had been slept in for a month."[9]

His suggestions were at first appreciated by Wellman, who agreed that fatigue and shock should be progressive and, as a result, most of the picture was shot in sequence. But as production continued, Wellman's patience started to wear thin. He did not like having a writer-turned-producer peering over his shoulder. It wasn't long before Pirosh found himself barred from the set permanently.

Schary didn't feel that he could intervene, so Pirosh left the studio in bitterness. His technical advisor chores were taken over by Lt. Colonel Harry Kinnard, G-3, the brains behind the defense of Bastogne.

Pfc. Holly (Van Johnson, right) contemplates cooking some eggs, while Pvt. Bettis (Richard Jaeckel) observes. The introduction of the eggs was based on an actual incident in screenwriter Robert Pirosh's diary. The sequence added some comic relief in the film, as it did in real life in the Ardennes.

To round out the roster of performers who would eventually fill the 18 principal speaking parts in the film, MGM acquired 20 of the original 101st Airborne paratroopers, then stationed with the 82nd Airborne Division at Fort Bragg, North Carolina.

On March 15, 1949, the 20 soldiers — 11 sergeants, five corporals and four PFC's — nominated by their fellow G.I.'s, were flown into Hollywood as a regular military unit on detached service, under the supervision of their regular division officers. Billeted in a motel down the street from the Culver City studios of MGM, the soldiers received $7 a day food allowance from the studio.

For these veterans, Bastogne had been just another hitch of patrolling outside the city in the deep snow and bitter cold of the Belgian winter, bringing in occasional prisoners, dodging enemy artillery, struggling to heat their food over tiny foxhole fires and wishing they were somewhere else.

Casting for *Battleground* at first presented a problem. Actors Robert Taylor, Bill Williams, Robert Ryan and Keenan Wynn all departed the project when a snag developed in contract

A foxhole, circa December 1944, with Jarvess (John Hodiak, right), sharing the limited space with Abner (Jerome Courtland).

negotiations. Taylor can still be seen in publicity photographs taken when the 101st Airborne soldiers arrived on the lot.

To replace Spangler Arlington Brugh (Robert Taylor's real name), Schary signed Van Johnson for the leading part of Holly, the playboy with a weakness for gags and girls. Johnson had a penchant for military roles, having recently completed *Command Decision* with Clark Gable. During the war, he had starred opposite Spencer Tracy and a young Robert Mitchum in *Thirty Seconds Over Tokyo*.

Newcomer Marshall Thompson was assigned the crucial role of Layton, the green replacement who slowly learns the true value of comradeship in Sergeant Kinnie's (James Whitmore) hard-pressed combat squad.

The other members of Wellman's amazing cast included future director Don Taylor (an Air Force veteran), Ricardo Montalban (a newcomer from the Mexican film industry), John Hodiak (who played Jarvess the ex-newspaperman), Jerome Courtland (who shone as Abner the hillbilly), Bruce Cowling (as no-nonsense platoon sergeant Wolowicz), Richard Jaeckle (the perpetual "kid" in countless war films, who finally grew up in *The Dirty Dozen*), Douglas Fowley (who had lost his teeth in an aircraft carrier explosion in the South Pacific) and the aforementioned James Whitmore (who, for his role as cigar-chewing, frostbitten Sgt. Kinnie, would be nominated for an Oscar for Best Supporting Actor).

Before principal photography began, the actors were put through a two-week mini-course in basic training. Every day, they fired weapons, practiced close order drill, grenade

Jarvess (John Hodiak, left) and Holly (Van Johnson) pay homage to their fallen comrade, Rodrigues (Ricardo Montalban).

throwing, creeping and crawling. They even watched an orientation film entitled "How to Get Killed in One Easy Lesson." The whole group, including the 20 veterans, fell out in fatigues early in the morning, moved from one area of the MGM backlot to another in 6x6 army trucks and smoked only during the ten-minute breaks.

Stars were paired with G.I.'s for individual coaching, the Army's buddy system which proved so effective in wartime. Pirosh's desire for dirtier uniforms was fulfilled. Laundering was strictly forbidden. As the first day of shooting commenced, army trucks began to bounce the cast over to Backlot 3.

There were two main sets on the backlot. One was a replica of Bastogne, rebuilt from an Italian village used by United Artists in 1944 for *The Story of G.I. Joe.*

The other set represented a pine forest in the Ardennes, reproduced on one of the MGM sound stages. A total of 528 trees were shipped to the studio from Northern California. These included giant pines, identical to the Bastogne species, and nearly 300 smaller trees and shrubs that would dot the terrain with such realism that one paratrooper declared that it gave him the creeps. To simulate cold, wintry Belgium, chemical snow was shipped in daily in a great mixmaster and blown about by wind machines.

True to its promise, the U.S. Army provided the necessary assortment of mobile transport and artillery. To duplicate the relief of Bastogne, a second-unit camera crew was sent to the State of Washington to photograph an armored division on maneuvers. Six years later, director Jesse Hibbs's Audie Murphy bio-pic, *To Hell and Back*, would also be shot there.

The Germans come to accept the Americans' surrender. Gen. Anthony McAuliffe's reply: "Nuts!"

One of Schary's challenges was in getting the censors to approve General Anthony McAuliffe's immortal answer to the German surrender demand. The single word "nuts" had been previously barred from the screen. Schary and Wellman claimed, justly, that there wasn't a synonym for such an historic reply. They eventually won over the censors and *Battleground* achieved its final touch of historical realism.

For the special jive drill sequence that opens the film, Schary secured the services of Master Sergeant Samuel Jaegers of the 94th Engineer Construction Battalion at Fort Belvoir, Virginia. Jaegers, a Southern University graduate, was one of the originators of "jive," a stepped-up version of regulation close-order drill, which served to brighten up the routine aspects of essential training methods.

"Bombshell ... March! ... To the Rear ... Freeze! And "T-Formation ... Hit it!" were typically unorthodox commands that became instantly popular with black troops and others.

Along with "jive" came the famous "Jody Chant," a song created to avoid the repetitious "left, right, left" of the marching cadence. Jody, of course, was the mythical female who remained at home to attend to financial and romantic matters, while her boyfriend or husband went off to war.

"You had a good home but you left. You're right! Jody was there when you left. You're right! Your baby was there when you left. You're right! Sound off! One, two. Sound off! Three, four. Cadence Count! One, two, three, four — One, two — three, four."

Each company would compose its own verse, some of which were quite obscene. In preparing the script, Pirosh had been guided by propriety, not memory.

Having completed principal photography routinely on June 3, 1949, *Battleground* was prepped for a Christmas release. It later opened at the Astor Theater in New York and then simultaneously at the Metro Theater in Antwerp, Belgium, the Forum Theater in Liege and

The platoon prepares to march to the rear. Notice how much Layton (Marshall Thompson, second from left) has matured. Sgt. Kinney (James Whitmore, right) calls the cadence; he would be nominated for the Academy Award for Best Supporting Actor of 1949. (Courtesy of the Academy of Motion Picture Arts and Sciences)

the General Patton Theater in Bastogne. The film arrived in Los Angeles for a major premiere on December 1, 1949.

As predicted by Dore Schary, *Battleground* became the big box-office champ of 1949. The public responded to the storytelling skills of Pirosh and the gritty attention to detail that William Wellman brought to the set. Van Johnson, John Hodiak, Ricardo Montalban, James Whitmore and the rest of the cast disappeared into their roles, bringing a combat squad to life for a postwar audience.

Slogging through mud with grim determination, and ignoring the constant smell of death around them, Sergeant Kinnie's soldiers had survived. Indicative of their never-failing spirit is the film's final scene — a poignant climax, created by a writer who was looking backwards, and still retained that "direct from the headlines" perspective.

Kinnie's men are sitting by the side of a Belgian road, preparing to march rearward. Their war is over. As they watch the reinforcements pass by in their new tanks and immaculate uniforms, the sun is shining and there is relief in the air.

Van Johnson, looking very fresh-faced in this pre-production still, takes a moment to pose on a modern American tank. (Courtesy of the Academy of Motion Picture Arts and Sciences)

Shouting an emphatic "Good luck!" to a passing tank crew, Kinnie orders his squad to its feet. Their clothes are filthy, their faces are dirtied, some of them are wounded and they're all bone-tired. It appears that they are headed back to the front, but Kinnie, playing out the drama, orders them "about face" and they march sullenly to the rear. They sluff along wearily, oblivious to their surroundings. The road is empty and their minds dwell on the luxuries of a bed and a warm shower. Holly taps Kinnie on the shoulder and points to a column of new recruits marching their way. The tattered Sergeant throws his cigar away and orders his shattered unit to look sharp. A cue is whispered and they begin the immortal Jody chant, slowly at first, and then, as they pick up the rhythm, they shout it out. The end titles appear as the full MGM orchestra joins in.

This upbeat, rousing ending had a distinct effect on postwar audiences. People emerged from the theater remembering the humanity of Pirosh's soldiers, not their victory over the Germans in the Bulge. They vividly remembered the platoon's spirit, their comical interplay, and the heroism which they displayed on a daily basis while surviving one of the worst military winters since Valley Forge — an experience that had brought them one step closer to home.

CHAPTER THREE

Twelve O'Clock High

RKO President Howard Hughes's decision to sell Dore Schary's *Battleground* project to MGM in the summer of 1948 was based on his conviction that postwar audiences were far more interested in aerial adventures than slow-moving infantry combat.

However prejudiced his decision seemed at the time (Hughes was already famous as an aircraft manufacturer and expert pilot), it was based on a gut feeling that the popularity of the Air Force in a series of post–World War I adventure dramas could be rekindled. Back in 1930, when war films were a considered a risky venture, Hughes had produced his highly successful film, *Hell's Angels*. Two decades later, under similar conditions, it seemed reasonable to believe that such fare would strike gold again.

Hell's Angels and the earlier *Wings* (1927) sparked the big World War I aviation cycle that continued in various forms until the beginning of World War II. Most of the air sagas of this period offered the very elements of flight extolled by Howard Hughes: escapist adventure, airborne romance and daredevil action. For two decades (1919–1939), the airplane was to symbolize an escape from the Depression. Various aspects of flying were featured in almost every film. A mechanical fascination, the airplane offered high adventure that lifted audiences out of their spiritual and financial funk.

Aviation sagas seldom dug deeper into the mentality of the pilot in the air, or the squadron commander on the ground. But there were some exceptions. One of them was *The Dawn Patrol* (1938), based on a story by Howard Hawks and John Monk Saunders, and released by Warner Bros. It was one of the only films of its time to explore a deeper meaning. Unfortunately, its symbolic warning was soon forgotten in the rush to a new war.

The film stars Errol Flynn and David Niven and tells the story of the 59th Squadron of the British Flying Corps, fighting in France during World War I, when the superior German Air Force was sweeping the British from the skies. Using obsolete planes and equipment, the unit valiantly tries to turn the tide, ultimately paying a heavy price in human life.

Although the aerial sequences were impressive in terms of realism, the film emphasized the low-key atmosphere at the aerodrome. Many scenes took place in the club bar where the names of downed airmen were erased from a blackboard and "Poor Butterfly" was played repeatedly on a small record player. An air of doomed camaraderie prevailed.

Released one year before Germany's invasion of Poland and the start of World War II, *The Dawn Patrol* was one of the last of the aerial anti-war films. For the American isolationists, it was their high-water mark. After Pearl Harbor and the London Blitz, pacifism became obsolete. Whatever the cost, America had to win the war. Hollywood went with the winner.

During the war, the true sacrifice of the airman depicted in films like *The Dawn Patrol* was seldom dramatized. Aerial warfare retained a distinct individualism and sense of adventure on the screen, while, in reality, military aviation had become more destructive than ever. Biplane chivalry had been buried in the rubble of Warsaw and Rotterdam. Individuality of the Eddie Rickenbacker variety had faded, crushed beneath the sheer magnitude of a modern air war.

Aerial combat was now a massive undertaking fought by thousands. The punitive squadron attack, so costly during the First World War, had been replaced by new tactics like the B-17 precision daylight bombing missions, the terror bombings of the German Luftwaffe and the night bombings of the British Bomber Command. To blacken the skies with aircraft was no longer fiction as wings and air divisions became common flying units, massing hundreds and thousands of bombers at once. Attended by wailing air-raid sirens, crumbling cities and homeless refugees, the airplane had become a dreaded symbol of cataclysmic death. Hiroshima and Nagasaki merely reinforced that fact on a massive, unbelievable level.

If you could hover suspended in space above a B-17 Flying Fortress you could visualize an imaginary clock. The nose of the plane would be at 12 o'clock, the tail at six, the wings at three and nine. The clock was the key to identifying the bomber's aerial defense against fighter attack. In describing the angle of an attacking German fighter, the pilot and the crew would pinpoint their direction by yelling out a time on the clock.

It wasn't long before the Germans realized that their best attack angle on a Fortress was from a position at 12 o'clock and high. Given the defensive weakness of the B-17's nose and the tremendous closing velocity which propelled fighter and bomber towards each other at a combined speed of over 800 miles an hour, a Messerschmitt ME-109 or a Focke-Wulf FW-190 (Germany's principal day fighters) could seriously damage a B-17 without committing suicide. The term "twelve o'clock high" was thus considered a synonym among airmen for potential danger. It was also the title of a very important war film of the 1940s.

Released at the same time as *Battleground, Twelve O'Clock High* was 20th Century–Fox president Darryl F. Zanuck's entry in the 1948-49 World War II film revival. While Howard Hughes kicked *Battleground* and production chief Dore Schary over to MGM, Zanuck whole-heartedly backed the tension-packed story of the early days of the Eighth Air Force, when it was an understrength combat unit. A classic study of the meaning of command and the danger of stress, the film returned to the spirit of *The Dawn Patrol,* placing character interaction on the ground consistently above combat spectacle in the air. Moreover, *Twelve O'Clock High* was the product of two Air Force officers who, like infantryman Robert Pirosh, were interested in putting their remembrances of dramatic times past on film for the world to see.

In the summer of 1931, the United States had no Air Force. Hampered by a tiny budget, the infant Army Air Corps was struggling for existence. Its fate varied from year to year. A generous appropriation from the War Department (highly uncommon) meant more cadets, newer planes and better facilities, while a minuscule appropriation (the rule during the Depression) meant far less of everything.

Fortunately for Yale graduate Beirne Lay, Jr., he entered the Air Corps during an upswing. The combined pressure applied to the Army General Staff by young officers like Carl Spaatz, Henry Arnold and George Kenney was having an effect. For the moment, there were openings for those whose motto would be "I Wanted Wings!"

Lay headed south that June to Randolph Field, Texas, for his first eight months of basic training. While headlines spoke of Wiley Post and his trip around the world in a plane named *Winnie May*, the Ivy Leaguer/turned pilot was encountering his own adventures. At Randolph, and later at nearby Kelly Field, where he spent four months in the bombardment section, flying ancient Keystone bombers, Lay gained the firsthand experiences about which he later wrote.

Almost a decade before he co-wrote *Twelve O'Clock High* with screenwriter Sy Bartlett, Lay wrote his first book, appropriately entitled, *I Wanted Wings!* Paramount Pictures producer Arthur Hornblow, Jr., later purchased the rights to the book and Lay was brought to Hollywood to write his first screenplay. Directed by Mitchell Leisen and released shortly before the events at Pearl Harbor in 1941, the film version of Lay's novel isolated a segment of the great American military buildup by following three air cadets through training. Hornblow Jr. would later go on to producer another terrific World War II drama about the Air Corps, the Steve McQueen, Robert Wagner vehicle, *The War Lover*.

Between 1933 and 1938, Lay served several tours of active duty at Langley Field, Virginia. Since Air Corps appropriations were so variable, he would alternate at times between inactive reserve and active status. Shortly after the German invasion of Poland on September 1, 1939, Lay was assigned to Ontario Field, California, as a primary flight-training instructor. Three months later, he was summoned to Air Corps headquarters in Washington, D.C. Colonel Ira Eaker had sent for him. Among other duties, Lay found himself assigned to the Air Corps Staff as General Henry "Hap" Arnold's speech writer. Waiting for a transfer to London and observer status, Lay was still in better shape than his future writing partner, Sy Bartlett.

Forever fascinated by flying and air power, Bartlett had been thrown into the Signal Corps, attached to the Army Pictorial Service. There it was felt he could utilize his film background to contribute a great deal to a new breed of training films. But Bartlett wanted to fly, or at least he wanted to be attached to a flying unit. A war was coming and the last thing he wanted to do was edit training documentaries.

It was Beirne Lay, Jr., who brought about Bartlett's transfer into the Air Corps. Although the two were strangers, Bartlett knew of Lay's work on *I Wanted Wings!* When orders transferred Bartlett to the Signal Corps Center in Washington, D.C., he asked his friend Arthur Hornblow, Jr., to set up a meeting with Lay Jr.

As a member of Colonel Eaker's staff, First Lieutenant Lay Jr. was on good terms with many of the Air Corps' senior officers. The two writers became close friends and it was not long before Captain Bartlett was introduced to General Walter Weaver, chief of the Air Corps. Through Weaver, he met Carl Spaatz, who would soon command the American Air Forces in Europe.

"Tooey" Spaatz had just returned from England, where he had been observing the Royal Air Force in combat. While the United States was sending bombers and destroyers to England as part of Lend-Lease, the rapidly growing Army Air Corps was keeping a wary eye on the European air war through a close liaison with RAF Bomber Command.

Upon his return, General Spaatz began to record his observations. He also organized a small staff, the nucleus of which later became the United States Army Air Force. Sy Bartlett joined Spaatz's staff as the general's aide.

Of the two writers, Lay Jr. now a captain, was the first to be ordered overseas. Eaker, who, like Spaatz, had served as a special observer with the RAF in 1941, returned the following year with the rank of brigadier general and orders to set up the Eighth Air Force. An integral

During World War II, screenwriter Sy Bartlett (third from left) served with Gen. Frank Armstrong (center), who was the inspiration for Gen. Frank Savage in *Twelve O'Clock High*. Standing on Armstrong's right is Richard Tregaskis, the author of *Guadalcanal Diary*.

part of the general's seven-man advanced detachment, Lay arrived in war-torn London on February 20, 1942.

His was an interesting tour of duty. When Eaker released him from his staff assignment with the Eighth Air Force as chief of its Film Unit, Lay began training on the newly arrived B-17s. He flew nine bombing missions with the "Bloody 100th" Bomb Group, including the disastrous raid on the Regensberg fighter plane factory in Germany. In late 1943, he was ordered stateside for advanced training on the B-24 "Liberator," an American heavy bomber then being put into mass production.

Barely six months later, Lay Jr. was flying again, this time as commanding officer of the 487th Bombardment Group, which he led overseas from Alamogordo, New Mexico, in March 1944. On May 11 of that year, the 487th was alerted for a strike against Chaumont, a railroad marshaling yard in Eastern France. About 120 miles southeast of Paris, Lay Jr.'s command ship was struck by anti-aircraft fire and shot down. He parachuted safely into occupied France and spent the next three months behind enemy lines, evading capture with the help of the French Underground.

Sy Bartlett had arrived in London on June 3, 1942. He quickly disengaged himself from Spaatz's staff and transferred into the Operational Intelligence Section of the Eighth Air Force.

While Eaker's group prepared for their first raids against the Germans, Bartlett observed the British, at times flying with the "Lancaster Bunch." While flying in one of the British bombers, he is credited as the first American flyer to drop a bomb on Berlin. It was during this association with British Bomber Command that Bartlett stumbled across "RT-Intercepts," a secret RAF operation that would be a plus for U.S. bomber defense.

Since 1940, English radar stations had been monitoring the Luftwaffe's radio traffic. Soon after its first mission, the RAF was receiving regular reports on German fighter reaction to their raids. At a secret communications complex in Gloucester, British military intelligence (MI-6) had trained German-speaking English girls to monitor Luftwaffe radio transmissions. Within weeks, the girls became familiar with the enemy pilots, instantly recognizing their peculiar "chatter."

When a British strike was launched, the tactical deployment of key German fighter units was observed and catalogued. These reports were extremely valuable. With the constant stream of information flowing into their planning rooms, British Bomber Command was able to counter the effective German fighter defense and, thus, neutralize the latter's ability to break up RAF bomber formations.

Still, the British did all of their bombing at night, a time when German fighter reaction was minimal. It was the American Army Air Force that opted for precision daylight bombing. Fighters would, thus, be a far more formidable threat to the Americans. Bartlett wanted those RT-Intercepts for Spaatz. If there was a way to save American lives, he meant to have it.

Bartlett's campaign to win for the Americans this vital information eventually proved successful. The program later became an important ingredient in the novel, *Twelve O'Clock High*. Patricia Mallory, a pretty young Wren officer who falls in love with General Savage, works in the underground complex at Gloucester, and tries to sell the General on the program's importance to the U.S. Army Air Corps.

As chief officer in charge of RT-Intercepts, Bartlett left Pinetree (Eighth Air Force headquarters at Wycombe Down) regularly to brief the front line commanders. He especially liked Colonel Frank Armstrong, the commander of the 306th Bombardment Group at Thurleigh Field. Armstrong, who had led the first ten missions against the Germans, was considered one of the Air Corps' most outstanding combat leaders. Beirne Lay, Jr., had known Armstrong before the war at Barksdale Field in Louisiana, when the latter commanded one of the Air Corps squadrons flying A-3 attack planes.

It was at Thurleigh, while visiting with Armstrong, that Lay Jr. and Bartlett began to discuss the possibility of writing an intimate narrative about the Eighth Air Force.

It was to be their last wartime meeting. Group Commander Lay Jr. had just returned from France, via the French Underground, and was headed home. Air Corps regulations prevented his return to a combat unit, not only for his own protection should he be shot down again, but for the protection of his French Underground contacts. Lay Jr.'s escape through enemy lines would later produce a book, appropriately entitled, *I've Had It!*

At Thurleigh Field, Bartlett told Lay Jr., "You know when this war ends, people are going to forget what happened here. They won't care anymore. To prevent that from happening, you and I are going to write a novel about the Air Corps. It will take place at a solitary field like this one and we'll have a central character like Frank Armstrong.

"And," he continued, "when we finish the novel, we'll write a screenplay. It will be the best war film ever. With your combat experience and my inside knowledge of the command structure, we can write this thing from a unique point of view."[1]

Bartlett remained in the Tactical Section of the Eighth Air Force until the war in Europe ended. After a brief tour of duty with a B-29 training command, he joined Brigadier General Armstrong's staff and headed for the Pacific where a war had still to be won.

Before Hiroshima and Nagasaki brought the Second World War to a close, Colonel Bartlett flew with the 315th Combat Wing. Apply tagged the "Gypsy Rose Lee Unit," Bartlett's aircraft were stripped of all armament in favor of a huge bomb load.

Twelve O'Clock High was born as a novel on a sunny day in the spring of 1946. The two Air Corps officers were once more civilians: Lay Jr. as an active freelance writer, Bartlett as a screenwriter under contract to 20th Century–Fox. Lay Jr. had invited his friend to Santa Barbara for a pleasant day of recollection, but Bartlett was still interested in writing the definitive Air Corps novel. Lay, Jr. immediately tried to sidestep the issue.

He told Bartlett, "I've been giving it a lot of thought, and it seems to me that it's too soon after the war for such a project. Sure, we could publish a book, but you know the real money is in a film. The time just isn't right, People are tired of war films."[2]

"You're right," replied Bartlett, "but forget about the film possibilities for now. Let's write the novel. I know Hollywood, when we finish the book, I guarantee we'll have no problem selling the film rights."[3] He concluded by appealing to Lay Jr.'s conscience. There was no way they could let people forget men like Armstrong or fields like Thurleigh Aerodrome. It was their responsibility to let people know.

That same day, they outlined their main character, a brigadier general named Frank Savage, a composite of generals Armstrong and Curtis LeMay: the former contributing his good looks, a rugged disposition and a blend of masterfully inspired leadership; the latter a sense of discipline that would lend Savage his over-powering sense of mission.

Brigadier General Savage would command the mythical 918th Bombardment Group, a numerical designation arrived at by Lay Jr., who simply multiplied Armstrong's own 306th group by three. Bomber command headquarters retained its code name, Pinetree. Thurleigh Aerodrome was changed to Archbury.

In the novel, an Air Corps colonel named Keith Davenport, the 918th's original commanding officer, sacrifices discipline and becomes overly identified with his men, ultimately losing his sense of command and strategic purpose. General Savage leaves his position at Pinetree to assume command of Davenport's seemingly jinxed bombardment group.

These events were based entirely on fact. Only five weeks after Armstrong left his own 97th Group to assume a staff position, he was asked to relieve "Chip" Overacker, commander of the 306th at Thurleigh.

Sy Bartlett had accompanied the general to Thurleigh on that fateful morning. "When we drove through the gate," he recalled, "past the sentry without being challenged, I knew it was going to be one of those days. Frank blew his stack. It was only the beginning. Thurleigh was a mess. The officers were drunk. All over the base, military protocol and discipline were completely lax. There was no pride whatsoever. Frank found it appalling."[4]

In addition to formulating the basic plot, each writer contributed his own brand of expertise. Bartlett gave *Twelve O'Clock High* its excellent sense of dramatic structure, drawing on his long experience as a screenwriter. His RT-Intercept program was a natural addition to the novel, as was the love affair between Wren Officer Patricia Mallory and Savage.

Beirne Lay, Jr., contributed a sense of realism and the actual experience of command responsibility as a pilot. As a bomb-group commander, he spoke from experience. On the Regensberg/Schweinfurt raid, one of the war's most dangerous bombing missions, he had flown as an observer with the 100th Bombardment Group. After the raid, General LeMay had asked him to submit a report on the mission. It was later published almost verbatim in the *Saturday Evening Post*. The bare facts needed no embellishment.

Like Robert Pirosh, Lay Jr. had experienced war first hand and could write lucidly about it. He didn't bog his writing down in tactics and strategy, names and places. He wrote with a certain honest feeling that more effectively conveyed the reality of the air war. Combining this talent with Bartlett's behind-the-scenes knowledge made *Twelve O'Clock High* the classic air war novel of World War II.

Months before it was published, in the winter of 1946-47, Bartlett had interested Fox producer Louis D. Lighton (a former story editor under David O. Selznick at MGM) in the project, and Lighton, in turn, began a personal campaign to win over Darryl F. Zanuck. It was no easy task. War films remained a cold topic in studio circles.

Fortunately, Lighton was not the only interested producer. Bartlett's friend, director William Wyler, had expressed enthusiasm from the beginning. It was only natural. Wyler was an Air Corps veteran, and as commander of a combat camera unit, had produced one of the war's finest aerial documentaries, *The Memphis Belle,* a film about a B-17's 25th mission.

As fate would have it, it was Beirne Lay, Jr., who had greeted Wyler when he arrived in

Twelve O'Clock High **begins when retired U.S. Army Air Corps Major Harvey Stovall (Dean Jagger, right) finds a special Toby mug in a London haberdashery; it is the same mug that graced the mantle in the Archbury officers' club. When the face of the Toby is looking at the room, a mission has been ordered.**

London in mid–1942. General Ira Eaker had ordered him to take temporary charge of the director's camera unit, get the men quartered and organize equipment and basic training for the combat cameramen.

Against orders, Wyler later flew as a waist gunner, camera in hand, on several raids (one, during which he lost most of his hearing when his plane was hit by anti-aircraft fire), much to the chagrin of Lay Jr., who had been ordered by Eaker to ground Wyler.

"Whatever his other qualities, he had enormous guts," Lay Jr. recalled. "This wasn't easy. Someone on a set might think he was a sonofabitch or a sadist because he wanted twenty takes of a scene, but here in aerial combat was the acid test. With his own skin on the line, he went out there and took the pictures he wanted."[5]

Bartlett, Lay Jr. and Wyler resumed their friendship in Hollywood four years later. A bidding war erupted between Wyler at Paramount Pictures and Lighton at Fox. Financially, such a competition was a windfall for the writers. Their agent quickly upped the novel's sale price to a whopping $100,000. The critical factor was Zanuck, who had remained lukewarm to the project until Wyler had entered the fray. He had great respect for Wyler and the box-office success of his latest film, *The Best Years of Our Lives*. With that in mind, he authorized Lighton to outbid Wyler and win *Twelve O'Clock High* for 20th Century–Fox.

In going over the novel with the writers, prior to the writing of the screenplay, "Bud" Lighton found several sub-themes and while they enhanced the book's realism, he felt that they would only create confusion in a motion picture. Lighton had already decided that these subordinate themes would have to go, so the writers began to make note of the proposed trims. As Selznick's former story editor, Lighton had learned the importance of a tightly written script, and with Zanuck's key interest in the project, he wasn't going to let his writers get carried away with a long, overproduced screenplay.

"You can only have one principle theme," Lighton told Bartlett. "If Savage is your main character, then we have to eliminate some of the other material — you can't have everything."[6] Primary among these subordinate themes was the bitter behind-the-scenes rivalry among the officers at Pinetree. This was Bartlett's arena. The command structure at Eighth Air Force headquarters resembled the batting order of a major-league baseball team. When an officer proved inefficient, he was bounced back to the minors, which, in Air Corps jargon, was a stateside-training command. Personal relationships were always to be sacrificed for the strategic good.

Bartlett, while working in operational intelligence, discovered that generals Spaatz and Arnold frequently surrounded themselves with a group of pre-war flying buddies who were neither effective leaders nor competent tacticians.

In the novel, Bartlett put these conflicts to work. Jealousy pervaded the atmosphere of Pinetree. Savage's superiors continually attempt to send him back to the States. Effective leadership was often canceled out as one superior after another tried to hamper the general's mission. This was strong material, but it watered down the impact of the main theme of the novel — which was the transformation of the 918th under Savage's leadership and how he begins to exhibit the very qualities of the man whom he replaced, Keith Davenport. In Lighton's eyes, the Pinetree rivalry was unnecessary. With a wince from Bartlett, it was eliminated.

The novel's love story was yet another victim. "However natural it is to have Wren officer Mallory skulking about," Lighton told Lay Jr., "it's damn distracting. Here we're trying to build Savage into a Rock of Gibraltar, and he has this convenient release."[7]

Lay Jr. fought for Mallory, arguing that it was this very release that contributed to Savage's eventual collapse. Lay Jr. told Lighton, "You get used to the pressure, because it remains steady. Sometimes it's almost unbearable, but you take it. Remember what Savage said at his first briefing at Archbury, 'Write yourself off. Tell yourself you're already dead. Once you accept that fact it will be easier to fly those missions.' That was his philosophy. He had already written himself off. But something happened when he met Patricia Mallory. Suddenly, he had a release, someone to think about. He was no longer effectively isolated. It was the kind of distraction that would eventually destroy him."[8]

Lighton accepted Lay Jr.'s reasoning, but when the script went 40 pages too long, the love story was doomed. Patricia Mallory, the infighting at Pinetree and Bartlett's RT-Intercept program all became casualties of the novel-to-script transformation. Although taskmaster Lighton continued trimming the screenplay and established a powerful overriding theme, he simultaneously stretched the remaining scenes with reams of dialogue. Work eventually ground to a halt. A conflict had developed in the crucial confrontation scene between Savage and playboy officer Ben Gately.

Zanuck was furious. In the subdued atmosphere of depressing Archbury, *Twelve O'Clock High*'s characters had become non-stop chatterboxes. Symbolism had disappeared in an unending amount of talk. Lighton was fired from the project and *Twelve O'Clock High* was put on Zanuck's "what the hell do we do with it now?" shelf.

Fox six months, from March to September 1948, the project stagnated. Zanuck and his writers could not agree on the revisions. Aside from the ponderous amount of dialogue, Bartlett agreed with his partner and later informed Zanuck that the impasse centered on the crucial hospital confrontation between Savage and a wounded Gately.

In the novel, Gately, Davenport's playboy chief air executive, is busted to airplane commander when Savage takes a dim view of his leisurely military attitude. "You're a coward and a disgrace to this whole outfit," the enraged Savage tells him. To complete the humiliation, Gately is placed in command of "The Leper Colony," a B-17 aptly named because it harbors nine other misfits.

The antagonism between the officers is maintained to the very end of the novel when Savage discovers a new side to the man he once called coward. The awakening occurs in the Archbury hospital. Through Doc Kaiser, the group's medical officer, Savage learns that Gately is in traction, suffering from a painful spinal fracture caused by his ditching in the English Channel on a previous mission. Despite excruciating pain, Gately continued to fly "The Leper Colony" on the next three raids.

"It was a very awkward situation for both men," said Bartlett, "as there is still this great tension between them. Savage sits quietly at Gately's side, unable to articulate his feelings, the latter equally powerless to accept favors from the man who had treated him so roughly."[9]

Bartlett thought the confrontation should end in stalemate. Lay Jr. disagreed, claiming that it was time the tension between the two men eased. Although he agreed that an outright commendation was out of character, Lay Jr. felt Savage should somehow communicate his regard for the officer's perseverance, and that Gately should accept the reevaluation.

It was a touching scene — Savage's hard shell was finally cracking; the question was, how much? Eventually, the two writers compromised. Both officers would retain their unyielding positions in person, but once outside the hospital, Savage would praise the fallen airman within earshot of Gately, who accepts the praise with a smile, and the conflict is resolved. In the novel, it was an effective solution.

It is important to remember that the Gately/Savage conflict was only one of many in the novel. While the change in Savage's attitude in the hospital scene was important, it was not critical to the outcome of the book. The screenplay, however, presented a whole new series of problems.

Lighton had previously eliminated all of the subsidiary conflicts, making Savage's character transformation from "Rock of Gibraltar" to caring individual that much more important. Thus, the final confrontation with Gately was crucial to the script. In the film's final scene, Gately would lead the group in Savage's absence. The man who was branded a coward returns to base with all but two aircraft. It was impossible to work the novel's compromise into the script. An overheard conversation (along with a smile) was cinematically ineffective. Zanuck also wanted the conflict to simmer until Gately finally proves himself.

In late September 1948, Bartlett, newly arrived director Henry King and Zanuck met in Palm Springs to discuss a suitable ending. It was clear to all that Savage could never outwardly express his feelings to Gately. It was too far out of character. For Savage to remain withdrawn was more in keeping with his disposition.

It was Sy Bartlett's solution that prevented another impasse and got *Twelve O'Clock High* moving again. He told Zanuck, "Darryl, let's bring in a third party, a nurse. We'll keep the conversation between the two men low key, no giving, no receiving. Then Savage will leave and the nurse will come back in and inform Gately, 'Colonel, I've been informed that you're a special case.'"[10]

"How do I address you?" asks newly arrived base commander, Gen. Frank Savage (Gregory Peck, right) to Sgt. McIlhenny (Robert Arthur), who is caught out of uniform.

Gen. Savage (Gregory Peck, center) takes over command of the 918th Bombardment Group at Archbury from Col. Keith Davenport (Gary Merrill, left). Maj. Harvey Stovall (Dean Jagger) stands by.

It was a brilliant solution to a knotty problem. Who can forget the tears in Gately's eyes when he hears the nurse's message. Zanuck took one look at Bartlett, then turned to King and told him to start scouting locations.

Henry King was one of Zanuck's favorite directors. He was also the movie industry's acknowledged aviation expert. In a space of 25 years, he had logged over one million air miles in his own plane. Combining his interest in flying with his work in film, King was the first Hollywood director to search out locations by plane. Recalled King:

> Most of *Twelve O'Clock High*'s exteriors were shot at Eglin Field in Florida. It's a tremendous field but hard to get to unless you're flying there. I had Zanuck charter a DC-6, which carried 96 people, and I shipped four tons of equipment by another plane. Thus, a cast of 60 and a crew of 40 were able to leave Hollywood in the morning, unload in Florida in the afternoon and begin shooting the next morning.
>
> When shooting was completed, I flew my private plane to Big Springs, Texas, stayed overnight and then went on to Hollywood the next day. Meanwhile, a DC-6 took off from Eglin at 9:00 A.M. with the crew and cast and checked into the Fox studio at 4:30 P.M., the same day. Then, after a good night's sleep, everybody was ready to start work the next morning.
>
> If this had been set up by train, at least ten days would have been lost in travel and even then you would not have a fresh cast ready to start work the next day. Plane travel has cut down to one week on an average what would have taken one month in the old days.[11]

King was also an Air Corps veteran who served two years of active duty with the Ferry Command, the Gulf of Mexico submarine patrol, and as liaison with the Mexican Air Force, which, during World War II, guarded the strategic Tampico and Hermosillo oilfields. His contacts with the U.S. Army Air Force headquarters served him well once Zanuck assigned him to *Twelve O'Clock High*.

Twelve O'Clock High is mostly about the high-tension waiting game that Frank Savage (Gregory Peck, left) and Harvey Stovall (Dean Jagger) undergo, as they wait for their group to return from a mission.

Four grueling months in Italy filming *Prince of Foxes* with Tyrone Power had done little to weather King. Ten minutes after his first talk with Zanuck, King was in touch with 20th Century–Fox's chief art director Lyle Wheeler. Through Wheeler, he discovered that former producer Lighton had picked Santa Maria, California, for the film's primary location. With misgivings, King flew north in his private plane with newly assigned art director Maurice Ransford. His premonitions were confirmed. Santa Maria was level, but the small agricultural community was surrounded by round hillocks and volcanic formations. Rural England it wasn't.

With Zanuck's authorization, King left for the east coast. In New Jersey, he stopped off at McGuire Air Force Base, which proved equally unsuitable. Despite its alluring complement of 11 functioning B-17s, McGuire was structurally too complex to resemble tiny Archbury. A camouflage job was also deemed impossible.

After securing Pentagon cooperation in Washington, D.C., King went south toward big

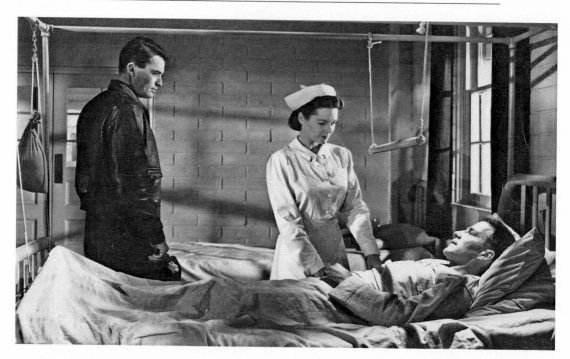

Gen. Frank Savage (Gregory Peck) visits Col. Ben Gately (Hugh Marlowe, right) in the hospital after it is revealed that Gately has been flying with a fractured spine. A nurse (Joyce Mackenzie) stands by.

Eglin Field in Florida. On the way, he picked up Colonel John DeRussy at the Army War College in Montgomery, Alabama. DeRussy, former commander of the 305th Bombardment Group, left his teaching job to become the film's principal technical advisor.

At Eglin, King resumed his wartime friendship with General Hoyt S. Vandenberg, former commander of the U.S. Ninth Air Force. Vandenberg cheerfully gave the director carte blanche at Eglin.

Ransford, the art director and Sy Bartlett were then summoned east to coordinate production plans. While Ransford measured the field and estimated construction costs, Bartlett underwent a concentrated 63-hour marathon story meeting with King. The topic was script revisions. Lighton's dialogue recommendations were being dumped like a cargo of bombs.

After that whirlwind effort, Bartlett returned to Hollywood to transcribe his notes and prepare the final shooting script. King soon followed. The script was mimeographed and sent directly to Zanuck. On January 24, 1949 — King's birthday — the director received a phone call from the studio. It was Zanuck. "Henry," he said, "it's the best script I've ever read. Happy Birthday."[12]

Two days later, Zanuck signed contract player Gregory Peck to portray General Savage. For Peck and King, it was the beginning of a relationship that accounted for four more successful films: *The Gun Fighter* (1950), *David and Bathsheba* (1951), *The Snows of Kilimanjaro* (1952) and *Beloved Infidel* (1959).

Not only was Peck fast becoming one of Hollywood's biggest box-office stars, but in a relatively short span, he had already been nominated three times for the Best Actor Oscar in *The Keys of the Kingdom* (1945), *The Yearling* (1946) and *Gentleman's Agreement* (1947). Tall, lanky Peck rose above his gentle personality to give one of the best performances of his career as General Savage.

Gregory Peck (left) didn't get a chance to smile too often in *Twelve O'Clock High*. Here, he gets a few moments of break time with Joyce MacKenzie, who portrays the nurse to Colonel Ben Gately.

Two other Fox contract players, Gary Merrill and Hugh Marlowe, were signed to play Davenport and Gately, respectively. Further augmenting the terrific cast was Dean Jagger in the crucial role of Major Harvey Stovall, the group adjutant. In many ways, Stovall became the film's conscience, a warm humanistic character through whom we see Archbury's and Savage's crucial transformation. He would win the Oscar for Best Supporting Actor that year, beating out *Battleground*'s James Whitmore.

Stovall fights his war from behind a desk. While he understands the long-term strategies, the logistics, the complications of modern war, his war is with a daily load of paperwork. Life at Archbury retains a human quality for him. He is surrounded by friends. Death becomes a swift-moving cloud.

"I'm a retread," he tells the general, "a mud merchant from World War I. I guess when I came over here they felt that I could only command a desk. But I'm a lawyer by profession, General. When I came to Archbury, I took on my biggest client, the 918th Bombardment Group. And, by God, I want to see it win its case at all costs."[13] Stovall's perseverance is a constant reminder to Savage that however mechanistic war has become, it is still waged with human blood.

That Stovall is a retread merely emphasized the fact that two former Air Corps officers-turned-writers were telling the story. Like *The Dawn Patrol,* 20 years earlier, the story of *Twelve O'Clock High* is told from the ground's point of view. It is the daily reactions of men like Stovall who wait for the planes to return that count. Had the writers endowed fighting characters like Savage and pilot Jesse Bishop with the major's insights, the film would have sacrificed its unique point of view.

The film, as well as the book, begins with a nostalgic flair. One year after the war, Harvey Stovall, now a civilian, discovers a slightly cracked Toby Mug in the window of a south London haberdashery. It is the very same mug that once graced the mantelpiece of the Officer's Club at Archbury. In the story, we quickly learn that when the mug is turned and its face is visible, a mission has been ordered.

For Stovall, the Toby unlocks a door to the recent past. After hurriedly purchasing the item, he travels by train, car, and then bicycle, to Archbury. He strolls across the deserted concrete air strip, now covered with cracks, weeds and disinterested cows. And, in the background, he begins to hear ghostly voices singing to him. He scans the field. Atop a decaying control tower, a battered windsock hangs lifelessly.

Then, abruptly, the air is filled with the sound of engines. The weeds are blown backwards by a burst of agitated air. The windsock comes to life with an energy of its own. Time disappears. It is World War II once more.

CHAPTER FOUR

The Bridge on the River Kwai

The curtain opens, the screen goes light and a solitary scavenger bird appears, gliding gracefully as it soars upward into the soft pale-blue sky. Evocative of freedom, it has all the time in the world to go about its business. Circling, searching for prey, it appears oblivious to all that is happening below. And there is a great deal, for this is 1943, and Siam has been overrun and occupied by the Japanese Imperial Army.

Below lies the jungle, a vast entangling carpet of teeming foliage, alive with the sounds of living things—birds, insects, reptiles, creatures of the land and water. The camera pans through this cacophony, waiting, wondering what will happen next. And then, beyond the rot, the untouched, unyielding mass of vegetation that one can almost smell, comes the sound of man.

It is a metallic retort, an alien presence in this atmosphere. But the sound is unmistakable. It is the steam whistle of a train, a Japanese military train moving on crudely laid tracks. There are sentries on the train, lazily holding their rifles. There is no human threat in this jungle, for the only enemy is a common one—nature. In any case, they are not worried; they are only herding the beaten survivors of the Singapore fiasco.

The train stops and a battalion of British prisoners disembarks. Shorn of its weapons and equipment, it is a military unit in name only. Physically, the men are a ragged lot with torn uniforms, skeletal bodies and wounds that are not healing. Nothing heals in this jungle. Many of them limp or are half-carried by their comrades. It appears to be another version of the Bataan Death March.

But there is something else here, something that cannot be seen, only felt. These men move purposefully. They have determination. They are not straggling along, but moving. It is a long way from the parade ground of Singapore, but this British battalion under the command of Lt. Colonel L. Nicholson (Alec Guinness), is a unit with spirit. Nicholson himself strides forward with a swagger stick, his chest thrown out, a symbol to his men, the defiant symbol of the British lion in captivity. His battalion is going to survive at all costs, even in this godforsaken jungle on the banks of the River Kwai.

The opening sequence to the 1957 film, *The Bridge on the River Kwai,* is a beautifully engineered example of *cinéma vérité*. There is no air of phony stage theatrics and there are no soundstage limitations. The jungle rot is the real thing, as is the scavenger bird, the Japanese train and the torn British uniforms. Together, they tell a story, a visual one that well complements the written word based on French author Pierre Boulle's novel.

49

Director David Lean's use of the outdoor locations to give the film its constant atmosphere of reality works almost effortlessly, as if nature herself had been painted and arranged carefully by an art director who, working with a sound-effects editor, simultaneously coordinated the noise of the jungle.

Although Hollywood movies had ventured outside before, especially in period adventure films and dramas like *The African Queen, Ivanhoe* and *From Here to Eternity, The Bridge on the River Kwai,* was, nonetheless, a trendsetter. In abandoning the soundstages for realistic backgrounds, this 1957 blockbuster expanded the general trend in Hollywood to move outside and give the new television audiences something they couldn't get on the small screen: true spectacle.

Soon, outdoor films were dazzling audiences with epic scope and running times. It was the age of the "road show," and movies suddenly became special events. Films like *The Ten Commandments, Around the World in Eighty Days, Ben-Hur, El Cid* and *Lawrence of Arabia* lured families into movie houses in record numbers, replenishing the coffers of a badly sagging industry.

Although the "big event" film was as old as Hollywood itself (D.W. Griffith's *The Birth of a Nation* was the first in a long line of spectacular films, followed later by David O. Selznick's *Gone with the Wind,* and the epics of Cecil B. DeMille), *The Bridge on the River Kwai* was really one of the first major motion pictures to open up the entire world of nature to the modern feature film camera. In terms of bringing greater realism to the war film genre, it marked a major turning point.

David Lean filmed in teeming jungles, amid the constant insect invasion, fighting for the proper atmosphere. His crew, which included Oscar-winning cameraman Jack Hildyard, waited for the proper sunsets, or the proper skies to add the right touch of nature to the story.

And *The Bridge on the River Kwai* was something else, too. It was a "thinking man's spectacle." Like later films such as *Spartacus* and *Lawrence of Arabia,* it avoided the mindlessness of spectacle by offering and emphasizing a superior story that introduced three-dimensional characters — real people. Here, in the jungle, a masterpiece of film engineering was to be created and it was all realized by flesh-and-blood actors and an equally talented crew.

Twenty years before Jack Hildyard ever pointed a camera, a disillusioned electrical engineering student named Pierre Boulle was contemplating an exodus. He was a bright young student in Paris, but he was bored with a tedious existence in secondary school. He yearned for adventure.

If Horace Greeley had lived in the City of Light during that spring of 1934, he would have beckoned young Boulle east, not west. In that year, scores of eager young Frenchmen, including some of Boulle's fellow classmates, were leaving France for the East Indian jungles. It was not a quest for gold or oil that was uprooting the youth of France. Nor was it an obsession with diamonds or other precious gems. It was rubber, and the world that now ran on automobile and truck tires was hungry for the stuff.

To the French, the rubber planters were the new pioneers. They were a tough adventuresome breed, men who had carved plantations out of the jungle, organized native labor and established a ready market for one of the world's most promising industries.

Seeking to join them, Boulle left school and headed for the city of Kuala Lumpur, the Malaysian gateway to the rubber country. He was soon introduced to Francois de Langlade, a mystery man who would one day become General Charles De Gaulle's clandestine representative in French Indochina. During a three-year apprenticeship, Boulle learned all about the rubber trade, and he made friends among the other rubber planters, a motley group of former Army officers, office managers and school teachers.

Meanwhile, political events were catching up with the French in Indochina. Following the invasion of China in the fall of 1937, Japanese imperialism proved far more urgent to the planters than the European war, which would engulf France two years later. The Japanese Army would soon be pushing into the rubber country, and Boulle realized that there was little to stop them.

When the French Army was demobilized in the late summer of 1941, which followed the fall of France to the Germans the previous year, a Japanese takeover of Malaysia became a foregone conclusion. With no army to protect them, the planters scattered. Boulle fled to Singapore, hoping to make contact with France's last line of defense, the Free French Forces.

At the bar of Singapore's Hotel Adelphi, he found his old boss, Langlade, and the other planters plotting guerrilla warfare against the advancing Japanese. As he listened, Pierre Boulle began a series of observations that would eventually lead to a novel entitled *Le Pont de la Rivière Kwai*.

In early 1941, only months before their Singapore base was overrun by General Yamashita's Imperial Guard, British Army Intelligence foresaw the importance and desirability of a future guerrilla operation and began secretly training the French planters as irregulars.

Their headquarters at Tanjong-Ralai (about 17 miles from Singapore) was disguised as a convent, and it was here that a commando group later known as 136th Army (*The Bridge on the River Kwai*'s Force 316) was born. In the huge plantation house located at the mouth of a river in the heart of a forest reserve (reconstructed tree for tree like the jungle), which would later become his theater of operations, Boulle received instruction in British commando tactics. He learned how to sink a cargo ship in port with the aid of a magnetic cupping glass, how to silently dispose of an enemy sentry, how to blacken the face with any means available, how to derail a train, how to destroy a bridge, and — even more importantly for his future book — how to blow up a train and a bridge.

British colonels Gavin and Chapman found their students to be avid learners, and it wasn't long before the French planters were ready to put their training to the test. Langlade, who had become their leader, suggested that they quickly organize an expedition to Indochina. Not only would the sortie apply a needed edge to their training, but, as the Japanese were steadily moving south, it would most likely be the last chance to disembark materials for their future sabotage operations.

The basic problem was transportation. Catalina seaplanes, the old inter-island workhorses, were now obsolete. British submarines were unavailable, and the American B-24 Liberator bomber (from which Boulle's future saboteurs were launched for the Kwai) was still a drawing on the table of a Consolidated Aircraft design engineer.

In desperation, the group commandeered a converted houseboat, which had only recently transported passengers along the Shanghai River. They departed Tanjong-Ralai in September 1941. Hugging the Malay Peninsula, they headed north, conserving fuel whenever possible in preparation for the dash across the South China Sea.

Fortunately, considering the unseaworthiness of their ancient vessel, a decoded radio message advised them that a major Japanese battle fleet stood in their way. Langlade canceled the operation and they turned around and headed back to Singapore, where Pierre Boulle resumed his work as an office clerk.

Three months later, Malaya and the Pacific Islands were invaded by the Japanese. It was soon obvious that the British would not be able to hold out, so it was decided that Langlade's Free French should go to China. In January 1942, Pierre Boulle left for Rangoon, Burma. Langlade had intimated that China would be a favorable meeting place for their projected forays into Indochina, so for three weeks Boulle waited for authorization to enter. Finally, he offered his services as a chauffeur, and, at the wheel of a Buick destined for the English consul general in Kunming, he drove through Burma. The spirit of adventure present throughout his later novel can be traced back to these chaotic days along the Burmese border.

Reunited once again with Langlade and the planters, Boulle contacted the Chinese military authorities to obtain their support in crossing the Indochina frontier. While the political and military picture along the border was slowly deteriorating, the Chinese continued their entanglement in ponderous bureaucratic procedures that would eventually handcuff their armies in the field. It was only after interminable feasts with overbearing Chinese authorities that permission to cross the frontier was finally granted.

In June 1942, Boulle and Langlade arrived by mule train in the village of Ba Van, which lay in the strategically located Nam Na River Valley, the waterway of which penetrated the Indochina frontier. On several occasions, Boulle journeyed to the frontier to scout out the land. He suggested to the weary Langlade that they journey to Hanoi by water. He figured that by utilizing the Nam Na River, they could cross into Indochina, branch off to the River Noire, and then ride the current to the Red River, which would lead them directly into Hanoi.

Meanwhile, the situation soon brightened. The supplies secretly acquired by Langlade finally arrived. Arms, radios, boxes of preserves, folding beds, and medications were all in their possession, and plans for their first operation were made.

To young Boulle, the descent of the rapids from Ba Van to Hanoi, a 450-mile journey, seemed an athletic exercise, which he hoped to accomplish in six nights, resting and hiding by day. Langlade, though, was skeptical. The more so since he could not accompany Boulle on the expedition, having been recalled to London by the Free French Committee. After many hesitations, he authorized Boulle to make the journey alone.

Boulle began by constructing a raft, which he reinforced with Chinese string and large bamboos to form a solid, if not comfortable, platform. With a few items of clothing, so as not to arrive in Hanoi too lightly dressed, and an English-Chinese dictionary (which could serve for code), all of which was carefully packed in a case of rainproof material, Pierre Boulle was ready for the great adventure.

The most difficult problem was to find a part of the Nam Na that was even theoretically navigable. The guides who had accompanied him to the frontier had left and Boulle found himself alone in the jungle darkness, on the bank of a stream. After attempting a descent and finding himself in the middle of a rice paddy, he finally discovered a tributary of the Nam Na capable of transporting him through a network of irrigation canals without risk of discovery. For three days and three nights, Boulle braved the jungle on the waterway, living the ordeal that the later film would reserve for Commander Shears (William Holden) — the escape from the River Kwai.

Caught by whirlpools which ensnared the raft for hours, buffeted brutally in his descent of the rapids, touched with fever, overwhelmed with fatigue, too exhausted to even light a cigarette to burn off the leeches that clung to his legs, or to fight against the invasion of ants that crawled over his body, Boulle continued to push towards Hanoi, still hundreds of miles to the east.

The dawn of the fourth day found him sick with dizziness. He could no longer find concealment. The jungle had given way to rice fields where Thai peasants curiously watched the exhausted white man drift by on the nightmarishly slow-moving river.

As his raft approached a forest, Boulle seized the opportunity to land, only to find himself facing 30 angry Thai villagers advancing towards him. His fate was sealed.

Instead of finding himself among friendly villagers, as Shears would in the film, Boulle had beached on military land in the territory of Laichau, about 250 miles northwest of Hanoi. He knew that the peasants had orders to stop all suspects found on such territory. Fearful of being handed over to the Japanese (he was unaware that they were still far to the east), Boulle pretended to be a tourist.

His captors carried him to the nearest village where he was inspected by the Thai militia and locked in a makeshift room. Meanwhile, his raft had been carefully stripped. In a state of exhaustion and fever, Boulle fell asleep. He was later awakened by a French-speaking native inspector of the guard, who entered his room and questioned him.

Boulle told his interrogator that he was from Ba Van, on the other side of the frontier, and that some emissaries he had sent to the Indochinese zone had assured him that the commander of the territory of Laichau was sympathetic to the Free French. The inspector listened intently, but said nothing. After 20 minutes, he excused himself and left.

Two days later, Boulle was taken to the French commander of the territory. After weighing the matter carefully, he had decided to reveal his true identity, as well as the reasons which had brought him, like a French Moses, to Laichau.

When brought before the Commander, he declared at once, "I am an officer of the Free French. Can you help me?"

The Commander looked at Boulle, got up slowly and began speaking in a confident manner. "I wish for the Allied victory, but the Gaullists are misled and acting against the best interests of France. I shall always remain faithful to the Marshal (Petain) who wants to maintain discipline at all costs. Discipline is essential at this moment above everything moral. I cannot help you. It is, thus, necessary for me to arrest you."[1]

In this incredibly stubborn Frenchman, Boulle had found the prototype for his main character in *The Bridge on the River Kwai*, the English Colonel, Nicholson. During a two-year prison sentence, Boulle began fashioning the notes that would eventually lead to his novel.

American screenwriter Carl Foreman was exiled in London when Boulle's original French novel, *Le Pont de la Rivière Kwai*, was published in 1952. Foreman's troubles had begun the previous fall. In a prepared statement read before the House Committee on Un-American Activities (then investigating reports of communist subversion in the motion picture industry), Foreman admitted a one-time association with the Communist Party, but assured the Committee that he had terminated all ties in 1949. His admission proved unsatisfactory. When asked to reveal names, Foreman refused, invoking the Fifth Amendment.

Producer Stanley Kramer immediately severed their partnership, which had included successful collaborations on such critically acclaimed Foreman scripts as *Champion*, *Home of the Brave*, *The Men* and *High Noon*. Foreman's name began to appear on the Committee's "uncooperative list," and blacklisting in Hollywood soon followed.

Unable to find work in California or New York, despite the support of staunch anti-communists such as actor Gary Cooper, Foreman went to London, a bitter and disillusioned writer. In the spring of 1952, he was confronted by State Department officials, who pulled his passport.

Fortunately for Foreman, English producer Alexander Korda had respect for his talents and, ignoring the blacklist situation in America, signed Foreman on as a producer/writer with Korda's own production company, London Films.

Foreman was struggling through Pierre Boulle's French prose when Major Ian Fielding's English translation of *The Bridge on the River Kwai* first appeared. It was one book that begged for dramatization. As Foreman recalled:

The thing that struck me about the book entirely apart from the fact that it technically was an English subject and could be a British film (and I had to make British films at that time because of the blacklist), was the fact that a Frenchman was taking a hard, objective, and yet cynical, look at both the British and Japanese military officer castes.

What Boulle was saying in terms of his two leading characters, Colonel Nicholson, and Colonel Saito, the commandant of the Japanese prison camp, was that they were very much alike. If anything, they were two sides of the same coin. He was making other statements as well, perhaps having fun with the notion that the English and Japanese were also similar because they were both island people.[2]

Although French producer Henri Georges Cluzot of *Les Diaboliques* fame had optioned screen rights immediately after Boulle's novel was published, he had been unable to raise enough money to begin production. Foreman purchased Cluzot's option for a paltry $850 (10 percent of the total purchase price, on a six-month option). The following day, Foreman presented the project to Korda as his first venture under the Union Jack. Korda was uninterested.

"In fact," said Foreman, "he hated the book. He failed to understand the character of Colonel Nicholson. He saw him as a madman. Holding that viewpoint, he felt that the English public could never accept such a character."[3]

Foreman did not want to give up the novel, but he couldn't bankroll the film himself, either. He would have to search for another producer to put up the funds. Two days after Korda rejected the project, Foreman heard from American producer Sam Spiegel, who was also in love with the Boulle novel.

Spiegel had just completed *On the Waterfront*, a film that was soon to sweep the 1954 Academy Awards. Interestingly, it was one of the few films Spiegel had ever filmed within the borders of the United States.

Like Pierre Boulle, Sam Spiegel was an adventurer at heart. Born in Jareslau, in what was known as the old Austro-Hungarian Empire, on November 11, 1901, he had spent much of his youth as a "young pioneer" in Palestine. In 1928, he arrived in Hollywood, where he began working as a production assistant at Universal Pictures. In 1930, production chief Carl Laemmle sent him to Europe to handle overseas production. It was a powerful position for the young adventurer and in his dealings with foreign governments (especially during the political chicanery associated with the marketing of Universal's *All Quiet on the Western Front* in Europe), Spiegel was introduced to such notables as Adolf Hitler, Joseph Goebbels and Benito Mussolini. But Spiegel was Jewish, and time was running out for the Jews in Europe. When Hitler rose to power in 1933, Spiegel fled to Hollywood.

After World War II, he formed Horizon Pictures with director John Huston. The pair's greatest success was *The African Queen* (1951), which was written by James Agee, and which won Humphrey Bogart his only Academy Award for Best Actor.

Following *On the Waterfront*, Spiegel left for Europe. In July 1954, he met director Elia Kazan in Paris, where they discussed a possible film version of Paul Osborne's 1939 play, *Morning's at Seven*. While in Paris, he became enchanted with the English translation of *The Bridge on the River Kwai*.

Through French producer Henri Cluzot, he learned that Foreman had already purchased an option on the screen rights, and later the same day he was told that Alexander Korda had promptly rejected the project. Spiegel contacted Foreman and, at a secret meeting place in England (Foreman could not journey to Paris because of his restricted passport), he bought the screen rights for $7,000. Foreman also agreed to write the screenplay for an additional $10,000.

Sam Spiegel (right) shows off a production sketch of the Kwai bridge during pre-production on *The Bridge on the River Kwai.*

That an American producer had purchased Boulle's novel proved quite significant in terms of the projected film's plot line and characters. One of Spiegel's first directives to Foreman was to create an American character in the story for box-office purposes.

Major Shears, the English commando in the novel, thus became Commander Shears, the American opportunist who makes a miraculous escape from the camp on the Kwai, only to be assigned to a commando mission that is sent in to blow up the bridge. Foreman still retained the overriding conflict between Nicholson and Japanese Colonel Saito, along with the important themes on madness and hypocrisy in the Siamese jungle of 1943. Foreman was also fascinated by Boulle's use of irony throughout the novel.

"After all," said Foreman, "the whole thrust of Boulle's novel was that whatever man planned or tried or essayed, he was always subject to natural law, which, in a sense, made him small and powerless. This was to be a recurring theme throughout the entire film."[4]

In the late winter of 1954-55, after signing British actors Jack Hawkins and Charles Laughton to play Warden and Nicholson, respectively, David Lean as director and Jack Hildyard as cinematographer, Sam Spiegel began the first of four trips around the world in search of locations. Columbia Pictures had agreed to finance the motion picture; the question remained, where to film?

Upon arriving to work at the finished prison camp, members of the cast and crew are feted by a local Ceylonese dance troupe. David Lean is seated in the first row on the far left, next to Alec Guinness and Sessue Hayakawa.

Hoping to find the actual bridge site, Spiegel, Lean and Hildyard embarked for the jungles of Siam, which turned out to be a major disappointment. Not only were there no roads to carry in or maneuver a cast of several hundred actors and a sizeable crew, but the River Kwai, which actually runs there, proved, from a purely cinematic point of view, to be quite small and uninteresting.

When Spiegel mentioned his observations to his guide, he was informed that the Malay Peninsula was unmatched in scenic beauty. The scouting unit moved south to the river country, only to see their potential locations overrun with Communist guerrillas. Two armored trucks were assigned to protect them, but when one of the vehicles was captured and half of its occupants killed, Spiegel called off the reconnaissance. Exhausted after a month's travel, Lean suggested that they recuperate at Mount Lavinia, a seaside resort on the island of Ceylon.

Ceylon (Sri Lanka today) is a magical island whose history is steeped in legend. According to one Islamic tale, it was to Ceylon that Adam and Eve fled once life became too harsh in the Garden of Eden. With its varied landscape, and breathtaking scenery, Spiegel quickly realized that Ceylon was ideally suited to Boulle's wide-ranging story.

Although not the first producer to stumble upon the island's native charm (between 1952 and 1955, the island had been used as a location in such films as *Outpost in Malaya, Elephant Walk, The Beachcomber* and *The Purple Plain*), Spiegel's crew would be the first to record its beauty with a Cinemascope wide-screen camera. With the location set, Spiegel returned to Hollywood to organize a major crew and to continue casting, leaving Lean and Hildyard in Colombo, the island's capital, to search out the exact location for the bridge and the prison camp. They were soon joined by art director Donald Ashton, his assistant Geoffrey Drake, and Carl Foreman, who delivered to Lean a completed first-draft screenplay.

Ashton was a particularly valuable asset. Stationed in Ceylon with the British Army during World War II, he had married a planter's daughter at war's end. With his keen knowledge of the countryside, the crew had little trouble finding locales to match the actual sites depicted in the completed screenplay.

In an abandoned stone quarry in Mahara, Ashton planted the Japanese Imperial Army pennant and began construction on Colonel Saito's prison camp, No. 16. It would take five months to complete. In the absence of dump trucks and steam shovels, elephants were the prime movers during the construction phase. On film, the finished camp is a nest of scraggly bamboo huts beset by swarms of mosquitoes and surrounded by hundreds of makeshift wooden crosses, marking the graves of Camp 16's former tenants.

It was the construction of the bridge, though, that symbolized Spiegel's supreme quest for ultimate authenticity. Based upon a sketch of an actual railroad bridge scribbled on a tattered piece of cigarette paper and smuggled across the Burma-Siam border into Lord Louis Mountbatten's Southeast Asia Headquarters in Ceylon, the Kwai bridge became one of the largest outdoor sets in motion picture history.

A third longer than a football field and as tall as a six-story building, it would take six months to build with Ceylonese labor and elephants, at a total cost of $250,000. With the original sketch in hand, Spiegel hired a London-based engineering firm to draw up the actual plans for the bridge.

Ashton surveyed several Ceylonese rivers before he spotted the proper location across the Kilaniya River at Kitulgala, 56 miles northeast of Colombo.

Reinforced by 48 elephants, numbered for easy identification like so many football running backs, several hundred workers began work on the bridge in the early spring of 1956. Fifteen hundred trees were cut down in the surrounding forest and fashioned into pillars, which were transported by elephants across man-made roads and a specially constructed trestle bridge to Kitulgala, where they were pile-driven into the ground to create a structure larger than any in Ceylon (425 feet long and 90 feet high).

As work progressed on the bridge throughout the summer and early fall of 1956, Spiegel resumed his international search for his cast. In August, he went to Tokyo and signed Sessue Hayakawa, a former American silent film star, for the important role of Colonel Saito, the prison camp commandant.

Back in Colombo, Carl Foreman was encountering increasing difficulties in fashioning the final shooting script. Between Spiegel's demand for commercialism and Lean's stubborn attention to detail, Foreman's patience was wearing very thin.

The primary sore point concerned the film's ending. In the novel, Nicholson discovers Force 316's demolition cables, betrays the sabotage to the Japanese and dies in a hail of shrapnel from Warden's mortar bombs. The bridge remains standing and Force 316's mission is a failure. Spiegel rejected Boulle's ending. He saw the explosion of the bridge as a potentially awesome cinematic event, rivaling Cecil B. DeMille's parting of the Red Sea in his just-released epic, *The Ten Commandments*. Accordingly, he ordered Foreman to rewrite Boulle's finale, having the British commandos succeed in blowing up the bridge just as a ceremonial Japanese train, loaded with dignitaries, enters the gorge.

Director David Lean was concerned with the question of whether or not Colonel Nicholson, by leading the Japanese to the demolition cables, was involved in an act of treason. Was it treason or insanity?

Says Foreman, "Being British, David was quite sensitive about the impression Nicholson would give to an audience. In my opinion, it was never treason. But it was the ultimate insanity. This man had built a bridge and the bridge had become more important to him than the entire war."[5]

Lean agreed with Foreman: "In most movies about war, people are conceived of as heroes. Aren't they wonderful? There was no question that Nicholson was a very brave man, but wasn't he also a fool who in the end became a blithering idiot."[6]

Although writer and director agreed upon Nicholson's basic motivation, a conflict revolved around the manner of his death and the fate of the bridge. Did Nicholson actually fall on the detonator plunger purposefully in the film, after being hit by Warden's mortar bombs? Or was it entirely an accident that he fell on the plunger just as the train hit the bridge?

"In my ending," explained Foreman, "the bridge was blown up, but again, by the same stroke of ironic chance that pervaded the whole film, it was only partially destroyed, and remained standing. The Colonel did not throw his body on the detonator. David and I dis-

Sam Spiegel (second from left), spends some time with his actors, William Holden (left), Sessue Hayakawa (second from right), and Alec Guinness.

cussed this scene many times and I thought this would be wrong. David always wanted Nicholson to do something that would expiate his previous actions, the discovery of the cables, the death of Lieutenant Joyce, the death of Shears, etc. I disagreed because any last-minute reformation would have been a serious copout."[7]

Neither Lean's desire for an honorable death nor Foreman's quest for irony prevailed. It was still Spiegel's show, and in his own mind, the destiny of the film lay in spectacle, not irony.

A frustrated Foreman bided his time, attempting to reconcile his differences with Lean. It was another development, however, that eventually forced the point. In the early summer of 1956, Foreman had written to the House Committee on Un-American Activities, requesting another interview. Foreman recalled the anxieties of his original appearance: "My mistake was in standing on the Fifth Amendment instead of the First. The First Amendment guarantees freedom of speech; the Fifth, against 'self incrimination,' implies you've got something to hide, something you feel guilty of, or ashamed of, something criminal. I had nothing to hide. But, at the time, I was ill advised."[8]

Granted a new interview, Foreman stood before the Committee that August, and after being termed a fine patriotic American, was given a clean bill of health. For the first time in five years, he could return to work in the United States. Rumors were rife that Columbia Pictures was offering him a multi-picture production contract. Foreman was no longer the blacklisted exile; he had unstuck himself.

It was certainly a good excuse to wave goodbye to Lean. Outnumbered and having lost his last measure of creative control on the project, Foreman left Ceylon and asked Spiegel for his release. Spiegel was sympathetic and asked Foreman to recommend another writer who could work with Lean.

Foreman recommended Michael Wilson, another blacklisted Hollywood exile, then living in Paris. He explained to Spiegel that Wilson would be quite willing to work anonymously for a reasonable sum. Spiegel thanked Foreman, took down Wilson's name and address and hired, instead, screenwriter Calder Willingham, who spent three horrid weeks in Colombo, became fed up with Lean and departed.

Foreman pointed out that Lean wanted a British writer if one could be found. "Underneath it all, this was our major problem. We were divided by a common language!"[9]

Eventually, Spiegel took Foreman's advice and persuaded Lean to try Wilson. At last, the collaboration succeeded. Wilson, who had previously worked with William Wyler on *Friendly Persuasion*, arrived from Paris, checked into Colombo's Galle-Face Hotel and began rewriting Foreman's screenplay. The first ten days were spent in conference with Lean and Spiegel, during which time an agreement was finally reached on the general thrust of his rewriting. It was pointed out that, aside from reworking the ending, his primary task was now to develop a new character for Commander Shears, the American, and to make his role equal in stature to that of the British and Japanese colonels. He was to do the same for the role of Major Warden, the British commando leader.

For nine weeks, throughout August and September of 1956, Wilson, working closely with Lean, rewrote and completed the final script of *The Bridge on the River Kwai*. At his insistence, there were no daily conferences, and meetings with Lean occurred only when he had completed a long sequence of 20 to 30 pages.

Remembered Wilson: "My relationship with David Lean was a good one, although he was not an easy man to please. Meticulous in all respects, he did not readily commit himself to some of my new ideas, although in time he came to accept most of them."[10]

One of Wilson's primary contributions was the conflict that develops between Shears

Col. Nicholson (Alec Guinness) proudly stands next to a plaque commemorating the British effort to build the River Kwai bridge.

and Warden, the commando and demolition expert. In the movie, Commander Shears arrives in Ceylon, after having survived a harrowing escape from the Kwai. As an officer, he's given first-class accommodations at the local hospital, he's allowed to date a beautiful nurse, and he even procures some alcohol to make martinis for his beach parties. Life isn't bad.

What we don't know is that Shears isn't an officer at all, but an "ordinary swab jockey" who switched uniforms with a dead man before he was captured. The last person he wants to meet right now is Major Warden, who invites Shears to join an expedition to blow up the bridge. Whereas Shears wants to survive the war at all costs, Warden is another duty-bound, "stiff-upper-lip" Englishman who considers duty first. Stoking this conflict, and turning Warden into another Colonel Nicholson, created an opportunity for a simmering conflict between Warden and Shears. This conflict reaches its height in the jungle when Warden is wounded and asks to be left behind.

When Spiegel signed actor William Holden to play Shears, Wilson was able to turn Shears into another Sefton — the opportunistic character from Billy Wilder's classic prisoner of war movie, *Stalag 17,* that had won Holden an Oscar in 1953 for Best Actor. Considering the fact that irony plays such a part in Boulle's novel, isn't it ironic that in a key scene in *Stalag 17,* Sefton is castigating his fellow prisoners over making dangerous escape attempts, when he suddenly says, "What do you guys think the chances are of getting out of here? And let's say

Escaping to Ceylon, Shears (William Holden, right) gets some much-needed R & R, with a lovely nurse (Ann Sears).

you make it to Switzerland, let's say to the States. So what. They ship you out to the Pacific, slap you into another plane and you get shot down again. Only this time you end up in a Japanese prison camp, that is, if you're lucky." In terms of William Holden's fate, truer words were never spoken.

In late September 1956, Charles Laughton, Spiegel's original choice for Colonel Nicholson, asked for his release so that he could rejoin the Broadway production of *Major Barbara*. Spiegel immediately contacted actor Alec Guinness who had already refused the part several times. Guinness, who, 20 years later, would be embraced by a new generation as Obi-Wan Kenobi in *Star Wars,* claimed that his fans knew him primarily as a comedian. Moviegoers, he concluded, could never accept him as the rabidly austere Colonel Nicholson.

But Spiegel wanted him. Accompanied by Lean, who had directed Guinness before in such films as *Great Expectations* (1946) and *Oliver Twist* (1948), he flew to London for one final effort and visited the actor, who was working on the stage production of *Hotel Paradiso*.

Spiegel invited him to dinner after a midweek performance. Guinness reiterated that it was useless to persuade him, but, nonetheless, accepted the dinner invitation graciously. It is a credit to Spiegel that, by dessert, Guinness had accepted the part.

While in London, Spiegel also signed actor James Donald to play Clifton, the dry, perpetually exasperated medical officer whose final cry of "Madness! Madness!" when the bridge is blown and everyone lies dead, ends the film.

From London, Spiegel winged west to Hollywood, leaving copies of the completed script with Cary Grant and William Holden. Before Grant could even glance at the script, Holden (then Hollywood's No. 1 box-office attraction) had read it, became enchanted with the Shears part, phoned Spiegel to accept the role and made preparations for his departure that winter.

Holden's new contract, signed one week after his arrival in Colombo, Ceylon, was a financial milestone. He would receive a basic salary of $250,000, plus 10 percent of the film's gross receipts in excess of $2.5 million. For his work on *The Bridge on the River Kwai,* Holden would eventually see over $2 million. Spiegel's cast now included two of the world's top stars. Jack Hawkins, whom he had previously cast as Major Warden, was then England's No.1 box-office attraction.

After a brief trip to Ceylon to witness the commencement of pre-production second unit photography, Spiegel began a concentrated search for a youthful actor to play Lieutenant Joyce, as well as several actresses to add still more production value to the film. Holden, without a love interest, was commercially unthinkable.

The search for Joyce, the young commando officer whose indecisiveness jeopardizes the

"Would you like to see where you were?" asks Maj. Warden (Jack Hawkins, right) of Force 316. Shears (William Holden, left) having miraculously escaped from the prison camp on the Kwai, registers his indifference.

entire mission, took a great deal of time. After a hundred unrewarding interviews, Spiegel paused in his search to attend the New York premiere of his latest film, *The Strange One*, which Horizon Pictures had filmed in Florida. In the small part of a military college cadet who is brutally beaten, Spiegel spotted young Geoffrey Horne and was immediately captivated by his sensitive performance. In a movie he had produced himself, Spiegel had discovered his green commando.

With principal photography due to begin in less than a month, Spiegel quickly signed lovely blonde Anne Sears to play opposite William Holden in the Ceylon love scenes (later filmed at Mount Lavinia, where a beach resort was hastily converted into a British Army hospital).

November 1956 dawned auspiciously. The bridge was completed, hundreds of extras were hired and David Lean was ready to begin work with the actors. Filming began in the prison camp at Mahara on November 26. Every day, the location company hired a special train to carry the hundreds of extras needed for the prison camp scenes. Dubbed the "Spiegel Special," it left Colombo every morning at 4:00 A.M. Shooting didn't begin until 9:00 A.M., but the task of transforming the huge number of extras, through makeup and costume, into half-starved prisoners of war took nearly four hours.

Lt. Joyce (Geoffrey Horne, right) is about to show his courage by taking out Col. Saito (Sessue Hayakawa, center), while the obsessed Col. Nicholson (Alec Guinness) is prepared to defend the bridge at all costs.

William Holden, protected by a sandbagged emplacement, prepares to photograph the bridge's destruction.

In keeping with the film's ever-present irony, most of the Japanese soldiers portrayed as camp guards were actually Chinese. Several of the British prisoners were Italians and Germans, many of the sunburnt Australians were fair-skinned Asiatics, and all of the Indians were Ceylonese.

After a spirited New Year's celebration, Lean shifted his cameras to the Kitulgala Valley location, site of Ceylon's newest tourist attraction, "The Bridge." He would return to Mahara briefly for a set of exteriors with newly arrived William Holden. The latter's arrival in Colombo on December 8, rivaled the welcome given Queen Elizabeth earlier in the year. Exotic dancers and musicians from Kandy piped him from his plane to customs while Ceylon's prettiest maidens threw perfumed flowers at his feet and a baby elephant carried his bag.

Surrounded by the lush Ceylonese landscape, and given his characteristic desire for perfection, David Lean seldom missed a chance to blend superb acting with symbolic atmosphere. Throughout the film, Lean used the colorful jungle backgrounds as integral parts of the film's action sequences. He often painted the jungle in several moods. Quiet and mysterious when Joyce and Warden track the lone Japanese soldier, it becomes cruel and unyielding during the final trek to the bridge when Warden limps along on a chipped bone in his foot. Composer Malcolm Arnold would later give these scenes a grandly adventuresome quality with what would be an Oscar-winning score.

The bridge is blown.

Lean portrays the River Kwai as being virtually silent at night when Shears and Joyce carefully float their raft down the rapids and place the explosive charges under the bridge piles. This continues in the morning when the river becomes foreboding, its exposed banks and wallows symbolic of a hidden truth.

With the bridge exteriors completed, Alec Guinness returned to London. Preparations were now made to blow up the $250,000 set.

Spiegel had been planning the demolition for two years. Several cameras would record the tremendous blast, the collapse of the bridge and the fall into the gorge of an overage train, which had been purchased from the Ceylonese government. It was obviously the film's single most delicate scene. If the train was blown off the bridge prematurely, there was no chance for a second take.

For the sabotage sequence, Spiegel imported a select team from Imperial Chemical in London. The demolition experts studied every plank of the bridge for weeks. While the film's Force 316 utilizes a relatively modest amount of plastic explosive in their handiwork, the men from Imperial surmised that it would take at least a thousand pounds of Glasgow dynamite to blow the train off the bridge.

"Even then," said one expert, "nobody knows whether the bridge will blow up or merely be knocked down. This is because the bridge is so heavy and so high. Also, if the explosives are placed underneath the log supports, the supports could break like matchsticks under the weight above, forcing the bridge to topple over into the river rather than lifting the bridge and train in the grand style which audiences, accustomed to watching Hollywood's explosives, expect."[11]

As a necessary precaution, Spiegel asked for and was given a detachment of soldiers to guard the bridge against premature sabotage. The night after the demolition charges had been carefully placed, a truck carrying gasoline mysteriously caught fire a few yards from the bridge. The driver jumped from the blazing vehicle, which headed, out of control, towards the bridge. Quick as lightning, the Ceylonese soldiers risked their lives to head the truck off and turn it down a steep precipice. It finally landed in the river, where it exploded at a safe distance from the bridge.

Finally, on the morning of March 11, 1957, everything was ready. Four cameras, safely dug into sandbagged emplacements, were in position to record the explosion at close range. Slightly out of range, members of the cast and crew waited expectantly in another series of bunkers, their own cameras trained on the doomed bridge. Hovering overhead, an RAF helicopter contained a fifth camera, ready to shoot the explosion from still another angle.

For the ground emplacements, it was arranged by Lean that the cameramen would all leave their cameras a few moments before the explosion and proceed to places of safety. All the ground units had been wired so that the cameramen could press a button, which would inform producer Spiegel, in a command bunker, that they were safe and that their cameras were in working order. Spiegel would then give the signal to the men from Imperial to blow the bridge.

A human error nearly cost Spiegel all the months of effort and expense. In his excitement, one cameraman forgot to press his safety button. As the now unstoppable train rolled forward, thoughts raced through the producer's head. This was the moment of the biggest scene in the film, but if one cameraman had not reached his place of safety, he might still be hurt, even killed.

Spiegel ordered the demolition halted. The 65-year-old locomotive rode across the bridge unharmed, over the few feet of rail extending beyond and ploughed off the track. Ironically, in Pierre Boulle's novel, the Japanese train actually makes it across the bridge, only to be blown over by a lone charge placed by a second-guessing Warden.

After this near disaster, the elephants were ordered forward and the repair work began. Throughout the day and night of March 11, the crew repaired the damage, lifted the train back onto the track and once more backed it to its starting point.

At two minutes before ten on the morning of March 12, the green lights began to flash in Spiegel's command bunker. Loud speakers blared forth a final warning to the few spectators within the danger area. Actors William Holden, Jack Hawkins and Geoffrey Horne retreated to their sandbagged emplacements. The sound mixer's tape recorder awoke to the sound of a train whistle. A thin puff of smoke signaled the approach of the doomed locomotive. Awakened from their sleep, a few jungle birds flew skyward.

At exactly 10:00 A.M., Spiegel gave the signal to Imperial Chemical. A thousand pounds of dynamite, ignited by a maze of circuitry, ripped the bridge apart. As the bridge collapsed, the locomotive arrived to fall expertly into the gorge along with its passenger cars. It was a spectacular sequence, well worth the effort and expense.

Locomotive steam was still rising above the Kitulgala Valley when a motorcycle escort convoyed the precious film cargo to Colombo Airport. Spiegel was taking no chances. Five different airplanes would transport the explosive footage to processing labs in London.

Minutes after the explosion, souvenir hunters, ignoring the repeated warnings, swarmed over the bridge's fallen timbers. Others took undamaged timber for practical purposes, like building fences and sheds, and parts of the train were gathered by junk men for scrap metal. Its man-made dam eliminated, the torrential Kilaniya River later swept away most of what remained.

The Bridge on the River Kwai swept the 1957 Academy Awards, won Best Picture of the year and became a box-office phenomenon in its day. Alec Guinness, fittingly, won the Best Actor Oscar for a part he had, at first, turned down.

In the ensuing years, when producers and directors were trying to convince tightfisted studio executives to allow them to shoot on location, they pointed out the success of Sam Spiegel and the spectacular use of actual locations in *The Bridge on the River Kwai*.

Section II

The Thin Red Line

Once war films regained their popularity with post–World War II audiences, filmmakers turned from purely battle action stories to films that explored the psychological motivations of fighting men.

It began in the same year that *Battleground* was released, with films like Stanley Kramer's *Home of the Brave*, which dealt effectively with racial prejudice on a Pacific Island. Through narcosynthesis, a young black Marine overcomes his handicap by reliving the nightmare of prejudice he suffered under combat conditions. *Home of the Brave* was the "sleeper" of 1949

In this scene from *The War Lover* (1962), Daphne (Shirley Anne Field) tells Army Air Force Captain Buzz Rickson (Steve McQueen), "You don't know how to love — you only know how to hate!"

and served to propel the careers of Kramer, director Mark Robson and writer Carl Foreman, all World War II veterans.

William Wyler's *The Best Years of Our Lives* (1946) had earlier explored the lives of returning soldiers, who found it difficult to make the adjustment from combat to civilian life. The scene in which young Army Air Force bombardier Fred Derry (Dana Andrews) wanders around an airplane graveyard and has an epiphany in the cockpit of a B-17 is an amazing cinematic moment, symbolizing the grounded flyer's loss of innocence and faith. The film was a huge success.

There were new filmmakers who followed Wyler and achieved dramatic success. In director Fred Zinnemann's 1950 film, *The Men*, a young Marlon Brando tries to readjust to society after a wartime injury makes him a paraplegic. It, too, was a success.

In *The War Lover*, Steve McQueen portrays an Army Air Force B-17 pilot who thrives on the danger of war; on the ground, he is out of control. McQueen had used much of the same character dynamic in *Hell Is for Heroes* (1962).

There were films that treated the "misfits" as a separate distinct class of fighting man. In *The War Lover* (1962), Steve McQueen portrayed Army Air Corps Captain Buzz Rickson, a hotshot pilot who cannot adjust to life on the ground. In the same year, McQueen played almost the same character in Don Siegel's *Hell Is for Heroes*.

Earlier, in 1953, Columbia Pictures released *From Here to Eternity*, a pre–World War II story, based on James Jones's bestseller that presented three outstanding portraits of soldiers under stress, in this case, during peacetime in Hawaii. Private Robert E. Lee Prewitt (Montgomery Clift), a stubborn bugler, Angelo Maggio (Frank Sinatra), a misfit private of Italian descent, and Sergeant Milton Warden (Burt Lancaster), a career soldier, all represented the pre–Pearl Harbor professional army at its rawest. It was an excellent film (an Academy Award winner as Best Picture of 1953), and it captured the interest as well as the hearts of audiences of its time.

Along with psychological motivation, there were many films that dealt effectively with stress and its relationship to command and responsibility among wartime officers. In *The Mountain Road* (1960), based on Theodore White's novel, an inexperienced demolitions officer

Two men on the very edge in *From Here to Eternity* (1953): Pvt. Robert E. Lee Prewitt (Montgomery Clift, left), a professional soldier who is tormented by his commanding officer for not joining the regimental boxing team, and Sgt. Milt Warden (Burt Lancaster), who picks the wrong time to fall in love with the wife of his superior.

(James Stewart) misuses his responsibility and puts the men under his command in jeopardy on a mountain road in East China in 1944. After witnessing the murder of three of his men, he becomes a vengeful fanatic, his own character balancing on what author James Jones referred to as "the thin red line" between the sane and the mad.

Marlon Brando would face that same balancing act as naïve German officer Christian Diestl in the film adaptation of Irwin Shaw's seminal World War II novel, *The Young Lions* (1958). Humphrey Bogart's Captain Queeg, the main character in the all-star adaptation of Herman Wouk's *The Caine Mutiny* (1954) offers another example of how far the psyche of a human being can be stretched, until it finally snaps.

In *Run Silent, Run Deep* (1958), Clark Gable portrayed Captain Rich Richardson, a submarine commander who drives his crew relentlessly with a "Moby Dick" obsession to destroy a Japanese destroyer. In producer Otto Preminger's *In Harm's Way* (1965), a naval commander (Kirk Douglas) survives the humiliating death of his wife, but forever harbors a deep mistrust of women. Once he rapes a young girl who was dating the son of his only friend (John Wayne), he virtually commits suicide by tracking the route of an attacking Japanese battle fleet.

In releasing films of this type, filmmakers were able to lend the war film genre a new sophistication that was in keeping with Hollywood's overall maturity. The big blockbuster war picture that offered only action and adventure was no longer the darling of the critics or the audience. The good-versus-evil simplicity of the 1940s and 1950s was replaced by a more balanced look at war and its cost in terms of humanity.

CHAPTER FIVE

Pork Chop Hill

The worldwide success of *The Bridge on the River Kwai* had an immediate impact on the war film genre. Not only was a strong effort now made to get away from soundstages and movie lots, but the films took on a harder edge. By the end of the 1950s, Hollywood had gone through a decade's worth of war film clichés. Patriotism was still alive, but the sober wars of the 1950s brought a new perspective to the plight of men in combat. The emphasis was more on the psychological impact of war, as opposed to racing to the top of the hill and planting the American flag. The kindhearted dogface with the girl back home was slowly being supplanted by soldiers suffering from what we would later call "post-traumatic stress syndrome" and a host of other maladies.

Although World War II inspired a steady, non-stop stream of war films, Hollywood had begun to explore more contemporary conflicts, particularly the Korean War, which ended in 1953.

U.S. Army combat veteran and maverick director Sam Fuller had taken the first shot with *The Steel Helmet,* a low-budget film that was released in February 1951, only seven months after North Korea invaded the south. Essentially a "squad in jeopardy" look at the Korean War, the story is told through the eyes of gritty veteran Sergeant Zack (Gene Evans) who steadies a group of outnumbered G.I.'s trapped in a Buddhist temple-turned-fortress. The movie may have lacked production values, but its no-nonsense look at G.I.s under stress has become a cult classic over the years and Sergeant Zack has become one of the archetype anti-heroes in film — the grizzled veteran with a heart of gold, who tries to help a young Korean orphan named Short Round, who is, nonetheless, killed by a communist sniper.

Even big-budgeted Hollywood pictures about Korea strayed from the clichés of the past. William Holden, Grace Kelly, Fredric March and Mickey Rooney starred in Mark Robson's colorful and tension-packed adaptation of James Michener's novel, *The Bridges at Toko-Ri* (1954), which dramatized the air war over Korea as seen through one disillusioned pilot's eyes.

In the past, the studio would have given the film a more upbeat ending, but under Robson's steady hand, the film ends badly for Lt. Harry Brubaker (Holden), who dies when his jet crash lands and he and his helicopter rescue pilot friend (Rooney) are machine-gunned by North Korean regulars.

Compare *The Bridges at Toko-Ri* with Dick Powell's *The Hunters* (1958), a flag-waving tribute to sabre jet pilots that starred Robert Mitchum and Robert Wagner. In that film, both Mitchum and Wagner are shot down, but rather than be gunned down by swarming enemy soldiers, *they* do the shooting, wiping out a platoon of soldiers sent out to capture them. They pay a price, though, as a group of innocent Koreans who tried to help them are lined up against a wall and shot by the enemy. As a little girl flees the scene, she, too, is shot.

However, while *The Hunters* didn't hesitate to wave the flag (the film plays liked a 1950s version of *Top Gun*), it also took spectacular CinemaScope advantage of live jet dogfights, using dozens of U.S. Air Force F-86 sabre jets. To woo American audiences away from their television sets, Hollywood was offering them spectacular widescreen action — and it worked.

Pork Chop Hill (1959) was much more than a gritty combat film about a desperate Korean War battle. It was one of the first Hollywood films to take an historical event, dispense with clichés, stock characters and meaningless dialogue and present it with near-documentary precision. Three years before Darryl F. Zanuck would apply similar care in producing an epic film based on author Cornelius Ryan's *The Longest Day,* actor-turned-producer Gregory Peck and his partner, *Twelve O'Clock High* producer Sy Bartlett, teamed with writer James R. Webb to adapt S.L.A. Marshall's 1956 book, *Pork Chop Hill.*

Brigadier General Samuel Lyman Atwood Marshall (1900–1977) enlisted in the U.S. Army in 1918, and, as the youngest commissioned officer in World War I, assisted in the demobilization of American troops at the end of the war. During World War II, he was an official U.S. Army historian who pioneered a method of extracting battle information by interviewing veteran soldiers in groups. In analyzing the effectiveness of American infantry, he discovered that only a small minority of the men he interviewed (25 percent) ever fired their weapons in combat.

While his research was later dismissed by other historians who questioned his assertions and cast doubt on his techniques, his work, nonetheless, encouraged the Army to adjust its combat training. In light of Marshall's theories, it is interesting that one of the lines of dialogue that Lt. Joseph Clemons (Gregory Peck) utters during the initial assault up Pork Chop Hill is, "The men are not firing their weapons."

When Marshall arrived in Korea in 1953, most of the press attention was focused on Freedom Village at Panmunjom, where peace talks were being held and the end of the Korean War was being contemplated. Because of the intense press focus on those talks, the bloody fighting around Pork Chop Hill had been virtually ignored.

As Marshall writes in his book:

I felt strongly that the ignoring of the fight by the press and the people only made it more important that some day the story should be told. The neglect was worse because in preceding weeks, this same division — the Seventh — had been lambasted for the loss of Old Baldy and the staging of Operation Mack. They had been described as weary, slipshod, demoralized troops and, while the Pork Chop Hill fight was on, this caustic criticism from home was repeated over Red Chinese loudspeakers to the American fighters. Then when the moment came that their brave deeds refuted all the disparagement of them, there were no witnesses to sing their praises. It was terribly unfair.

One at a time, we formed the companies which had taken the main blows on Pork Chop, Dale and Arsenal (two other hills that were part of the Seventh Infantry Division's defensive line). Already, units which were 200 strong when the fight began were down to 40 or 50 men. Some of the platoons mustered not more than five or six men. These little bands were still chins up.... The average length of the question and answer session with each company was seven and one-half hours, during which we worked steadily together, except for two or three short breaks for coffee and to uncramp my fingers.

But when we finished, we knew practically everything that had happened to these units during the fight, the determining events were in almost chronological order, and we could account for the manner in which most of the men had been killed or wounded, as well as how effectively the weapons had been used.

The in-fighting which took place in the entrenched works of the outposts was as hard pressed and bloody as Cold Harbor, Attu or the Argonne. The Americans won, not simply by the superior weight of their artillery, but because the infantry, man for man in the hand-to-hand battle, outgamed the Red Chinese. In two vital particulars these Americans outshone any of our troops with whom I have ever dealt; there was a superior command presence in their young officers, and a higher ratio of enlisted men exercised strong initiative in the most dangerous moments.[1]

Screenwriter James R. Webb was rummaging around Martindale's Book Store in Beverly Hills in 1956 when he came across a copy of Marshall's newly published book. Being a history buff, Webb knew of Marshall and his previous work in military history, and, when he read the book, he was particularly intrigued with its focus on a small, barren Korean hilltop and the lives of the infantry soldiers who sought to conquer and hold it. When he learned that Marshall was an editorial writer and military critic for the *Detroit News*, he contacted him directly, tracking him down in Washington, D.C. Within a few minutes, Webb had an option and carte blanche to do what he wanted with the book.

Webb was a World War II veteran, having served on the staff of Lieutenant General Lloyd Fredendall's II Corps in North Africa. After graduating from Stanford, he had started his career in Hollywood by writing mostly westerns. Three years before John Ford commissioned Frank Nugent to write *The Searchers*, Webb wrote *The Charge at Feather River* (1953), which also told a story about a search for two captive white girls. And although this 3-D programmer (starring Guy Madison and Frank Lovejoy) lacks the polish or reputation of the Ford film, it shows off Webb's passionate love of history and the Old West. The following year, he wrote the energetic Civil War–era western, *Vera Cruz* (1954) for actors Gary Cooper and Burt Lancaster.

(I worked for James R. Webb. As a college student at U.C.L.A, in the early 1970s, Webb hired me to research a spec book he was writing on popular inventions. I discovered that he was, indeed, a passionate lover of history and took delight in the little facts that I unearthed while combing through the patent office in downtown Los Angeles. Had I known he was the writer of *Pork Chop Hill*, I would have interviewed him right away. Unfortunately, in the era before Google and IMDb, I had no list of his credits, although I did know that he had written an early draft for *Patton* [see Chapter Ten].)

In 1957, actor Gregory Peck, now producing under his Melville Productions banner, brought Webb in to clean up a screenwriting mess on William Wyler's epic western, *The Big Country*. Sy Bartlett had also contributed to the screenplay on *The Big Country* and he was Peck's producing partner at Melville.

It had been a decade since Bartlett had worked with Gregory Peck on *Twelve O'Clock High*. During that period, he had written two films for future James Bond director, Terence Young — the Alan Ladd World War II saga, *Paratrooper* (a.k.a. *The Red Beret*) and *That Lady*, a swashbuckler with probably the worst title of all time (you often wonder if marketing people just give up on a film). On a more positive note, he wrote the story for Republic Pictures' *The Last Command*, an enthusiastically produced depiction of the siege of the Alamo that was supposed to star John Wayne, but ended up starring a terrific Sterling Hayden as Jim Bowie. Gregory Peck needed a partner to help run his production company, and Bartlett — the man who had co-created General Frank Savage in *Twelve O'Clock High*—fit the bill.

It was Webb who introduced Peck and Bartlett to the Marshall book. They were so delighted with the idea that they pulled Webb off his next assignment (which was supposed to be a film entitled *Thieves Market*) and put him on *Pork Chop Hill*. He commenced the screenplay on Tuesday, March 12, 1957. According to a letter from attorney Evarts Ziegler to producer Sy Bartlett, Webb's compensation was $5,000, payable immediately against $25,000, plus 5 percent of the profits if Mr. Peck appeared in the picture. If Peck did not appear in the picture, he would get 7 percent of the profits. Webb also agreed to deliver his first draft on June 15, 1957.

Although Marshall's book covered the unit histories of a number of U.S. Army infantry companies that fought in the celebrated battle, Webb chose to adapt only one of his scenarios—a chapter entitled "All the King's Men." Given that he was writing for actor Gregory Peck, he decided that Lieutenant Joe Clemons, commanding officer of King Company, 31st Infantry Regiment, Seventh Infantry Division, was the perfect character for Peck to play.

Joseph Clemons enlisted in the U.S. Army right out of high school, hoping to become eligible for the G.I. Bill so he could go to college. He wanted to join the infantry, but he was assigned to the Army Air Corps instead. In the summer of 1946, he served in the Philippines when the country became independent from the United States. He was placed in the photo lab of an air recon squadron that was mapping the islands. He was about to be designated as an aerial photographer when his superior officers discovered that he had a high IQ and asked him if he wanted to go to West Point. Clemons said yes, and he was appointed to the service academy where he eventually graduated eighth in his class.

In 1950, while still a student, he and his brother-in-law and fellow classmate, Walter Russell, went on a trip to Japan to study the economic, military and sociological effects of the U.S. occupation of Japan. It was while they were in Japan that North Korea crossed the 38th Parallel into South Korea and the Korean War began.

Clemons, Russell and another classmate of theirs, Tom Harrold (all three of whom would serve on Pork Chop Hill) returned to the States. They graduated from West Point in 1951, received their commissions and were assigned to the 82nd Airborne Division. When they arrived in Korea in October 1952, they were transferred to the Seventh Infantry Division. Lt. Clemons was given the command of King Company, 31st Regiment; Russell commanded George Company in the 17th Regiment; Harrold was commanding Easy Company.

All three units would be heavily involved in the Battle of Pork Chop Hill. When Easy Company was overrun, Harrold himself managed to barricade himself and a few of his surviving infantrymen in their command bunker atop Pork Chop. Lt. Clemons was summoned by his commanding officer, Colonel John Davis, and given the mission to take his 135 men and recapture the hill, which was now heavily defended by Chinese Communist forces.

Gregory Peck and his wife, Veronique, socialize with Capt. Joseph G. Clemons and his wife, Cecil. Peck portrayed Clemons in *Pork Chop Hill* (1959).

"I had three rifle platoons that went up," Clemons would later say. "My weapons platoon with mortars and 57mm recoilless rifles, did not come with us. It was detached for fire support. The hill was too steep for armor. We had a couple of tanks that were supposedly down at the bottom of the hill, but I was never aware of them."[2]

As written by Marshall, and closely dramatized by Webb, the fighting men of Clemons's King Company ended up getting hammered by artillery, mortar, machine gun and rifle fire. Every bunker, every trench, every pillbox on the hill was a separate firefight and by the time Clemons reached the top, he had only 25 men left. Artillery fire from communist positions on nearby hills continually slammed into the dirt of Pork Chop. It is quite possible that more artillery shells were fired on Pork Chop Hill during those few days in April 1953 than had ever been fired on a single target in the history of modern warfare. The hill was covered with shell craters, collapsed trenches and bunkers, and a steady rain of artillery fire continued throughout the battle.

"We stayed in the bunkers," related Clemons. "I was cut off from the rear and no one was responding to our radio messages. I finally gave up sending coded messages and we just sent it in the clear that we were down to 25 men. There was no answer. When a public information officer showed up on the hill, I gave him a written message to take back."[3]

Of all people, considering his unit was from a different regiment, it was Clemons's brother-in-law, Lt. Walter Russell, and George Company that fought their way to the summit to relieve him.

Recalled Russell, now a retired state legislature from Georgia: "My orders were to reinforce K Company on Pork Chop. We didn't have any personnel carriers, so we had to go up on foot and we were almost immediately under Chinese artillery fire from Old Baldy. They had all the roads zeroed in. It eventually took us eight hours to get to the top of that hill through all that shelling.

"I had a little over a hundred men when we started and we took casualties right away. I knew Joe was up there because we had lunch about ten days before the battle and he told me he was commanding K."[4]

By the time Russell reached Clemons in the command bunker (Clemons had relieved Harrold), George Company was down to half its strength. The first thing he said to Clemons, who was in the process of interrogating five Chinese prisoners was, "What the hell is going on around here?"

"He was very happy to see us," Russell continues. "We immediately called all the platoon leaders together and I deployed my company on the far right of the hill, while Joe mainly stayed in the middle. We also had some men from Love Company."[5]

As Webb would relate in the film, Russell had previously been stationed on Chejudo Island, where his 17th Regiment was sent to guard Chinese prisoners. When the regiment returned to the mainland, he was given command of Love Company until March 1953, when he took command of George.

Back on Pork Chop Hill, Clemons and Russell had little to celebrate. Division headquarters had decided not to risk Russell's remaining 50 men and had ordered him to withdraw his company by 3:00 P.M. that day.

Russell immediately got on the radio and informed Clemons's battalion commander, Colonel Davis, that he had 50 men and Joe only had 25, and that Russell should stay on the hill with George Company. With orders from his own superiors at the regimental and division level, Davis's response was negative. Clemons would be left alone.

"If I was a major, I might have felt differently about that response," said Russell. "I was still a 23-year-old first lieutenant. My last words to Joe were, 'Goodbye, and I'll hug Cecil (Clemons' wife, Russell's sister) for you.' And I knew that Cecil would kill me if I left Joe up there and something happened to him. I was very glad to get off the goddamn hill, but I was sorry to leave Joe."[6]

"When Walt left, I got on the radio and told Davis that if he couldn't reinforce, I asked if they would withdraw us,"[7] Clemons remembered. The answer was no. According to Marshall's book, Division headquarters was not aware that Clemons was down to a handful of men and that he was literally hanging on by his fingernails. When General Trudeau, the commander of the Seventh Infantry Division found out the true strength of King Company, he contacted his own superiors to determine if they really wanted to hold on to Pork Chop.

Low on ammunition, food, water and medical supplies (not to mention morale), Clemons and the King Company survivors stayed behind and withstood a furious enemy attack, once again taking refuge in the command bunker. Fortunately, battalion, regiment, division and corps had come to their senses and relieved him in force.

To help him dramatize the events of the Battle of Pork Chop Hill, Webb contacted Clemons, who, in 1958, was stationed at Fort Benning, Georgia. Webb had to flesh out the characters, making them more than just names and ranks on the page.

For instance, based on Clemons's recollections, Webb created the character of Private Franklin, a nervous African American soldier who tries to duck the fighting.

Remembered Clemons: "What really happened is that he came in as a new replacement and he was welcomed by the battalion adjutant. And next to the adjutant's bunker were 20 American body bags, men that had been killed on a patrol that had been ambushed the night before. So he was spooked when he got there and he later deserted. He was rounded up and brought back to the unit and general court martial charges were filed. However, he fought well enough in the actual battle to get the charges dropped."[8]

In a letter to Gregory Peck, dated April 27, 1957, Webb commented on the Private Franklin character and any possible controversy, "It has a swell payoff and I don't think we need to worry about offending anyone, but, if necessary, we can always make one of the featured sergeants a Negro, which I am sure will put us completely in the clear."[9] Eventually, the producers cast African American actor James Edwards (*Home of the Brave, Patton*) as Corporal Jurgens, to keep Franklin in line. Relative newcomer Woody Strode got the Franklin part. He was so intense and effective that actor/producer Kirk Douglas and director Stanley Kubrick cast him to play Draba the Ethiopian gladiator in *Spartacus* the following year.

Webb also developed Clemons's close relationship with his executive officer, Lt. Suki Ohashi, a Japanese American officer who commanded the first platoon of King Company. In real life, his name was Tsugio "Eddie" Ohashi and he was a World War II veteran of the Fifth Infantry Division and a native of Waipahu, Kauai, Hawaii. At the time of the filming, the real Ohashi was assistant principal at August Ahrens Elementary School in Waipahu. Peck would later meet him in Hawaii and he gave the veteran a private screening of the final film. In the screenplay, Ohashi is a major character, who shares virtually every moment of hell up on Pork Chop with Clemons. Interestingly, it was the one character that central casting had trouble with on the picture.

In late February 1958, Joe and Cecil Clemons were in downtown Los Angeles, having just gone to see *The Brothers Karamazov*, when they bumped into another of Clemons' West Point classmates — George Shibata. George had been the first Japanese American to ever graduate from the service academy and he had gone on to fly F-86 sabre jets in Korea. He was a practicing attorney in Los Angeles when Clemons encouraged him to come in and read for the part of Ohashi. On a lark, he took Clemons's advice and he got the role. Shibata, however, was more interested in becoming a lawyer than an actor, so his Hollywood career was fairly short. He did make a strong impression in *Pork Chop Hill,* and later he portrayed Jeffrey Hunter's older stepbrother in *Hell to Eternity* (1960) and the part of the young Japanese officer and UCLA grad in *The Wackiest Ship in the Army* (1960).

Webb spent a great deal of time establishing the fact that the Panmunjom peace talks were taking place only 60 miles away from the Battle of Pork Chop Hill. In the original screenplay, Webb showed the activity at Panmunjom and even featured a scene with dialogue at the beginning of the movie. However, all of this was cut, except for some peace talk images that play over the credits. The Panmunjom sequence was moved towards the very end of the movie, when we begin to see why the Chinese are fighting so hard to take an obscure, worthless hill. As the negotiating American admiral says to an American general, "I'm beginning to think they picked it because it's worth nothing. Its value is that it has no value. That makes it a test of strength pure and simple. They're willing to spend lives for nothing, or what seems nothing. That's what they want to know. Are we as willing to do that as they are?"[10]

Given the importance that propaganda played in the world of 1953, particularly in communist countries, Webb came up with a unique story element in which a skilled young Chinese propagandist broadcasts directly to the Americans troops fighting on the hill. Although his speeches would be distilled over many of Webb's drafts, here is an early example of the first broadcast heard, in this case, by Easy Company defenders:

Chinese Broadcaster
    For two years, seventeen thousand five hundred and twenty weary hours ... you have sweated
    it out in your little ant hills ... wasting away your lives, living in filth and misery ... fighting and
    dying to defend the Thirty-eighth Parallel, a mere line on a map.... What are you doing in this
    political war, anyway? Your own newspapers are already describing you as weary, ineffective and
    demoralized. Well, why shouldn't you be?[11]

During the rewrite process, the propagandist was softened and became genuinely interested in getting the Americans to surrender. But they listened about as much as American Marines listened to Tokyo Rose in World War II. It was just a very unique and contrasting visual. One moment you're knee-deep in the furious fighting for the hill and then suddenly it would be quiet and the loudspeakers would suddenly blare, "Congratulations King Company." It was almost as if the Americans were fighting on some kind of giant competitive game board where every move they made was recorded, observed and commented upon by their enemies. After a particularly heartfelt exhortation to give up meets with deaf ears, those same loudspeakers were filled with the blasts of Chinese trumpets sounding the charge, while the number of background voices made it sound like all China was attacking.

Said Clemons, "We heard some broadcasts but not to the extent they were used in the movie. It didn't bother me. It was obviously part of the story."[12]

Who was going to direct *Pork Chop Hill?* Peck offered the film to Nicholas Ray, who had just won plaudits for directing James Dean and Natalie Wood in *Rebel Without a Cause* (1955), but Ray turned him down (although he recommended that Peck hire newcomer Leonard Rosenman to score the film, and Peck agreed). Then, Lewis Milestone's name came up. The veteran of *A Walk in the Sun* and *All Quiet on the Western Front* certainly had the chops, particularly with a military subject, but recently, Milestone's record had been sketchy — it had been five years since he had directed a feature, and he had been working primarily in television. However, Peck and Bartlett knew his work and his reputation for gritty, non-compromising war sagas and he was hired.

With Milestone on board, and a new draft of Webb's script available, casting began in earnest. It would be quite a challenge — there were 83 speaking parts in the film — all men. Initial casting ideas indicate that Gregory Peck wasn't necessarily going to play Clemons. A casting memo to United Artists from Peck's producing partner, Sy Bartlett, dated July 9, 1957, listed the following actors as possible leads: Jeff Chandler, Richard Egan, Tony Curtis, Paul Newman, Audie Murphy, Tony Perkins, Jack Palance, Ben Gazzara, Henry Fonda, Gene Kelly, Charlton Heston, Richard Widmark, Robert Stack and Robert Ryan. Hmm, Gene Kelly as Joe Clemons, now that would have been casting against-type.[13]

Two weeks later, casting director Helen Moore came up with some additional possibilities: John Cassavetes, Farley Granger, John Ericson, Vince Edwards, Gene Evans, Peter Graves, Sterling Hayden, Earl Holliman, Richard Jaeckel (what 1950s war movie would be complete without him?), Van Johnson, Ben Johnson, Joe Mantell, Dewey Martin, Barry Nelson, Carl "Alfalfa" Switzer, Darryl Hickman, Gil Stratton, Jr., Aaron Spelling and Stuart Whitman.

(By the way, notice how many American leading men were in the pool to play Clemons in 1957 — and this list didn't include a number of pricey leading men who were considered out of contention because of budget issues. If you were casting Lt. Clemons today, odds are he'd be British, Australian, Irish or a New Zealander. As my friend, screenwriter Steve Mitchell is fond of saying, where are the manly American leading men under 40 today?)

When Gregory Peck decided to take on the role of Lt. Joseph Clemons, a decision was made that would affect the entire casting process and provide a boon to a number of actors. Accompanying the breakdown of all the available parts in *Pork Chop Hill* was a directive from Melville Productions:

> Though some of these characters may not have a great deal of footage, every part listed below must stand out sharply and require a highly experienced acting background. However, we are interested in only new faces so far as motion pictures are concerned. Though some of these characters have humorous lines, we don't want any "comedy relief."[14]

Here are some of the casting guidelines given to agents at the time for some of the key characters:

Lt. Ohashi — A Japanese American with no accent whatsoever. Tall and slender. Very American in his movement and conduct, just that he is unmistakably of Japanese origin. Dry sense of humor. Please do not bring any Chinese or other nationality for this Japanese part. He is Gregory Peck's confidante and close friend and plays most of his scenes with Mr. Peck. About 30. (As previously mentioned, this part went to Clemons's West Point classmate, George Shibata.)

1st Lieutenant Russell — Should look from 28 to 35. Russell is Mr. Peck's brother-in-law in the picture. He is regular army, comes from a good background. This part requires a very fine actor. (A 27-year-old newcomer by the name of Rip Torn won the part of Lt. Russell. His real name was Elmore Rual Torn, Jr. "Rip" was his father's nickname, too).

Payne — Radio Operator — About 30. A tall, lean, Maine farmer, with a distinctive face and New England accent. He has many scenes with Mr. Peck. (When Cliff Ketchum was cast, Payne became a Texas farmer with a distinct Texas accent.)

Corporal Fedderson — Machine Gunner — At least 30. He is a capable, two-fisted American guy. Reliable, unafraid, but a young man who can control what he feels. He is a teammate of Forstman. (The part went to newcomer George Peppard, who was on the cusp of stardom. Two years later, he would star opposite Audrey Hepburn in *Breakfast at Tiffany's*.)

PFC Forstman — He is Fedderson's assistant gunner, somewhat younger than Fedderson.

This part calls for a splendid actor. Though he became Fedderson's teammate on the gun, simply in the line of duty, a strong bond has grown between the two men. Forstman thinks he should have been rotated out of Korea before this action starts, but nevertheless primarily because of Fedderson, he is a willing soldier. (When top television actor Harry Guardino was cast as Forstman in 1958, Fedderson, his buddy, became Forstman's assistant on the machine gun.)

Private Velie— Small, no more than 18, extremely sensitive and nervous. This boy is completely dazed and bewildered by the war ("little boy lost"), but he finds himself as a soldier, and his story is really the story of all men who discover hidden strength when the chips are down. This part requires a very fine actor, and, if possible, he should be a naturally nervous type. (a 24-year-old Robert Blake was cast as Velie and he was perfectly nervous in the part. Before he was fired and replaced by television director Leslie Martinson, director Lewis Milestone cast Blake in *PT 109*.)

Lt. Colonel Davis— He is regular army, 35–40. Though he knows his job, he is capable of anxiety. Here again, we do not want "typical" casting. (Top television character actor Barry Atwater claimed this part. Later in his career, Atwater would play the seemingly unstoppable vampire, Janos Skorzeny, in the classic ABC movie-of-the-week, *The Night Stalker*.)

Public Information Officer— A young lieutenant not used to front line combat, probably has been a cub reporter for a small-town newspaper, drafted into the army. (Character actor Lew Gallo would claim this role. Although he would become very friendly with Milestone, the first few minutes on the set were nerve-wracking for the 29-year-old stage actor.)

"I was new in Hollywood," Gallo recalled, "and I wanted to make it [*sic*] good. I got the part and waited six weeks to work my two days on the picture. During the six weeks, I worked on the part every day. I was to play a Public Information Officer, who, during the most dire moment in the battle for Pork Chop Hill, shows up with a photographer to take pictures for 'the folks back home.' I finally went to work and on the first rehearsal, the cast and crew broke up, and well they should as I had the only comic relief in the movie. Then Milestone went to work. He saw immediately that I was a stage actor giving a stage performance. Without putting me down, he talked character, character relationships, and "took me down" to a motion picture performance, which is more intimate and smaller. I got a crash course in acting for the camera, but, more importantly, I gained a teacher and friend."[15] (Gallo would also be cast by Milestone in *PT 109* and later worked for the director on *Ocean's 11*.)

Judging from the casting memos that were flying back and forth from Melville Productions that winter and spring of 1958, every male actor in Hollywood was seen by Milestone and Bartlett. In one letter from MCA agent Maynard Morris to producer Sy Bartlett, dated February 21, 1958, Morris noted that, in addition to MCA clients Harry Guardino and George Peppard, the production appeared to be interested in Jack Klugman for the part of Kuzmick, Gene Lyons for Russell, Warren Beatty for Forstman or Velie, James Congdon for Jordan and Read Morgan for Big Smith.

Simultaneously, agent David B. Graham of the William Shifrin Agency recommended Clint Eastwood to play Coleman, the radio operator; Dennis Hopper to play Velie; Lyle Bettger to play Lt. Russell; Sterling Hayden to play Colonel Kern; Robert Bray to play Colonel Davis; Pat O'Brien or Frankie Laine to play General Trudeau and Dan O'Herlihy to play Chief of Staff. None of them made the final cut.

Peppard turned out to be the first supporting actor cast. He was signed for $1,000 a week, on a three-week guarantee. He was given first class transportation from New York City and back, but, curiously, he was given no living expense money. To show how much Harry

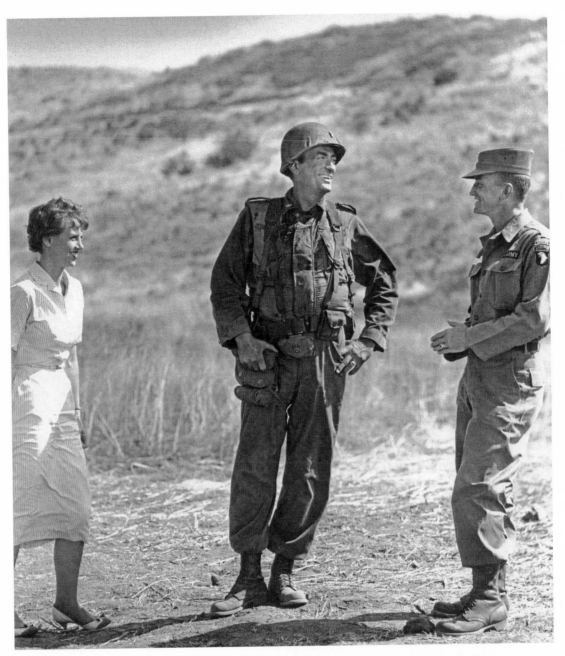

Gregory Peck (center) takes time out to chat with Joe Clemons (the man he portrays in the film), and Clemons's wife, Cecil. (Note: Clemons was a captain when he reported for work on *Pork Chop Hill*). (Courtesy of Joseph and Cecil Clemons)

Guardino meant in 1958, he was signed for $3,500 per week for two weeks, a contract that was later amended to $15,000 for eight weeks (when Forstman's role was expanded).

Meanwhile, Jack Lord was being considered for Lt. Harrold of Easy Company, a part that turned out to be just a bit role (Charles Aidman got it). And future *Where Eagles Dare* and *Kelly's Heroes* director, Brian Hutton, then acting up a storm on television and running the Beverly Hills Playhouse, was also auditioning. One of his students, Harry Dean Stanton (then known as Dean Stanton), grabbed the small role of MacFarland who, prior to the battle, was asked if regular army Lieutenant Clemons knows anything. He replied, "Probably just enough to bury you according to regulations."[16]

Robert Ellenstein, who would shortly join Martin Landau on Alfred Hitchcock's *North by Northwest,* was in the running because Bartlett thought he had "a lot of humor in his face." He had also just given a superb performance on *The Robert Montgomery Show* about a Stork Club musician unjustly accused of theft. Ellenstein was eventually given another tiny bit part, as one of Lt. Harrold's Easy Company platoon leaders whom Clemons and his men liberate when they take the hill.

On April 21, a number of MCA clients came in to read for the parts of radiomen, Payne and Coleman. They included Dick Van Patten, Kevin Hagen, James Franciscus, Bert Remson, Jerry Paris and Simon Oakland. Although the radioman parts went to Norman Fell and Cliff Ketchum, Hagen and Remson both took bit parts in the film.

The following day, Woody Strode came in and read for the part of Franklin. In their notes on Strode, he's referred to as a wrestler and football player who had been acting since 1951.

With production scheduled to start on Monday May 26, 1958, the final parts were quickly cast. Rip Torn was signed as Lt. Russell at $1,000 a week, with a three-week guarantee; Gavin MacLeod gave an excellent reading and won the part of Saxon, who complains about the weight of his bulletproof vest, then gets his foot shot off; Martin Landau read for Lt. Harrold but ended up taking the small part of Lt. Marshall, the last surviving officer of Love Company; and former western icon Bob Steele was cast as Colonel Kern. Interestingly, *A Walk in the Sun*'s Herbert Rudley also read for that part; Viraj Amonsen was cast as the Chinese propagandist.

In addition to the actors, Sy Bartlett hired a rough-and-ready stunt crew headed by Chuck Roberson, who was doubling Gregory Peck. Roberson, in turn, brought in Hal Needham, Chuck Hayward, Eddie Saenz, Billy Shannon, Ronnie Rondell and others. Although there would be some Asian stuntmen, the Caucasian stuntmen often played Koreans.

Veteran stuntman Hal Needham, who had started in the business two years earlier on *The Spirit of St. Louis,* remembers *Pork Chop Hill*: "They needed some young athletic stunt guys and there was myself, a kid named Ronnie Rondell and four or five of us, and we looked the part because we were young. I also played a lot of Koreans, getting blown up and things like that. It's like doing a western; you're an Indian in one shot and a cowboy in the next."[17]

While casting was going on, a decision was made to shoot the film on the Albertson Ranch in Thousand Oaks, California, which was approximately 38 miles from the Goldwyn Studio, in the western San Fernando Valley. Unlike *The Bridge on the River Kwai*, which required a lush tropical jungle, sweeping vistas and river gorges, *Pork Chop Hill* required one ugly, cratered, rock-strewn, barren hill.

Although an initial location survey was made to the U.S. Army base at Camp Carson, Colorado, it was determined that the terrain was perfect on the Albertson Ranch, which had recently hosted MGM's World War II service comedy, *Imitation General.*

The 70-year-old production designer, Nicolai Remisoff, who had worked with Milestone as early as 1939 on *Of Mice and Men*, was in charge of turning a barren Calabasas hill into the title location, complete with sand-bagged trenches, pillboxes, bunkers and concertina wire. After production signed a contract with C.L. Austin of the Albertson Company (the property would cost $50 a day during construction and $150 during shooting), the bulldozers moved in and the fine-tuning began.

Meanwhile, producer Sy Bartlett had sent the completed Webb script to the Production

Code Administration of the Motion Picture Association of America (the primary rating organization in 1958). They accepted the script, but also commented, "We notice, however, that the present version contains a rather liberal usage of the words 'hell' and 'damn.' While it might be possible to argue the dramatic validity of these words, in particular instances, we feel that the cumulative effect of their repeated employment would prove offensive to many members of the audience, and as such would be in violation of the code provision governing the use of these words. We will not attempt to list the number of times they are used, but will simply leave it to your discretion to select those instances which are of the greatest importance to you, asking that while retaining these, you can change or eliminate the majority. As you know, our final judgment will be based on the finished picture."[18]

The MPAA wasn't the only organization with objections. Hiram W. Kwan, the Chairman of the Citizens Rights Committee for the Chinese American Citizens Alliance, had seen an advance copy of James Webb's script and was objecting to the fact that the enemy soldiers in the film were referred to as "Chinks." Screenwriter James Webb personally wrote back to Mr. Kwan.

"Apparently," he wrote, "you have been misinformed as to the content of our script. In our opinion, there is nothing in the dialogue or otherwise that could be considered derogatory to the Chinese American people. Our purpose in making this picture is to portray war itself, not to stir up hatreds, even where the Communist Chinese are concerned. A very few times, the enemy Chinese are called 'Chinks' in dialogue, and as we are trying to make a realistic picture, we feel that it would seem artificial to do otherwise, but we have made sure that no officer refers to them as 'Chinks.' The inference, we feel, is that this is merely slang and has no real derogatory meaning."[19]

Production on *Pork Chop Hill* began with a 7:00 A.M. call on Monday May 26, 1958, at the Albertson Ranch in Thousand Oaks. Work on the film began right in the thick of the fighting, with action in the Third Platoon foxholes and near the checkpoint bunker. George Shibata was the only principal actor working that day.

Stuntman Hal Needham remembers noticing that Lewis Milestone was the first director he had ever seen who had sketches of every action sequence laid out in his script. He didn't realize that Milestone himself had made the sketches.

Needham had worked with Gregory Peck on two previous films, *The Man in the Grey Flannel Suit* (1956) and *The Big Country* (1958). One of Needham's first stunt sequences on *Pork Chop Hill* was when the Americans reach the concertina barbed wire. A number of soldiers throw themselves on the barbed wire to become human bridges and soldiers then run across their backs. Needham was one of those running soldiers in what became a signature Milestone tracking shot. Needham recalled, "As we jumped over the wire, the explosions were supposed to blow up behind us. Well, they got their wires mixed up, and as I started to cross the wire, they blew it off right in my face, burning all the hair below my helmet, knocking the helmet off my head and knocking me down. It was night, I couldn't see anything and I thought I was blinded. And I was for a few minutes."[20]

Another one of Needham's assignments was to play a Chinese defender. When the American searchlights suddenly came on and exposed Clemons's company, the Chinese jumped out of their trenches and opened fire on the Americans. The maneuver involved a gymnastics move, which Needham described: "We did what we call a "nip up," where you lay on your back, kick your feet up in the air and land on your feet. And we had to do it with a rifle in our hands. We'd nip-up, spray the Americans and fall back down again. A nip-up is hard to do, especially if you're holding a rifle and I was one of only two stuntmen who could do it."[21]

Capt. Joe Clemons, U.S. Army (Ret.), instructs Gregory Peck on the proper technique for throwing a hand grenade. (Courtesy of Joseph and Cecil Clemons)

Joe Clemons found the whole process of moviemaking an educational experience. He found it amusing that many of the actors had sponge-rubber hand grenades and flak vests that had no real armor in them. When George Shibata arrived on set, Clemons played a trick on him, getting the wardrobe man to supply his vest with real armor. Shibata didn't figure it out for a couple of weeks. It was his personal revenge for the fact that Air Force pilots were allowed to go home each night after a mission and sleep on clean sheets.

"I was out there with the crew every day," Clemons remembered. "I wanted to be there to observe as much as possible. They were making the movie for the teenage high schoolers, which is what I was told. I was surprised that bombshells would go off right next to people and they wouldn't get hurt. That wasn't accurate, but they were obviously making allowances. The assistant director who set up each scene told me to tell them if something didn't look right. They really tried to make it as realistic as possible, sometimes they couldn't do it."[22]

Battleground director William Wellman's son, Bill Wellman, Jr., took a small part in *Pork Chop Hill* as Iron Man, Joe Clemons' radioman, who takes over communications when Payne and Coleman are killed by an artillery burst. Before he did six months' active duty service in the infantry, Wellman had done three military pictures in a row — *Lafayette Escadrille* (for his dad), *Sayonara* and *Darby's Rangers*. "I was beginning to think I was never going to get out of uniform," he quipped, and then *Pork Chop Hill* came up and I couldn't pass up the opportunity to work with Lewis Milestone, the director of *All Quiet on the Western Front* and all those actors."

"I knew George Peppard because he was a close friend of Jim Franciscus, who would later marry my sister, Kitty. But I was really excited to see Bob Steele, who was one of my favorite actors. I used to see him at The Hitching Post theaters in the 1940s. They were theaters in Los Angeles that showed almost exclusively westerns and Bob Steele was a big western star."[23]

Wellman described the hill on Albertson's Ranch: "I don't think they had to do a lot, because it was pretty stark out there and evidently looked like Korea. There was almost no vegetation, no trees, it was lifeless. But it was a tough shoot — not a fun location.

"Milestone was of the old guard — he wasn't going to take any nonsense from anyone. I always got the impression that his production crew was a little frightened of him."[24]

Gregory Peck reported for work on Day Two at the Albertson Ranch, shooting a night sequence as the platoon heads up Pork Chop Hill. Joining him on their first day of shooting were Cliff Ketchum, Norman Feld (he would change his name shortly to Norman Fell), Abel Fernandez (McKinley), John Alderman (Lt. Waldorf) and 42 G.I. extras.

On Day Three, weather forced the unit back to the Samuel Goldwyn Studios where the unit shot the night interior of King Company Reserve, (in the scene when Clemons gets his orders and where Forstman (Harry Guardino) learns he's one point short of rotation back to the States. To maintain the schedule, the crew call was still a night shoot, even though they were shooting on a soundstage.

Location shooting on the Albertson Ranch resumed on Monday, June 2, and that Thursday Woody Strode (Pvt. Franklin) and Robert Blake (Pvt. Velie) reported to work for their scene in which Franklin feigns an ankle sprain, Velie tries to help him and then Franklin gets upbraided by Clemons.

Although actor Martin Landau only has a brief scene in the finished movie — the one during which he's introduced as Lt. Marshall, the last surviving officer of Love Company who arrives on the hill with ten men — it is clear that there was much more of Marshall in the early cut, because Landau worked a series of nights on the Albertson Ranch. Unfortunately, all of that footage ended up on the cutting room floor. Landau's arrival sequence was shot in daylight on Thursday, June 19.

Location shooting continued at Albertson Ranch throughout June and July with no weather problems. Special effects chief, David Koehler, and his ten assistants were particularly busy. According to the official estimates, some 85,000 U.S. artillery shells slammed into Pork Chop Hill during the course of the battle, in addition to countless enemy shells. Obviously, Koehler couldn't replicate those conditions. The producers decided to focus more on enemy small arms and grenade fire than on constant artillery barrages. It was a wise choice. Milestone's only alternative would have been to shoot his cast with their faces constantly wedged into the dirt of a shell crater or hunkered down deep in the belly of a concrete bunker.

Koehler's team made its own rubber hand grenades, flamethrowers, carbines, army flares, potato mashers (Chinese grenades), burp guns and rifles, all manufactured from official specifications.

Location filming was completed on Wednesday, July 23, 1958. Actor Gavin MacLeod (Pvt. Saxon) was brought back to Albertson for one day of shooting, most likely the sequence where he is carried down the hill on a stretcher after his foot is blown off ("Come on, fellas, it hurts!").[25]

The following day, Milestone's company established its beachhead at the Samuel Goldwyn Studios where work began inside the Command Post (C.P.) Bunker. It was Day 42, and the unit was ten days behind schedule. Lew Gallo, as the public relations officer, worked his one day on Tuesday, July 29; Rip Torn finished his part at Lt. Russell on July 31 and Barry Atwater took on the role of Clemons's battalion commander, Colonel Davis, on Wednesday, August 6. Production on *Pork Chop Hill* wrapped on Friday, August 8. However, this wasn't quite the end.

The entire sequence involving the peace talks at Panmunjom was shot nearly two and a

Having finally been relieved by fresh U.S. Army units, Lt. Joe Clemons (Gregory Peck) leads the weary survivors of King Company off Pork Chop Hill.

half months later at the Hal Roach Studios in Culver City. Although there is a brief sequence in Webb's early drafts that indicates a scene at the peace talks, apparently this sequence was jettisoned in favor of starting the movie with Lt. Clemons's position in reserve, as he is about to get his orders to take Pork Chop. However, when the first rough cut of the film was screened by Milestone, Peck and Bartlett, it was determined that a visit to Panmunjom was necessary, but not until the end of the film.

Such a sequence served two purposes. First, it gave context to the battle — reinforcing the fact that while men were fighting and dying in combat, the American negotiators at Panmunjom were facing their own stonewall of resistance from the Koreans and Chinese. Secondly, it allowed the audience to hear the American admiral in charge of the negotiations explain why the Chinese were investing so much effort to take Pork Chop Hill and what was at stake in sending reinforcements to save Clemons and the remnants of King Company.

Where to put the peace talks was just one of the problems dealt with in the reshoots. The other concerned the Chinese propagandist who is broadcasting directly to the troops on the hill. Apparently, the producers weren't satisfied with just hearing the broadcaster; they wanted to see him too. So, actor Viraj Amonsin was cast as the propagandist. He reported for work on Halloween, 1958, in the Int. Chinese Underground set at the Samuel Goldwyn Studios. Gregory Peck himself directed the various sequences in which Viraj broadcasts to the troops.

A month later, Amonsin wrote to Peck, "I wanted to tell you how much I enjoyed working for you on *Pork Chop Hill*. I liked the script very much and I am proud that I was involved in a work of such quality and taste. I especially enjoyed our rehearsals and our discussion as to the character of the broadcaster. Frankly, I was overwhelmed by your sensitivity as a director (for all practical purposes where I was concerned, you directed). Before that, I had only thought of you as a fine actor! And I look forward in the near future to a work in which you will star as well as direct. Your directorial talents, the kindness and friendliness of every one of your associates and above all, your personal qualities as a human being, all these impressed me profoundly and if I worked as well as I hope I did, it was because I felt 'at home.'"[26]

When *Pork Chop Hill* was screened for the first European critics, reports came back through United Artists' Arnold Picker that there were some objections to the film's final narration bit. In Webb's shooting draft, it read:

> Pork Chop Hill was held, bought and paid for at the same price we commemorate in monuments at Bunker Hill and Gettysburg. Yet you will find no monuments on Pork Chop. Victory is a fragile thing and history does not linger long in our century. But those who fought there know what they did and the meaning of it. Millions live in freedom today because of what they did.[27]

In a letter to Picker, dated June 9, 1959, shortly before the film was released in France (it had opened to favorable reviews in the States on May 29), Peck wrote: "I notice in the London reviews that the end narration antagonized a couple of critics. It seemed to them to over glorify the American contribution and struck a discordant note. If this end narration is going to offend Europeans generally it might well be removed. The effect of having the men march off the hill without comment from a narrator gives the whole film a great anti-war, 'futility of war' impact. It leaves the audience free as they walk out to speculate and draw their own conclusions on the meaning of the film. What would seem to us to be a 'down beat' ending might be the very thing that would put the picture over in Europe. This can easily be done and I would appreciate your giving the problem some serious consideration and letting me know your decision at once."[28]

Picker wrote back a week later, "As regards your feelings concerning the end narration, I must tell you that I honestly believe it is helpful, essential and gives superb meaning to the whole picture. If the decision were to be mine alone, I would say we should not change it. However, to be completely fair and objective, I have sent your thoughts to Europe, without in any way conveying to them my own opinion and, if their reaction on the spot is different than mine, I will certainly recommend to you that we drop it out. I feel, however, in the first instance, that I must truthfully and forthrightly give you my own opinion."[29]

On June 23, Picker wrote Peck again, with a plan of action: "Quote cable from Europe, 'We believe eliminating end narration Pork Chop Hill makes for too abrupt unsatisfactory ending. Suggest de-emphasizing American contribution by changing narration in subtitling and dubbing for Europe as follows: Pork Chop Hill was held, bought and paid for at the same price we commemorated in monuments at other great battlefields. Yet you will find no monuments on Pork Chop. Victory is a fragile thing and history does not linger long in our century. But those who fought there know what they did and the meaning of it. What they did helped millions live in freedom today. Please advise if satisfactory.'"[30]

Peck, Milestone and Bartlett agreed and narration changes were made on European prints, all paid for by United Artists. In 1959, in the relatively peaceful Eisenhower era, it was not considered unusual for American filmmakers to go out of their way to satisfy international audiences — even if it involved downplaying our own country's historical legacy. Today, if a European critic had problems with an American historical reference, I doubt if anyone would consider changing it.

CHAPTER SIX

The Longest Day

For showman Darryl Francis Zanuck and 20th Century–Fox Film Corporation, the fall of 1960 was a crucial period.

One of Hollywood's all-time most successful producers and studio executives, Zanuck had turned independent in 1956 and, in the space of four short years, he turned a series of worthwhile film properties into costly, overblown productions, each one a major disappointment at the box-office. These less-than-successful 20th Century–Fox releases included *The Sun Also Rises* (1957), *The Roots of Heaven* (1958) and *Crack in the Mirror* (1960).

Earlier, in 1952, the seeds of disintegration were sown with the appearance of Bella Wegier or Bella Darvi, as she was billed in another series of costly duds: *Hell and High Water* (1954), *The Egyptian* (1954) and *The Racers* (1955). Zanuck's infatuation with this talentless girl of Polish/French descent, not only clouded his film sense but it brought about the dissolution of his 30-year marriage to Virginia Zanuck. (Incidentally, Bella Wegier's stage name, Darvi, is composed of the first parts of the names Darryl and Virginia.)

Throughout this period, 20th Century–Fox was in increasingly desperate financial straits. Its investments in Zanuck's personal productions were proving painfully unprofitable and the studio was about to enter the *Cleopatra* era, a period of even further financial decline and creative stagnation.

Zanuck left the studio in 1956, surrendering production chores to Buddy Adler, formerly of Columbia Pictures, who had produced *From Here to Eternity* in 1953. Adler worked hard to reorganize the unwieldy studio structure and return it to solvency, but when he died suddenly four years later, the task was left unfinished.

Zanuck refused to stay down, nor let the studio that had always been his home crumble into receivership. In 1960, he returned to produce *The Longest Day*, the most important film of his career.

Like a ruptured artery, the spiraling costs of *Cleopatra* would eventually drain the studio's lifeblood. It was up to Zanuck to replenish the loss with the infusion of box-office plasma. Darryl Zanuck saw *The Longest Day* as the chance of a lifetime. He was right. And his timing proved perfect. The film eventually became a huge success and saved 20th Century–Fox from financial ruin.

In many ways, the production of this blockbuster recreation of the June 6, 1944 Normandy invasion resembled the complexity of the original historical event known as D-Day. Zanuck's war epic eventually cost more money, took up more screen time, featured more directors and international stars, and included more technical assistance than any other American war film up to that time. But it was worth every penny and every minute and, to this day, it represents the perfect image of what pioneer director D.W. Griffith originally viewed as a history lesson on film.

Although critics later attacked the film as lacking serious comment on the true cost of the invasion, *The Longest Day* was lauded by others for its documentary style, the accuracy of its historical framework, and its professional, fast-moving storytelling.

In April 1969, a few weeks before the 25th anniversary of D-Day, author and journalist Cornelius Ryan, writing a retrospective story for *TV Guide,* stood on the wind-swept beaches of Normandy, remembering the seminal events that led to the conclusion of World War II in Europe. Ryan had been a war correspondent for the *London Daily Express,* assigned to cover the Normandy landings when the Allies hit the beach on June 6, 1944. For all his experience and expertise, Ryan still found it difficult to write meaningfully about the invasion.

He later wrote, "Out of the dawn, a million men plowed ashore through the surf, flags flying and marched on Berlin. Ridiculous. On that gray and misty morning, fewer than 9,000 men landed on a 50-mile stretch in the first wave. They came in a thin straggly line of landing craft.[1] It seemed more like a Madison Avenue affair. The organization was fantastic. Five thousand ships, fifteen thousand planes, hundreds of correspondents. You couldn't help asking yourself, What's that soldier thinking about? Had anyone considered the villagers on the coast? What did the Free French feel as they fired on their homeland?"[2]

Ryan felt totally inadequate to report the historical event. He felt there was no way to tell the whole story without getting inside the men who were living it. As he explained: "I knew I had to get this down on paper in an informed way. I had to be able to say, '*This* is the way it was!' If I had been a soldier, I might not have been interested in finding out why, why it was the way it was. But I was just young enough to be angry with myself for not knowing ... not understanding. I was determined to find out everything I could, the stupid things, the mad things, and the courageous things. I had to know."[3]

But D-Day ended and Ryan left to join General Patton's Third Army. And, after the war ended in Europe, he was ordered to the Far East. The idea for a book on D-Day did not return to him until 1949 when a group of the original correspondents returned to Normandy for the fifth anniversary of D-Day.

Ryan recalled, "I walked along the beach and saw the flotsam and jetsam of war still cluttering the area, burned-out vehicles, weapons.... I watched as a fisherman dragged a howitzer out of the sea with his net. A skeleton, helmet still in place, protecting the empty skull, was tangled up somehow in the cannon's wheels. Who was he? Nobody, nobody anywhere, knew. Nobody knew which men landed on D-Day in the first wave. What an appalling thing.

"And yet, who was there to keep track? Who possibly had the time to record the happenings? Not the participants. It was then that I began to think seriously about writing a book about the happenings of Normandy on that fateful day."[4]

At that time, Ryan was working for *Collier's* magazine, but he could not interest his employer, nor any other magazine, in financing his proposed project. He started anyway, sustaining himself with his own money. He began searching for records, for people. He ran advertisements that asked: "Where were you on June 6, 1944? Contact me if you took part in D-Day."

"I began writing to survivors. I sent out 6,000 questionnaires. Two thousand answered. Out of the 2,000 came 700 interviews. There were some 240 books written on D-Day. I read them all."[5]

In 1956, *Collier's* magazine went bankrupt. Ryan was about $20,000 in debt, money he had borrowed to cover his travel, correspondence and translation expenses.

"My wife Kathryn was then an editor at *House and Home*, and we talked it over and decided that I should devote full time to the book," Ryan explained. "I began writing in earnest, and when I took the first pages of the book to Simon & Schuster, they gave me an advance of $7,500.

"I finished *The Longest Day* three years later. Kathryn and I had worked seven days a week with absolutely no time off for at least three or four years. Even though I finally received financial and research help from *Reader's Digest*, by the time we finished, we were still about $60,000 in debt.

"I turned the manuscript in and walked directly over to the *Digest* to ask for an assignment. Then I went home to Kathryn and we stared at each other. Suddenly, we didn't know what to do with ourselves."[6]

Reader's Digest condensed Ryan's book and *The Longest Day* first appeared in the spring of 1959. One month later, Simon & Schuster published the hard-cover version.

It became a landmark work of non-fiction, establishing Ryan as one of the country's top military historians. Ryan used this reputation to go on and write two more epic war stories, *The Last Battle* (about the battle for Berlin in the final days of World War II in Europe) and *A Bridge Too Far* (a fascinating study of the tragic Operation Market Garden airborne landings in Holland in September 1944, which, in 1977, became an epic film directed by Richard Attenborough).

French film producer Raoul J. Levy, the man who discovered curvaceous French sex symbol Brigitte Bardot, took an option on *The Longest* Day, and on March 23, 1960, he closed a deal with Simon & Schuster to acquire all film rights. Ryan was to receive $100,000 for those rights, plus another $35,000 to write the screenplay.

Within a week, in an attempt to set up a financing/distribution deal, Levy contacted several major American studios, including Columbia Pictures, which had first refusal on all Levy projects.

Levy envisioned *The Longest Day* as a true blockbuster that would cost at least $6 million to produce. He also announced his intention to seek military cooperation from Britain, France, Germany and the United States. He predicted that filming would begin in the spring of 1961.

While Cornelius Ryan was beginning what was to be a very long screenplay, Levy was busy filming *La Vérité* starring Mademoiselle Bardot. When that project was finished, Levy began arrangements for *The Longest Day*. Failing to secure an American studio or production company, he set up a deal with Associated British Picture Corporation, and then flew to Washington, D.C., to confer with members of the Defense Department.

At Dulles International Airport, he informed reporters that Englishman Michael Anderson had been signed as director, with cameraman Erwin Hillier, who had been the cinematographer on *The Dam Busters,* joining the production as well.

In an interview with *Daily Variety,* Levy revealed that Ryan had been hired to write the script, and that "although the cast is not as yet set ... there will be around 300 speaking parts in the film, and of these about 50 will be of star caliber American, British, French and German performers. Most of the top French actors we've contacted are eager to be in the film."[7]

His plans were to get production rolling by March 1961; interiors would be done at Elstree Studios outside London; other shooting would be on the English coast and in France. To handle the broad sweep of the film, he envisioned as many as 20 camera crews working on the production at once. He further predicted that *The Longest Day* would be the first contemporary epic.

Levy's plans, however, came to an abrupt and unexpected halt when the executives of Associated British Pictures informed him that they were unable to come up with the projected budget of $6 million.

Like Samuel Bronston's experience 16 years earlier on *A Walk in the Sun,* Levy learned the hard way that independent producers — even successful ones — ran into critical snares when attempting to independently bankroll a costly picture.

No sooner was Levy shot down by the British, than Zanuck stepped in to revive the project. He had been filming *The Big Gamble* with Stephen Boyd and Juliette Greco, on Africa's Ivory Coast, when Ryan's book had been published. When Levy grabbed a first option, Zanuck waited to see what he would do with the project. When it fell through, he stepped in and purchased Levy's option.

Although somewhat wary about putting up large sums of money for a war picture, the Fox executives were even more anxious to back a winner that could lift the studio out of the deepening red ink that had engulfed them. Production bills on *Cleopatra* were arriving from Italy in horrendous numbers and amounts. Filming had gone from bad in London to worse in Rome.

One of the basic mistakes had been in picking rainy England for the shooting of a sunny Egyptian story, and that error had been compounded by two more strokes of bad fortune. Actress Elizabeth Taylor fell in love with her co-star Richard Burton (both were married to others at the time) and then Ms. Taylor contracted pneumonia in London. Both events were almost fatal, the former to the studio and the latter to the new Queen of the Nile.

Another two and a half million dollars trickled down the drain when Joseph Mankiewicz was hired to write at night and direct by day an unbelievable off-the-cuff operation that, by 1962, had pyramided production costs to over $35 million.

In an effort to save the studio from ruin, the Fox executives decided that if Zanuck would indeed acquire *The Longest Day,* they would gamble the studio's last financial reserves on the venture.

Elmo Williams, a 20th Century–Fox second-unit director and the future producer of *Tora! Tora! Tora!,* had reinforced Zanuck's belief in the potential of the film, as well as pointing out its logistical demands. He laid out in cold figures the mountain of equipment that would be required to re-stage what some people considered the largest military invasion in modern history, the manpower and directorial skill it would take to capture it on film, and the challenge of finding a huge cast of international players.

Zanuck understood the complexities. He felt, as did Levy, that to do justice to the tremendous scope of the story, shooting would have to be done on authentic location sites whenever possible. And, despite the obvious cost, only great stars of international renown would be cast.

On December 2, 1960, Zanuck purchased the film rights to Ryan's novel from Levy for $175,000. The large sum included the writer's compensation for a new screenplay. In a news conference, it was Zanuck's turn to announce his plans. Ever the showman, he didn't mince words: "I feel that it will probably be the most ambitious undertaking since *Gone with the Wind* and *Birth of a Nation.* What will it cost? God knows! I don't know. Certainly millions. Either I will go broke, or make the greatest picture ever. I believe that from a patriotic standpoint, we can get stars to fill all of the major roles."[8]

Zanuck emphasized that the production would not "be a war picture as such" but rather "the story of the little people, of the underground, of the civilians who were there, of the unknown men who made the first assault, of the general confusion." He concluded, "My picture will hate the institution of war, but be fair about it."[9]

With Elmo Williams taking charge of the logistical aspects of the battle scenes and Ryan working on the new script, Zanuck sent producer Frank McCarthy first to Washington, D.C., and then to Europe to secure the military cooperation vital to the success of the film.

McCarthy, a brigadier general during World War II and aide to Chief of Staff General Marshall, recalled his mission for Zanuck: "General Lauris Norstad was then commander of the NATO forces and I went to him after script approval from Washington. Norstad promised us complete cooperation and 700 Special Forces troops. These soldiers were stationed far from the border and they were selected on the theory that should there be any trouble with the Russians in Berlin, they could be sent to the capital from Normandy just as readily as they could from their bases in Southern Germany."[10]

To better coordinate the pre-production phase of *The Longest Day*, Zanuck moved an army of secretaries, translators, researchers and agents to the Rue de Bac, in Paris. Ryan continued writing the screenplay in his hotel room at the Prince de Galles Hotel, which he had converted into an office.

Originally, it had been decided to have Williams coordinate and direct each battle scene in the film, but Zanuck soon realized that with eight major battle segments, it would be more practical to have multiple directors filming simultaneously on the different locations.

One of the directors subsequently hired to film these sequences was Gerd Oswald, who had directed action sequences on two previous 20th Century–Fox war films, *Decision Before Dawn* and *The Desert Fox*.

Recalled Oswald, "Zanuck's notion at the time was, I believe, to hire a group of directors who are known in the movie industry as 'lightweights.' He avoided strong, well-established directors who could possibly stray from Darryl's law. Zanuck wanted to run the whole show and he decided to hire only those directors he felt he could control and who would not question his decisions."[11]

In addition to Oswald, Zanuck's staff of directors would include Andrew "Bundy" Marton, Ken Annakin and Bernhard Wicki. Later in the filming, during the interiors shot at the Boulogne Studios in Paris, Zanuck directed a great part of the film on his own — a first in his career.

Teaming with Cornelius Ryan, Elmo Williams laid out eight major battle sequences, the largest number ever featured in a motion picture. The sequences covered the Omaha Beach landing, the Utah Beach landing, the Ranger assault on Pointe du Hoc, the French commando attack on Ouistreham, the airborne landing in Ste. Mère Église, the glider assault on the Orne River bridge, the British landings on Sword Beach and the destruction of the Colleville strongpoint. Because of the film's

With his trademark cigar in place, Darryl F. Zanuck goes over a production detail with Peter Lawford (right), while Zanuck's girlfriend, actress Irina Demich, observes.

length, the Colleville segment ended up on the cutting room floor, much to Williams's dismay.

"I didn't mind giving up any other battle sequence, except that one," Williams said. "It would have been the greatest ever seen on the screen, but it would have taken up 20 minutes of screen time.

"We had a group of German S.S. troops holed up in a blockhouse behind the American invasion beach, near the town of Colleville. When the Americans go ashore, they drive the Germans back, and many of the beach defenders also wind up in the crowded blockhouse. These were the ordinary Wehrmacht troops, and they wanted to give up, but the S.S. fanatics wouldn't let them. They ended up forcing the Wehrmacht to fight at gunpoint. They actually had machine guns inside the blockhouse pointed at their own men, and they held out for quite a long time because their strongpoint was well fortified. Finally, after naval bombardment proved ineffective, the Army brought up flamethrowers and fired into the air vents on top of the bunker. They kept firing until all of the oxygen inside the blockhouse was burned off.

"It was an unusual sequence because the S.S. officers knew what was going on outside, and they tried to get the soldiers to conserve their air. They were actually counting when the soldiers could breathe. It was really eerie, but we had to take it out of the picture because we already had close to a four-hour film, which was much too long."[12]

Regarding the logistics for filming these ambitious battle scenes, Zanuck wrote a letter to Lord Mountbatten, stating, "I believe I have a tougher job than Ike had on D-Day. At least he had the equipment, I have to find it, rebuild it and transport it to Normandy."[13]

Thus began one of the greatest scavenger hunts in war film history. For the Orne River glider assault, Zanuck ordered two Horsa gliders from a British piano company, the same firm that had constructed the original gliders during wartime. For the film's strafing sequences, Zanuck needed functioning World War II Spitfires and Messerschmitts, which were practically non-existent by that time. Fortunately, Williams found three Spitfires serving with the Belgian Air Force and two Messerschmitts in Spain, attached to General Franco's small air force.

At several locations along the Normandy coast, work gangs were rebuilding and refurbishing many of the surviving Nazi fortifications, once part of Hitler's so-called *Festung Europa* (Fortress Europe). Milk cans once used by the Germans as mines but later dug up and reused by the French for their original purpose, were bought by Zanuck and once more restored, this time as dummy explosives.

To provide one of the film's lighter moments, Zanuck acquired the designs for the Rupert Decoy. Dropped from a plane behind the Normandy coast in the dark morning hours of D-Day, Rupert engaged large groups of German soldiers and fought pitched battles with them amid the confusion of the hedgerow country. It was only after the Germans had surrounded the enemy and had blasted him to shreds that they discovered the Allied trick. Rupert was a rubber dummy, covered with firecrackers. There were thousands of Ruperts and they served two purposes. Not only did they draw off and confuse the Germans, but they lulled them into the belief that reported paratroop landings were nothing more than purposeful diversions from the real invasion, which was expected to the north, at the Pas de Calais, which was the closest French soil to England.

The amount of ammunition needed to supply the two movie armies was one of Zanuck's biggest headaches. Over 600,000 rounds of blank ammunition had to be hand manufactured in the United States, Great Britain, Germany, Holland and Norway.

One Belgian gunsmith was commissioned to produce a supply of handmade blanks for a German anti-aircraft gun, at $10 a shell.

Zanuck complained, "The S.O.B. wanted screen credit — ammunition by so and so. We eventually shot off about $8,000 worth in one night outside Ste. Mère Église."[14]

France's Secret Army Organization, a terrorist organization which was at the peak of its activity during the filming of *The Longest Day* in 1961, became a complicating factor for the production. The French government frequently voiced its nervousness over Zanuck's vast cache of arms and ammunition. As a security precaution, most of the automatic weapons were kept under police guard at all times, as were the Frenchmen cast in the various German roles in the film.

The French memory was long and the German uniforms were still a hated and feared ensemble in France. When a swastika was flown over the ancient castle of Chantilly, near Paris (simulating German headquarters at La Roche Guyon), it nearly started a riot.

Besides the 700 Special Forces troops promised by the NATO command, Britain, through Lord Mountbatten, pledged a fleet of 66 ships of World War II vintage and 150 men from the East Anglia and Green Jackets brigades. France, despite pressing problems in Algeria, provided over 2,000 men. West Germany could muster no soldiers, but the civilian government did promise all the World War II material it could find, along with valuable technical assistance.

"I negotiated for nearly eight months," recalled Zanuck in a 1962 article in *Life* magazine. "I needed a great deal of material for a period of almost a year. In return, I agreed that each of the participating governments could review the finished film and censor anything that might appear to be offensive."[15]

Along the Normandy coast, Zanuck's corps of movie engineers continued to pave the way for the production crews, clearing out any vintage mines and burning off the overgrown shrubbery to reveal the pockmarked terrain of D-Day Normandy.

During the clearing operation, they unearthed a British tank in the sands where it had been buried for 17 years. With a little help from the art department, it was restored to serviceable condition, joining Zanuck's small, but capable, tank corps.

Uniforms for the Allies were no problem. The regular troops were already outfitted in battle dress that needed few alterations to bring them back to 1944 standards.

British and U.S. military depots were amply stocked with uniforms for the additional civilian extras who masqueraded as soldiers. But the German uniforms had to be especially tailored. The West German Army had previously destroyed all reminders of Nazi days. Since Chancellor Konrad Adenauer, alone among Zanuck's "allies," could not spare any genuine soldiers for the production, the German soldiers themselves presented another special problem.

The solution became an elite corps of 60 French and German actors who were recruited in Paris and packed off to basic training near Versailles for a one-month course in the Nazi manual of arms and the goosestep, under the supervision of former Wehrmacht paratrooper, Johnny Jendrich.

How much sensitivity remained in Normandy in 1961 was vividly demonstrated at Ste. Mère Église. On the first night of production, Jendrich thought it would be amusing to have his little "army" march into town smartly, heavy boots hitting the cobblestones in well-remembered and fearfully recalled cadence. The large French crowd that had gathered to watch the filming burst into violent anger, stones started flying and the loudspeaker echoed across the angry mob, trying to explain that these were movie extras and not German storm troopers.

Jendrich's unit of 60 men later proved to be the workhorses of the film. They were defeated at the Orne River bridge, overrun on Omaha Beach, surrounded at Ouistreham, ambushed by the French underground, strafed by Spitfires, and surprised by the Rangers at Pointe du Hoc.

The equipment continued to pour into Zanuck's forward base of operations in Caen, Normandy. A 20mm Wehrmacht cannon was found in England. It had been captured at Dieppe during the war. Several 50mm anti-aircraft guns used by the Germans were found in bunkers on the Il de Rey near La Rochelle. A British Piat gun, which resembled the American bazooka, was loaned from a London museum, and a German Maxim heavy machine gun was located in Paris and sent to Caen with hundreds of rifles and submachine guns.

Special props, such as Rommel's ceremonial baton, had to be manufactured. It was copied from a photograph supplied by Mrs. Lucy Rommel, who was later credited as a technical advisor on the film.

Propmaster Sam Gordon was unable to find two items. One was the Indian type of machete knives which the Free French commandos carried during the invasion. They had obtained the long-bladed weapons while training in India. The other was a simple item: a 48-star American flag. This had to be custom manufactured for the production.

Throughout the spring of 1961, Darryl F. Zanuck, a movie Eisenhower with a perpetual cigar shoved between his teeth, organized his "armada." Elmo Williams's original plan had called for all of the actual invasion scenes to be filmed on the actual locations. But practicality, a strained budget, and the French tourist season, forced a change in those carefully laid plans.

When it was announced that the U.S. Marines would invade Corsica as part of a training exercise, Darryl F. Zanuck not only received permission to film the event, but he was allowed to outfit the Marines to look like G.I.'s, circa 1944, and to build beach obstacles.

Zanuck considered transferring Sword Beach, where the main British forces landed, to the other side of the English Channel, where there would be a ready supply of English natives on hand to fill the ranks of the movie army. A level beach, similar to the broad sandy plain characteristic of Sword was discovered, but production plans were shelved when a group of irate bird enthusiasts warned the producer that a sanctuary was too near the beaches.

Finding Lord Mountbatten's naval flotilla useless because of its great fuel bill (a cost that Her Majesty's Navy was not going to foot), Zanuck soon found himself in drastic need of a naval flotilla and an invasion beach free of tourists and rare pheasants.

The battle action required almost two miles of uninhabited beach to film with the required sweep (especially aerial shots taken from a diving Messerschmitt's point of view). This was not going to be one of those tightly shot sequences showing two dozen Marines scrambling ashore near San Diego. It would be the real thing, with at least 1,000 extras in landing craft sweeping onto a beach fortified with actual defenses. Close-ups could be shot later, in the off season, on the original landing beaches in Normandy, but Zanuck could not afford to keep his second-unit crews idle during the entire summer while he filmed indoors at the Boulogne Studios in Paris. He needed beaches right away.

In May 1961, the producer was able to train his cameras on a major British-staged paratroop drop on the island of Cyprus, but landing beaches remained elusive.

While Zanuck and his staff were scouting equipment and locations, Cornelius Ryan was in Paris, completing the script. On May 15, Zanuck arrived to find Ryan and the fattest screenplay he had ever seen.

Recalled Zanuck: "He had things completely out of proportion, 26 pages for something that should take three lines and three lines for something that should have taken 26 pages. It was a painstaking thing. Rewriting, and rewriting and rewriting, and more rewriting."[16] Working in each other's pockets (the uneasy relationship between writer and producer would later explode), the pair eventually finished the script.

To celebrate the occasion, Frank McCarthy brought good news from Washington. The U.S. Sixth Fleet was planning major amphibious maneuvers with the Marine complement and McCarthy reported that motion picture coverage could be arranged. Leaving Ken Annakin and Bernhard Wicki behind to supervise the construction of the interiors at the Boulogne Studios, Zanuck, Elmo Williams, Oswald, Marton and a crew of 165 left Paris for Naples, Italy. Their final destination: the broiling sands of Saleccia Beach in Northern Corsica.

Permission had been granted to fortify the Corsican beach so that it would resemble Omaha Beach in 1944. Steel obstacles were constructed along a two-mile stretch and special-effects charges were buried in the water and sand. Machine gun simulators, firing tiny ball-bearings, were stationed to cover the surf.

But there were problems. The subtropical beach was obviously not the English Channel and the wedgewood skies of Corsica bore no resemblance to the brooding clouds over Normandy. However, since the Marines were going to land over a two-day period, Zanuck and his directors were able to work out the details. Early each morning, before the Marines stormed ashore, the movie crew hosed down the beaches to make them look as dark as the Norman shore. The billowing smoke of burning tires, combined with several varieties of camera filters, turned the sky to an acceptable gray.

Zanuck's personal intelligence corps warned him that a nudist colony, just two miles inland from the beach, posed a potential hazard. It was arranged, therefore, for the local authorities to post signs warning the nudists not to go near the water during the landings.

During the voyage from Naples to Saleccia, Zanuck had kept his unit busy photographing

Navy transports en route, lecturing the troops and arranging the proposed camera coverage with the Admiral in charge.

Gerd Oswald remembered the shipboard routine: "Our base of operations was in the flagship. Every night, Elmo, Bundy [Marton] and I would go to a different ship and try to explain to the Marines what we were filming. Unfortunately, with a vast number of people like this [1600 Marines] we were unable to give personal directions to everyone. We couldn't say, 'you drop dead here, you get hit by a bullet in the leg, and you do this.' We had to trust them.

"We tried to make the Marines realize that a couple of them had to 'die' and a couple of them had to be 'wounded.' Some of the guys told us that the Marines always made it. 'Yes,' we replied, 'but we're making a movie, not a commercial!'"[17]

At the end of the voyage, the Sixth Fleet entered French waters and rendezvoused with a squadron of French ships that would act as a liaison during the Corsican maneuvers.

With the refreshing taste of wine and the aroma of fresh-baked bread (a pleasant change after the U.S. Navy diet of Coca-Cola and hash), Zanuck prepared his unit for disembarkation. Pleased with the two-mile stretch of fortified beach constructed by his art department, he began to place his camera crews with all of the precision of a defending field marshal.

With the combined fleet of 22 ships in the background representing the D-Day armada (which, in reality, had closer to 5,000 ships), everything was ready for the Marines. Shortly before H-Hour, however, Zanuck noticed an aircraft carrier riding at anchor near the Marine transports. Since there were no carriers present in the channel on D-Day, Zanuck requested that it stay 2000 yards to the right of camera. If it could remain in that position, Zanuck figured he could still photograph the rest of the fleet. The Navy complied and Saleccia Beach received its last touch of realism.

At 2:00 P.M. on June 21, 1961, the first wave of assault boats, carrying the men of the Third Marine Battalion (reinforced) arrived at the beach. Ramps dropped down and the attackers came wading through the deep water, wearing 1944-type leggings and net-covered helmets.

Since most of the Marines were seasick (a gale wind was blowing that day) they could hardly wait to get off the landing craft and, instead of coming up smiling (which was one of Zanuck's worries), they looked as grim as though they were entering actual combat. Zanuck's crew was aided by the French LST *Argens,* which ferried in supplies.

Oswald summed up the Corsica shoot: "We didn't really know what the men would do. I was supervising three cameras and whenever I saw something interesting, I told my crew to shoot it. We just shot on a one-take deal. Eventually, in the cutting room, the best scenes were all put together."[18]

While cameras were recording invasions and paratroop drops in documentary fashion, a great international cast was being assembled.

Oddly enough, the first people cast were a group of young American rock and roll singers. Related Elmo Williams, "Darryl and I were having lunch at *Fouquettes* in Paris when an agent friend came over and said, 'Hey, I hear you're going to make this film, why don't you let me give you a hell of a bargain with some names.' So he told us about these singers. Darryl asked me what I thought, so I said, honestly, that 'you can't tell one guy from another when he's wearing a helmet, so why not?' Zanuck said okay, and they were the first actors signed."[19]

One month later, Fabian, Tommy Sands and Paul Anka, all American teen idols, were "processed" in Paris and shipped to Andrew Marton's unit at Pointe du Hoc. Their mission: don Ranger uniforms and scale the 80-foot cliffs in four minutes.

Meanwhile, vivacious redhead Irina Demich became one of only three women in *The Longest Day*. Zanuck discovered her at a cocktail party in Paris and immediately signed her for the part of Janine Boitard, the French resistance worker, who, in real life, saved 68 Allied flyers from the Germans. Off-camera, she replaced Juliette Greco as Zanuck's main squeeze.

In all, Zanuck spent over $2 million on major talent casting, which, considering the number of name actors in the cast, was amazingly cheap, even by 1961 standards. After the rock and roll singers were signed, it was superstar John Wayne who opened the floodgates of talent. When a deal could not be struck with William

On location at Pointe du Hoc in Normandy, Darryl F. Zanuck chats with Robert Wagner (right), who portrays a U.S Army Ranger assigned to scale the cliffs. Singer/actor Fabian is in the center.

Holden, it was the Duke who took on the key part of Lt. Colonel Benjamin Vandervoort, the 82nd Airborne Division officer whose broken ankle did not prevent him from leading his men into Ste. Mère Église on D-Day.

After Wayne signed, other major American actors soon followed. They included Robert Mitchum, Rod Steiger, Jeffrey Hunter, Eddie Albert, Henry Fonda, Robert Ryan, Red Buttons, Robert Wagner, George Segal, Edmond O'Brien, Richard Beymer (fresh from *West Side Story*) and Tom Tryon. In all, there were 28 American actors portraying everyone from Ike on down. Henry Grace, an MGM set designer and a virtual look-alike for Dwight Eisenhower, won the coveted role of the Supreme Commander. It was his acting debut.

Leading the British cast, which featured 15 stars, were Richard Burton, who, along with Roddy McDowall, was shuttling back and forth between *Cleopatra* and *The Longest Day*.

For one English part, Zanuck had to choose between Sean Connery, Patrick McGoohan and John Gregson. It was Connery who first approached Zanuck about the part of an outspoken British private fighting on Sword Beach. But, there was a conflict. The young Scot had a commitment with United Artists for a film in Jamaica, which would begin shooting in January 1962. Through some heavy negotiating, Connery was able to squeeze in *The Longest Day*, while still honoring his commitment on the other project. The latter film turned out to be *Dr. No*, the first James Bond movie and Connery's ticket to superstardom. Interestingly, Zanuck also cast German actor Gert Frobe in a small part as a rotund German sergeant who delivers milk to the beach gunners on his horse. Three years later, Connery and Frobe would match wits in *Goldfinger*.

The 24 French and German actors completed the star-studded cast that ranks as one of the largest in motion picture history, and probably will never be duplicated. Frank McCarthy describes the methods used to employ the massive group of top performers: "Although Ryan's finished screenplay was very much like his book, certain liberties were taken to accommodate

Nancy Sinatra (left) visits Fabian and Robert Wagner on the beach at Pointe du Hoc, in Normandy.

the large cast. For example, if a character was very strong in a scene in the first ten minutes of the film, Ryan would find a way to lace him in somewhere else for a couple of minutes. You would see a little bit of Richard Todd and, later on, you would see him a little more. This was done with many of the actors."[20]

To add crucial factors of realism to the characterizations, as well as the action, Zanuck received a great deal of advice and assistance from a group of actual D-Day participants. Lord Mountbatten led a British advisory team that included the Earl of Lovat and Major John Howard. Zanuck, who had served with Mountbatten during World War II, was still apprehensive about going to the British for substantial help.

"I found a slightly hostile feeling," said Zanuck, "based on the fact that they thought this was another one of those American movies which showed how the Americans won the war. They wanted to be sure I wasn't interested in making it a one-man show. I told them what I was planning and that, realistically, I had to have their cooperation."[21]

Having fought his way inland from Sword Beach, British Army officer Lord Lovat (Peter Lawford, left) links up with British paratrooper, Maj. John Howard (Richard Todd, center) and an unidentified cast member during fighting for the Orne River bridge.

Lord Lovat eventually coached actor Peter Lawford to dramatize Lovat's own D-Day experience, leading British commandos onto Sword Beach and later linking up with Major John Howard's glider-born infantry, who were holding the Orne River bridge.

Actor Richard Todd would play Howard, and Howard himself was his advisor. Todd was no stranger to D-Day Normandy. A veteran of the paratroops, he had jumped a few miles from the Orne River bridge on invasion day.

Through General Norstad of NATO, Zanuck contacted veterans on the German side, as well. Senior among them was Vice Admiral Friedrich Ruge, retiring commander in chief of the German Navy, who was Field Marshal Erwin Rommel's naval aide during D-Day. He, in turn, found General Gunther Blumentritt (Field Marshal von Rundstedt's chief of staff), Lt. General Max Pemsel (the Seventh Army chief of staff) and Major Werner Pluskat (an officer of the 352nd Coast Artillery Division, and one of the first German officers to see the approaching Allied armada).

With the valuable assistance of these officers, actors Curt Jurgens (Blumentritt), Wolfgang Preiss (Pemsel) and Hans Christian Blech (Pluskat) were able to bring another level of realism to the atmosphere of chaos that pervaded the German Seventh Army Command on June 6, 1944.

It was Rommel's comment (spoken by actor Werner Hinz) that gave the film its name. Speaking above the sands of Normandy in early spring 1944, the Field Marshal enunciated his strategy on defeating the invasion:

> Look out there, gentlemen," he told his subordinates, "how calm, how peaceful it is. A narrow strip of water between the continent and England, between us and the Allies. And beyond that peaceful horizon? A maelstrom! A coiled spring of men, tanks and planes waiting to be unleashed against us. Not a single Anglo-American shall reach the shore. Not a single Anglo-American shall set foot on the beaches. Whenever and wherever it comes, I intend to defeat the invasion right there. Right there, gentlemen, at the water's edge. Believe me, gentlemen; the first twenty-four hours of the invasion will be decisive. For the Allies, as well as Germany, it will be the longest day … the longest day."[22]

With his cast assembled, his equipment concentrated at the French ordnance depot in Caen, and his directors on alert for action, Darryl F. Zanuck launched his own movie armada into filmed battle. *The Longest Day* had begun.

Andrew "Bundy" Marton, with his singers and 150 Rangers of the U.S. Eighth Division as "extras," was assigned the task of recreating the June 6 assault on Pointe du Hoc. On D-Day, 17 years earlier, Lt. James E. Rudder of the Second Ranger Battalion led three companies against the 80-foot cliffs, located on the right flank of Omaha Beach. Their target: heavy caliber naval guns that could wreak havoc with landing craft.

Before filming began, a cleanup crew similar to the art department unit employed in Corsica, transformed the plant-overgrown cliffs to their circa 1944 rockiness.

After clearing out 600 live land mines, the crew used flamethrowers to burn off the shrubbery and reduce the shrub trees to charcoal. Shell craters were reblasted, a bunker was refurbished and draped with camouflage, and the familiar rubber tires were brought in as burning smudge pots.

Johnny Jendrich's defense force of Germans arrived soon after, spending most of their free time drinking wine and Calvados, and playing chess with the Rangers. On location, Zanuck had his own canvas chair and a French-built Alouette helicopter standing by, ready to transport him to Gerd Oswald's crew filming in nearby Ste. Mère Église.

Besides Tommy Sands, Paul Anka and Fabian, the Ranger assault for Marton's cameras would include Robert Wagner and George Segal. Wagner had read Ryan's book on his own and hadn't waited to be invited to the filming. He had applied for a part. Moreover, after visiting the

British Army veteran Lord Lovat (left) served as a technical advisor on *The Longest Day*. He is seen chatting with Peter Lawford, who plays him in the film.

American cemetery at Omaha Beach, he had come to believe that the movie was his personal responsibility. Then, too, Zanuck had been luck for him in the past — he had been a contract player at Fox since the early 1950s.

The attack on Pointe du Hoc closely resembled the storming of a medieval castle. Following a murderous naval and air bombardment (off camera, of course, to save money), the movie Rangers came ashore on a narrow gravel beach. Using mortars to launch hundreds of grappling hooks into the barbed wire nine stories up, the three companies of Ranger extras began their version of the historical climb.

The oft-repeated phrase that "three grandmothers with brooms could have swept the cliff clean" is made frighteningly apparent as the Rangers make the agonizing, nearly vertical, climb with their ropes and ladders while a small German force keeps them pinned down with machine gun fire and hand grenades.

Inevitably, there were injuries. Anka suffered a deep cut in his hand. Tommy Sands lacerated his knee and received several stitches, and Wagner injured his back in a collision with Fabian. All the actors, though, had been subjected to a full week's intensive training before Zanuck permitted them to make the actual climb.

For 12 days, Marton filmed the Battle of Pointe du Hoc. The final cost, which included the expense of transporting the U.S. Army Ranger unit from their base in Wiesbaden, Germany, was a half-million dollars. Total screen time was less than ten minutes.

On August 13, ominous news reached Zanuck from Berlin. The Russians had erected a wall between the eastern and western halves of the capital. The Berlin crisis had begun. U.S.

German director Bernhard Wicki (left) with actor Werner Hinz (right), who portrayed German Field Marshal Erwin Rommel, and actor Michael Hinz, Hinz's real-life son, as Rommel's son, Manfred, in *The Longest Day*.

Army units throughout Europe were placed on full alert. At Pointe du Hoc, a direct telephone line to the Ranger's headquarters in Wiesbaden was kept open in case the soldiers were needed in the German capital.

It was during the early days of the Berlin Crisis that a controversy first erupted over the use of American troops in a motion picture production. What originated as a low-key congressional request for information later escalated into a major governmental policy revision concerning military cooperation with the motion picture industry.

On September 13, 1961, Representative Robert Wilson, a Republican from California, fired a telegram to Arthur Sylvester, Assistant Defense Secretary for Public Affairs. Prompted by a questionable massing of U.S. troops for a Jack Paar telecast from the Berlin Wall (which resulted in disciplinary action against the Army officers), Wilson was anxious to know the extent to which cooperation was being offered to Zanuck's crew operating in Normandy.

On October 3, Sylvester defended the use of the Ranger company at Pointe du Hoc: "It was our considered opinion that, basically, such a story has historical importance and that the film will give the public a better understanding of a most crucial combat operation. The film would show the U.S. Armed Forces in gallant action and, although it deals with war in its roughest form, it should prove beneficial for recruiting and in creating general interest in the Armed Forces."[23]

Sylvester further stressed, from the facts obtained via the European command, that no violation of Army regulations apparently was involved. "The Rangers," he concluded, "were not taken from Berlin, but from elsewhere in Germany. As reported previously, the troops were not paid as extras because the deployment was regarded as an opportunity for the Ranger-type troops to participate in cliff-scaling training. Consequently, any wages in addition to their military pay would not be justified. As a result of all the facts on hand, there is no thought of reprimanding anyone concerned."[24]

For the moment, members of Congress were satisfied. But the repercussions of the first investigation were already beginning to open the whole spectrum of military cooperation to closer scrutiny. An era was coming to an end, and Darryl Zanuck would soon find himself in the middle of a major policy shift.

To the North, in the little Norman town of Ste. Mère Église, director Gerd Oswald prepared to film one of history's most dangerous paratroop landings. Designed to disrupt German communications behind the invasion beaches on the night before D-Day, the American airborne landings were a costly success. Although both the 82nd and 101st Airborne Divisions accomplished their missions, many paratroopers were drowned in flooded swamplands, shot out of the sky by German anti-aircraft guns and often blown, by powerful winds, miles from their drop zones.

In his book, Cornelius Ryan had concentrated on the catastrophic landing in the town of Ste. Mère Église. In planning the movie battle action, Elmo Williams saw the confrontation where a paratroop company is wiped out, as playing from a unique angle.

"This particular battle," he said, "was laid out specifically from the paratrooper's point of view, every setup in the sequence was vertical, either made from the ground looking up or from the paratrooper's point of view looking down. It was one of those battles that was unique and the only thing that made it unique was having an actor like Red Buttons (portraying Pvt. John Steele of the 82nd Airborne Division) hung up on that church steeple, watching the slaughter below him."[25]

When director Gerd Oswald began filming several hand-to-hand combat sequences on the ground to add realism to the battle, Williams ordered him to stop. "There was nothing wrong with what he was doing," Williams explained, "except that it took away from the pattern we were trying to set, a strictly vertical pattern. There were other battles to film on the ground and we wanted to reserve that type of action for those sequences."[26]

Pressure from Williams and Zanuck was not Oswald's only problem. History was repeating itself as the strong Normandy coastal winds played havoc with the unit's helicopter-borne paratroopers.

"The Normandy winds were simply terrible," laments Oswald. "Our groups, which consisted of about 25 French stuntmen, some English paratroopers and a contingent of soldiers from a nearby French Air Force base, could never land in the proper places. They were always being blown away. Week after week, we had to resign ourselves to getting little pieces of film at a time."[27]

As a last resort, Oswald put in a request for a group of construction cranes. During the last two days of shooting, guidelines were strung and the paratroopers were mechanically dropped on their targets. To further create the illusion of a large-scale airborne operation, full-size dummy paratroopers (as opposed to the Ruperts) were also dumped from the helicopters. Filming in the actual village of Ste. Mère Église gave the sequence its ultimate sense of realism. Throughout the three-week shoot, the 1,500 residents of Ste. Mère Église were given a nightly front-row seat at their own history.

John Wayne (third from left) portrayed 82nd Airborne Division Lt. Col. Benjamin Vandervoort, who, despite breaking an ankle upon landing, led his men into Ste. Mère Église. Joining him in the assault are Captain Harding (Steve Forrest, far left), Lt. Wilson (Tom Tryon, to Wayne's right) and Lt. Sheen (Stuart Whitman, to Tryon's right). Other cast members are unidentified.

Christian Marquand portrayed French Commando leader Philippe Kieffer, who led his men against heavily defended Ouistreham.

Frequently, Zanuck's Alouette would appear, producer and director would confer on the progress of the day, and then the special helicopter would wing northeast to Ken Annakin's unit filming near the Orne River bridge.

By the beginning of September 1961, Marton had completed the Pointe du Hoc sequence and was halfway through the Spitfire strafing attack. Annakin had finished the Orne River assault and was preparing an important train wreck with the cooperation of the French National Railroad Bureau. Oswald, having finished Ste. Mère Église, was preparing the French commando assault on Ouistreham.

Upon his return from the Corsican landings in June, Elmo Williams had begun the major chore of scouting the locations for the close-up beach landings. These sequences would include both American beach landings, the British landing on Sword and the French assault on Ouistreham.

With Chomat, an expert French helicopter pilot, at the controls, Williams began to scour Normandy for a town similar to wartime Ouistreham. "The real Ouistreham," explained Williams, "lies at the mouth of the Orne River, a very flat uninteresting area. The casino, the focal point of the French attack, had been ripped down. Since there was nothing left resembling the town the way it was during wartime, Chomat, Oswald and I began to look for a new place where we could get the same effect but in a more confined area that lent itself to dramatization.

"Our first day out we found the perfect location, a town on the coast called Port-en-Bessin. It was perfect because there were still some bombed-out buildings in existence. The French mayor, a former member of the resistance (as everyone turned out to be) was delighted to cooperate with us.

"We told him that we wanted to repair the shell holes and then blow them out again. At first, he thought we were crazy, but he eventually gave us all the cooperation he could."[28]

Before filming could begin, Oswald went to Zanuck, dissatisfied with Williams' choice of location. The director, battle-hardened after the disasters in Ste. Mère Église, preferred a small fishing village only three miles from Ouistreham. Faced with a difference of opinion, Zanuck deferred to Williams. Williams and production manager Lee Katz then proceeded to compare the two locations, eventually opting for Port-en-Bessin. Recalled Oswald: "I was overruled because of a basic logistical problem. My little fishing village was unacceptable because of inadequate housing and catering facilities."[29]

Forced to accept the new location, Oswald penciled in several changes in Williams's battle plan. The casino — the focal point of German resistance in the original Ouistreham — was constructed at the vertex of two angles, one stretching along an estuary, the other past a ruined castle and some bombed-out buildings. The French commando attack could converge on the casino from two sides. Unlike Pointe du Hoc, or Ste. Mère Église, the Ouistreham battle sequence was blocked out horizontally to be, for the most part, one long helicopter shot, here described by Williams: "In the screen version of the attack, you start at the bridge and come down the estuary past the fishing boats. You pull up to the casino, pan right and, near the ruined castle, you see the other attack force. Originally, we planned it differently. You started up beyond the round tower of the castle, and you came down towards the fortified casino. As the attack progressed, the camera panned left, this time revealing the estuary as it came alive with troops."[30]

Quarreling between Williams and Oswald on the nature of the battle sequence continued, and when Zanuck finally entered the fracas, Oswald was fired from the picture. Oswald's name does not appear in the final credits. Oswald explained: "In the original contract, Darryl had stipulated that each director's contribution had to equal one-fourth of the picture to be credited. This was almost impossible to establish, since he was also directing a great deal. But, certainly, the Ste. Mère Église sequence was not a fourth of the film. So, contractually, he could eliminate my name, which he did." Andrew Marton later completed the Ouistreham sequence under Williams's supervision.

It was during the middle of October 1961 that Zanuck was forced to make a fateful decision concerning the proposed filming off the French coast on the Il de Rey.

The tiny islet off the Brittany coast, near La Rochelle, had been accidentally discovered by Williams during a prolonged search for landing craft. A full 24 hours later, Zanuck was surveying the bunker-strewn beaches, pronouncing the island perfect for the close-ups of the beach landings. Before he could mobilize his forces, there were two major problems.

First came the weather. Winter was coming and it simply was not the time to film a landing sequence off the Brittany coast. The seasons were changing and massive storms centering in the Central Atlantic could be expected at any time.

Williams preached caution. The logical move was to postpone the exteriors and film them the following spring. But to Zanuck, any postponement spelled disaster. It had taken him six months to gather and organize a vast number of international stars. Could he predict that they would still be available for principal photography eights months from now? Aside from the weather, the other problem was the financial state of 20th Century–Fox.

The studio was sinking into ruin. The debt for 1961 had been a hefty $22 million. *Cleopatra* was still ridiculously out of control, further draining the monetary reserves of the strife-torn studio. Zanuck began to think, rightfully so, that should the production be postponed, it might never start up again. He vividly recalled his first confrontation with management.

In the spring of 1961, the Fox executives had launched a powerful assault on *The Longest Day*. One of the prominent board members, John Loeb, demanded that Zanuck take a $3 million loss and get out. But Zanuck would not withdraw — he reasoned that it was stupid to even consider it. Author Mel Gussow, in his biography of Zanuck, describes the fateful moment on May 24, 1961, when the producer faced the board:

> Outnumbered, outflanked and seemingly defeated before he began, Zanuck got up and began fighting with his mouth, which in moments of peril had always been one of his best weapons. He began talking about D-Day, about the worldwide interest in the subject and the limited knowledge that people had about it. This would be the final word on the subject.
>
> General James Van Fleet (a member of the board) came to Zanuck's rescue. "He lost his temper," says Zanuck. "He practically called them idiots. He had landed in the first wave on D-Day. Usually at board meetings, he never said anything, but now he said, 'This picture will make more than any other picture.' Then Robert Clarkson began to sway for me. Robert Lehman began to sway for me. They asked me to leave the meeting and wait outside. They then called me in and said I could go ahead, but if I spent more than $8 million, they would take my cameras away. I think the vote was six to five in my favor."[31]

With this less-than-enthusiastic vote of confidence, Zanuck returned to France. That was in the spring. Now it was the late fall and the weather factor was launching a more concentrated assault on *The Longest Day*.

In the ballroom of the Hotel Malherb in Caen, in front of his entire crew, Zanuck asked for opinions on whether to postpone or gamble. Predictably, a majority favored postponement. Many of them recalled a similar situation confronting 20th Century–Fox director Edward Dmytryk's production of *The Young Lions*, which faced tremendous weather problems in 1956, while filming outside Paris.

Zanuck, battling for the very lifeblood of the studio, was unconvinced. Two days later, he told Williams to get the crews moving. It was time to finish the picture.

No sooner had Zanuck decided to move his crews to the Il de Rey, than another problem surfaced concerning the film's use of American troops. Ever since the Jack Paar incident in Berlin, the Department of Defense had come under increasing scrutiny by Congress in regards to its dealings with the motion picture industry. Although Arthur Sylvester had defended the use of the Ranger company in the filming at Pointe du Hoc, he was still in favor of eliminating the excesses of military cooperation.

Only one week before shooting began on the Il de Rey, Defense Secretary Robert McNamara personally ordered that Zanuck's issue of troops be cut from 700 to 250 men.

A statement from the Pentagon read: "Participation in the film, *The Longest Day,* has been lowered from 700 to 250 at the direction of the Secretary of Defense. This decision was based on the fact that the number originally planned was much larger than is normal in military cooperation. The curtailed participation is being authorized on the basis that it is in the national interest to do so."[32]

The Pentagon decision and a new series of strictly enforced regulations deeply affected the course of future military cooperation with Hollywood. It was an historic judgment. For Zanuck, it was just another headache.

Luckily, it was the French this time who came to the rescue, ordering over 2,000 soldiers to the Il de Rey to help Zanuck finish his film.

Filming began on October 21, 1961, and stretched for over a month. Zanuck had hauled in his overworked construction crews to recreate the inhabited portion of Sword Beach on D-Day. Additional machine shops, wardrobe tents and catering facilities were also constructed behind the deserted beaches that looked west towards the stormy Atlantic.

While director Andrew Marton filmed the American exteriors and Annakin the British, Bernhard Wicki, who had been working mostly in Paris on the German interiors, arrived to film the opening shots of Rommel philosophizing above the Normandy bluffs. With the arrival of Jendrich's "Germans" (it was at Omaha Beach that they offered their stiffest resistance), the final phase of action sequences began.

Unlike the Corsican maneuvers, where Zanuck had virtually no direct control over his "extras," at the Il de Rey, the landings were planned on a precise timetable with a group of second assistant directors sprinkled amongst the French assault troops. Some 36 years later, Captain Dale Dye, the military advisor to director Steven Spielberg on *Saving Private Ryan,* would use a similar system to create their version of D-Day.

Zanuck, himself, described the first day's shooting on "Omaha Beach":

> It was the only time outside the big paratroop jump in Ste. Mère Église, where we had actual casualties. I had about 30 second assistants in uniforms as my squad leaders. One of the 30 handled each assault group. They picked which "extras" would fall as casualties, or who would make the beach. We ran a tape from the edge of the shore to the cliff [to form] alleys, so that the men wouldn't bunch up. We then covered the tape with light sand and planted 150 explosives.
>
> Unfortunately, we never thought about smoke. In the final take, I shot a pistol. That signaled the cameras on the ground and in the air. *Bang,* it starts and it's the goddamndest mess I've ever seen in my life.
>
> They couldn't see because of the smoke. They were bumping into each other ... and we, at the cameras, couldn't see either. People were sitting, holding their faces in their hands. Some had facial cuts where they had run into explosives. In one scene, where guys blow up in the air, that wasn't staged. They were running blind. We stayed up all night working out non-smoke or white smoke. I got two takes that were good and decided we wouldn't do it again. We would have killed somebody."[33]

The battle sequences completed, Zanuck withdrew his crews to Paris. There, in the Boulogne Studios, the producer personally directed many of the final scenes in the film involving the American performers.

Zanuck screened the rough cut of *The Longest Day* on March 5, 1962. Although he was quite satisfied that the film was the blockbuster needed to revive the sagging fortunes of 20th Century–Fox, he immediately detected that the ending of the film lacked a certain comment on the true meaning of D-Day among the participants. The producer saw that it was time to slow the pace of the film and add one last scene.

A quick phone call was placed to Rome where Richard Burton was courting Elizabeth

Brigadier Gen. Norman Cota of the U.S. 29th Division (Robert Mitchum) stands on the recently taken Omaha Beach.

Taylor, both on and off the screen. Zanuck told Burton he had another great scene for him and asked him to come up to Paris for a couple of days. Burton agreed to appear as a wounded Spitfire pilot, philosophizing on the meaning of war. He treated the short sequence like a scene out of a Shakespearean play. He flew into Paris on April 8. By that time, the major production crews had completed their work on the film and had departed. Zanuck personally opened the studio for Burton and a small crew.

The short scene summed up the excitement, exhaustion, courage, confusion, stupidity and horror of D-Day. One of the film's few contemplative moments, it retains a distinct sense of individuality. Burton, his badly wounded thigh held together with safety pins, lies by the side of a road. Actor Richard Beymer (as Private Dutch Schultz), a lost paratrooper, lies next to him, exhausted by his night's ordeal. Through all the confusion of trying to find his unit, he has yet to fire his weapon. Nearby, a dead German officer lies sprawled against a fencepost ("He was coming to make sure of me," growls Burton).

"It's funny," utters Burton, an injection of morphine causing him to slur his words. "He's dead, I'm crippled and you're lost. I suppose it's always like that. I mean, war."

An explosion sounds far away. Both men hardly stir.

"I wonder who won?" asks Beymer.[34] Zanuck smiled as he listened to Beymer's last line. In his mind, there had never been any doubt.

CHAPTER SEVEN

Hell Is for Heroes

A year before he began writing his Oscar-winning screenplay for *Battleground,* screenwriter Robert Pirosh accidentally stumbled upon the details to one of World War II's most bizarre incidents: a multi-unit deception that would lead the Americans to victory in the Battle of the Bulge, and Pirosh to one of the best combat films of the sixties: *Hell Is for Heroes.*

In the spring of 1946, Pirosh was enroute to his new writing assignment at the Samuel Goldwyn Studios, in Hollywood, when he stopped in a gas station for a fill-up. New clothing was still scarce in postwar California, so the combat veteran was still wearing his army uniform, which included the "ruptured duck" insignia of all discharges. Noticing the emblem, the service station attendant, himself a veteran, struck up a conversation, during which Pirosh revealed that he was a veteran of the 35th Infantry Division.

"The 35th Division!" cried the attendant, "I'll never forget that outfit. When they pulled you guys out of the Vosges Mountains and sent you to the Bulge, they sent in my unit to cover your positions. It was a secret move, a deception, and we were small. Our job was to spread out very thin and hold, hoping that the Germans wouldn't discover the switch."[1]

At the moment, Pirosh did not know he was listening to a military secret. Or that the deception pulled in the Ardennes that winter of 1944, a secret maneuver that allowed the Allies to quickly shift the axis of General George S. Patton's Third Army and deploy it against the German counter-offensive, would remain classified until 1960. Pirosh recorded the details of the maneuver in his diary, thanked the attendant, and reported to work. For nine years, the story remained buried in his notebook.

In the summer of 1955, after completing the script for *The Girl Rush,* a minor musical starring Rosalind Russell, he began searching for a new project. While thumbing through his wartime diary, he discovered the few scribbles he had once haphazardly recorded in the filling station.

A new war film project seemed appealing to him. He had enjoyed the success of *Battleground,* and *Go for Broke,* the latter a combat film depicting the story of the 442nd Regimental Combat Team, the Japanese American Nisei regiment that was the most decorated military unit in the United States Army in World War II.

Pirosh put through a call to an established contact in Washington, but the response was unsettling. The "Vosges (rhymes with Rose) Deception" was still classified. So much for writing a new combat film.

Pirosh was pondering his next move when the telephone rang. It was Ray Stark, a major theatrical agent (later a top producer) with an offer. The Kirk Douglas Company was producing a film version of the popular television show, *Spring Reunion*. A director was needed and Pirosh had been highly recommended (he had made his directing debut in 1951 with *Go for Broke*).

Just the thought of a long research trip to Washington, D.C., with the possibility of major haggling with the Pentagon, made him opt for the new project. The war film could wait. There was, after all, no danger of anyone stealing his idea — Army red tape would see to that.

Spring Reunion, which featured Betty Hutton, Dana Andrews and Jean Hagen, was released in late 1957. Filmed at a rented studio and allowed a cramped budget, it turned out to be less than the interesting project Pirosh had envisioned. Three years went by. For producer Selig J. Seligman and ABC Television, Pirosh began developing an idea for a series based on his wartime diary. *Combat!*, the product of his labors, debuted in the fall of 1962. Starring Vic Morrow and Rick Jason, it remains the most successful military action drama ever shown on national television.

On October 5, 1960, good news arrived from Washington, D.C. The 1944 deception had been declassified and was no longer considered a top military secret. Would Pirosh like the details? Delighted, he dusted off his original five-page treatment, filled in the gaps with historical details provided by the Pentagon and went to visit his friend, Martin Rackin, head of production at Paramount Studios. Rackin, a relative newcomer at Paramount (he was in the middle of his second year there), was himself a combat veteran, having served as a bomber pilot with General George C. Kenney's Fifth Air Force in the Philippines. A few years after the war, he had written *Fighter Squadron* (1948), a World War II air saga that predated *Twelve O'Clock High* by one year.

In what he later referred to as a "real razzle dazzle,"[2] Pirosh gave Rackin a rough insight into the 1944 deception: "Marty, it's an amazing story. A ten-man squad is ordered to defend a company's position on the Siegfried Line. I've worked out about five pages to give you an idea as to what kind of gimmicks the men use to trick the enemy."[3]

The gimmicks were unusual and helped to sell the story to Rackin. In the short treatment, Pirosh had his quad modify the engine on an ordinary jeep to make it sound either like a truck or a tank. When the "tank" was driven back and forth behind their positions, it would give the Germans the impression that they were opposed by a company with armored support. Pirosh also had the men string wires in front of their positions. To these, they attached empty ammunition cans filled with rocks. The cans were placed at strategic points, so that when they were tripped, it appeared that patrols were out.

Rackin was impressed. Aware of Pirosh's background and professionalism in combat films, coupled with an excellent track record at MGM, Rackin signed him to write, produce and direct the proposed film. For the first time in his life, Pirosh would wear all three hats.

Before he left, Rackin asked, "Do you have a title, something I can send to the New York office?

"I thought we would call it 'Separation Hill,' Pirosh replied. "It's a term we used in the Army when you're on your first big hike and you're going up a steep hill. As trainees began to drop out, the sergeant would start yelling, 'Come on boys, this is separation hill. It'll separate the men from the boys.'"[4]

With a fat contract under his belt, Pirosh resumed a personal interest in the life of the combat infantryman, begun so successfully with *Battleground*. He retained the squad as his basic unit, developing a group of soldiers with certain individual characteristics. In the new film, he introduced Pvt. Reese, the loner, who carries a butcher knife for close encounters; Sergeant Pike, the tough, experienced platoon sergeant; Sgt. Larkin, the courageous, by-the-book squad leader; Private Corby, the scrounger; Henshaw, the fixer, whose only friend is a duck; and Homer, the Polish refugee, one of the story's most unique characters.

The idea of Homer (later portrayed by Nick Adams) came from a true incident depicted in Pirosh's wartime diary. During the last months of the war, after the 35th Division had crossed the Rhine River and was moving through Germany, Pirosh's squad was assigned the task of reconnoitering evacuated villages. Conversant in German, the master sergeant, with the makeshift diary in his pack, was frequently ordered to take five men and investigate tiny enclaves on the road to Berlin.

During one of these patrols, his unit discovered two German soldiers cowering in a cellar. After a few choice words, they surrendered. Aside from these ragged remnants of the once-proud Wehrmacht, there was another resident of the filthy cellar, a wide-eyed Polish youngster, barely 17 years old, and a recent escapee from a slave labor camp. In Germany, the boy communicated his sole desire: he wanted to become an American soldier.

Pirosh took the boy back with him and, for the next month, he tried, through every channel, to get him inducted. In the meantime, he became the unit's mascot, learning American mannerisms, and mastering those peculiar American cuss words, ever-present in the military ranks. The perpetually cussing youngster, whose name the unit could never pronounce, was christened Homer.

Recalled Pirosh, "Homer was given a uniform, but we never gave him a rifle. The Army wouldn't let him have one, and rightfully so, for he could have shot one of our own men by mistake."[5]

Eventually, Pirosh regretted his decision to adopt Homer into the unit's ranks. He would get drunk, and though he was a good-natured and fun-loving kid, he was also very immature and he frequently embarrassed the squad behind the lines. Somehow, he managed to ingratiate himself into another platoon, and the last Pirosh saw of him, he was still in uniform.

The script was half-finished when Pirosh began to encounter "writer's block." The characters were intriguing, at times highly amusing. The plot was interesting enough, the deception downright ingenious. But something was lacking, a certain driving force. There was little motivation to all the characters. They were fast becoming just another platoon of guys. And by 1962, audiences had already seen too many platoons of guys. The unorthodox deception was in danger of becoming routine.

"I couldn't get off the ground," Pirosh recalled. "There I had this big contract, the biggest I had ever had by far, and I couldn't write the complete story. I was stuck, and I floundered for weeks."[6]

Experienced screenwriter that he was, Pirosh had a plan of action covering any writing emergency. This time he went for advice to his former writing partner, George Seaton. The pair had a useful arrangement, dating back to the 1930s, by which script problems were solved in conference. After reading the story for *Separation Hill*, Seaton said that he enjoyed the suspense of the story, but agreed that it lacked the crucial internal conflict. He suggested that Pirosh take one of the characters and turn him into a more interesting person, someone, in fact, a little off center.

"Why don't you make this guy Reese a real psychotic?" Seaton advised. "He's a nut and he likes combat. He's also a bastard and the squad stays away from him. But at the same time, they respect him because he's a good soldier."[7]

Seaton felt that with a central conflict between Reese and the men, especially Sergeant

Sgt. Pike (Fess Parker, right) finds Reese (Steve McQueen) in an off-limits French tavern. One could almost strike a match off the intensity projected by McQueen in this scene.

Larkin, who's a book soldier, Pirosh would be able to divide the focus of the screenplay between the deception and Reese.

Pirosh was pleased with the suggestion and began to modify the Reese character. Originally just an eager-beaver G.I. with a liking for combat, he became a man obsessed. He cannot adjust to life behind the lines. Once, after winning a battlefield commission, Reese went on furlough and cracked up, nearly killing a superior officer in the process. In the Pirosh script, he lands in Pike's squad, having been busted down to private. He's a loner, waiting for the next move. He does not identify with his fellow squad members, who are thinking of the war's end and a return to their homes. Reese doesn't want to go home—he wants to fight.

To play this character, Rackin signed Steve McQueen, the youthful hero of the *Wanted: Dead or Alive* television series and the co-star of the recent box-office smash, director John Sturges's *The Magnificent Seven*. Pirosh also called Rackin's attention to another star of *The Magnificent Seven*, James Coburn, who was signed to play Henshaw, the fixer. Another television personality, Nick Adams of *The Rebel*, was hired to play the Homer character.

Said Pirosh: "I tried very hard to get a real Polish kid to play the part. I figured we could make an actor out of him, like we did in *Go for Broke* with the Nisei. But I just couldn't find anybody that was right for the role. Rackin, who was very good at casting, suggested Nick Adams. I liked Nick and he was a talented guy, but I still think he was too old for the part."

Television's Davy Crockett, Fess Parker, was signed to play Sergeant Pike, the stalwart

When Homer (Nick Adams, left) tells Reese (Steve McQueen) that he is going to show up on the line and kill the so-called "Krauts," Reese replies: "You show up on the line, I'll blow your head off."

platoon leader; singer Bobby Darin became the perfect Corby, the scrounger. Character actor Harry Guardino, fresh from *Pork Chop Hill*, became Sergeant Larkin, Reese's major nemesis.

One of the more unusual parts in the film was added at the last minute. This was Private Driscoll, the naïve headquarters clerk, a bumbling typist, who is "drafted" by Larkin's hard-pressed combat squad. He would be played by newcomer Bob Newhart.

Having met the 32-year-old comic at Charlie Morrison's Mocambo Club, Rackin asked Pirosh whether there was some way they could get Newhart into the picture. Together, the two men conceived of the Driscoll character, whose particular talent for gabbing on a tapped field telephone aids the deception on the Siegfried Line. Director Don Siegel, who later replaced Pirosh as the film's director, criticized the way in which Newhart's talent for monologue was exploited: "Bob Newhart could have been accepted if I didn't have to put him through that ridiculous telephone conversation [in the film Larkin asks Driscoll to imitate a real phone conversation with headquarters for the benefit of the German listeners who've wired the unit's command post]. He could have been amusing and scared and all that, but I wouldn't have him going through his 'shtick' routine. It had no place in the film. I wouldn't even have Bobby Darin singing, something I know the studio would have loved."[8]

In the shadows of Mount Shasta, outside Redding in Northern California, Pirosh and his art director, Howard Richmond, found the ideal setting that would represent the desolation of the Siegfried Line, Hitler's last line of defense. Supplied with photographs, Richmond began designing the look of the battlefield, complete with simulated concrete anti-tank obstacles called "dragon's teeth," pillboxes and wrecked tanks. Simultaneously, a series of conferences and rehearsals were held with the young actors. Pirosh was immediately taken with McQueen.

"Steve was very stimulating to work with during the script stage," recalled Pirosh. "He was fun, and he had some terrific ideas, which helped me develop the Reese character. He came up with little bits of dialogue and I thought the guy was great. He was going to give a great performance and I was going to get some credit for it."[9]

Although he admired McQueen and strove to develop the Reese character into the film's major driving force, Pirosh still considered *Separation Hill* as a film, not unlike *Battleground*, about a group of soldiers, not a starring vehicle for any one actor. But Steve McQueen's star was on the rise and he was tired of playing subordinate roles in films loaded with established name talent. Since *Separation Hill* featured a group of relatively unknown players and given the key role of Reese, McQueen saw the film as a major stepping-stone in his march toward stardom.

Undaunted by Pirosh's desires, McQueen demanded that his part be built up. The writer/director stood his ground. Facing a decision similar to director John Sturges's face-off with McQueen, a year later on *The Great Escape*, Rackin also went to his screenwriting bench, bringing in writer Richard Carr to rework the Reese character. It was a move that could damage his relationship with Pirosh, but Rackin didn't want to lose McQueen, either.

Carr, who knew Pirosh through their mutual friend, actor John Cassavetes, was surprised to find himself working on the war script. "What they wanted," he recalled, "was an inexpensive writer. They were primarily concerned with the opening. McQueen felt, and I think rightfully so, that his character wasn't clearly defined and that there was no empathy for him. So, I rewrote the opening after discussing it with Bob. It gave Reese an entrance. Whereas Bob had opened with him joining the unit in the field, I began the film in a village behind the lines. In this way, I simply introduced the characters in a more effective way. I didn't change them."[10]

Pirosh accepted Carr's new opening and continued to prepare the unit for location shooting near Mount Shasta. Problems continued, though, with both Rackin and McQueen. With new script changes forthcoming and his relationship with the actor slowly deteriorating, Pirosh decided one afternoon in late May 1961 to drop the entire project. He was disgusted and he approached Rackin, asking for his release.

"Marty, I've done the script," he told the producer. "And you've paid me. You also paid for my expenses in scouting the locations. But as far as directing the film, I'm through. I'm not getting along with McQueen. Cut off my salary right now!"[11] Rackin's half-hearted plea for the director to reconsider was rejected and Pirosh left the office at Paramount, never to return.

With the prospect of production costs spiraling in the event of a delay, Rackin wasted little time in choosing a new director. He hired Don Siegel. During World War II, Siegel was in Hollywood directing short subjects, two of which won Oscars. He was an interesting contrast to Pirosh. When he read the script for *Separation Hill*, he was immediately dismayed at the amount of humor in the story, and although he thought occasional humor at times was an excellent device, he couldn't see anything funny about the desperate situation depicted in the film. Like Carr, he too was shocked that Pirosh had left the project.

"Pirosh was a personal friend of mine," Siegel admitted, "and I told Marty Rackin how much I thought of Bob. He acknowledged my admiration, saying, 'I too must have liked him or I wouldn't have given him the job, but I'm telling you right now that he's not going to do the picture. Somebody's going to, and if you don't, I'll get someone who will.' I told Rackin that I would have to talk to Bob first, but he told me to wait until the deal was set."[12]

But Siegel didn't wait. He phoned his friend that night and gave it to him. "What the hell are you doing? Are you as big an idiot as I am? Why are you throwing this project away?"

"Look, Don," Pirosh said, "I don't want to talk about it. I'm not getting along with either McQueen or Rackin."

Siegel replied, "Rackin offered me the project, but I know it's your picture. Do you have any feelings about me taking over?"

Pirosh calmed down, "No, but thanks for asking. I'd just as soon have you direct than somebody I didn't know."

"At least," Siegel pleaded, "why not carry on as producer, and certainly as the writer?"

"No thanks," said Pirosh with finality, thinking of Carr already rewriting his script. In desperation, Siegel launched one last assault on Pirosh's pride.

"Bob, I think you're making a very serious mistake. It isn't necessary to be a triple-threat man. As long as you're having problems, let someone else come and direct. But don't desert the whole project!"[13]

The plea failed. Siegel hung up and went to sleep. The next morning, he called Rackin and accepted the directing assignment.

With a new director in charge, the script revisions took on a more serious turn. Siegel began to eliminate much of Pirosh's original humor. Henshaw's duck was cut out of the story; Corby, the Bobby Darin character, was given a fresh approach and new dialogue was added to several key scenes.

Carr later explained that the original characters were expertly drawn, but lacked certain movements that would have explained their individual natures.

"For instance," he explained, "James Coburn played Henshaw, a guy who fixes things, a mechanic. Coburn wanted to wear glasses and appear studious. So instead of just talking about what he did, at the beginning of the story, we introduced him working underneath a truck. Larkin comes over and asks, 'Whose truck is that?' and Henshaw looks absentmindedly back at him, replying, 'I don't know, Sergeant.' Now, with a little scene like that, you could tell that he was a quiet, reserved sort of guy. It was one of those pictures where there had to be little touches like that to build the character."[14]

Carr also added a scene in the early part of the film, featuring the film's only woman, actress Michelle Montau, portraying a seductive French bartender. "The purpose of that scene," Carr explains, "was to show Reese breaking the rules. He disregards the standing order that the town bar is off limits. He was getting drunk because he was unhappy. Pike comes into the bar, doesn't necessarily reprimand Reese (because they're old friends and they respect one another) and tells him that the unit is not going home, they're going back on the line.

"Suddenly, all the moroseness leaves Reese. He picks up a bottle, tucks it in his jacket, puts on his garrison cap, and goes back to the squad. His life now has purpose once more. It was an illuminating scene that established Reese's rebellious nature early in the story."[15]

Director Don Siegel was working with his army of stuntmen and extras when word reached him that the title of the film had changed. Since *Separation Hill* was now considered too similar to *Pork Chop Hill*, the title had been switched to *Hell Is for Heroes*, a typically commercial title dreamed up by the New York publicity office of Paramount Pictures. But, as Siegel explained, there was an association between the title and theme: "'Hell Is for Heroes' means that the ones that are heroic wind up in hell, they lose their legs or their lives. They have nothing to gain by being heroes. It's an exercise in futility, and hell is for heroes when you're brave enough, depending on your point of view, or stupid enough to go and attack a pillbox like Reese did. Where else are you going to end up?"[16]

Henshaw (James Coburn), the bookish fix-all who handles the flame thrower.

To keep the film's budget under control (*Hell Is for Heroes* would eventually cost $2.5 million), Rackin brought in Henry Blanke to produce the film. Blanke was a financial genius, having enjoyed a strong producing career, particularly in the 1930s, with such films as *Anthony Adverse, The Life of Emile Zola,* and *Jezebel.* He was expensive, but Rackin needed a professional to control the film's spiraling budget. Blanke took over financial control of the film on June 21, 1961, nine days after Siegel had begun principal photography.

Pirosh had originally planned to shoot the film in the snow of winter. It was supposed to be cold on the Siegfried Line. But with the script revisions and production delays, the crew did not arrive in Redding until the high summer, when temperatures soared to 117 degrees, giving rise to Siegel's belief that Redding was indeed "the hell hole of the world."[17]

Since the actors were forced to wear their heavy issue G.I. uniforms, Siegel decided to shoot a major portion of the film at night. It was one of the director's best moves. Not only were the "troops" more comfortable, but the film itself benefited from the increased tension and atmosphere of night action.

Aside from the terrible weather conditions and the potential dangers of shooting night battle sequences with large quantities of explosives, Siegel was continuing to have script problems. Seldom has there been more controversy over the definition and general philosophy of one character. In Pirosh's original script, Reese was portrayed as what the writer referred to as a "cowboy," a guy who went looking for trouble.[18] The part had been drawn from the writer's wartime diary.

While his unit was advancing in the Ardennes, it was joined by a young major, whom Pirosh later referred to as a "typical eager beaver." This was the major's introduction to combat and Pirosh relates how this young officer spotted some German tanks in a nearby field and decided on a suicidal attack.

"This major comes running up and asks, 'What's going on here? Who's in charge?' I told him that I was and that we were pinned down.

"'Sergeant,' he told me, 'get this platoon moving so that we can get at those tanks!' Five minutes later, the major was dead and two of my men were wounded. That was a cowboy. Who the hell did he think he was, trying to take on those tanks?"[19]

In reworking the introduction of the Reese character, Richard Carr felt that he did not change the original portrait of the wayward soldier that Reese was. Pirosh disagrees, claiming that Reese suffered a shift in emphasis, particularly in his climactic assault on the German pillbox, in which he is killed.

Said Pirosh: "For my money, it lost the authentic attitude of the G.I. There was a tendency to glorify and go for spectacular effects. And, in the end, Steve McQueen goes with that 'gang-busters' attitude. I had worked out that last scene differently. I used a technical advisor who helped me come up with the moves, how he could take the pillbox on his own, and what kind of demolition he could use. I worked out every detail of it, but I didn't have him go in with that attitude."[20]

Classifying Reese as a psychotic, something the critics later saw in the Steve McQueen character, was something with which Richard Carr failed to agree:

In the film, *War Hunt*, John Saxon portrayed a depraved killer who puts on blackface and goes out alone to kill Koreans, cutting off their ears and bringing them back. The commanding officer knows he's a psycho, but he lets him continue because he's valuable. Now, as I see it, Reese in *Hell Is for Heroes*, was just a guy who probably couldn't make it on the outside, away from the Army, and who had terrible feelings about going back to civilian life.

In fact, when the men believed they were going back to civilian life, Reese was very morose about it. He only perks up when Pike tells him that they're going back on the line. Reese probably hoped for the battlefield commission he had once lost, so that he could go back as an officer.

He was an off-center guy, a misfit, a killer, but not a psychopath. He got behind the lines and simply had nothing to do. Reese doesn't become heroic at the end, he's just being the most professional soldier there. The way he attempts to take the pillbox in the ill-fated night attack, by using Henshaw to shield him with the flamethrower, was strictly legitimate.

Later, during the massed attack at dawn, when he throws the satchel charge into the pillbox, he immediately dashes for a foxhole. He doesn't expect to get hit. But then, once he is hit and dying, his whole aim is for revenge. He sees the Germans throw out the charge and he gets up with his last ounce of energy, grabs the charge and rolls inside with it. He's dead anyway, his insides are all shot up. I don't think that his action in the end is really inconsistent with his other actions all along, which are solely professional.

He did take too many chances to be classified as a true professional. Who's to say that Larkin wasn't the better soldier. He knew how to take orders. Reese thrived on the danger of combat. But there is a line which a man crosses to become a psycho and Reese never did cross that line."[21]

To clarify the character of Reese, Siegel and Carr had originally worked out a scene, later cut, that takes place after the failure of the abortive night raid on the pillbox — during which both Henshaw (James Coburn) and Colinsky (Mike Kellin) are killed.

As Carr recalled, "Originally, we had planned that this would be the scene where Reese reveals his true character. Pike would come over and ask him, 'Were you right?' and Reese would respond with an illuminating speech.

"Unfortunately, it came out stilted. McQueen and I worked on the speech and we tried

The final assault on the German pillbox. Reese (Steve McQueen) is on the far left, holding his signature grease gun.

Still beset by the German pillbox, Pike's platoon heads for the Dragon's Teeth, a German anti-tank obstacle.

After finishing *Hell Is for Heroes*, Steve McQueen (left) went to England to star in another World War II movie, *The War Lover*, co-starring Robert Wagner. McQueen, incidentally, was never too far from a motorcycle.

to cut it down. Finally, it was Steve's idea that there would be no explanation, just a simple, 'How do I know?' And that carried a lot more impact than a bunch of words or phony Freudian explanations. In a situation like that, a guy isn't going to start talking anyway."[22]

Director Siegel saw Reese as an emotionally tormented individual, especially after the disastrous night raid. "I don't see how you could possibly go about killing people and not be affected by it," he says. "All soldiers are psychotic in some sense of the word. Certainly, Reese wasn't above the horror of his particular situation. He had enough emotion to burst into tears when he returned from the raid, and this was the last thing in the world that you'd expect. He was about to desert, but he stops, with tears in his eyes, realizing that he can't quit. His guilt over the death of two men was terrific. He had to stay and fight."[23]

For the crying sequence, which was later edited out of the film, Siegel found it almost impossible to get Steve McQueen to cry. There was no simple way. He used onions to no avail. Finally, he slapped the actor as hard as he could in the face.

"After that," Siegel recalled, "I wanted to be as far away as possible. Then, when he comes up in a close-up, you can see his tears and his anger.

Says Siegel, "In making the film as realistic as possible, I found one way was to play Steve as a professional, a real pro who was surrounded by amateurs. Certainly, with our cast, which came from all walks of life in the entertainment world, there was hardly a professional aura, and that made Steve stand out all the more."[24]

Hell Is for Heroes was completed in the late summer of 1961. Paramount Pictures released the film the following summer. Critically and commercially overshadowed by the more technically ambitious war films of the day — *The Longest Day, The Guns of Navarone, Merrill's Marauders* and *PT 109, Hell Is for Heroes* was, nonetheless, a minor classic that holds up well. Like *Pork Chop Hill,* it also featured the terrific work of musical composer Leonard Rosenman, who also scored Pirosh's *Combat!* television series. In the capable hands of Don Siegel, it was directed in a straightforward, no-nonsense manner and managed to sidestep spectacle for its own sake, emphasizing performance and atmosphere, two factors that successfully dramatized an incident from Robert Pirosh's wartime diary, and served to elevate the war film to a more sophisticated level of artistic achievement.

CHAPTER EIGHT

The Great Escape

It is the afternoon of September 21, 1962. For the first time in many weeks, the lush green foothills of Bavaria are awash in sunshine. High in these meadowlands, within sight of the Alpine peaks of Austria and not far from the tiny Germany town of Füssen, a crowd of spectators has gathered.

Along a dirt road that winds through the lush green pastureland, a German catering truck is making labored progress. Visible beyond a little hillock, its steel radial outlined against the distant mountains, is a Chapman camera crane. The crane's arm carries the words, "The Great Escape."

The caterer pulls into a makeshift parking lot adjacent to an endless barbed wire fence. He cuts his engine and looks around. Nearby are motorcycles with sidecars, ten-ton Mercedes trucks, a Mercedes touring car (circa 1940), and fully uniformed German soldiers, armed with sub machine guns and Mauser rifles. Shaking his head in astonishment, the little man turns and presses an electronic horn. The blaring klaxon echoes across the meadow, signaling that lunch has arrived.

Near the fence and gathered around the Chapman crane is a crowd of nearly 100 people. A few turn at the sound, but for the most part, their attention is riveted on two young men dressed in identical blue sweatshirts and dirty beige slacks. Actor Steve McQueen and his friend Bud Ekins, a stuntman and motorcycle expert, are standing next to a customized British Triumph racing bike. Camouflaged in Wehrmacht military green and disguised as a German BMW, the machine will shortly catapult Ekins over a six-foot barbed wire entanglement, a crucial sequence in this, the 1963 war adventure classic, *The Great Escape*.

There is little doubt that the stunt will succeed. Tim Gibbs, the Australian stunt rider, has already made the jump successfully. Here, in the afternoon sun, Ekins will duplicate the feat for the cameras. Steve McQueen, a fanatical motorcyclist who would rather ride than eat, must sit this one out. He is simply too valuable to the production, and insurance regulations forbid him to do many of the film's more dangerous motorcycle stunts. Ekins, who is a perfect double for McQueen, is to be the sacrificial lamb. The pair shake hands and Ekins climbs aboard the converted Triumph. As he revs up the crackling engine, easing up on the throttle, the crowd presses forward. There is electricity in the air, that peculiar magic that surrounds the shooting of a motion picture.

Before he takes off for his final run, Ekins nods to the man atop the Chapman crane. Director John Elliott Sturges turns to his cinematographer, Daniel Fapp, and nods.

Mentally recording the time on his watch (it is just two o'clock), he adjusts his sunglasses and concentrates intently on the Triumph.

The Great Escape, the most challenging film in his directing career, is nearly finished. Most of the actors have shot their final scenes and have flown back to their respective countries, and the extras, mostly college students from the University of Munich, have returned to their classrooms. It is just a matter of a few days before he, too, can depart for Hollywood to edit and score his masterwork.

Nearly 20 years earlier, in March 1943, Canadian Paul Brickhill, who would ultimately pen *The Great Escape* was flying his Spitfire over the Tunisian Desert in North Africa, when his fighter was struck by 20mm cannon fire from a German ME-109. His controls shattered and his engine on fire, Brickhill bailed out and was almost immediately captured by the remnants of Rommel's Afrika Korps.

When the Germans began to evacuate the continent in late March, Brickhill, along with a large group of British and American flyers, was transferred first to the Italian mainland and then, by train, to Sagan, Germany, a small town 90 miles southeast of Berlin, in the territory of Silesia, Germany's dustbowl. Carved right out of a nearby forest, and erected by Russian prisoners, was their final destination: Stalag Luft III.

Brickhill entered the German prison compound just as its 700 British and American officers were moving into the newly constructed north compound. The camp was 300 yards square and surrounded by the latest security precautions, including two nine-foot barbed wire fences, machine gun towers and a fully armed German garrison; it was considered escape proof. Squadron leader Roger Bushell's X Organization, an ultra-refined escape machine, would soon put the Germans to the test.

The 30-year-old Bushell had spent the last three years behind German wire. His captivity had begun on May 23, 1940, when his 12 Spitfires on patrol over the Dunkirk beaches were jumped by 40 twin-engine ME-110s. Bushell claimed two enemy fighters before he was, in turn, shot down and captured. Three years and several escape attempts later, he was incarcerated in a Gestapo prison until the Luftwaffe had him transferred to Stalag Luft III. He was never the same again, as Brickhill observes in an early chapter of *The Great Escape*:

"This was a changed Roger — not the old boisterous soul who thought escape was good, risky sport like skiing ... Now he was moodier, and the gaze from that twisted eye was more foreboding. In Berlin, he'd seen the Gestapo torturing people and he could not tolerate Germans anymore.... His frustrated energy was beginning to focus on the people responsible for his captivity. He cursed all Germans indiscriminately ... but inside was a clear, cool-headed hatred, and it found sublimation in outwitting them."[1]

As Big X, it would be Bushell who would plan and execute *The Great Escape*. At Sagan, Brickhill became one of 700 Allied prisoners of war who worked for Bushell's escape machine. As a cog in the machine, he bossed a gang of stooges who guarded the camp forgers, working in their exposed position at the hut windows. Brickhill was all set to escape with 250 others when Bushell excluded him because of claustrophobia.

On the moonless night of March 23, 1944, the squadron leader executed his plan. Supplied with civilian clothes, maps, compasses and forged identity papers, 76 officers broke out of Stalag Luft III through an elaborate tunnel and made a brief but spectacular dash for freedom across Germany.

Two weeks later, on direct orders from Hitler, Bushell and 49 others who had been recaptured, were murdered by the Gestapo. Only three officers escaped to England; the rest of the survivors were returned to Stalag Luft III and other prisons, including the concentration camp at Sachsenhausen.

The tragedy of the 50 redoubled the prisoners' desire for freedom. Brickhill helped engineer a new tunnel, which by July 1944, was creeping out under the campground towards the wire. But in January 1945, before it was completed, the Germans evacuated the camp to avoid the advancing Russian winter offensive. The prisoners were force-marched 60 miles to Spemberg and then taken by cattle truck to the German seaport of Bremen, where they were settled in an old condemned camp.

The Germans were soon under attack from two sides, however, and the prisoners were moved once again. Brickhill describes their final days of captivity: "We were sheltering in barns up near Lubeck, when we heard the barrage as the British First Army crossed the Elbe. Two days later on May 2, we heard firing down the road and two tanks rumbled through the trees from the south. We didn't know whether they were Germans or British and you could practically see the nerves sticking out of everyone's skin and vibrating like piano wire. The hatch of the front tank opened and two Tommies stuck their heads out. We ran up to them screaming at the top of our voices."[2]

After his discharge, Brickhill resumed writing, concentrating on stories about the Royal Air Force and prisoner escapes. It took him four and a half years to finish *The Great Escape*.

Twice after the war, he returned to Germany to research the actual sites of the tragedy, and once he was given permission by the Soviet Union to cross the "Iron Curtain" and walk through the scenes of the murders. After the principal Gestapo chiefs were hanged in 1948, Brickhill leafed through several thousand pages of unpublished reports, including those of Wing Commander Bowes of the RAF Special Investigation Branch, who conducted the postwar investigation into the crimes. The last quarter of the book was devoted to the aftermath of the escape. He then searched out the important survivors and filled in the few gaps left.

First published by W.W. Norton & Company in August 1950, *The Great Escape* became a rousing testament to the freedom and spirit of mankind. The details and drama of escaping POWs were later incorporated into other British screenplays about the war, including *The Colditz Story* (1957) and *The Password Is Courage* (1962).

Despite the surefire dramatic qualities of his book, Brickhill adamantly refused to sell the film rights. He spurned lucrative offers and promises to treat the material factually. He claimed that it was simply not his story to sell and that there were too many others involved, including the families of the slain officers who preferred to forget the horrible wartime tragedy.

Brickhill was quite satisfied with his book royalties and felt he had been justly compensated for his research. There was no reason to carry the project further. He continued to write about prisoners of war (*Escape or Die* in 1952), and when the punitive British taxation system proved unbearable, he moved to Australia. *The Great Escape* went through four printings in eight years and in March 1961, the Fawcett World Library purchased the paperback rights. As late as 1960, Brickhill was still declining movie offers. Meanwhile, 8,000 miles away, a hard-driving film director was trying to kindle interest in the very book that Brickhill wished Hollywood would forget.

Army Air Corps First Lieutenant John Sturges was in Washington, D.C., when the March 1944 breakout from Stalag Luft III took place. Barely three months before D-Day, he was sweating out his transfer overseas to an Air Corps photographic unit. On direct orders from General Henry "Hap" Arnold, Sturges was to accompany director William Wyler to Corsica where the pair would create *Thunderbolt*, a brilliant documentary detailing the daily life of a typical P-47 fighter bomber squadron operating against German troop and supply concentrations in Northern Italy.

A film editor at RKO studios before the war, Sturges was on detached service from the First Motion Picture Base Unit in Culver City, California. Like many creative individuals in Hollywood, he had spent the early years of the war editing scores of military training films, both at "Fort Roach" in Culver City, and at Wright Field, Ohio.

On June 9, 1944, he arrived in Caserta, 20 miles north of Naples. Rome had been liberated and the Allies were moving inland from the Normandy beaches. To prevent the resupply of German units still deployed to the north of Rome, Army Air Force General Ira Eaker, commander in chief of Allied Air Forces, Mediterranean, was planning Operation Strangle, an aerial offensive that would become the primary focus of *Thunderbolt*.

In Caserta, Wyler asked for and received permission to work with a front line fighter-bomber squadron. Two weeks later, Sturges was on Corsica, attached to the 12th Combat Camera Unit. For the next nine months, he was part of a unit that filmed numerous raids from the windows of a converted B-25 Mitchell bomber that bristled with cameras. Following the chubby P-47 "Thunderbolts" over the Mediterranean and on to their targets over the port of Spezia won Wyler's unit four battle stars and a Unit Citation.

After his discharge from the Army Air Corps in early 1946, Sturges worked as an assistant director at Columbia Pictures, and it was there, under studio head Harry Cohn's tutelage that he directed his first film, the crime drama, *The Man Who Dared*. He later transferred to Metro-Goldwyn-Mayer, where he was signed as a contract director. In the summer of

James Garner (left) and Steve McQueen pose in front of a photograph of the original Allied officers who participated in the actual "Great Escape."

1950, he picked up a copy of *Reader's Digest* and began reading the serialization of *The Great Escape*.

"It was the perfect embodiment of why our side won!" explained Sturges. "Here was the German military machine, the sparkling uniforms and the absolute obedience to orders. On the other side of the wire, there were men from every country, every background, makeup and language, doing everything they pleased. With no arbitrary rules, they voluntarily formulated an organization which eventually clobbered the German machine."[3]

While reading through the Brickhill book for the first time, Sturges recalled an incident in Italy that reinforced his belief in the book's theme. During a tourist visit to the front lines, he was delayed in a massive tie-up at a rural intersection where an American PFC was directing traffic. A general arrived by Jeep and demanded the right of way. According to Sturges, the PFC shouted, "Sorry, Bud, you'll have to wait your turn!"

"By the side of the road," Sturges recalled, "I noticed this small group of German prisoners. One of them was a captain, which was a high rank in the Wehrmacht. He saw what was going on and I knew he understood English because he was reading an American *Superman* comic book. What I saw in the German's face was utter disbelief, the whole collapse of what he'd been led to believe."[4]

Convinced that *The Great Escape* was the perfect film project, Sturges decided to go right to the top. On a pleasant sunny Southern California day, he drove to the MGM lot with the express purpose of selling the book to studio head Louis B. Mayer. He was embarking on a crusade that would stretch through 13 years of his life.

Contract directors are not generally part of the upper strata of the studio hierarchy, and it had taken Sturges a long time to get an appointment with Mayer. And when the meeting finally occurred, it was brief and disturbing. In a nutshell, Mayer and his studio executives were disquieted by the story's tragic climax.

"What kind of a great escape is this?" they chorused, "no one escapes! Even if we did change the ending, how could we tell a unified story with so many characters and entangling elements. This will be another $10 million film. Forget it!"[5]

Sturges could not forget it. He remained convinced that the project was workable. It would just take time. Through the grapevine, he had already learned that Brickhill was rejecting film offers in his own country and he was confident that only he, John Sturges, could convince the author to let his book be filmed.

After each of his increasingly prestigious films — *Bad Day at Black Rock* (1954), *Gunfight at the OK Corral* (1957), *The Old Man and the Sea* (1958) and *Never So Few* (1959) — Sturges tried to interest studios in his pet project, but he met with virtually the same stonewall everywhere.

Impressed with the new freedom of his director friends who were operating independently for the first time, Sturges left MGM in 1959 and signed a partnership agreement with the Mirisch Brothers, one of Hollywood's first successful independent production entities.

It was here among directors like William Wyler, Robert Wise, Billy Wilder and John Ford, that he found the creative freedom he had been seeking. The Mirisch brothers — Walter, Harold and Marvin — shrewdly gave complete autonomy over their productions to a group of directors considered to be Hollywood's finest. All financial and distribution responsibility, however, remained with the brothers.

During the period when the major studios were becoming more and more cautious about fostering and financing ambitious and expensive film projects, the Mirisch brothers and their distribution partner, United Artists, continued to offer freedom to their creative people. The results were such successful films as *West Side Story, One Two Three, The Horse Soldiers* and *The Children's Hour.*

Sturges's first project for the Mirisch Brothers was *The Magnificent Seven,* a film that won worldwide success and became a western classic. With star Yul Brynner surrounded by a group of virtually unknown actors — Steve McQueen, James Coburn, Charles Bronson, Brad Dexter, Robert Vaughn and Horst Buchholz — Sturges established a clarity of character and a sense of pace rarely achieved in the western genre. The film won him the mandate to produce *The Great Escape.*

"After *The Magnificent Seven,*" he recalled, "if I had walked in and asked to direct the phone book, they would have given me a hearing!"[6]

In the spring of 1960, Sturges met with the Mirisch brothers and Arthur Krim and Robert Benjamin of United Artists. An agreement was reached to advance Sturges the desired front money to purchase the rights to Brickhill's book and hire a screenwriter to adapt it. It was generally agreed that another multi-character adventure like *The Magnificent Seven* was commercially attractive, especially if Sturges could bring back many of the young actors who had made the western such a success.

Immediately, Sturges wrote a letter to Paul Brickhill in Australia, describing his decade-long campaign to sell the project. The Britisher, who previously had considered the thought of selling his book to the money-mad Yanks an outrageous move, agreed to meet Sturges in Hollywood to discuss the project.

Sturges treated Brickhill with mink gloves. He promised that there would be no half-measures in the telling of the story. Everything would be filmed just as it happened, and Brickhill — responding to the director's honesty and sincerity — agreed to sell his book to Sturges and to become a partner in the venture.

With Brickhill's help, Sturges located Wally Floody, the former "Tunnel King" of Stalag Luft III, who was signed on as the film's technical advisor. He also obtained the cooperation and help of senior British officers Wings Day and Group Captain Massey. In South Africa, he convinced the parents of Roger Bushell that their son's death would be treated with dignity, giving context to the historical events of the escape.

In Hollywood, Sturges gave the task of preparing the screen treatment to 47-year-old William Roberts, who had previously written *The Magnificent Seven.* In *The Great Escape,* Paul Brickhill had concentrated on facts and events, rather than characterization. The Allied officers in Stalag Luft III were necessarily overshadowed by the sometimes bizarre details of the escape. To create a scenario that would breed effective audience identification and give substance to the breakout, Robert's task was to flesh out Brickhill's one-dimensional freedom seekers.

Knowing that, for security precautions, only 12 men had actually known the entire escape plan, Sturges asked his writer to reduce the principal participants to about a dozen officers and to tell the story entirely through their eyes. He also gave Roberts a scrapbook in which the Brickhill book was cut apart, pasted on individual pages and divided into sections, each one describing a separate entity — tunnels, traps, the camp itself, Big X, the scroungers, the tailors, the manufacturers, the forgers, the stooges, the Gestapo, the ferrets, etc. The scrapbook became an indispensable tool.

The problems confronting Roberts were quite similar to those he had faced on *The Magnificent Seven.* As he recalled, "In *The Great Escape,* we needed an authority figure like the Yul Brynner character in *The Magnificent Seven.* By telling a great deal of action through his eyes, we could, in turn, introduce other characters. Luckily, we had the cool, calculating Big X as a handy mold."[7]

In his 64-page treatment, Big X dominates. Roberts also developed characters that became the future prototypes for "the cooler king," the American scrounger, the Royal Navy dispersal chief and the limping Senior British Officer (SBO).

In the meantime, Sturges had begun filming *By Love Possessed*, with Lana Turner and Efrem Zimbalist, Jr. He again ran into script difficulties, and, once more, Roberts came to his rescue, helping unravel and coordinate the enormously complex James Gould Cozzens novel. Since Roberts had completed his primary task, *The Great Escape* treatment, Sturges began searching for another writer to carry the ball further and develop a shooting script.

In an elevator at Columbia Pictures, Sturges bumped into screenwriter Walter Newman. After a moment of uncomfortable silence (their stormy relationship on *The Magnificent Seven* was still fresh in their memories), Sturges discussed the new project. "It's about a group of American and British flyers escaping from a German Stalag. I'd like you to look at the book and consider doing a script."[8]

It sounded good to Newman and he accepted the assignment. While he too was concerned with the one-dimensional characters, the majority of his time was spent in workably dramatizing the complicated events of the escape. Once the technical flow of the film was completed, he hoped to backtrack and flesh out the characters. But, although his character names do appear in the final film, Newman was not to complete his script.

Another schism occurred when the normally hands-off Mirisch brothers demanded to see a portion of Newman's unfinished script. Sturges found himself torn between divided loyalties. In order to secure the proper commitments from actors like Steve McQueen and James Garner, he needed to negotiate now, and the Mirisches couldn't make deals without a script. On the other hand, the last thing he wanted to do was antagonize Newman, whom he considered a fine writer and who needed time to finish his first draft.

Newman later complained that Sturges was difficult to work with because he was involved in too many projects and couldn't concentrate his ideas and suggestions and present them in succinct form.

The script was at last progressing and with two new films coming up for him to direct in the near future, Sturges was once again too busy to critique his screenwriter's work. It was an exasperated Newman who solved the director's problem by departing for another assignment.

Although the first draft satisfied the Mirisch brothers, who immediately signed McQueen and Garner, it was hardly the polished shooting script that Sturges needed. It was overly long and lacked central continuity. Several times, Newman had followed the book into sidetracking subplots. And the characters weren't yet completely developed and well rounded.

A constructionist was needed, someone who could tighten the Newman script and eliminate some of the unnecessary subplots. Writer W. R. Burnett's name was mentioned, for, in his novel *The Asphalt Jungle* (a famous crime novel of the 1950s, which had been turned into a terrific John Huston film), Burnett had dealt quite successfully with a multi-character story.

Frank Sinatra played the matchmaker in the spring of 1961 when he hired Sturges and Burnett to create *Sergeants Three*, a satirical comedy-western remake of Rudyard Kipling's *Gunga Din*, starring Sinatra and his Rat Pack.

During the script stage on the latter film, Sturges phoned Burnett and invited him to his home in Studio City where "The Great Headache" was being reorganized. Having heard about the film, Burnett was eager to apply his skill to the script, so much so, in fact, that he slammed a car door on his thumb on the way over. He arrived at the director's home with his injured thumb in a splint, but ready to talk business.

With the muddy fields drying in the background, John Sturges, standing on a crane, begins filming exteriors in Stalag Luft III. James Garner and Richard Attenborough stand by (bottom right).

Sturges greeted the writer and showed him the previous draft of the script. "Bill," he confessed to Burnett, "I'm getting nowhere fast on this project. The Mirisch brothers are being as patient as possible, but since we're most likely going to be shooting next spring, time is running out. There's something of value in both of these scripts, but I need your help to pull it together and make it work. Can you do it?"[9]

Despite the pain in his thumb, Burnett gripped Sturges's offered palm firmly. Writer number three was about to put his talents to the test.

Screenwriter W.R. Burnett ripped Newman's script apart, developing a straight line narrative that emphasized the complexities of the tunnel operation. As *The Great Escape* was destined to benefit from sharp cutting, Burnett began developing short, penetrating scenes that pinpointed action and introduced character. He felt that narration (a technique used extensively by both previous writers) was unnecessary if the scenes were simply composed and realistic in nature.

After the completion of *Sergeants Three* in September 1961, Sturges began a closer relationship with his writer, the result being that the pair spent a great deal of time together developing, among other things, the humorous interplay between the film's three American characters, Hilts, Hendley and Goff and their British compatriots.

Once Burnett's first draft was finished, Sturges sent off copies to his first two choices for the crucial role of Big X—John Mills and Richard Harris. Mills, a veteran British actor who had appeared in *The Colditz Story*, declined the offer, claiming in part that the material lacked a certain freshness. Harris, a much younger actor whom Sturges had found excellent in his recent role opposite Marlon Brando in *Mutiny on the Bounty*, fell in love with the role of Big X and accepted the assignment, provided he could finish *This Sporting Life* for producer Karel Reisz.

It was after his interview with Harris that Sturges considered hiring yet another writer to work on the script. Something in Burnett's final draft bothered him and it wasn't the writer's fault. Richard Harris had pointed out that it was obvious that somewhere between Brickhill and Burnett, the English feeling of the story had been lost. Sturges was now worried that such an error could ultimately affect the authenticity of the film. Assistants Robert Relyea and Jack Reddish, both competent second unit directors, were already preparing to scout locations for the second unit in Germany. Time was of the essence.

So, in February 1962, Sturges hired James Clavell, a former resident of Japan's notorious Changi Prison during World War II and the future author of *King Rat* and *Shogun*, to redevelop the British characters in *The Great Escape*, particularly Big X, and instill in their makeup a properly British philosophy and bearing.

Clavell brought forth Big X's most important characteristics, namely his ruthless hatred of the enemy and overwhelming desire to "mess up the works." It was during Clavell's tenure on the script that Sturges decided once more to change the film's principal focus and reduce the importance of Big X to just another one of the 12 leading characters, giving him equal billing with the two Americans, Hilts and Hendley.

Meanwhile, for his next directing project, *A Girl Names Tamiko*, Sturges, producer Hal Wallis, cameraman Charles Lang and a large crew traveled to Japan in the winter of 1961, spending weeks selecting and photographing every location called for in the script. This photography was later matched entirely on the Samuel Goldwyn Studios backlot.

Sturges planned to follow the same pattern for *The Great Escape*. He revealed to reporters on February 19, 1962, that only 10 percent of the film was to be shot abroad. The camp itself was to be constructed in the San Gabriel Mountains near Big Bear Lake, a two-hour drive from Hollywood. With such a plan in mind, Sturges assembled his scouting unit, which consisted of old friends Robert Relyea and Jack Reddish (Relyea had worked on both *Never So Few* and *The Magnificent Seven*; Reddish was a veteran of *Sergeants Three*), and art director Fernando Carrere. The trio arrived in Munich in the middle of February and, working out of a rented office at the Geisel Gasteig Studios, they circled Germany twice in search of potential locations.

Relyea applied to the American consul for permission to visit Sagan, but the Cold War had escalated and the authorities were reluctant to allow any Americans into the Russian zone. The scouting unit would have to rely on photographs and the help of their technical advisors.

After the first scouting trip, the group received ominous news from Sturges in Hollywood. The Pandora's Box opened by entertainer Jack Parr the previous summer (when American troops were exploited during a television broadcast in Berlin) was impacting *The Great Escape*. Sturges was also competing with Darryl F. Zanuck's *The Longest Day*, which was in need of its own extra "army."

The military would not cooperate with Sturges in Hollywood, so plans were now being formulated to use a large group of college students and non-professionals to avoid the cost of hiring professional extras. "Impossible!" came the response from the Screen Extras Guild. There was a standing rule, they pointed out, that all productions filmed within a 300-mile radius of the corner of Hollywood and Vine, must exclusively hire professional extras. There were to be no exceptions. Faced with such a prohibitive cost, Sturges reluctantly decided to take the entire film aboard. Relyea had already advised it.

"I went up to Big Bear, as John requested, and I found some pine trees and a place where we could have built the camp," Relyea remembered. "But when I went to Germany, I told John that there was really no comparison between our little stand of pines in Big Bear and the locations outside Munich — Germany was Germany. And he eventually agreed."[10]

In April 1962, Sturges arrived in Germany. The basic problem now was where to build the camp. Since Geisel Gasteig Studios was located out in the Bavarian countryside, amid forested frontier, Sturges soon found that he could construct the camp virtually on the backlot. There was snow on the ground when he first spied his location. He brought the studio president out to see his choice and was quickly told that there were tiny pine saplings beneath the snow — part of the protected German National Forest.

Since the location was so ideal, being only a few hundred yards from the sound stages where art director Fernando Carrere was already designing the huge tunnel sets, Sturges decided to send Relyea to the German Minister of the Interior for permission to remove the trees.

Relyea found the minister in Munich and brought him out to the studio where Sturges took him up on a Chapman crane and showed him the area planned for the prison camp exterior. The minister was told that the studio would replant the trees elsewhere, two for one, and as the saplings were still young and could be safely removed, the minister agreed to the deal. After Sturges's crew finished in Germany, the prison camp was dismantled and the vacant area was replanted. (I visited that backlot in 1993, for *Return to The Great Escape*, a docu-

John Sturges (right) goes over the Independence Day sequence with Steve McQueen (left) and James Garner.

mentary on the making of the film which I produced for Showtime. I can testify that Sturges kept his promise; there is a thriving forest back there where guard towers and barracks once stood.)

In early May, Richard Harris withdrew from the project. Having read the new Clavell script, he became dissatisfied with his deflated role as Big X. In any case, *This Sporting Life* (in which Harris portrayed a British rugby player) was badly behind schedule and Harris couldn't possibly meet Sturges's deadlines.

To replace Harris, Sturges signed 38-year-old veteran British actor Richard Attenborough, who had been a staple in military movies since *In Which We Serve* in 1942, and had co-starred in such war films as *The Ship That Died of Shame* (1955), *Dunkirk* (1958), *Sea of Sand* (1958) and *Breakout* (1959), the latter another World War II escape yarn set in an Italian prisoner of war camp. He was virtually unknown to American audiences — but not after *The Great Escape*.

Despite the script's new pecking order — with Big X sharing screen time with Hilts and Hendley — Attenborough was still fascinated by Big X, a flying officer, who, despite torture, constant threats, and the crucial responsibility of command, continued to defy his captors in every way possible, retaining his fiery passion to the very end.

With principal photography scheduled for the first week in June 1962, Sturges had already gathered the remainder of his crew in Munich. Daniel Fapp, a Mirisch Company cinematographer who had just returned from Geisel Gasteig (where he had worked with Billy Wilder on *One, Two, Three*), was assigned to Sturges on Robert Relyea's advice (the pair had worked together on *West Side Story*, which had just won the Best Picture Oscar for 1961).

Squadron Leader Roger Bartlett (Richard Attenborough, standing) informs his X Organization that they're going to dig three tunnels and get 250 men out of Stalag Luft III.

Sturges chose his stuntmen carefully. At Steve McQueen's suggestion, it had been decided that the Hilts character would steal a German motorcycle during the escape. The director liked the idea, and although a motorcycle had not been used in the March 1944 breakout, there was proof that escaping prisoners had, in some cases, stolen motorcycles.

The prisoners had taken the idea from the French underground, as Sturges related: "What they would do was wait until nightfall along the forest roads where the dispatch cars ran. No one knew who rode in them, high brass or couriers, but they would often travel like a bat out of hell, with motorcycle guards running escort, front and rear. The French quickly got the notion of stretching piano wire across the road at a 45-degree angle, terminating in a gully. They would let all these fellows pass by and then lift the wire on the last rider, who was immediately clobbered.

"By the time the next-to-last guy looked around, they would be gone. Since the couriers ran on strict timetables, it was dangerous for him to turn around and search for his buddy. He usually just kept right on going."[11]

Since Steve McQueen was already a highly capable motorcycle rider, Sturges gave him authority to purchase the motorcycles and hire a stuntman. The actor immediately contacted his good friend and riding buddy, Bud Ekins, who operated a North Hollywood motorcycle repair shop. Once Sturges saw how much Ekins looked like McQueen, he was hired as the chief motorcycle stuntman on the film.

Before he left for four months in Germany, Ekins purchased two British Triumph motorcycles and began the major conversion job that would turn them into vintage German BMWs. He described the transformation process, which was completed in ten hours: "I gave them both a solo seat, a rack in the back and a different front fender that was flared like the German bikes. I put special competition forks in them and I rigged the suspension like racing bikes of the period. Finally, I painted them both Germany Army green and gave them a balsa wood battery."[12]

The motorcycles completed, Ekins and three other stuntmen — Chuck Hayward, Roy Jenson and Roy Sickner — left for Munich, arriving at Geisel Gasteig Studios on June 8, 1962. They were soon joined by Tim Gibbs, who would also be riding motorcycles in the film.

Despite the rainstorms that pelted Germany throughout the spring and summer of 1962, creating seas of mud in the newly cleared backlot, Fernando Carrere completed the camp on time. The barracks themselves were merely shells with no interior, but there was no denying the camp's overall realism.

Said actor Jud Taylor, who portrayed Hilts' comical American friend, Goff: "It was really impressive, because when you came out of the woods into this clearing there really was a camp with towers and barbed wire. I was walking out there one afternoon and I saw this man walking his dog through the woods. He looked very distressed when he saw the camp. He didn't know where it had come from and it wasn't until I told him in broken German, that it was a movie set, that he was relieved."[13]

Beyond the trees and only 1,000 feet from the camp were the sound stages where Carrere had constructed the tunnel sets. Brickhill had been very explicit in describing the underground escape route. Organized and designed after years of trial and error, the tunnels dug by the X Organization were the most sophisticated ever seen and served to give the finished film its uniqueness, authenticity and sense of claustrophobia.

Extending along the entire length of a stage, the tunnels were constructed with wood and skins filled with plaster and dirt, simulating the dirt interiors of the real tunnels. An entire side was left open, through which Fapp's cameras would capture the action. To photograph the prisoners as they rolled through the tunnels on their underground trolley cars, a lengthy dolly track was constructed. On another soundstage, he constructed the full-sized barracks rooms where the prisoners toiled, slept and plotted their escape.

In nearby Munich, the theatrical center of Germany, Sturges found his German actors. The handsome Hannes Messemer was signed to play the critical role of the camp commandant, Colonel von Luger. During World War II, Messemer was captured by the Russians on the Eastern Front, and escaped by walking hundreds of miles to the German border, a feat duplicated by few Germans. Interestingly, Messemer knew very little English and he had to learn his lines phonetically.

For the role of Werner, the chronically nervous ferret, Sturges found Robert Graf who, despite the loss of an arm to cancer, was superb as the innocent young German who is later blackmailed by Hendley (James Garner). For Straachwitz, the menacing sergeant who brandishes a Schmeisser MP-40 submachine gun as readily as a notebook, the director signed musical comedy star Harry Riebauer. There was nothing funny about Straachwitz.

Til Kiwe, who portrayed Frick, the ferret who discovers the prisoners when they tunnel into the forest, was another former P.O.W. who spent most of the war as prisoner of the Americans in Arizona, an interesting experience described by Relyea who knew Kiwe well: "Kiwe came from our own Stalag Luft III in the Arizona desert. This was where we kept our own rotten eggs and, interestingly enough, he made 17 escape attempts from that camp. He used to tell us how he and his mates contemplated escaping to California, stealing aboard a freighter and making it back to the war zone."[14]

Another fine German actor was Robert Freitag, who portrayed Captain Posen, von Luger's adjutant. It was a small role, but as Relyea points out, John Sturges excelled at casting excellent actors in supporting roles.

"John's theory," Relyea explained, "has always been to put superb actors into the so-called gut of the picture. When he has a critical role, he will usually fall back on the finest actor he can find for the part. In one of his early films, *Bad Day at Black Rock*, the heavies were Robert Ryan, Ernest Borgnine and Lee Marvin, and audiences weren't familiar with the work of two of those actors. Yet, they gave excellent performances that contributed heavily to the success of the film."[15]

A career article, later published on Sturges in *Films and Filming* magazine expanded on Sturges' eye for talent: "He is not a director with a notable talent for deep or penetrating character studies. But he is marvelously adept at establishing the identity and individuality of his characters, even minor ones, with a few telling, economical touches (aided certainly by his excellent eye for casting actors with strong and distinctive personalities). Here, as in all his best films, we come to be involved with and concerned for the escapees, and in this instance to root for them."[16]

June 4, 1962 dawned cold, dark and forbidding. At approximately 7:00 A.M., Sturges arrived at Geisel Gasteig Studios in a driving rainstorm. There was snow on the ground — snow in June — and the work of the flamethrower trucks the previous day had done little but create more mud and slush in the prison compound.

All thoughts of filming exteriors discarded, the director called a meeting of the cast and crew to decide what to do. So as not to waste valuable time, the crew voted to go indoors and begin filming *The Great Escape* somewhere in the middle of the picture. Even if the rain did let up, it was virtually impossible to work in the mud: once the dry season arrived, the cameras could never match the two settings.

Actors James Garner and Donald Pleasence (who was playing gentle-spirited Colin Blythe,

John Sturges points to the area in which the German ferrets will arrive, during interior sequences in the barracks. Charles Bronson (right) portraying Danny "The Tunnel King," is in the "Harry" tunnel entrance. John Leyton (left) plays the other "Tunnel King," Willy. The crew member standing is unidentified.

the forger) were given the call and Sturges began shooting in one of the cavernous Geisel Gasteig sound stages, where Carrere had erected the interior of Hendley and Blythe's sleeping quarters.

It continued to rain for several days and Sturges began to wonder whether he would ever see the sun again. Two weeks later, the weather did improve enough to begin shooting exteriors, in this case the film's opening where the prisoners arrive at the camp.

Inclement weather wasn't the only problem that Sturges was facing. Steve McQueen had been expressing doubts about his part for weeks, and a showdown was brewing. Steve had arrived in Munich with his wife, Neile, and their two children, Terry and Chad. A beautiful house had been rented for him, he had a gull-winged Mercedes for transportation and every other perk he needed. However, when he showed up for costume fittings, he took one look at James Garner's turtleneck sweater and pressed uniform, and became defensive. McQueen had demonstrated how competitive he could be in films like *The Magnificent Seven*, in which he constantly upstaged Yul Brynner, and he didn't like the fact that Garner's scrounger character was much more prevalent in the camp sequences, not to mention the fact that he was better dressed.

In McQueen's defense, he does spend a lot of time in the "cooler." In Clavell's shooting script, Hilts is introduced in the film's opening sequence when he discovers a "blind spot" in the wire, carries on in the "mole maneuver," an abortive escape attempt with Flying Officer Archie Ives (Angus Lennie), spends a great deal of time in the cooler, and then disappears after Ive's death on the wire. He reappears in the escape tunnel, but there is nothing of Steve McQueen for nearly 30 minutes. And the repetitiveness of the cooler sequences began to gnaw at him.

He had just fought and won a major battle with Robert Pirosh and Paramount on *Hell Is for Heroes,* the result of which was that his part rose above the ensemble. McQueen decided to use the same tactics again. However, Sturges was no Robert Pirosh, and he stood his ground. To add scenes at this point was impossible. The script was ridiculously overlong, and with the weather so erratic, they were already behind schedule. He considered eliminating the Hilts character altogether, having his actions absorbed by other characters. But, Sturges was adamant; there would be no rewrite.

The result: Steve McQueen went on strike. For six weeks, he sat in his Munich house and refused to work until the script was fixed. Sturges tried to be patient, but eventually he told McQueen's agent, Stan Kamen of ICM, that he was through with Steve's attitude and, if he didn't go to work, he was going to get fired.

Kamen flew to Munich and tried to bring the parties together, and had thought he had succeeded. However, McQueen and Sturges continued to lock horns, and, according to both James Garner and Robert Relyea, McQueen was indeed fired at one point. Sturges gathered his crew together during the filming of the sequence in which Garner and Pleasence steal an airplane, and announced that McQueen was leaving and that Garner would be taking over elements of his part.

Kamen had just arrived back in Los Angeles, when he got the exasperated call from Sturges that Steve was done. Kamen immediately boarded another plane and headed back to Germany. Fortunately for McQueen, the future of *The Great Escape* and all the fans of that film over the years, a compromise was reached. Screenwriter Ivan Moffit was brought in to beef up Hilts's role.

Recalled Garner, "Coburn and I took Steve to lunch one day and tried to get him to open up. It turned out that Steve wanted to be the hero, but he didn't want to do anything heroic. But he wanted to do something other than just sit in the cooler and ride the motorcycle at the end, so Moffit came up with a sequence where Roger convinces him to escape, make maps of the countryside and get recaptured. That placated Steve."[17]

Satisfied with his character's newfound identity, McQueen settled down, worked hard and contributed a great deal to the final film. In a role similar to that of hotshot American B-17 pilot Buzz Rickson in *The War Lover*, which Steve had just shot in London, McQueen excels as the brash American pilot who insults the Germans, has no patience for the British

Hiltz (Steve McQueen, left) gets another stretch in the cooler—hence his title, "The Cooler King."

and devotes all of his thoughts towards escape. The motorcycle chase in which Hilts leads half the German Army on a wild chase was the perfect *coup de grâce* and gave the film an overflowing sense of movement, in addition to its signature action sequence. But more on that later.

Meanwhile, Sturges had started shooting outdoors. The first shot was the opening of the movie in which the convoy of new prisoners arrive in Stalag Luft III. For this evocative opening sequence, Relyea and Reddish had already gathered the motorized equipment necessary. The arrival sequence was eventually finished on the network of roads west of Geisel Gasteig.

Interestingly, in the Burnett script (which followed the Brickhill book closely), the film had opened differently, showing the way in which many of the flyers were actually captured. In addition, the promotion department of United Artists had asked that Burnett work some women into the story.

"We had several openings," said Burnett. "In one, Hendley, our American scrounger, was shacking up with a German girl who had said, 'The hell with Germany,' when the Gestapo broke into their house and sent him off to prison. We also had a scene showing Big X being worked over by the Gestapo. In the original script, we also went into greater detail with the Ashley-Pitt character [portrayed by a pre–*The Man from U.N.C.L.E.* David McCallum]. He was portrayed very snobbishly as the upper class Britisher, third son of a duke. Eventually, though, he became a hero by killing the Gestapo chief and saving Big X and MacDonald (Gordon Jackson) from capture. The hero came through in the film, but the snobbery was eventually lost when the script proved too long."[18]

John Sturges poses alongside a display of equipment used in the actual escape, including one of the trolleys.

A month after shooting began, Sturges's assistant, Robert Relyea, was still getting letters from United Artists, asking politely that they put more women in the story.

"One," he recalled, "said that we might be guaranteed big box-office if, when David McCallum was killed in the train station, he could be cradled in the lap of a beautiful girl wearing a low-cut blouse and showing a lot of leg. They even wanted us to select her by organizing a Miss Prison Camp contest in Munich."[19] Whatever the commercial possibilities of such promotional hokum, Sturges just ignored it.

After two months of shooting in the camp, Sturges began to shoot the escape exteriors that predominate in the last hour of the film. Since he was already running out of money, the escape sequences could not be as elaborate as originally planned. Instead of filming through many cities and villages, simulating the prisoners' race for freedom, Sturges decided to concentrate his location sequences in and around the small Bavarian town of Fussen, about 57 miles southwest of Munich, near the Austrian border.

In the little town, which the scouting unit had previously found desirable, he found everything he needed — a train station, narrow streets, a distinct Alpine quality (in the film, the prisoners are making for Switzerland), a little river, and, not far away, meadowlands — in short — "motorcycle country."

Motorcycle stuntman and double Bud Ekins was, by now, eager to work on the motorcycle stunts. His first assignment was to trip the German rider so Hilts can steal his motorcycle, but Sturges's hope that a motorcycle rider could be tripped right into a gully seemed impossible.

"Something," said Ekins, "must have been lost in the translation, because when a rider hits the wire, he's going to fall off the bike and that's it. But John wanted the feeling of the bike coming at the wire, changing directions and then flying off into a ditch. He just wasn't satisfied with the bike plopping down in the middle of the highway."[20]

With the sun shining on the Stalag Luft III outdoor set, James Coburn (left), James Garner (center), and Steve McQueen prepare for a ride on a German motorcycle with sidecar. At right, an unidentified crew member.

In order to take advantage of some intricate shadows, Sturges had hoped to find a patch of road enclosed by the trees. Since such a setting was unavailable, the motorcycle-snatching scene was shot on a stretch of open highway outside Füssen.

Throttling up to 40 miles an hour, Ekins would fly off the bike, trying to land in a ditch, but each time he would only end up on the road with a sore behind. Tim Gibbs, the Australian stunt rider, was then given a chance on the stunt. Donning a German motorcycle rider uniform, he skidded the bike 50 feet down the highway on his first try. Relyea, who was handling the logistics of this sequence under Sturges's supervision, thought it was perfect. Relyea suggested to Sturges that they shoot the stunt in two sections; a simple cut would switch from the skid to a shot of the bike hitting the ditch.

Gibbs limped over and asked if his stunt was good enough. "It's fine," said Relyea, "but could you try it once more?"

Ekins hurried over and slapped the Australian on the back, "Come on, they're paying you good money for this!"[21] Gibbs grunted and did the stunt twice more for the cameras. For the role of the unlucky German rider, he also dumped the bike into the roadside ditch.

Leaving Relyea to coordinate the next motorcycle sequence, which included a chase through a little village on the outskirts of Füssen (simulating a German military checkpoint), Sturges returned to Geisel Gasteig Studios to arrange cooperation with the German National Railroad Bureau for the train-escape sequences.

"Come on, Colin," says Hendley (James Garner, right) to Colin Blythe (Donald Pleasence, second from left), as MacDonald (Gordon Jackson, left) and Bartlett (Richard Attenborough) wait for their turn to escape.

Steve McQueen, ready to roll for motorcycle chase sequences, shot on location in Bavaria in 1962. (Note: the British Triumph motorcycle has been altered by Bud Ekins to look like a German BMW.)

Outside Munich, art director Fernando Carrere purchased two vintage passenger cars and a flat car which were assigned to a "special" engine that would transport them up the main line. On one of the passenger cars, they fitted platforms designed to accommodate the huge arc lamps that would illuminate the train interiors, where the escaping prisoners would be nervously seated. On the flat car, Sturges mounted his Chapman crane, which was designed to swing over the passenger car and film the jump by two stuntmen, who were doubling for Garner and Pleasence. The scene called for the two actors to jump off the train when the Gestapo arrive.

When Sturges's train was rolling, the railroad bureau attached a special radio operator to the camera crew, who would alert the engineer to oncoming trains.

"We had to squeeze in our shooting before actual trains came onto the line," remembered Sturges. "So they would organize our times and we'd go out on a section of track, run a certain distance at speed, and then retreat to a siding just as another passenger train raced by at 80 miles an hour."[22]

In terms of which stations to dress, Carrere chose a small station near Geisel Gasteig for the sequence where Hendley (James Garner), Blythe (Donald Pleasence), Roger (Richard Attenborough), MacDonald (Gordon Jackson), Ashley-Pitt (David McCallum), Haines (Lawrence Montaigne) and Nemmo (Tom Adams) board the train. The station where they get off, and where Ashley-Pitt kills a Gestapo agent and is, in turn, shot by soldiers, was the Füssen station.

When the railroad sequences were finished, John Sturges went looking for a Luftwaffe aerodrome for yet another escape vignette. In early September, he found one north of Munich. Although it was equipped with the latest jet aircraft, the field also boasted a complement of AT-6 "Texan" training planes which were painted German aviation gray and outfitted with the appropriate German cross and swastika insignias. In Florida, that same month, Warner Bros. was using similar AT-6s for Japanese Zero fighters, launching winged assaults on a naval base for their feature film, *PT-109.*

In the aerodrome scene, Hendley and Blythe, who is now virtually blind, sneak onto the field, clobber a German sentry and commandeer a special trainer for a quick escape-hop through the nearby Alps. The plane was a little vintage Buker 181 low-level observation plane, purchased in Hamburg for $325.

After Carrere's crew got the AT-6s and the Buker ready for the cameras, Sturges asked that the field be watered down with fire hoses, to simulate early morning. He could not risk his actors in the rickety old Buker, so Bob Relyea, a qualified amateur pilot, volunteered to fly the plane for the brief aerial sequences.

According to Relyea, the Buker was an unusual plane. Its throttle was located on the left side of the cockpit and, in order to start the engine, a crank was employed. This presented special problems because Relyea soon found that the plane had a bad habit of stalling in midair. Since you couldn't re-crank the plane at 6,000 feet, he began to land in some very strange places.

"I was beginning to think that when we landed on an airfield, we were lucky," Relyea quipped. "There is a segment of the film where the Buker is supposedly losing power and I was asked to hedgehop with a camera plane alongside, simulating the descent over a line of trees. There was this old farmer plowing a field and he looked up and saw the Buker with its swastikas, and, out of natural reaction, he threw his rake and almost got me. I always thought that had I been killed, someone would have to explain to my children that I had been shot down by a rake."[23]

On another occasion, Relyea landed in an innocent looking field that just happened to be the backyard of the local German aviation official. Because he was flying without a valid license in an obsolete and dangerous aircraft painted with illegal markings, Relyea was arrested and detained until explanations from Sturges engineered his escape.

A decision had not been reached as to who would actually crash the Buker, so the finale was postponed. Since both Garner and Pleasence were due to leave Europe, Sturges decided to first shoot the after-action sequence showing the two actors stumbling out of the Buker's flaming wreckage.

"We weren't very smart then," related Relyea, "because there's a golden rule that you

Captain Virgil Hiltz (Steve McQueen), having stolen the uniform and motorcycle, heads for Switzerland.

never shoot after-action until you know what the action looks like. When you're dealing with a crashed plane, you don't really know where it's going to land until you actually crash the plane. While we were still working on the aerial sequence, we took a mock-up body of the Buker and placed it down on the road below some trees. The actors climbed out of the burning plane and the scene was completed. It was very picturesque and it worked just swell. But I put in the back of my mind, that some day soon I would have to get the real crash shot for John. It was not something I was looking forward to."[24]

Having dumped the German dispatch rider's uniform, Hiltz (Steve McQueen) races for the Swiss border. These sequences were shot on the network of roads outside the small Bavarian town of Füssen.

To recreate the wartime border between Germany and Switzerland, Sturges worked out a deal with five local farmers so that his art department could erect a mile and a half long double barrier. The motorcycle chase to that border fence begins when Hilts (Steve McQueen), now dressed in the uniform of the tripped motorcyclist, attempts to sneak past a checkpoint near the border. He is spotted by a guard (stuntman Roy Jensen) and questioned. Since he lacks the proper papers, Hilts kicks the soldier and frantically rides off, only to be followed by several motorcyclists, some with sidecars.

This particular scene, one of the film's most dramatic, had McQueen take off on one of the repainted and tricked-out Triumphs, followed by a sidecar manned by Bud Ekins and Chuck Hayward. The action called for Hilts to cut a corner and race across a little foot bridge, while the Germans misjudge the turn and crash through a fence, falling into a gully.

"It wasn't a breakaway fence," related Ekins, "but the real thing. And buried beneath the grass was another board which changed the direction of the bike at the last minute, clipping Chuck in the groin. He was thrown to the ground and ended up in the hospital. I was okay, although my neck hurt. I fell with the bike and got thrown against the sidecar."[25]

To Sturges's dismay, the German stunt riders hired in Munich could not keep up with the hard-riding McQueen. They were primarily experienced as highway racers and were out of their element on the dirt roads that crisscrossed the green meadowlands.

One morning, Sturges was mulling over the problem when he felt a tap on his shoulder. He turned around and was greeted by a fully dressed German soldier with little beer-bottle eyeglasses. It was Steve McQueen. Before Sturges could say anything, McQueen said, "Now you know they wouldn't recognize me." And Sturges agreed, "By God, they wouldn't."[26]

As a result, in one scene, McQueen rides off as Hilts, the action is stopped, he changes clothes and rides back over the same ground as a German rider, chasing himself. The sequence worked perfectly, and it wasn't until years later that Sturges revealed that the swift-moving German stunt rider was actually McQueen.

As Sturges explained, "The Germans had a lot of guts, but they weren't really stuntmen. Curiously enough, if you're a real motorcyclist, you're not necessarily a good stuntman, because a stuntman knows how to fall off a bike. Whereas, a real professional bike rider's whole purpose is to try and stay on the bike. We were lucky to have Steve with us. With exceptional cutting, he could have played the entire German Motorcycle Corps."[27]

The most spectacular scene in the film is Hilts's motorcycle jump for freedom, in which he negotiates a six-foot barbed wire fence. Originally, Sturges wanted Ekins to achieve the necessary height with a wooden ramp, but it was clear that a ramp, even one well camouflaged, was too obvious.

Early in September, while Sturges completed the train and aerial sequences, Ekins, Tim Gibbs and a German special-effects technician spent a few hours near the new fence discussing the stunt. They soon discovered a natural wallow that curved down and then upright. Taking the barrier down in one place, they started racing into the wallow to see how high they could actually jump. Gibbs tried it first and jumped the motorcycle six feet across the wallow and two feet off the ground. Retrieving shovels from their Volkswagen bus, the trio started digging to create a sharper incline.

Ekins now took the handlebars and raced into the wallow, doubling Gibbs's previous attempt. The digging continued. Steve McQueen arrived and was promptly handed a shovel. Soon, everyone, including McQueen, was racing the motorcycle while the special-effects man stood by, measuring each jump with a piece of string.

When the digging was completed, the wallow resembled the shape of a jai alai racket. As the motorcycles hit the ditch, the suspension would drop, the bike would hit the incline sharply and simply pop out of the hole. The scientific logistics became so sensitive that Ekins was digging an inch at a time. By evening, the bikes were sailing 40 and 50 feet. They were ready for the cameras.

Far to the north, Robert Relyea was planning an even more critical stunt. After two weeks of careful planning, the special-effects crew had determined that there were exactly three ways to crash the tiny Buker. They could put the plane up on a chute, like a ski jump, and glide it in mechanically. This, they reasoned, would involve a very short entry, zero control, and they could end up wrecking the airplane without being sure of a good scene. Or they could guide the Buker in with wires, which would allow more effective control. However, the entry distance would have been greatly reduced, further inhibiting the plane's velocity at point of impact, and thus reducing the realism of the stunt.

The third choice was obvious: have a stuntman fly the plane into the trees. This way, someone could direct the plane up until the moment of impact. Had he been given the choice, Relyea would have definitely eliminated the third alternative as it was far too dangerous. However, since the after-action had already been filmed and there could be no room for error to match the shots, there was to be no choice.

Bravely resolving that he alone could destroy the Buker (everyone else, including Sturges, thought he was crazy), Relyea selected six camera positions and began practicing the run in a nearby field dotted with little flags, simulating the distance between his adversaries: the trees.

He was doing well until Reddish asked him to bring up his tail by taxiing a little faster to simulate a landing. While practicing such a maneuver, Relyea crashed into a flag head-on. Had it been one of the trees, the engine of the Buker would have had to pass through the cockpit, leaving Relyea with a permanent naval ornament. It was a frightening experience and Relyea considered forgetting the entire sequence.

While he rationalized that model work was prohibitively expensive, the crew prepared the stunt for the next morning. The weather that had remained pleasant enough for motorcycle work suddenly changed for the worse and the next day dawned dark and cloudy. Since the crash could only be filmed in blazing sunshine because it had to be done in one shot and the cameras needed maximum lighting, Relyea was granted a temporary reprieve.

The clouds stood guard over the crash site for two days. As dawn broke on the third day, Relyea's fear was intense. His wife arrived in time to inform him that if he went ahead with the crazy stunt, she would never speak to him again.

The special-effects crew prepared the vulnerable little Buker for its appointment with disaster, sawing off the control stick, taking the glass out of the canopy, constructing a special reinforced seat and carefully draining off the excess gasoline. As the Buker was 90 percent wood, a fire crew stood by. Every time Relyea went behind a bush to be sick, he would see

Against insurance agents' orders, Steve McQueen tests the motorcycle jump that Bud Ekins will perform for the cameras.

the firemen standing by with their buckets of crushed ice. It was enough to drain any man's confidence.

At last, everything was ready. As he revved up the engine, and the crew prepared to remove the blocks which held the plane in place, Reddish came running up, climbed onto the wing and shouted above the deafening roar, "Camera Five wants to change to a 50mm, what do you think?"

Relyea screamed, "I don't care if he puts a Coke bottle on it, if I don't go in the next five seconds, we're forgetting the whole thing!"[28]

His anchor gone, Relyea cut his flaps, pulled back on the miniature throttle and rolled forward. When halfway across his makeshift runway (actually a cow pasture), he noticed the Buker rolling toward the right tree. He compensated by hitting his right rudder pedal. Fearful that he would accidentally cut power while adjusting his rudder, Relyea rammed the throttle forward and removed his hand, hoping that he could hang on and be able to jab a little rudder at the last minute and avoid the telltale tree.

Removing his hand from the throttle nearly killed him. Hoping to hit the tree at 45 miles an hour, he looked down at his indicators a second before impact and noticed the Buker pushing 100. It was much too fast.

He remembered, "I realized how fast I was going, and I had just enough time to hit the left rudder before the plane struck. I involuntarily closed my eyes and felt a terribly slight shudder. And then it was over and I thought, 'That wasn't bad!' I opened my eyes and all I saw was blue sky, which was funny because I expected to be down in the dirt near the road. It then dawned on me that I had hit so hard that I had ripped the Buker's landing gear and wings off and that I was headed towards the Austrian border."[29]

When Relyea did hit the ground, the force of the crash knocked him unconscious. Seconds later, the four firemen arrived to unstrap him and cover the plane with ice. "They took me to a Munich hospital," Relyea continues, "because when I recovered my senses, I had a sharp pain in my back. The wet X-rays showed a line down my spinal column, so I was sure I was paralyzed for life. Fortunately, wet X-rays do lie, and I was okay. I had a little trouble for a couple of years, as a long drive would tire me out, but on the whole, I survived unscathed."[30]

Bud Ekins's heart was pounding. Sturges' wristwatch read 2:01 P.M. On a little saddleback ridge, assistant directors Jack Reddish and John Flynn signaled that the cameras were ready. The director raised his arm, signaling Ekins. The crowd around the Chapman crane pushed forward. Steve McQueen leaned against a tire and waited for his "twin" to streak by. The crackle of the Triumph's engine echoed across the meadowland.

And then he was off, the streaking illusion of Steve McQueen, blue sweatshirt and dirty beige pants, fluttering nervously in the Triumph's air stream. With considerable ease, and traveling at nearly 60 miles an hour, Ekins took the Triumph into the jai alai racket-shaped wallow, expertly jumping the motorcycle 65 feet, hurtling the six-foot barrier with a foot to spare.

A cheer went up from the crowd of onlookers. The German soldiers whistled their approval, and Steve McQueen leaned over to offer his congratulations. John Sturges simply smiled at cameraman Daniel Fapp and climbed down from the Chapman crane. Spying the catering truck, he remembered he was hungry.

SECTION III

THE NEW HEROES

Looking back into the era which followed the Vietnam War's escalation in the summer of 1964, the effects of the conflict on the quality and success of war films are clearly discernable. Author James Jones's *The Thin Red Line*, perhaps the finest combat novel of World War II, became a darkly flavored, sterile tale of warfare that failed to generate much interest. Despite young actor Keir Dullea's excellent portrayal of Private Don Doll, the picture was a commercial failure. While World War II continued to provide the conventional background for the dwindling entries in the epic war adventure genre (*The Dirty Dozen, Kelly's Heroes, Where Eagles Dare, Midway*), a new group of controversial military films appeared.

Dealing effectively, pointedly and, thus, controversially, with the realities of the nuclear age, the new films continued to dissect the military culture, expanding immensely on the mature portrait of fighting men, painted a decade earlier in films like *From Here to Eternity*.

One of the most memorable pictures of the period was director Stanley Kubrick's satirical triumph, *Dr. Strangelove or: How I Learned to Stop Worrying and Love the Bomb* (1964), which attacked both militarism and the A-Bomb reality with an almost farcical blend of factual drama, sharp satirical comment and allegory. Primarily a comedy, *Dr. Strangelove* still represents a realistic scenario, demonstrating the threat of nuclear aggression in a nightmare world of political, military and sexual psychosis.

Dr. Strangelove or: How I Learned to Stop Worrying and Love the Bomb was Stanley Kubrick's brilliant satire of Cold War tensions. Here, mad-as-a-hatter Air Force General Jack Ripper (Sterling Hayden, right) comforts British liaison officer Group Captain Lionel Mandrake (Peter Sellers) and begins to explain the importance of his "precious bodily fluids."

149

Of course, to an impressionable 12 year old, the film was just plain "shake-your-head" weird. What else would you think about a modern movie about the Strategic Air Force which talks about "Rooshin phrase books," and issues of prophylactics, introduces us to military officers named General Jack Ripper and Colonel Bat Guano, and finally presents the title character as a wheel-chair bound ex–Nazi who can barely restrain his Heil Hitler salute.

It is not surprising that the United States Air Force refused to offer Kubrick military cooperation, the result being that the entire film was completed in England. However, *Dr. Strangelove* was a commercially successful film that established director Stanley Kubrick as one of America's top creators. It was as wild and wooly a statement on the hazards of the nuclear age that could be depicted at the time. However, there was enough truth in it to give the film serious power and meaning.

A year later, in 1965, Columbia Pictures released *The Bedford Incident*, which carried the military re–examination a step further, dealing with a nuclear missile-equipped American destroyer tracking a Russian submarine in the North Atlantic. Captain Eric Findlander (Richard Widmark), a tough naval officer of the World War II mold, is obsessed with tracking down the encroaching submarine, and his resultant obsession becomes a personal war that leads to another nuclear exchange.

Attached to Finlander's destroyer, the USS *Bedford*, is liberal magazine correspondent Ben Munsford (Sidney Poitier) who questions Finlander's strategy, and through those eyes we appraise a Captain Queeg of the Atomic Age. Like General Jack Ripper in *Dr. Strangelove*, Finlander's bravado is no longer practical.

In *Seven Days in May*, director John Frankenheimer and writer Rod Serling's nightmarish portrait of a possible military takeover of the United States, Kirk Douglas portrayed Marine Colonel Jiggs Casey, a modern warrior who helps save the country by challenging the man he once idolized.

His relentless pressure for efficiency cripples young Ensign Ralston (James MacArthur) who soon develops a chronic case of nerves. If such a relationship had developed during World War II (as it did in such films as *The Enemy Below*, and, much later, *Das Boot*), the captain would have instilled courage and individual spirit in his nervous subaltern, and both would have turned their anxieties towards the enemy. But aboard the nuclear destroyer *Bedford*, such tension is no longer allowed a viable outlet.

In the film's apocalyptic ending, Finlander is instructing Munsford on the specifics of the *Bedford's* missile system when young Ralston misunderstands a command and accidentally launches a nuclear strike, which obliterates the Russian submarine. In turn, the *Bedford* is eliminated by a spread of atomic torpedoes that were fired just before the submarine was hit. If you want to see a movie that lays out the clear tension and stakes of the Cold War, then you should see *The Bedford Incident*.

Films like *The Bedford Incident* portray the military at the mercy of their machines.

In *Seven Days in May*, Burt Lancaster portrays an anachronistic American Air Force general who not only challenges the president's nuclear treaty with the Russians, but plans to take over the United States himself.

Handcuffed by the demands of an age that continually preached prudence to fighting men, military leaders with World War II experience found themselves unable to deal rationally with their assignments. They failed to understand the meaning of the Cold War and the need for maintaining the peace. Such weakness proved devastating.

In *Seven Days in May* (1964) — written by Rod Serling, who adapted Fletcher Knebel and Charles W. Bailey II's novel — U.S. Air Force General James Scott (Burt Lancaster) dismisses President Jordan Lyman's (Fredric March) nuclear treaty with the Russians as "an act of criminal negligence" and plans a military takeover of the United States. Scott, another veteran of the Second World War, is thrust into the world of Cold War power politics and inaction. This man of combat, by all its definitions, puts no faith in papers, especially when he is dealing with a country like the Soviet Union, which, he claims, has "never honored one treaty in its entire history."* Scott symbolizes the basic military strategy that the only good defense is a strong offence. That the world is to survive under a perpetual threat of nuclear war is a situation the general deems inevitable.

The general's aide, Marine Colonel "Jiggs" Casey (Kirk Douglas) is a more modern warrior. Having stumbled upon his superior's plot, Casey contacts the president and actively participates in President Lyman's countermeasures. Still, he holds the deepest respect for and even defends Scott, until it is finally proven that his general is, indeed, immersed in treason. When one of the president's advisors castigates Scott as "a jackal," Casey explodes in anger,

Seven Days in May, Paramount Pictures, 1964

prompting President Lyman's closing speech, which chastises, not the conspirators, but the age of insecurity that produced their conspiracy. The clearly defined realities and clarity of World War II had vanished, and it is through President Lyman's eyes that we see the murkiness and confusion of the Cold War and how anachronistic our former military strategies could be.

As the war in Vietnam raged, other factors affected the portrayal of war on the big screen. To make up for the loss of such a violent and adventuresome genre, Hollywood suddenly and graphically transferred mass bloodshed to more conventional genres such as the western and police drama. The killing machines were being reprogrammed. The tough soldier was replaced by tough cops like Dirty Harry and Bullitt and western heroes like those in *The Wild Bunch*, *The Professionals* and every character played by Clint Eastwood. Ironically, in the new crime dramas, many of these men were Vietnam veterans.

Drug smugglers, early 20th century Mexican banditos and the Mafia substituted often for the conventional enemies of World War II. It was the reversal of the trend of the later 1930s, when Hollywood abandoned the war on crime and corruption and geared instead for the conflict against fascism.

CHAPTER NINE

The Sand Pebbles

When director Robert Wise mentioned Steve McQueen's name to 20th Century–Fox in mid–1963 as a possible candidate for the leading role in his projected film adaptation of author Richard Milton McKenna's best-selling book *The Sand Pebbles*, the word came back from the studio that Steve was not bankable.

Needless to say, after the release of *The Great Escape* in the summer of 1963, statements like that were no longer heard in Hollywood. After *The Great Escape*, Steve McQueen was one of the fastest-rising stars in the world — one of the first superstars — and everyone wanted him. What the iconic photographs of James Dean and Marlon Brando had done for 1950s pop culture, the publicity shots of Steve McQueen riding the motorcycle in *The Great Escape* did for the iconography of the 1960s. Steve was now the "King of Cool" and the 1960s became, in many ways, the McQueen decade.

Robert Wise was also on a roll. Having won two Oscars for producing and directing *West Side Story* in 1961, he was about to take the helm of *The Sound of Music*, an epic motion picture musical that would help save 20th Century–Fox from bankruptcy. But Wise was much more than a maker of epic musicals. His career dated back to the 1930s, when he started out as a sound effects editor, segued to film editor and worked closely with Orson Welles on *Citizen Kane*.

It was horror impresario Val Lewton who gave Wise one of his first directing gigs — the always-creepy *The Curse of the Cat People* in 1944. Wise took the ball and ran with it, re-teaming with Lewton on *The Body Snatcher* and then becoming one of Darryl Zanuck's busiest contract directors in the 1950s.

It was Wise who directed the science-fiction classic *The Day the Earth Stood Still* in 1951. He was a director without a signature style, but his films were all solid pieces of work and were enormously entertaining. Whereas Hitchcock only did thrillers and Ford did mostly westerns, Wise worked in all genres.

His World War II films were particularly memorable. In 1953, he did two World War II desert films: *The Desert Rats*, an action-packed sequel to *The Desert Fox*, the 1951 film biography of Rommel, in which a gritty Richard Burton portrays a British officer assigned to green Australian troops defending the escarpments of Tobruk from the pick of Hitler's troops; and *Destination Gobi*, set in Inner Mongolia, where a ragtag band of Navy weathermen (under the able stewardship of Richard Widmark) battle the desert, bandits, shady Mongols and Japanese cavalry. Both films featured good doses of comedy, which was also a Wise touch in many of his dramatic films.

Five years later, he got a chance to work with two acting icons — Clark Gable and Burt Lancaster — in the World War II submarine drama, *Run Silent, Run Deep*. Years before *Das Boot* raised the realism level seriously in World War II submarine dramas, Wise gave us a very edgy, claustrophobic, psychological account of life aboard a fleet submarine fighting in Japan's Bungo Straits. His experience maneuvering the two superstars through the sweaty corridors of the USS *Nerka* would serve him well in the narrow engine spaces of a Yangtse gunboat in *The Sand Pebbles*.

Because he was so eclectic in his tastes, it is not surprising that Wise responded to Richard McKenna's *The Sand Pebbles*. To westerners, there has always been a mysterious quality to Asia, and McKenna's book served as a doorway into a little-known aspect of that world, namely the gunboat diplomacy of the 1920s.

"I liked the story very very much," said Wise. "I liked what it had to say about our world today and the need to get along with each other…. I met Richard McKenna once in New York. He lived in the Carolinas and he came up to meet me and talked about the book and his experiences. He was a very big hulk of a man, but a very sweet man. But I never got his reaction to the film because he died before I got the film done."[1]

There was an epic quality to this slice of world history, and given his new clout with the success of *West Side Story* and the upcoming *The Sound of Music, The Sand Pebbles* was, in many ways, a perfect Robert Wise project.

An ex-gunboat sailor and U.S. Navy veteran (he also served aboard a naval transport in World War II), Richard M. McKenna had worked in the engine rooms of naval ships, had spent a great deal of time around sailors in the Far East and certainly understood their daily drills and nightly rituals. He had been writing and selling short stories for years when he began his novel and the results were extraordinary.

The Sand Pebbles introduces us to Jake Holman, a U.S. navy engineer who is assigned to duty aboard the USS *San Pablo*, a gunboat on patrol along China's Yangtze River in 1925-26. To the indigent Chinese living in a warlord-dominated culture, the sailors of the *San Pablo* are known as "The Sand Pebbles." Although McKenna's naval service aboard gunboats took place in the 1930s, he decided to set his novel in the earlier period, when China was in dramatic flux. The era of the warlords was ending and the Nationalists under ex-warlord turned visionary Chiang Kai-Shek were on the move. The Sand Pebbles would soon find themselves caught between the tides of revolution, with orders that no longer made sense.

Steve McQueen starred in *The Sand Pebbles* as engineer Jake Holman, who transfers to the U.S.S. *San Pablo*, a gunboat patrolling the Yangtze River in 1920s China.

It's not difficult to picture Steve McQueen reading the novel and appreciating the makeup of Jake Holman — or Ho-mang as the Chinese coolies would call him. Jake was a salty, two-fisted loner, endlessly fascinated with anything mechanical and determined to make the *San Pablo*'s engine room the envy of the fleet. As long as everything was going well with the engine, Jake Holman was happy, but tamper with the engine and his quick-tempered rebellious nature began to emerge.

He immediately disdained the fact that the *San Pablo* employed dozens of Chinese coolies who did virtually everything, from cooking, cleaning and laundry, to working in the engine spaces. Whereas his shipmates did their duty, stood their watches and stayed ready for what action might come their way, they were also a lazy bunch who spent more time ashore in bars and brothels than in military action. It was easy duty and Jake was advised to just let it go; the engine would run itself as it always had.

Holman is offended and his determination to change the culture of the *San Pablo*'s engine room caused problems at every turn. Captain Collins, the stalwart skipper, had carefully integrated the coolies into the ship's culture and he was loath to change anything. In the novel, Holman isn't initially resented by the crew — he becomes an effective gunboat sailor and engineer — but the seeds of discontent are eventually sown and Holman does have to face down the bulk of the engine crew who resent him and his individualism.

The movie later followed much of the book's plot. Jake befriends watertender Frenchy Burgoyne; he trains Po-han the bilge coolie to replace Shing, the boss coolie who is killed while repairing the engine; and he meets and falls in love with young missionary Shirley Eckhardt, who lives at China Light, a missionary compound up river from Changsha, one of the *San Pablo*'s ports of call.

McKenna brought an exquisite amount of detail to his descriptions of the life of a Yangtze gunboat sailor. For instance, he points out that the *San Pablo* shares the waterways and ports of call with the gunboats of England and Japan, and there was a great deal of camaraderie between the sailors of different countries. They all drink at the same tawdry bars and brothels. When Jake takes it upon himself to completely dismantle the *San Pablo*'s steam plant and rebuild the engine, he receives critical support from other gunboat sailors and civilian mechanics who bring him tools, equipment and labor. McKenna carefully walks the viewer through the unscrewing of every rusted bolt as sweaty sailors, coolies and helpers work to get the *San Pablo* ready for the open waters of the Yangtze.

In the book, Po-han had a wife and family and they became friendly with saloon girl, Maily, who, thanks to her lover Frenchy, escapes the grasps of servitude from underworld figure, Victor Shu. Shirley Eckhardt, meanwhile, begins teaching at China Light and she meets a brilliant young student and rising Nationalist leader named Cho-jen, who is more fully developed in the book.

The book is also heavy with the political atmosphere of mainland China and its transition to a country run by the Nationalist government of Chiang Kai-Shek. Chinese nationalism is everywhere, with soldiers and sympathizers vanquishing the warlords, flying the new Chinese nationalist flag, turning in traitors and gradually turning against the gunboat sailors with the new tools of boycott and propaganda.

All of these elements were new to American readers, and Wise correctly surmised that they would make a terrific movie. However, his failure to convince Fox in 1963 to hire McQueen as Jake Holman, plus the enormous logistics that were involved in putting together an epic film set in China, put the project on the back burner and he turned, instead, to *The Sound of Music*.

However, he did get the studio to put the project in development, and Robert Anderson was chosen to adapt the McKenna Novel. Anderson was the perfect choice. He was an accomplished screenwriter and playwright who had adapted *Tea and Sympathy,* his own play, into a motion picture and had written *The Nun's Story* (starring Audrey Hepburn), which was nominated for eight Oscars in 1960. Anderson was also a U.S. Navy officer in the Pacific during World War II, so he was comfortable writing about navy men and their idiosyncratic world.

Wise was in London working on *The Haunting* when he sent Anderson the book. The playwright liked McKenna's novel very much and flew to England right away to discuss the adaptation with Wise. Later, Anderson was working on the script in New York in the fall of 1963 when Wise came to visit. The pair ducked out of Wise's hotel room to have a soufflé, and when they came back they discovered that President John F. Kennedy had been assassinated in Dallas. Wise was so shaken up that he excused himself and made immediate arrangements to return to Los Angeles. He needed to get home.

We are not privy to the script discussions between Wise and Anderson, but the latter produced a masterful adaptation of the McKenna novel. And this was no small task. As good as the book was, it is episodic and the dramatic confrontation between Holman and the crew comes late, in the last 50 pages of the book.

Anderson kept McKenna's basic story line, but shifted some events around, eliminated others, and focused on how the *San Pablo* and its crew are gradually becoming an anachronism, the victim of a changing China that is sweeping away its old ways and embracing the new nationalism. It is, thus, becoming increasingly more dangerous to protect American missionaries and civilians who are living in China. At one point, gunboat sailors were allowed to use their guns; now the *San Pablo's* directives from the fleet preach diplomacy instead.

Nowhere is this more dramatically shown than in the capture and torture of Po-han. In previous times, Captain Collins would have led a heavily armed shore party against the fanatics; now, he and his men must stand idly by as their beloved bilge coolie is flayed in plain sight by a scary mob. If they fire, they can touch off an international incident. If they don't fire, Po-han will suffer the Death of a Thousand Cuts. It's a brutal scene to watch in the final movie because you share Holman's and Collins's enormous frustration. When Steve McQueen finally grabs a rifle and aims at the coolie who has become his good friend, you can barely breath. When, against Collins' orders, he finally opens fire and kills Po-han with a single bullet, you're in horrified shock. To this day, the death of Po-Han remains as one of the most difficult sequences to watch in any mainstream Hollywood epic.

Anderson needed to flesh out Frenchy and Maily and integrate them into Holman's world, since everything would revolve around him. Stawski, the machinist mate, who is a background character in the book, despite the fact that he does fight Po-han in the celebrated boxing match, became Holman's number-one antagonist.

It is clear that Wise wanted Holman to be much more of a loner in the movie. When Steve McQueen was signed, Holman's character evolved even more, becoming pure Steve McQueen — laconic, rebellious and ready for action. Only Captain Collins and Shirley Eckhardt were close to their literary origins. Anderson did eliminate practically all of Cho-jen's back story and, in the movie, he is reduced to a bit player whom Jake kills in the fight to destroy the junk boom.

But it was Anderson's clear understanding of dramatic structure that took McKenna's fascinating, but undisciplined, story and turned it into a compelling, thinking man's epic.

And, despite what appeared to be an obvious parallel, Anderson had no intention of comparing the events of China in 1925 with the growing horror of the Vietnam War. Vietnam was barely a blip in 1963 when Anderson began his screenplay. And, although President Johnson orchestrated a massive buildup in Vietnam after the death of President Kennedy, Anderson was not interested in making a direct parallel to Vietnam stick.

However, to this day, whenever I see the last scene in the movie, in which Jake Holman yells, "What the hell happened?," I think that the whole debacle of the Vietnam War was being summed up by those words, uttered by a mortally wounded gunboat sailor in 1925. What the hell happened? Indeed.

Pre-production on *The Sand Pebbles* began in earnest in mid–1965. It was considered impossible to shoot the film in Red China, so efforts were initiated to film on the only other possible location for a realistic movie featuring thousands of Chinese — Taiwan, Formosa. Wise planned to shoot the bulk of the movie on location in Taipei, the capital of Taiwan, with a second location to be shot in the New Territories, near Hong Kong, with interior soundstage sequences to be organized on the 20th Century–Fox lot in West Los Angeles.

Robert Liu, a native of China, was a young cinematographer attending USC in Los Angeles in the early 1960s when he met Robert Wise. When the latter made his first location scout to Taipei in 1965, Liu tracked him down and offered his services as a cameraman. Wise was traveling with director of photography Ted McCord, who had just served in that capacity on *The Sound of Music*. They met at the Grand Hotel in Taipei (owned by Madame Chiang Kai-Shek), and Wise offered young Liu the camera operator position on the test footage they were going to shoot on Tam Sui River waterfront.

Said Liu, "They wanted to make sure it looked like Shanghai, where the movie begins. They would eventually shoot the opening sequence in Keelung, which we called Rain Harbor, because it rained 360 days a year. And Mr. McCord said that when they came back to do the show, he wanted me to be the second unit director of photography."[2]

Unfortunately, McCord dropped out of *The Sand Pebbles* and was replaced by Joe McDonald, who brought his own second-unit cameraman from the States, so Liu lost his position. However, Wise was impressed with Liu's knowledge of the local film community, so he hired him to be an assistant director, in charge of the sequences involving large numbers of Chinese.

Wise returned to the States and began the casting process. McQueen was in, although he was not Wise's first choice. Paul Newman had turned down the role, feeling that he was wrong for Jake Holman. (And he was right — Paul Newman was much too handsome to play a career gunboat sailor and although pool shark Eddie Felson, Newman's character in his signature film, *The Hustler,* showed the range of this fantastic actor, McQueen was much better suited to the part.)

Wise had one previous experience with McQueen. They had worked together in 1956 on *Somebody Up There Likes Me*, the Rocky Graziano boxing biopic, which was one of McQueen's first film roles. McQueen appears briefly as a young tough named Fidel, opposite Paul Newman's starring role as Graziano. Ironically, the following year, Wise would direct Steve McQueen's future wife, Neile Adams, in the comedy *This Could Be the Night*. So *The Sand Pebbles* would be something of a reunion for the Wise and McQueen clans.

Although Eli Wallach read for the part of American gunboat sailor, Frenchy Burgoyne, Wise cast Richard Attenborough to play Jake Holman's friend who falls in love with a wayward Chinese girl.

"Why in God's name Bobby Wise should decide to cast me, an English actor, as a member of the United States Navy was a total puzzlement to me," said Richard Attenborough to film historian Michael Thomas in 2004. "I suspect that Steve McQueen had something to do with it. But I will always be profoundly grateful because not only did it give me an opportunity to continue my friendship with Steve, but I got a chance to go to a part of the world — Taiwan — where, goodness knows, I would never possibly have ever gone."[3]

For Captain Collins, Wise was interested in 38-year-old television leading man Richard Crenna (*Our Miss Brooks, The Real McCoys*). Having successfully broken away from comic typecasting, Crenna, unfortunately, had to turn Wise down because he was in the second season of the political drama *Slattery's People*. Fate, however, intervened when the television show was canceled, allowing Crenna to take on the role of Collins.

Crenna walked into Wise's office at Fox and found himself in the company of Hollywood royalty. Wise told him to hurry and get his shots because he had to be on a plane right away. A few days later, Crenna flew to Taiwan with his entire family, except for his one-month-old daughter who would join him later.

Crenna remembered his first meeting with McQueen: "We were checking into our hotel in Taiwan and the phone rang and it was Steve McQueen. He said, 'Hi Dick, how are ya?' And I said, 'Fine, Steve, I'm really pleased to be in the picture with you.' And he said, 'I'd

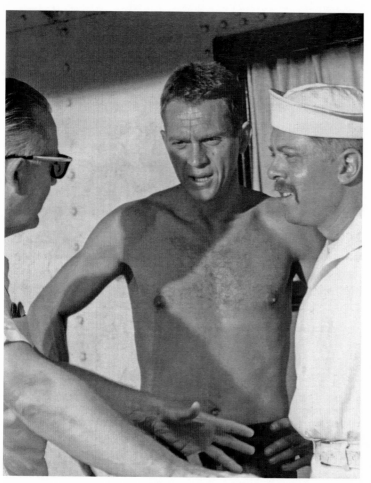

like to come over and shuck.' "And I looked at my wife and said, 'What the hell is shuck?' I later found out that it meant to talk and kibbitz. He really wanted to come over and see how we all fit together in the great scheme of things, whether this was going to be a collaborative effort or a competition. So after we sat down and talked for about ten minutes, I saw him relax, I relaxed and I realized we were going to have quite a journey."[4]

The 19-year-old model-turned-actress Candice Bergen was the neophyte of the group, with only one film under her belt: *The Group,* Sidney Lumet's period study of a private girls' school. However, that very innocence and inexperience was just what the part of missionary-to-be Shirley Eckert needed.

Bergen, like Attenborough, wondered how she ended up in such a prestige production. She recalled,

Robert Wise (left) chats with Steve McQueen (center) and Richard Attenborough during sequences aboard the *San Pablo*. (Courtesy of the Lee Pfeiffer Collection)

I was so naïve at the time and I had fallen into acting so quickly and precipitously. I had just been kicked out of college actually and I was studying the history of art and journalism and I hadn't had a chance to study acting.

I didn't know how to prepare for a role. I did some reading, whatever I could find about the time period, about missionaries in China. I really was an innocent and I suppose that came across.... It was only in later years that I came to appreciate not only the tremendous content and the depth of content in the story and film, but also Bob Wise's political commitment ... he is a man of such passionate beliefs, of such strong political principles. I don't think I appreciated the scope of the opportunity that was presented to me.[5]

Like John Sturges, Robert Wise had demonstrated in all of his films an ability to cast wonderful supporting actors that not only made the leads look good, but also gave the film an amazing tapestry of faces, body-types and personalities. *The Sand Pebbles* was no exception. To fill out the colorful cast of gunboat sailors, Wise picked such character legends as Simon Oakland (as beefy "Ski" Stawski), Ford Rainey (as foul-mouthed gunner's mate Harris), Joe Turkel (as Bronson), Joe Di Reda (as Shanahan), Gavin MacLeod (as Crosley), and Tom Middleton (as Jennings the medic). Middleton would simultaneously coach Richard Attenborough, helping him lose his British accent for the role of Frenchy.

And to play the pivotal role of bilge coolie, Po-han, Wise chose 31-year-old Japanese actor Mako, whose full name was Makoto Iwamatsu. Mako was known primarily as a television actor. Interestingly, he had worked in a Steve McQueen film before, taking a small uncredited role as a wounded soldier in John Sturges's *Never So Few.* The role of Po-han and his relationship with Jake Holman was a critical part of *The Sand Pebbles* and Mako rose to the occasion, eventually receiving an Oscar nomination (he would lose to Walter Matthau for *The Fortune Cookie*).

It is said that casting is 90 percent of a director's job. However, on *The Sand Pebbles,* the physical preparation for the epic film was enormous. Production designer Boris Leven, who had worked on both *West Side Story* and *The Sound of Music,* was brought in to recreate China, circa 1926. It was a tall order.

McKenna had set his story on the Yangtze backwaters of mainland China and the first thing Leven had to assemble were photographs of the period. Questions had to be answered. What did Changsha look like? How did people dress in 1926? What did an American gunboat look like? What was the terrain in Hunan Province? How did the Chien River look?

Some consideration was given to shooting *The Sand Pebbles* in the United States. As Wise told Y.C. Lee, who was freelancing for the *Los Angeles Times* that fall, "We could have built cities on the Sacramento River, but no one had a quick answer about obtaining 20 river junks, dozens of sampans and thousands of authentic Chinese extras. For some scenes, I needed a thousand and I doubt that even San Francisco could guarantee that many on any given day.

"Besides," he continued, "if you make a picture this costly and you don't have the feel of authenticity, you've lost."[6]

Once it was decided to shoot the film in Taiwan, locations matching the photographs had to be found. Production illustrator Maurice Zuberano then took those photographs and rendered scale drawings of each set as it would finally appear in the film.

Leven's biggest challenge was a character in itself—the USS *San Pablo.* U.S. Navy gunboats no longer existed in 1965, so Leven's challenging mission was to build the *San Pablo* from scratch.

The ship would be an exact duplicate of the old USS *Villa Lobos,* taken as booty from Spain after the Spanish American War. The *Villa Lobos* served in the Far East until 1929, when she was sunk as a target off the Philippines.

Due to the demands of the principal Taiwanese locations, namely the extremely shallow Keelung and Tam Sui rivers, the *San Pablo* had to be built with an equally extreme shallow draft. However, this same vessel had to be ocean-going, since it was decided that the end battle between the *San Pablo* and a line of junks blocking the Chien River, had to be filmed outside Hong Kong. The *San Pablo* would have to be towed across the often-treacherous Formosa Straits.

Leven teamed with naval architect David Logan of Long Beach, California, to design the 150-foot steel-hulled gunboat, which would be built by Vaughn & Jung Engineering, Ltd., of Hong Kong. Authentic fittings for her, long ago sold as antique pieces in maritime shops, had to be designed and cast. Her vintage guns — a workable three-inch gun on the bow and a one-pounder on the stern — had to be located; every detail of a Yangtze gunboat, within practical reason, had to be duplicated.

Steve McQueen takes time out to sign an autograph during the making of *The Sand Pebbles.* (Courtesy of the Lee Pfeiffer Collection)

Fortunately, nothing below decks had to be constructed — the crew's quarters, the engine room, the captain's cabin, were all film sets that would be constructed on soundstages at 20th Century–Fox. In actuality, the ship slept six, which was all the crew she needed in 1965. She was commanded by Captain Shih Hsien Miao, a graduate of the Chinese Naval Academy, who fled the communists in 1949 and served in high posts with the Nationalist Chinese Navy, retiring three months before shooting began on *The Sand Pebbles.*

Fully fitted, she cost $200,000. Her power source: twin Cummins diesel engines. However, she also ran a steam boiler, coal fired, which was used to belch smoke from the *San Pablo*'s faux stack and for summoning up live steam for such sequences as repelling boarders. The ship itself had but 30 inches of draft, enabling her to maneuver in the shallow Taiwanese river locations.

She may have been a Hollywood-engineered prop, but the *San Pablo* looked solid and amazingly realistic. A great deal of effort was made to keep her paint job appro-

Another star of *The Sand Pebbles:* the U.S. Navy gunboat *San Pablo*, built especially for the movie.

priate to the scene. Initially, she is a bright-white ship of the line, with swabbed decks and glistening brass fittings. President Calvin Coolidge would have been proud to ride in her. When she's trapped in Changsha harbor by a low winter tide and angry mobs, the *San Pablo* begins to decay, with her complexion turning from pristine white to rust streaked gray and brown.

One of the busiest crew members on *The Sand Pebbles* would be standby painter Joe Krutak. Because of extreme weather conditions in this part of the world, location filming was often determined at the last minute. It wasn't uncommon for Wise to shoot the *San Pablo* in the morning in her pristine white condition and then, due to a lack of sunshine, move to the dirty winter gunboat look for an afternoon shot. And that's what Krutak and his Chinese crew of seven painters did — they either slapped white paint on, or dirtied it up, sometimes within a few hours.

In order to make the engine room set at 20th Century–Fox look realistic, Leven bought a rundown steam engine in Northern California and had it carefully re-assembled on a soundstage. One of the special-effects technicians assigned to the film turned out to be a steam engineer who was able to get the plant up and running again. So even though it was a set, the engine was real, as was the sweat on Steve McQueen's brow.

In addition to the *San Pablo*, Leven had to assemble a fleet of period Chinese sampans, junks, and support craft that were constantly deployed in the background for various scenes. Hours were spent getting the various vessels in place, then keeping them there despite the demands of wind and current.

Unfortunately, Wise could not find everything he needed in Taiwan. It was thus determined that the crew would spend the first four months in Taiwan, then segue to Hong Kong, still independent in 1966, where the crew would shoot necessary exteriors. For instance, the scene where Mr. Bordelles (Charles Robinson) leads a squad of sailors through a downtown street while angry residents dump their breakfast on their heads was shot in an old section of Hong Kong. However, the crew would shoot the final battle against the Chien River junks along a river in the New Territories district of Hong Kong. Wise needed a river channel where both banks could be visible and he couldn't find that in Taiwan.

Weather and logistics were not the only challenges for Wise and his production team. They would be the first American crew to shoot on Taiwan, and it should not be forgotten that the island was, in 1965, literally at war with Mainland China. The entire island, which is only 240 miles long and 85 miles wide, was a virtual military base, with army trucks rumbling continually through the busy streets of Taipei and uniformed military personnel in sight everywhere.

Ten days prior to the start of production, a defecting communist pilot crash-landed a Russian-built IL28 jet bomber near Taipei. Nationalist Chinese gunboats fought a pitched battle in the Formosa Straits and then limped into Keelung victoriously. During filming, Nationalist Chinese frogmen were seen on maneuvers in the very river channels where Wise's team was working and Chinese gunboats kept a keen eye on the film production when it moved across the Formosa Strait to Hong Kong.

Interestingly, the first scene of the film was supposed to show Jake Holman leaving the battleship USS *Texas*, anchored in Shanghai harbor and motoring to the dock. Wise had located the vintage American battleship resting in anchorage in the Houston Ship Channel, and plans were made to film onboard the ship in April 1966, after the crew returned from the Far East. That location shooting with Steve McQueen took place, but the footage was eventually cut from the finished film.

The exodus to the Far East began on November 2, 1965, when a Pan American World Airways jet transported 166 actors, crew members and dependents to Taipei, Taiwan. Wise traveled with his associate producer and second-unit director, Charles Maguire.

Production on *The San Pebbles* began officially on the gloomy morning of November 22, 1965, exactly two years after Robert Wise and Robert Anderson had heard the terrible news about JFK's assassination. The location was the military port of Keelung, Taiwan, playing Shanghai, Mainland China, circa 1926.

Assistant director Robert Liu had helped assemble an enormous extra cast of 5,000 people who would be playing period citizens of Shanghai. Many of these extras were recent escapees from Mainland China, some of whom had lived in Shanghai. They were organized in groups of 10, 50 and 100, each group with its own leader, and they were told to bring their own wardrobe. Liu maintained contact with the various groups through walkie-talkie. In the harbor, the "Sand Pebbles navy" was deployed—14 big junks, four of which had been built from the keel up for the production, plus more than 100 sampans. This flotilla would be deployed again in the Changsha harbor sequences.

Actor Richard Crenna had just arrived on location when he observed the first days shooting at Keelung from a nearby rooftop: "Dickie [Attenborough] and I arrived on location together and we were able to observe that first day's shooting.... As far as you could see, Boris Leven had recreated Shanghai 1926, and it was just incredible and I looked at Dickie and said, 'Dickie, we are going to be in a movie!' And I'm standing there thinking that I'm going to be in a Robert Wise film."[7]

Although it is true of all of his films, Wise's military films always featured actors who gave their military characters an esprit de corps. In *The Desert Rats* (1953), for example, Richard Burton was utterly believable as a British officer commanding Australian troops fighting in the Libyan Desert of 1941. When a sandstorm provides cover for Rommel's tanks as they attack the Tobruk garrison, Wise puts you in the dirty foxholes and caves with these ragged, but tenacious fighters, waiting for waves of steely German infantry to follow the tanks. The battle has a documentary quality, especially when the sandstorm is over and full-fledged combat is waged all along the front. Wise keeps you close to the front lines, observing real men fighting a real war.

In *Destination Gobi* (1953), the tone may be less serious, but the realism never flags. This time, the viewer is with a group of young Navy weathermen, operating deep in Inner Mongolia under the watchful command of Chief Bosun's Mate Sam McHale (Richard Widmark). Inside their tents, these self-styled "balloon chasers" are not your typical salty sailor types. They correlate data, transmit their reports, gripe about the sizzling Mongolian sun and freezing night wind, praying for the moment their relief plane arrives and takes them out of this desert hell hole. Once again, Wise assembled a terrific team of character actors — Casey Adams, Don Taylor, Martin Milner, Earl Holliman, Ross Bagdasarian, Darryl Hickman — and he transforms them into seasoned Navy men who eventually cross half of Asia to get to the sea where they pilot a junk to Okinawa.

In *The Sand Pebbles,* Wise works on his biggest military canvas, aboard the biggest movie prop ever created and, once again, realism is the key. The Sand Pebbles of 1926 China not only looked good in their sterling white Navy uniforms, but they were entirely believable as the crew of a gunboat on the Yangtze. These weren't rock hard physical specimens from the Naval Academy. These are China sailors, a long way from Pearl Harbor. They're beefy, foulmouthed, quick-tempered and lazy, epitomized by actor Simon Oakland's flabby "Ski" Stawski, who eventually boxes Po-han in what appears to be a one-sided match, but turns into a surprise victory for the young bilge coolie.

When Jake Holman arrives on the *San Pablo,* he meets a group of salty China sailors who have been patrolling the Yangtze for years. They know every whorehouse and prostitute, every bar, every nuance of what appears to be a monotonous duty. They are a sloppy team, but a team nonetheless and Captain Collins keeps them in line to the best of his abilities. Robert Wise made sure that his actors were completely

Steve McQueen and Candice Bergen have lunch on the set of *The Sand Pebbles.* (Courtesy of the Lee Pfeiffer Collection)

comfortable and realistic in their uniforms and that they knew their action stations. When the *San Pablo* alarm bells go off, they know what to do.

Holman not only represented the antithesis of the *San Pablo* crew, but Steve McQueen brought a whole new level of attention to detail to his role. Ever since McQueen had first attracted the notice of moviegoers with the supporting role of resourceful Bill Ringa in John Sturges's *Never Say Few,* he had been perfecting a unique onscreen style that was less about dialogue and more about his physical reaction to people, places and things. As critics constantly observed, McQueen could say with a glance what other actors needed pages of dialogue to communicate.

Jake Holman may have been the most complicated character McQueen ever had to play on a location shoot; it was also the most grueling role he ever undertook. He spent seven months in the Far East, perfecting every detail of Holman. The result is his most enduring, multi-dimensional performance. The fact that it won him his only Oscar nomination is a fitting tribute, but, more importantly, it showed how his acting ability had matured.

As Attenborough recalled, "Steve was as good a screen actor as I have ever witnessed and I have worked with some wonderful ones. If Steve had lived I think he would have been comparable, maybe equal, to the greatest screen actor that America has produced, which is Spencer Tracy, and Steve could have been another Spence.

"Steve was a wonderfully butch character, which tended to make you think that he wasn't as bright. He was as bright as a cart load of monkeys. He was just terrific. The characters that he played he had to identify with, it was a prerequisite. If he couldn't identify with them, he had to believe absolutely in that man. He understood absolutely the difference between acting in the theater and acting in the cinema. Acting in the cinema was, in its own right, a unique and special art and Steve had it par excellence, and because he had such an available persona, he could put across, to an audience, emotions and feelings and thoughts which suspended their sense of disbelief ... he was totally acceptable."[8]

Richard Crenna added, "Watch Steve carry his sea bag up the gangplank to the *San Pablo.* The way he's carrying it, you know that guy has carried that gear a hundred times to a hundred ships in a hundred different ports in the world.

"Steve has never been better than he is in this film. You hear the comment 'born to play a role.' He was born to play this role. His use of props, his use of weapons, his use of the engine — the engine becomes an integral part of the story, the engine was a character and Steve plays with that character as if he's with another actor. He just brings such a realism to what he does. Young actors should sit and watch and see how Steve operates logistically as an actor. It's incredible.... He's always been a physical actor, his movement is very athletic, very sure, very strong. Even stationary, Steve is moving."[9]

The key to Steve's performance in *The Sand Pebbles* is his relationship with Mako's Po-han character. In the story, Jake Holman selects the bilge coolie to become the chief engine room coolie. It's not what he wants to do. He doesn't trust the Chinese because he doesn't think they're intelligent enough to learn about the engine. In McKenna's novel, his tirade against the whole coolie system on the *San Pablo* gets him in trouble with Captain Collins. In the film, Holman has one outburst in Collins's cabin before he's persuaded to train the young Chinese.

However, Po-han does begin to pick up the nuances of a steam engine and Holman marvels at how fast he learns — their relationship begins to warm and the hard shell that seems to surround Holman begins to soften. McQueen's ability to express himself with very few words, plus the absolute realism that Mako brought to his role, elevate the entire film. However, the rest of the Navy engine crew doesn't share in his camaraderie with Po-han, and when Stawski finds the coolie drinking coffee, he is incensed, slapping the coffee cup out of his hand. Holman punches Stawski in the stomach, an act that leads to a celebrated boxing match between Stawski and Po-han. The stakes: if Po-han wins, he can stay on the ship and be the chief engine coolie.

The boxing match was shot on a soundstage at Fox in July 1966, after the crew's return from the Far East. Mushy Callahan, the famed boxing consultant, who had worked with actor Montgomery Clift on the boxing sequences in *From Here to Eternity*, was brought in to choreograph the semi-comic bout between the overweight, beer-slugging Ski and the slight, inexperienced Po-han.

Remembered Mako, "Mushy Callahan was assigned to choreograph and he was hard of hearing, so he only hears what he wants to hear and he would say things like, 'I'm going to make you look like a real boxer.' After about a week of rehearsing with him, I kept saying to Mushy that this wasn't working. It finally took Mr. Wise to set him straight and we finally got it.... The only difference between the rehearsal and shooting was that in rehearsal our gloves were dry and during the course of shooting, we wetted the gloves, soaking them in water—so that when you swung it was as if you were making full contact and sweat would splatter. During the shooting, every time Mr. Wise would yell 'cut,' Simon [Oakland] would come over and say, 'Are you all right? I'm sorry, I'm sorry, I really didn't mean it. He was such a pussycat."[10]

Crenna points out how much surprising comedy pops up in this dramatic scene. "There is a comic element to it—Mako's reaction, the way he fights, his fear of the man who's pummeling him. And you can't help but smile. You just had to like Mako's character and you just hoped he'd hit this big bastard in the belly."[11] Wise understood the value of comedy in dramatic story telling—how it serviced the story, opened up scenes and made the dramatic elements that more powerful. It was a device he used in many films, particularly his war pictures (i.e., Casey Adams wooing of the Mongolian girl in *Destination Gobi*; Robert Newton's drunkenness in *The Desert Rats*; and the patting of the photograph of Betty Grable's derriere as the men go to battle stations in *Run Silent Run Deep*).

The warmth of the relationship between Steve McQueen's Jake and Mako's Po-han, and the comic relief present in the boxing scene, are stark contrasts to what happens to Po-han next. Called to shore, he's seen fleeing back to the *San Pablo*, chased by a horrifying mob of anti–Imperialist fanatics who are not only dead-set on torturing and killing Po-han, but daring the *San Pablo* to open fire to save him.

Filmed on the beach of Tam Sui, which was duplicating the village of Paoshan in the McKenna book, the sequence involved dramatizing "The Death of a Thousand Cuts" where a victim would be literally sliced to death in a slow torturous manner that is horrifying to watch. Wise liked Tam Sui because it had similarities to the river villages of Hunan Province where the sequence takes place in the book.

Mako described his assailants, "They weren't experienced extras so they were kind of running at half speed. So assistant director Reggie Callow offered a reward of $100 in local Taiwanese currency for the guy who caught me. So then they started chasing me and the street was rather muddy and it became difficult because in rehearsal I pulled my hamstring."[12]

It was also challenging to perform once he's strung up, "It's kind of hard to balance when your hands are tied in the back and there is no way to steady yourself once you're suspended."[13]

When I met Mako on the set of *Sidekicks*, a Chuck Norris family action film in 1992, he told me that the actor who was torturing him with a knife blade had a device in the hilt that projected a stream of blood every time he sliced.

Boxing specialist Mushy Callahan, seen here on the set of *From Here to Eternity* with actor Montgomery Clift (left), was later attached to *The Sand Pebbles* to work with actors Mako and Simon Oakland on their bout in the ring.

According to assistant director Robert Liu, "The guy who played the heavy was a very good friend of mine. I cast him after I read the script because I thought he would fit the appearance of the leader. He was actually a director and writer at Taiwan Film Studio, on their regular staff. They liked his appearance. His name was Wong Da Chuen."[14]

"It was a horrific scene to watch," relates Crenna. "And Steve does some of his best acting in the film, silently watching what's happening to his dear friend. What is amazing is the background actors in this film, how effective they are, how real it is. You look at that crowd, those are not actors, those are Taiwanese extras and what a job they do. This was a terrifying scene to experience."[15]

The sequence involving American sailors in a potential combat situation, who have their hands tied, until Jake Holman disobeys orders and shoots his friend, was a harbinger of what military confrontations in future foreign lands would be like. Long before *Platoon, Black Hawk Down* and *The Hurt Locker,* Robert Wise was showing us how the world was changing, how the rules of engagement for American military personnel were no longer so black and white.

Tam Sui village also filled in for Changsha on the mainland, one of the main ports of call for *San Pablo.* It was in Changsha where the sailors hang out at the Red Candle bar and brothel and where Po-han fights Ski Stawski; it's where Mr. Jameson and Shirley Eckert are dropped off at Nationalist Chinese headquarters and it's also where the *San Pablo* is quarantined after Frenchy dies of hypothermia, Maily is murdered by anti-imperialist fanatics and Jake Holman is accused of her death. The *San Pablo's* introductory shot at a military pier was shot at Eight-Foot Gate, a Taiwanese naval base near Keelung.

Weather continuously delayed production, but there were other logistical problems that put Wise's crew behind. Because the *San Pablo* only had a few inches of draft, she could float off her mark with ease. It was like trying to man a high-flying kite. Meanwhile, on the long daily drive to Tam Sui, Steve McQueen was busy destroying cars and causing havoc along the motorway. He was still himself.

Weekends were more relaxed. Wise invited cast and crew to a lunch buffet and a screening of dailies, which became a popular weekly ritual. Recalled Crenna, "At that time, they didn't have a sound system, so all we saw was a silent version of the film in the theater. It became a kind of contest among us to mouth our dialogue to the soundless film and it became kind of funny, because we would change dialogue to get a few laughs."[16]

The long shoot was beginning to get to many of the actors, especially young Candice Bergen: "I think I was in Taiwan for three months and I worked three or four weeks out of that time. We were all basically going nuts, so we would go on excursions in Taiwan. We'd go to the beach and suddenly we'd be surrounded by Chinese military personnel, guys with rifles, and all of the beaches were lined with bunkers as far as you could see because they were always waiting for Mainland China to attack. It was extremely clandestine and furtive in those days. We were staying in the Golden Compound at the Grand Hotel in Taipei. I was always on call so I had to stay in my room. It was pretty primitive in the days before CNN. I was so glad to get to Hong Kong, where we shot for a month. Mail took five weeks to arrive, phone calls were almost inaudible and extremely expensive, so you were basically incommunicado, eating sweet-and-sour soup every night."[17]

To pass the time, Bergen practiced her skills as a stills photographer. Actor Larry Gates, who was playing Mr. Jameson the missionary (Craddock in the book), hired a Mandarin teacher so that he could order in restaurants. Richard Attenborough was trying to put together financing on a film about Mahatma Gandhi, which would take him another 15 years to complete.

While traveling to Taiwan had been a logistical challenge, the move across the Formosa Straits to Hong Kong, in March 1966, was a potential political powder keg. Although still a British Crown Colony, Hong Kong was, nevertheless, next door to Communist China, which had a big problem with movie crews who were covering subject matter about Nationalist China, regardless of how long ago it had occurred. When Wise and Company finally did get their permission from the colony, there were ground rules:

1. No Nationalist "gear-wheel" flag was to enter the colony.
2. No Nationalist army uniform was to be permitted in the colony.
3. No press release announcing filming in the colony would be permitted.
4. In dealing with queries of the press, any sticky fielding question had to be relayed to British authorities.
5. Any incident of any nature involving the American personnel in anything political could cause cancellation of permits within two hours.

As PR representative Tsai Chien reported from Kowloon, reminders of Mao's presence in the colony were everywhere. Communist junks from Canton plodded by the gunboat *San Pablo* on their way to the Victoria docks with fresh fruits and vegetables. Another time, burlap sandbags were ordered for a barricading scene on the bridge of the *San Pablo*. Crew personnel discovered that each bag had been prominently labeled, "Made in People's Republic of China." Fortunately, they were discovered in time and painted over.

Chien also reported that when it came time to make a high shot from a waterfront building on the Kowloon side, it was ascertained that the ideal platform was a rooftop owned by the head of Hong Kong's communist party. It was predicted he would not truck with the Hollywood barbarians. However, it was soon found that as much as he hated American capitalists, he liked their green money, and the shooting platform was secured.

It wasn't until April 24 that the colony's leading communist newspaper attacked Wise as an "Imperialist American Provocateur." In a two-part article, the paper stated that Wise was making the film to further aggression in Vietnam and also to justify American aggression in China during the twenties and thirties. Considering that Robert Anderson's script was based on a book written before most people had ever heard of Vietnam, the former charges were considered ridiculous. As for the latter, anyone who had bothered to crack open McKenna's tome should have realized that, if anything, the book was more sympathetic to the plight of the Chinese than the salacious gunboat sailors who patrolled her inner waterways.

The most logistically complex sequence in the movie, and its biggest set piece, is the furious and bloody battle between the American gunboat sailors of the *San Pablo* and the young Nationalists who man the Chien River junk blockade. Stretched from shore to shore, it's a formidable obstacle to the *San Pablo*'s mission to rescue the missionaries up river at China Light. Some 14 junks, spaced 100 feet apart, are connected by a two-foot bamboo rope — the boom —1,000 feet in length and shackled to the prows of the junk armada. A significant number of anti-foreign Nationalists man the junks which are equipped with obsolete cannons and rifles.

The sequence required the *San Pablo* to sail up the Chien River and attack the blockade, land two boarding parties on the main junk and break the bamboo rope boom with an axe. Who would be manning that axe? Who do you think? During the course of his work to break the boom, Jake Holman is jumped by Cho-jen, Shirley Eckert's young student leader from China Light, and Jake kills him with an axe thrust to the belly. Like the death of Po-han, it's another traumatizing moment for Holman.

The Chien River battle sequences were shot at Three Fathom Cove, on the Kowloon side of the crown colony and in a broad expanse of water that flanks Tai Yu Shan Island. The *San Pablo* would sail up Tolo Channel, in New Territories waters, some ten miles from the Communist Chinese border.

Once again, weather bedeviled the Wise production crew. Boris Leven's art department had just assembled the junk blockade when the first hurricane of the season struck Kowloon and wiped out the whole set, turning Leven's armada of junks into, well, a bunch of junk.

Once the debris was cleared and the junk blockade restaged, Wise carefully rehearsed a choreographed movement that would bring the gunboat sailors into action, led by Captain Collins.

Remembered Richard Crenna, "For my boarding sequence, Wise asked me to jump onto one of the junks and I said, 'No problem.' My stunt double, Ben Wilder, asked me if he could try it first and I said, 'No, I'll do it.' But he insisted, and, finally, I said, 'Fine.' Well, Wilder tried it and he jumped right through the deck of the junk. Fortunately, he didn't get hurt. If it had been me, I probably would have broken my leg."[18] Wilder looked at Crenna and reminded him why stunt doubles were there. Crenna wholeheartedly agreed.

This sea battle was not only a key action sequence in *The Sand Pebbles,* it also showed that, however ragged, dirty and slothful the crew of the *San Pablo* had become, they were ready to unite, perform their duty and prove their worth as gunboat sailors. Once again, director Robert Wise was able to show his skill in planning and shooting realistic military action sequences.

Up until now, we have not seen the combat fighting ability of the gunboat sailors. The rules of engagement in the Far East had changed and they were spending more time eyeballing the enemy than fighting with them. Welcome to a new kind of warfare. But the Chien River engagement changes all that. In a bloody hand-to-hand battle, the gunboat sailors of the *San Pablo,* storm aboard the lead junk, rout the defenders, taking heavy casualties, and Jake breaks the boom with his trusty axe. He also demonstrates considerable skill with the new Browning Automatic rifle (B.A.R.), which he will use later at China Light.

McQueen is pure McQueen in this sequence. He's the guy you want handling the B.A.R. and the way McQueen uses the heavy assault weapon makes you believe that he's been firing that gun all his life. McQueen had always been skilled with weapons, going back to the sawed-off Mare's Leg in *Wanted: Dead or Alive,* his six-shooters in *The Magnificent Seven,* and the grease gun in *Hell Is for Heroes.* He doesn't disappoint with the B.A.R.

First-unit principal photography was completed in the Far East on May 15, 1966, a total of six months and one week on location. A second-unit crew would continue to get additional shots while the main crew segued to California, where Boris Leven had built China Light monastery on the Fox Ranch in Malibu. Much more stylized than Richard McKenna's nondescript portrait from the book, China Light's walled monastery becomes downright mysterious at night, especially when Jake Holman and his small landing crew are forced to defend themselves against Nationalist sharpshooters.

Although Wise loved Jerry Goldsmith's musical scoring work on *The Sand Pebbles,* it was decided to use very little or no music for the film's climax. The result is enormously suspenseful, with heavy emphasis placed on the sound effects of B.A.R. and rifle fire and the frightening repartee between the Nationalist militiamen.

After the amazing production values of the assault on the Chien River junk blockade, the final battle at China Light is much more minimalist, but equally effective. Who can forget McQueen, now alone, facing an unknown number of unseen enemies, repeating what his Captain had tried, calling to fellow sailors who aren't really there, talking to himself and trying to make it seem like there are plenty of good guys available.

After work was finished on the monastery set, Wise would continue to work on the Fox lot where almost every interior was built on several sound stages. On June 18, 1966, he would take a crew to Texas to film McQueen departing the deck of the battleship USS *Texas.* Why Wise decided to eliminate the shots of the *Texas* we will never know.

The Sand Pebbles was the most honored film of Steve McQueen's career, receiving eight

Oscar nominations. Although it lost in all eight categories, including Best Picture to *A Man for All Seasons* (that film's Paul Scofield had bested McQueen for Best Actor), it has become a timeless classic that seems to mirror the events of every succeeding decade. Richard McKenna had written a book that had introduced readers to a new China and a new breed of American warrior. Robert Wise's magnificent film brought them to life and Steve McQueen gave us an unforgettable portrait of a good man, defending his country's flag at all costs.

CHAPTER TEN

Patton

I want you to remember that no bastard ever won a war by dying for his country. He won it by making the other poor dumb bastard die for his country!—Actor George C. Scott as Patton (1970)

To say that George C. Scott's opening speech in the 1970 film *Patton* was outrageous would be one of the great understatements in film history. It was writer Francis Ford Coppola's idea to let Patton speak in the vernacular of the day, all expletives intact. And, in a way, such frank discourse put the final nail in the coffin of the long war against a prohibitive censorship code that forbade men of war to speak realistically. Such an unorthodox approach to a complex character won Coppola and Edmund H. North an Oscar for Best Screenplay that year, and launched a film that became a true phenomenon. Patton's speech was merely the introduction to a complex character study.

Draped behind the imposing figure of Scott's Patton was a giant replica of the Stars and Stripes. The American general was exquisitely manicured, down to the shine on his ivory-handled revolvers, and his profanities, delivered in a raspy tirade, instead of being an affront, demonstrated, instead, the general's overall sense of command and his supreme confidence. It was all a carefully planned pep talk that inspired everyone who heard it — the soldiers who heard it back in 1942, and the moviegoers who were stunned by its impact some 28 years later.

In 1970, at the height of the Vietnam War, at a time when militarism was the dirtiest of all possible words, when the government of the United States and the Pentagon were the targets of a great swell of organized, outspoken and frequently violent anti-war criticism from all levels of society, when the motion picture industry practically shunned all World War II combat films as unmarketable, 20th Century–Fox, the studio that had once gambled its reserves on Darryl F. Zanuck's *The Longest Day*, gambled another $12 million on a mammoth screen dramatization of one of World War II's most controversial field commanders.

And, yet, was it really a gamble at all? In 1948, MGM executive Dore Schary had defended his studio's film, *Battleground*, by maintaining that story and not topic was the deciding factor. Some 20 years later, Fox producer Frank McCarthy voiced similar sentiments. He had a screenplay that could surmount the enormous wave of anti-militarism and unite a divided audience in a fascinating character experience. He also had George C. Scott, perhaps America's finest actor.

There was nothing typical about *Patton*: The movie, or the man. Like his nemesis in the

171

Tunisian Desert, Rommel "The Desert Fox," Patton was a fighting general, a master of move-ment and audacity. He was also a competent poet, a vivid writer, a student of history, a very religious man and someone who believed strongly in reincarnation. Thus, he was a veritable treasure trove for any competent writer.

The film begins shortly after the American landings in North Africa in November 1942 and ends shortly before Patton's death in an automobile accident in Germany in December 1945. A triumph of historical drama and objectivity, *Patton* presented a tapestry of moods, emotions and visions of war, as seen through the general's eyes — a portrait that allowed the audience to form its own judgment of the character's actions.

Thus, *Patton* became a mirror through which warring doves and hawks viewed the confir-mation of their own deeply emotional beliefs. To the former, General Patton was the anti–Christ, who symbolized the reckless and irresponsible brand of militarism that had led to the debacle in Vietnam. And yet, as an audience, they found it difficult to criticize a film that was so overtly honest. It would be the key to the film's success, for there was no need to embellish or disparage the character of Patton; the paradox of his makeup was obvious from the beginning.

To the hawks, *Patton* offered a nostalgic look at a simpler time, a period when superheroes were also super patriots, and when victory was made possible through decisive military action. With his earthy vocabulary, dashing leadership, and unorthodox tactics, Patton personified to them a man of action, the absence of which was a major factor in Vietnam. In essence, he symbolized their impossible dream. At the same time, they could not deny the offensiveness of the man's attitude towards subordinate officers, his lack of sympathy for soldiers who couldn't handle the pressures of combat, and his pompous demand for military protocol and correctness, even on the front lines.

While the film pleased ideological extremists, it also appealed to the discriminating viewer who was seeking entertainment. As Patton, actor George C. Scott met their equally demanding standards magnificently, and despite the grandeur of the production, they never lost sight of the principal focus.

A product of the new generation of actors that had followed the Golden Age class of Spencer Tracy, Laurence Olivier, Fredric March, Clark Gable and Jimmy Stewart, Scott influenced every scene and every action. He was well suited to the demanding role, for he lacked the stigma of superstardom, an established image that might have neutralized the effec-tiveness of his characterization. For instance, picture John Wayne or Robert Mitchum in the lead role — and they had been considered. Somehow, those actors would have brought a little too much Wayne or Mitchum to the role. *Patton* needed the modern-actor equivalent of a chameleon — Scott fit the bill perfectly and, throughout the film, he remained the complex historical figure, faithfully depicting every mannerism and every insult.

Darryl F. Zanuck was the patriarchal war horse at 20th Century–Fox. Now chairman of the board, he persuaded his fellow board members and his son, Richard (Fox's head of pro-duction) that producer Frank McCarthy's *Patton* project was a good bet. With pleasant mem-ories of *The Longest Day* and his talent for organization, Zanuck Sr. began to lay the groundwork for potential military cooperation from the Pentagon.

It was retired Brigadier General Frank McCarthy's memo to Darryl Zanuck, dated Octo-ber 23, 1951, that originally initiated the idea of a film about America's colorful wartime hero. Such a project was made possible by the death of General Patton's widow, a woman who had vehemently opposed a film dramatization of her husband's life.

In 1951, McCarthy urged his superior to consider the *Patton* project and all its apparent possibilities. But, for 13 years, he was denied Pentagon assistance because two of Patton's children were in, or were directly tied to the service (Patton's son was an Army officer and his daughter was married to a soldier).

"And then," relates McCarthy, "after many years, it occurred to me that we might make the picture in Spain. At the end of World War II, we needed airfields in the Mediterranean, and the Spaniards, with a very poorly equipped army, decided to trade us the airfields we needed for surplus military hardware.

"They got tanks, aircraft, modes of transportation, rifles and artillery. Spain remained poor and they were unable to replace the surplus material with more modern equipment. By 1969, when we went on location for *Patton*, the Spaniards still had everything and we were able to rent their entire army for the film."[1]

Both former Signal Corps Colonel Darryl Zanuck and retired General McCarthy were fascinated by the project's creative potential, and they were able to transfer their enthusiasm to the rest of the 20th Century–Fox board. Fox was in much better straits than it had been in the early 1960s. Films like *The Sound of Music* and *Planet of the Apes* had seen to that. Given such a secure foundation, the Fox executives were willing to invest $12 million in *Patton*.

The iconic image from *Patton*: George C. Scott as General George S. Patton, Jr., addressing the troops.

Zanuck spelled out his feeling for Patton in a detailed memorandum to his son in February 1966: "Personally, I look upon him as a great man. I think he was correct in kicking his soldiers in the ass. I think he was right in wanting to use ex-Nazis as German administrators in Bavaria. I am not sure if he was entirely wrong about taking on the Russians at the River Elbe. I admire him and believe, most instances, that he was absolutely right. I wonder, however, especially in these times, if American audiences will understand or appreciate him as much as I do. Perhaps this will provide the controversy we want in the picture."[2]

Producer Frank McCarthy was also convinced that an honest character study could transcend the film's obvious military setting: "Darryl and I believed that this was to be a story of a man of World War II. It didn't relate whatsoever to Vietnam. We were dealing with history and to many of today's young people, World War II is ancient history, just as the Civil War was remote to me when I was a youngster, growing up with two grandfathers who had fought for the Confederacy."[3]

Gut-level enthusiasm and passion aside, it was young Francis Ford Coppola's intriguing first draft screenplay that convinced everyone, including actor George C. Scott, that *Patton* was a movie. Only 26 at the time, Coppola was something of phenomenon in Hollywood. The son of a classical flautist, Coppola was born in Detroit, Michigan, on April 7, 1939. He was barely five when Patton's Third Army crossed France and raced for the German border.

At eight, Coppola was already tinkering with the family's 8mm projector, and, two years later, during a painful bout with polio, he fitted homemade soundtracks to silent 16mm films. Later, at Hofstra University on Long Island, New York, he wrote and directed several musicals, and in 1962, at UCLA, won the Samuel Goldwyn Award for a hastily written screenplay.

In 1964, the shrewd, bearded filmmaker was already a veteran of the Hollywood wars. Fighting his battles in the cutting room while fellow film students debated Eisenstein and Renoir, Coppola was already writing and selling screenplays to Warner Bros. (11 in two years) when he was assigned to his first military project, the film dramatization of the Larry Collins/Dominique LaPierre novel, *Is Paris Burning?*— a baptism of fire which became a political nightmare.

Assigned to adapt and dramatize a fascinating leftist uprising against the retreating Nazis in Occupied Paris, Coppola was instead restrained by a series of political maneuvers, which eventually diluted the entire impact of the story. The months spent in Paris with co-writer Gore Vidal, director René Clement and two French writers, were enlightening, if nothing else.

Although the crux of the story was the uneasy alliance between the Gaullist and communist factions for control of the city, the writers weren't allowed to mention the communists or use their names. The regime of Charles de Gaulle didn't acknowledge their existence then or now. Without the ability to draw on the actual historical facts, especially the critical involvement of the communists, Coppola wasn't sure the movie would work.

Convinced by Vidal that they could overcome their difficulties, Coppola controlled his frustration, finished the script and happily left Paris. Despite location shooting and an all-star international cast (that included Kirk Douglas as General Patton), *Is Paris Burning?* became one of the most disappointing films of 1966.

Young Coppola's film savvy impressed Frank McCarthy, who was searching for a young, disciplined writer who would bring no preconceived ideas to the *Patton* project. The producer desired such a scribe to dive into his painstakingly assembled research materials and surface with an entirely fresh perspective. Ironically, Coppola's problems on *Is Paris Burning?* not only won him the *Patton* project, but they prepared him for the political demands of the new script. Politics and creativity are strange bedfellows in the motion picture business, and Coppola suffered through enough sleepless Parisian nights to understand the complex tightrope he would soon walk at Fox.

On a cool, clear spring morning in 1965, Coppola arrived at General McCarthy's campaign tent (actually an air-conditioned office on the Fox lot) and was issued his field equipment. Assigned to him were no less than 12 biographies of Patton, including the most comprehensive, author Ladislas Farago's *Ordeal and Triumph*, which the studio had just purchased. He also received a packet of research materials prepared by Robert S. Allen, a syndicated columnist who had served with the intelligence section of Patton's Third Army.

Patton (George C. Scott) at the map. The actor's transformation into the general was uncanny.

On that very first night, Coppola conceived of the film's opening scene, the long illuminating monologue sequence before the giant American flag. Coppola was experienced enough to realize that a film of this nature needed an opening of sheer shock value, evocative of the film's unique tone. Coppola believed that Patton was at his most colorful while addressing the men under his command. He became their military leader, their father, their priest and their God. He believed strongly in a no-holds-barred, gut-level appeal to his men on the eve of battle.

Patton cursed, joked, related anecdotes of courage and impressed his men with a strong fighting resolve. Their immediate superiors enlightened them as to the "where" and "when," Patton instructed them in the more important "why." Like Attila the Hun, Patton appeared above them on a raised platform as their "scourge of God," and still his speeches were warmly appreciated. The men of the U.S. Third Army believed that they were the finest combat troops in the world. It was this type of indoctrination that would contribute to their spectacular success in battle.

Coppola also felt that it was important to create the proper setting for the speech. He formulated the paradox of having a vast American flag draped behind the General, and Patton would appear in his dressiest garb. The monologue would set the tone for the entire film. The speech itself was completely authentic, much of it drawn from the general's wartime speeches. Coppola searched for revealing phrases and profanity was included indiscriminately. As far as Coppola was concerned, it was the age of the new morality and soldiers were able to speak naturally for the first time.

> Now, an army is a team. It lives, eats, sleeps and fights like a team. The bilious bastards who wrote that stuff about individuality for the *Saturday Evening Post* don't know any more about real battle than they do about fornicating![4]

George S. Patton, Jr., was at his most colorful when revealing his basic military strategy and his obsession with movement. More than any other General in history, Patton symbolized the birth of armored warfare and the death of static defense.

> I don't want to get any messages saying, "We are holding our position." We're not holding anything. Let the Hun do that. We are advancing constantly and are not interested in holding onto anything except the enemy. We're going to hold onto him by the nose and kick him in the ass We'll kick the hell out of him all the time and we'll go through him like crap through a goose![5]

Patton always concluded his speeches with a special brand of poignancy, which Coppola preserved:

> There's one thing you men will be able to say when you get home and you may all thank God for it. Thirty years from now when you are sitting around the fireside with your grandson on your knee and he asks what you did in the great World War II, you won't have to say, "Well, I shoveled shit in Louisiana."[6]

Director George Seaton, who was present at the film's 1970 premiere, recalled the audience's reaction to the opening prologue: "There were hisses and boos when the curtain went up and everyone saw the American flag draped cross the entire screen. But this attitude was slowly altered by the texture and candor of the speech, until, at the very end, the 'shoveling shit in Louisiana' line broke up the entire audience. Everyone laughed, and it was a wonderful touch that gave the film an immediate anti-war feeling."[7]

In his first draft screenplay, Coppola revealed General Patton's vision of himself as a reincarnated warrior, the classic military leader destined to lead the Allied armies to victory against the Hun. As such, he saw war, battle and death in the classical sense. To convert this vision to the screen, Coppola frequently prefaced many of his scenes with descriptive phrases that would aid both the director and the cinematographer in deciding what technical effects they could use to dramatize Patton's moody concept of war. It was the incubating director side of Coppola coming out — he was still about six years away from directing *The Godfather*.

For example, before the Battle of El Guettar, where Patton's II Corps defeated Rommel's 10th Panzer Division, Coppola wrote, "The Sun begins its roast of the desert sand. The music is dissonant and ancient as though the battlefield is strangely eternal."[8]

Coppola was also deeply aware of symbolism and how it could reveal Patton's inner character. He reasoned that careful attention should be paid to the general's appearance and that every mannerism should be carefully used by the actor playing the role.

Coppola's 202-page first draft roughly follows the Farago book, covering the general's involvement in World War II, without going into his life before the war. Much of the dramatic conflict in the screenplay is provided by the relationship between Patton and his subordinate in North Africa, and later superior in Western Europe, General Omar Bradley. Remarked McCarthy in a story conference with Coppola, "The steadfastness, sanity and calm of Bradley accentuates the flamboyance and rashness of Patton, although we do not lose sight of the fact that both men are magnificent soldiers. The more we strengthen Bradley, the better will be the contrast between the two."[9]

Like the Harvey Stovall character in *Twelve O'Clock High*, we see much of the action in *Patton* over Bradley's shoulders. This is a war of movement, grand decisions, high-level strategy and personality clashes. Battle is seen, once again, from a distance.

Coppola added another perspective on his own by creating scenes behind German lines at the Reichschancellory in Berlin, where the enemy's reaction to Patton's success is gauged. General Alfred Jodl assigns Captain Steiger, a former professor of literature, to compile a complete dossier on Patton, and it is through such a device that we learn additional factors about Patton before the war. His functional belief that the lessons of history needed to be learned and re-learned leads Steiger to believe that Patton will follow the Athenian example and invade Sicily after his success in North Africa.

Despite his script's unusual format and brilliant pace, Coppola's first draft lacked a certain cohesiveness. In McCarthy's words, "it was like having a handful of pearls and no string.[10]

Coppola turned in his first draft on New Year's Eve 1965, and, with a new bankroll, began preparing two new films. One of them, *You're a Big Boy Now*, was to become his master's thesis at UCLA.

While telegrams sailed back and forth between McCarthy and the Zanucks, appraising the script, preparing for the film's military cooperation and gauging the cost of the Spanish Army, a director was sought to take over the production. Everyone's first choice was William Wyler, a good friend of McCarthy.

Unfortunately, Wyler disliked the Coppola script. He failed to see the writer's objective viewpoint. And Wyler, who was forever making profound and deeply significant motion pictures, desired a more concrete approach to the mysterious Patton. Coppola had developed the general through his wartime experiences, which provided a structured plot. Wyler was far more interested in the general's background and the factors that contributed to his unusual behavior.

In the early spring of 1966, Wyler confronted producer Frank McCarthy: "Frank, we ought to start over and get Jim Webb to do the script. He was with Patton in North Africa. I know he'll do a wonderful job."[11]

It was literally the last thing that McCarthy wanted to hear and the producer objected. Plans were already being finalized to shoot the film in Spain that summer. To junk Coppola's unpolished screenplay and begin anew was madness, so Wyler backed out and McCarthy tried to interest another director, a difficult chore because the Zanucks were obviously looking for a good investment. Between prior commitments, executive preference and just plain apathy towards the material, McCarthy could find no one.

While correspondence with the Spanish military resumed, the shooting date was postponed. Since everyone respected Wyler's creative savvy and alternates were definitely lacking, Richard Zanuck gave McCarthy the authority to assign Webb to the project.

Webb, who wrote *Pork Chop Hill* in 1959, was still the preeminent history specialist in Hollywood, having won the Oscar for screenwriting in 1962 for *How the West Was Won*. The *Patton* project was also a natural for him. First Lieutenant James Ruffin Webb was attached to II Corps in North Africa when George Patton replaced General Lloyd R. Fredendall after the disastrous Battle of the Kasserine Pass. Throughout the remainder of the North African campaign, Webb observed the colorful Patton in his native habitat. Webb knew Patton, a fact that convinced Wyler that he was the perfect writer for the project. Webb had also co-written Wyler's 1958 western, *The Big Country*.

A stickler for detail and accuracy, Webb began researching anew and it was not until the winter of 1966-67 that he was ready to begin a script. Meanwhile, McCarthy had secured the help of Omar Bradley, who agreed to read and annotate the final screenplay.

Webb's script also begins in North Africa in 1942, but during the course of the story, it flashes back to the general's life before the war. Preliminary scenes showed Patton with General Pershing in Mexico, chasing Pancho Villa; playing polo in Hawaii to the consternation of General Drum; demonstrating armored tactics and equipment during the Louisiana maneuvers of 1941; and much of his early life as a young aristocrat growing up in Pasadena, California.

Webb also treated Patton's campaigns in a more detailed and historical manner. He discussed behind-the-scenes strategy, and many of the scenes were portrayed as if taken right out of the official campaign summaries. Dealing historically with a topic that held a special appeal for him, Webb's final script was a cohesive tribute to the wayward life of Patton. But, as McCarthy soon put it, "It was a beautifully structured script, but the pearls had disappeared and now I had the string."[12]

At a time when even the most controversial stratagem lacked any intrinsic fascination, Webb had concentrated on the general's battlefield savvy, failing to emphasize the unique mystery of the reincarnate. Still, Wyler was happy with the script, as it delved expertly into the general's background. On this basis, McCarthy began searching for an actor to play Patton. In one of the most frustrating casting searches in film history, he was turned down by almost every major actor in Hollywood. Even George C. Scott, who had been interested in the project from the beginning, declined the offer based on the new Webb script.

"Most of the actors," recalled McCarthy, "were simply afraid of the Webb script, because they thought it was too much of a glorification. I was afraid of this, but I was also convinced that Wyler could turn such interesting material into a beautiful film."[13]

Further complicating George C. Scott's interest in the project was Wyler himself, who had recently fired him off the set of *How to Steal a Million*. In the spring of 1968, Wyler announced

General Patton (George C. Scott, left) nods to local Tunisian children as he arrives to take over II Corps in North Africa. An aide, Captain Jensen (Morgan Paul), follows.

his own departure. Partially deaf and no longer at his physical peak, he was now convinced that the rigors of filming outdoors in a multiplicity of Spanish locations and climates would prove too arduous. It was a difficult decision because Wyler was quite taken with the subject.

McCarthy felt beaten. After three years of concentrated effort, he possessed two unworkable scripts, no director and no star. It appeared as if George Patton had lost his greatest battle. There were, fortunately, other good forces at work. On June 12, 1968, Fox producer David Brown was lunching in New York when he was approached by George C. Scott's agent, Jane Deacy. Brown expressed regret over Wyler's departure form the *Patton* project, which prompted her to say that Scott was still interested in the project if McCarthy would return to the original Coppola material.

Brown cabled McCarthy that very same day. Jolted into action, the producer signed Scott with assurances, dusted off the Coppola script and called in veteran writer Edmund H. North (*The Day the Earth Stood Still*) to string the pearls.

With General Bradley operating as a mine of information, North, who later shared Academy Award credit with Coppola (a man he never met), tightened the script, adding anecdotes, some of which were supplied by Patton's daughter. Building the Bradley character into an important counterforce prompted the studio to purchase the general's autobiography, *A Soldier's Story*.

An expert constructionist, North had dealt with complex military strategy in 1959 on *Sink the Bismarck*, another Fox project. As North worked diligently on the final draft, McCarthy searched once more for a director who, like Coppola, could approach the subject objectively, but with a firm hand.

At that time, the 20th Century–Fox lot was teeming with characters from an ambitious new science-fiction film based on French author Pierre Boulle's novel, *Planet of the Apes*. Directing the army of simian soldiers was Franklin Schaffner. McCarthy knew Schaffner's work and was impressed with the realistic medieval battle scenes he had filmed for *The War Lord* three years earlier.

No mere director of movement, Schaffner had an experienced eye for performance, culled from years of work in live television in New York. In 1964, the year of the political thriller, he had directed the film adaptation of Gore Vidal's play, *The Best Man*, a fascinating study of political intrigue during a presidential convention which starred Henry Fonda and Cliff Robertson. In later films such as *Papillon, Islands in the Stream* and *The Boys from Brazil*, Schaffner would demonstrate his adeptness at filling the screen with sweeping adventure and three-dimensional characters. He was a new breed of director.

Franklin Schaffner, fresh from helming *Planet of the Apes*, was given the job of directing *Patton*. He replaced William Wyler, who originally developed the project with producer Frank McCarthy.

Impressed with his vitality and versatility, McCarthy signed Schaffner to direct *Patton*. It was a bold and decisive move that eventually

George C. Scott with his family on location in Spain for *Patton*.

paid off handsomely. Schaffner took to battle sequences naturally, and with his mind a constant maze of logistics, he would be at home in Spain during the spring of 1969. From the snows of Segovia, which was simulating snowy Bastogne during the Battle of the Bulge, to the sand and scrub of Almeria, which was playing the sandy wastes of Tunisia, Schaffner and his ace cinematographer, Fred Koenekamp, created the perfect tapestry of moods, visions and actions.

The hour is late, the house is silent, except for one room where the steady clickety-click of a motion picture projector can be heard. Surrounded by empty beer cans, his head resting against a sofa, his knees drawn up to his chest, George C. Scott watches a silent film intently. Piled beside him is a stack of archaic film canisters with official U.S. Army titles. As one reel is completed, he replaces it with another. The projector once more clicks to life as the titles appear on screen — "Patton arrives in Sicily."

Scott watches a landing craft approach a beach. The ramp comes down and General George S. Patton, Jr., steps triumphantly onto Sicilian soil. Scott studies Patton, alert for the characteristic mannerisms, the general's walk, his posture, his facial expressions, the cut of his uniform, the reaction of his subordinates. Nothing escapes his trained eye. Having studied this man constantly for six months, preparing himself mentally for all of the general's complexities, Scott is now undergoing phase two of this indoctrination — the physical transformation.

In later interviews, Scott pointed out that one of the keys to bringing Patton to life was

George C. Scott on the set. He would win the Oscar for Best Actor of 1970, but he declined the award.

imitating his carriage. In watching all of the available documentary footage on the general, he never saw him slouch or appear as less than an erect human being. Scott was convinced that Patton slept straight and never adopted a fetal position, even as a child. His research further revealed that the general was a publicly emotional person who would cry at the sight of green grass. His emotions were always close to the surface.

The documentary film continues as Patton greets his victorious II Corps commanders and strides towards a jeep that will take him farther inland. Despite his fatigue, Scott's eyes never falter. It is 1969. Some 24 years have passed since the end of World War II. But the fascination has not withered. In the living room of a Beverly Hills mansion, the final synthesis of a great American war story is being nurtured over warm beer.

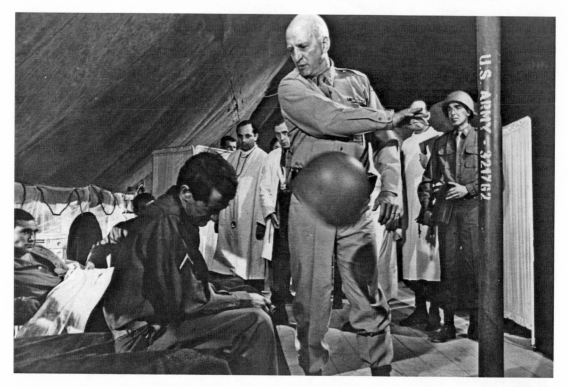

The slap heard around the world: General Patton's (George C. Scott) indiscretion against a nerve-wracked soldier in Sicily (Tim Considine) probably cost him command of U.S. Forces in Italy.

It is May Day in Madrid. *Patton* is nearly finished. There is only one more scene to be shot. On the northern wall of a vast soundstage, a huge American flag has been professionally tacked. Fred Koenekamp expertly places his cameras and the crew waits expectantly for the "General." At precisely 12:00 noon, George C. Scott strides up to the platform.

With his hair close cropped and dyed white, his nose reshaped and his jaw lengthened, he has become Patton, a perfect replica created out of the magic kit of the makeup and wardrobe departments. But the transformation is more than physical.

Scott walks steadily and erect, his chest thrown out, his head upright, his eyes on fire. In a raspy voice he informs Schaffner that he is ready. The lights dim and the camera sweeps the stage. McCarthy, who is standing next to Schaffner, whispers his approval.

For a moment, Scott stands quietly, majestically, soaking in the mood of the moment. Absolute stillness prevails over the large stage as he begins to speak. As the crew listens and watches in fascination, Scott disappears and Patton emerges. The general has reincarnated.

The speech is given in one flawless take and Schaffner yells, "Cut!" Magic lingers for another moment before the crew breaks into spontaneous applause. Scott smiles, acknowledges their plaudits with a polite nod and walks off the set.

When it was released in the spring of 1970, *Patton* succeeded in uniting a badly fragmented audience, one disgusted with the debacle of Vietnam. Hawks and Doves alike embraced Scott's marvelous performance, also giving high marks to the script by Coppola and North, as well as Schaffner's ability to fill the frame simultaneously with spectacle as well as intimacy.

The critical and commercial success of the film proved that the fascination with World War II, with its characters, battles, atmosphere, courage and clarity of purpose, was far from over.

CHAPTER ELEVEN

Platoon

The release of *Patton* in 1970 was a huge success for 20th Century–Fox, but, in terms of the popularity and viability of war films, it was an exception. America was now embroiled in the fifth year of the war in Vietnam, and the protests against that war were becoming increasingly violent. This was the year of the shootings at Kent State and college campuses were at their boiling point everywhere. On the one hand, President Richard Nixon was telling the nation that he wanted to end the war; on the other, he was sending combat troops into Cambodia.

How was Hollywood treating the war? Two years earlier, an aging John Wayne had starred in *The Green Berets*, a formulaic, rabidly pro–American-involvement film that played like a 1950s war picture cliché. But, for the most part, the studios steered clear of Vietnam. Even an enormously popular service comedy like *M*A*S*H*, avoided the war, and set its story 20 years earlier, in Korea.

When America finally withdrew from Southeast Asia and peace was declared in 1973, filmmakers began to consider Vietnam War projects, but studios were either loath to greenlight them, or they slowed down the development process to a crawl. America needed time to heal, and Hollywood wasn't in a hurry to stir the painful pot of a polarized America. However, major filmmakers with clout were already at work on seminal, albeit fanciful, depictions of the Vietnam cauldron of war.

Fresh from the enormous success of *The Godfather* (1972) and *The Godfather Part II* (1974), Francis Ford Coppola was developing *Apocalypse Now*, an enormous, yet fictionalized, Vietnam epic inspired by Joseph Conrad's book, *Heart of Darkness*. Although shot in 1976, the film wasn't released until 1979, and was more a filmmaker's fanciful take on Vietnam rather than anything related to history. Granted, it created some amazingly memorable characters, including actor Robert Duvall's gung-ho Colonel Kilgore ("I love the smell of napalm in the morning") and Martin Sheen's shell-shocked Captain Willard, who is sent upriver to assassinate an American Army officer who has gone off the deep end — Colonel Walter Kurtz.

However, Marlon Brando's nearly unintelligible performance as Kurtz and Coppola's emphasis on the surreal, make this a flawed attempt to encapsulate the Vietnam experience, despite the amazing visuals and the innovative Dolby soundtrack. It's still a hugely memorable, even iconic, film.

Meanwhile, another filmmaking giant — Stanley Kubrick of *Spartacus* and *Paths of Glory* fame — was percolating with his own look at Vietnam — *Full Metal Jacket*. The movie, which would be released in 1987, was based on Vietnam war correspondent Gustav Hasford's novel *The Short Timers,* which takes place in Hue during the Tet Offensive of 1968 and includes the siege of Khe Sanh. In dramatizing Hasford's short-but-brutal novel, Kubrick's emphasis, like Coppola's, was more stylized and visceral, than historical and realistic. However, the movie is intensely absorbing, offering a sobering look at the life of a combat infantryman. Interestingly, considering how filmmakers had followed director David Lean's example to shoot on locations around the world to achieve verisimilitude in their productions, Kubrick shot the whole film in England, recreating the trauma of the Tet Offensive in the abandoned Beckton Gasworks in East London. It was an unusual location, which works in the dramatic structure of the film, but, in retrospect, seems far from the reality of Vietnam.

Another look at the Vietnam experience (perhaps an even stranger one) was director Michael Cimino's *The Deer Hunter,* which was less about the combat experience than the unique camaraderie of a group of friends from the Pennsylvania steel country and how the war affects their lives. Although the film was a huge success and won the Oscar for Best Picture in 1978, it's hardly an historical portrait.

Someone else would have to make the definitive Vietnam War film.

Enter Oliver Stone.

Platoon was much more than a big commercial movie release in 1986 — it was a revelation. For over a decade, Vietnam veterans had tried to tell their stories, to come to grips with the legacy of a ten-year war in Southeast Asia. With *Platoon,* audiences started to listen and, because of that, our nation started to heal. Before *Platoon,* the Vietnam War was not about the soldier's experience. The public didn't seem to care. They associated Vietnam with political discourse, the anti-war movement, the failure of President Nixon, the My Lai massacre and Agent Orange. American soldiers were demonized as "baby killers."

After *Platoon,* the Vietnam veteran had a face.

In Lewis Milestone's *All Quiet on the Western Front,* the German soldier reaches out to touch a butterfly and gets shot. That one image summed up the futility of a horrific war and humanized an enemy soldier. *Platoon* humanized an entire platoon of soldiers, gave them faces and personalities and allowed the audience to wade into the jungle with them. Their guide is a baby-faced U.S. Army volunteer soldier named Chris Taylor (Charlie Sheen) who has no idea what to expect. And because we were right there, taking every dangerous step with him, with no fantasy or exaggeration between us, the experience of the Vietnam soldier became clear, perhaps for the first time.

Like Robert Pirosh and *Battleground,* Oliver Stone wrote *Platoon* from the first-hand recollection of a combat infantryman. And, although the snows of Bastogne in 1944 are quite different from the teeming jungles of South Vietnam in 1969, the scripts share the unblemished truth of combat. Stone, particularly, knew the responsibility he carried in dramatizing the legacy of his fellow Vietnam "grunts." Clichés would have not only destroyed the impact of his film, they would have been an insult to the memory of the men who died there. A decade later, Tom Hanks and Steven Spielberg would carry similar thoughts when they set out to dramatize Robert Rodat's script for *Saving Private Ryan.*

Oliver Stone grew up with war. He remembers spending summers in France with his French grandfather who was himself a combat infantry veteran of World War I, who fought in the Battle of the Marne and was gassed. In France of the 1950s, Stone recalled sleeping at his grandparents' house in the country and seeing his grandfather wrap a bandage on his wound, which never properly healed. He learned how horrible mustard gas really was.

Stone's father, Lou Stone, was a lieutenant colonel in World War II, who served in

Oliver Stone begins to show the wear and tear of a grueling schedule in the heat and humidity of the Philippines. (Courtesy of Ixtlan)

SHAEF (Supreme Headquarters Allied Expeditionary Force) under General Walter Bedell Smith. As part of Smith's economic policy brain trust, he helped formulate plans that would affect the postwar world in Europe. He would meet Oliver's mother, a French Catholic, in Paris.

Stone grew up in a privileged family in New York. But his life changed at 16 when his parents divorced. Shipped off to a tough boarding school (The Hill School in Pennsylvania), Stone found comfort in reading novels that transported him to other worlds. His heroes were James Joyce, J.P. Dunleavy, John Dos Passos, Ernest Hemingway and Norman Mailer. He read everything he could find, and started to dabble in novel writing himself.

He attended Yale, his father's alma mater, and although an outsider he could appear to be an Ivy League student who was in George W. Bush's class. In truth he was burned out. Four years of boarding school plus his parent's split had left their imprint. If it had been 1936, there is no doubt that Stone would have signed up for the ambulance corps and gone to Civil War–ravaged Spain. For Stone, the equivalent in 1965 was South Vietnam.

Stone was drawn to Asia partly because of Joseph Conrad's adventure novel *Lord Jim*, and partly because he didn't know anything about it.

Recalled Stone, "I had to see the world. In fact, in 1964, I came very close to going to the Belgian Congo as a mercenary. I wanted action and I wanted to get away from Yale.... I didn't believe in the intellectual life."[1]

Dropping out of Yale, Stone signed up as a teacher with the Free Pacific Institute, a Catholic group, which Stone later found out was a front for the Central Intelligence Agency. He arrived in Saigon in June 1965.

"It was like Iraq," he remembered, "the First Infantry Division was there, the Marines were arriving, but there were also a lot of civilian contractors. I wasn't hired by the government; I was there on my own passport as an independent teacher."[2]

Stone mixed with all the groups — teachers, contractors, soldiers, civil servants, and he saw the war at the earliest stages. "It was fascinating," he said, "because Saigon in those days was pretty much Dodge City with the troops walking around the streets at night with unconcealed weapons and there were Viet Cong all over the place. At night it was pretty spooky and there were shootouts."[3]

Stone taught English and history at the Free Pacific Institute of Cho Lon, a big suburb of Saigon. His students were mostly Chinese kids (25 to a class), and he quickly grew restless. At every opportunity, he went off exploring, traveling to Laos and Cambodia, getting into one adventure after another. He was offered a job as a merchant sailor by a French company, but it would involve working in a port and Stone wanted to get back to sea.

So at the first opportunity, he shipped out on a freighter heading back to the States. On the ship, he was made a wiper, the lowest rung on the merchant marine job chart. He cleaned the boilers and the toilets, swabbed the engine and held on for dear life when the ship almost foundered in a storm off Taiwan.

Back in the United States, Stone drifted around, went to Mexico, stayed in Guadalajara long enough to write a novel called *A Child's Night Dream* (which was universally rejected) and wound up back at Yale. He would last four months, dropping out in January 1967 with zeros in all of his classes. According to the media, American troops were kicking butt in Vietnam, especially after the battles in the Ia Drang Valley, and Stone was now worried that the war would be over before he could get there.

He thus volunteered for the draft in April 1967. "I wanted to go infantry, I wanted to see the bottom," Stone recalled. "Like the Chris character in *Platoon*. I didn't want any phony job and I got what I wanted. I just never figured what I was going to get."[4]

After basic and advanced infantry training at Fort Jackson, South Carolina, Stone arrived in Vietnam on his 21st birthday — September 15, 1967. The days of a limited U.S. force in Vietnam were over, and Stone was part of an expeditionary force that now numbered in excess of 500,000 men. He would eventually see action with three different combat platoons. He even served as an auxiliary MP in Saigon. But his first assignment was with the Second Platoon, Third Battalion, 25th Infantry Division, U.S. Army.

If you want to know what his combat service was really like, just listen to Charlie Sheen's running narration in *Platoon*. It's Stone speaking from memory. And when he shows an exhausted and nearly delirious Chris Taylor hacking his way through heavy jungle on, essentially, his first day in country — that was Stone's memory of his introduction to Vietnam.

Stone has a photographic memory of his Vietnam experience and he drew on it often. The images were hard to forget, and he had problems with practically everything he saw. He had a particular problem with career soldiers who "were gaming the system."

Recalled Stone, "There were these master sergeants, I couldn't stand these guys, they had all the ribbons, they knew the system and they got the jobs, the PX jobs, the rear echelon jobs, all the maintenance jobs where they make the dough. Tons of shit was coming over, TV sets, cars, everything you can f**king dream of from the American life style was being shipped to the PXs and half the stuff would vanish into their pockets. Plus they had the bar and liquor concessions. Big money was involved, it was like shipping Vegas to Vietnam.

"They were corrupt motherf*****s who would do anything to stay out of the field. I never saw officers, maybe some captains, and an occasional major in battalion operations, but they weren't on the front. And the leadership was just lousy. There were some good officers, but you can't get guys like Creighton Abrams, who was a tank commander, to understand this shit, much less an artillery guy like Westmoreland. It was a joke."[5]

During combat operations, Stone would collect information and maps and send them back and they would vanish into the maw of intelligence. "All of these assholes would come out and know everything and do nothing. So we'd go back to the same area a month or two later and get more guys killed and wounded. And we'd sit there and wonder why we were going back to the same area. It was a pointless exercise."[6]

During combat operations in Vietnam, Oliver Stone was shot twice. The first time, he got hit in the neck (as does Charlie Sheen' character in *Platoon*). If the bullet had entered an inch farther, he would have died. His second wound occurred when he was attached to a platoon of the 25th Infantry Division. Just before the beginning of the Tet Offensive in January 1968, he was blown up by a satchel charge during a full ambush. It knocked him out, but he was evacuated and survived.

It was during his next assignment with the military police in Saigon that he got into a scuffle with a master sergeant who was complaining about Stone's un-shined boots. Instead of a jail sentence, Stone volunteered to go back into combat as part of a Long Range Reconnaissance Patrol (LRP) section of the First Cavalry Division. It was with the LRPs that Stone met a native American character who inspired the Sergeant Elias (Willem Dafoe) character in *Platoon*.

"Elias was LRPs," Stone explained. "LRPs would go out on the trail and just sit. You don't fight. You just observe and then you get out. But sometimes you run into some shit. Elias was killed by his own men by mistake — friendly fire accounted for 15–20 percent of our casualties, at least."[7]

Stone got kicked out of the LRPs for getting into a fight with another master sergeant. He went across the road and joined the First Regiment of the Ninth Infantry Division, and that's where he met another soldier who would serve as the inspiration for a character in *Platoon*, Sergeant Barnes (Tom Berenger).

"I was his radio operator for the first month or two," said Stone. "He never yelled at me, but his cold, quiet stare withered and terrified me as no man has ever done since. He was the best soldier I ever saw, except, possibly Elias ... but unlike Elias, there was a sickness in him, he wanted to kill too much. The gooks had shot him right above his left eye in '66, and the bullet somehow lodged in there and he spent a year in a hospital in Japan. The resulting scar ran the whole left side of his face in a large, sickle-shaped pattern layered with grafted skin from the indentation above his eye to his lower jaw. It was a massive job, indicative of equally massive damage to the nerves and possibly the brain.

"Yet, when he got out," Stone continued, "he came back to Nam because he *wanted* to. To get even, I guess — either with the gooks or, if they weren't around, with us. When Barnes looked you in the eye, you felt it all the way down to your balls. But there was a tenderness and sensuality in the man's quietude that made him fascinating. He'd get drunk at poker and occasionally crack a country smile, but never let you in. The only vulnerability in the man was the scar, and such a massive thing it was that it provoked the deepest empathy."[8]

"The guy wanted back — he hated the gooks — like the Ahab character in *Moby-Dick*. I liked the guy in a strange kind of way. He taught me a lot about staying alive. He was good at it, damn good. We lost fewer men than when I was in the 25th, but the missions were tougher and very different. We'd go to villages, whereas in the 25th we spent most of our time in the jungle."[9]

It was while fighting with the Ninth Division that Stone began to see what he terms the "hinge point" in America's involvement. He explains, "Johnson decided to withdraw from running for president in March 1968, which meant it was over, this thing was a charade. So that's when things got really bad — the drugs, the mutinies started to happen. It was definitely bad when I got there, but by late 1967, you'd find from official reports that we were kidding ourselves. The NVA [North Vietnamese Army] were never going to give up. They told us we were fighting the Viet Cong, but they were definitely NVA."[10]

Stone had an inkling that a North Vietnamese offensive was coming in early 1968. "We were in more and more engagements and we were taking more combat casualties, so we knew something was coming up."[11] In a battle that would inspire the final engagement in *Platoon* when the American position is overrun, Stone was stationed along the Cambodian border when his unit was attacked by an NVA regiment.

"I was on the inner perimeter that night and they hit us with at least two battalions on two sides," he recalled. "I made it through, but it was a horrible night because they were in the perimeter. It started at 9:00 P.M. and lasted all night. The jets came down and eventually bombed our own positions.

"The greatest message I could get from that war, that I learned philosophically, was to keep your compassion alive. To keep your humanity was the hardest thing. Day by day, they grind you down. When you wanted to kill, kill, kill, when you wanted to kill the other guy and you're willing to kill villagers, innocent people, when you don't give a f*** and a gook is a gook and you don't see the difference anymore. When you're willing to rape or kill a 16-

According to Oliver Stone, *Platoon* was heavily influenced by Homer's *Iliad,* and its internecine warfare amongst the Greeks — here transposed to Vietnam and the ongoing battle between Sgt. Barnes (Tom Berenger, left) and Sgt. Elias (Willem Dafoe, right). The lieutenant (Mark Moses), unfortunately, has no power in the field over these two. (Courtesy of Ixtlan)

year-old girl, you've lost your f***ing mind. You're the casualty, and that's what I kept seeing in these platoons. I saw the polarization we see in our country today. Polarization is really a sick thing, a sad thing, between the guys who can say we're going to win this war and the guys who were saying, 'Survive man, get along with your neighbor, try to make it, try to keep your soul because that's what's really at stake here.'

"And America lost its soul in that war. Half the population of this country still thinks that war was a good war — they're out of their minds."[12]

Determined to get out of Vietnam and the military, Stone opted to extend his combat tour by three months to avoid having to spend six more months on duty in the States. He spent his last 12 days in Vietnam on a mountaintop in the rain. Eight days after he returned to Saigon, he was shipped back home.

Oliver Stone wrote the first draft of *Platoon* in the bicentennial summer of 1976 — he actually began the script on the Fourth of July, while he was making his living as a cab driver. He felt it was time to tell a Vietnam story from the grunt's point of view. It was his 12th screenplay.

Stone told journalist Fred Schruers, "I came out of this spin I'd been in…. I thought, 'I've forgotten a lot in eight years. If I don't do it now, I'm gonna forget.' It's a pocket of our history nobody understands — what it was like over there, how the everyday American, wild crazy boys from little towns in Ohio who grew up by the 7-Eleven stores with the souped-up cars and the girls on Friday night, turn into these little monster killers."[13]

Although fiction, every aspect of the screenplay would be based on his own experiences, and Chris Taylor was essentially playing Stone. In the screenplay, the setting is the triple canopy jungle northwest of Saigon, near the Cambodian border. Taylor finds himself assigned to a combat platoon run by two sergeants — Barnes (Tom Berenger), an excellent soldier but a scarred warrior who hates the enemy with a great passion; and Elias (Willem Dafoe), the "good" sergeant who takes care of his men and whose stand against Barnes's brutality eventually costs him his life.

Stone populated the story with a colorful group of characters who are doing everything they can to survive the meat grinder that combat in Vietnam had become. Among them are Bunny (Kevin Dillon), the baby-faced killer who hangs with the rednecks and worships Barnes; Sgt. O'Neill (John C. McGinley), another nervous redneck and compatriot of Barnes who is a bully and a coward at heart; King (Keith David), a kind-hearted but war-weary soldier who befriends Taylor; Lt. Wolfe (Mark Moses), the clueless college boy who lets Barnes run the platoon; Lerner (Johnny Depp), the skilled interpreter who can't paint the Vietnamese with a color that Barnes can accept; and Junior (Reggie Johnson), the wise-cracking private who nearly gets the platoon slaughtered when he falls asleep on guard duty.

As for the ongoing feud between Barnes and Elias (who has been in-country much longer), Stone's inspiration was none other than Homer's Iliad. He had remembered the tremendous infighting amongst the Greeks who were fighting the Trojans. He also wanted to expose the falsehood that all soldiers fight as a united front, something he termed "officer bullshit."[14]

It would take ten years to get *Platoon* financed. Studio after studio, financier after financier, turned the project down saying it was too depressing. He was told that America wasn't ready for a Vietnam War film as gritty as *Platoon*. As frustrating as that was for the young writer, his script got him other assignments — major assignments — and, in 1979, he won the Academy Award for adapting the Billy Hayes/William Hoffer book, *Midnight Express*. Four years later, he wrote what became one of the most oft-quoted screenplays of the 1980s, *Scarface*, for director Brian DePalma. Between the squalor of a Turkish prison in *Midnight*

Express and the gritty drug-dealing world of Tony Montana (Al Pacino) in *Scarface,* Stone was getting a reputation for unflinching drama and edgy, brutal and controversial characters.

Meanwhile, Stone had begun to direct, albeit infrequently, starting with the cultish horror film *The Seizure* (1974) and, much later on, *The Hand,* an evocative but little-seen 1981 horror film that starred Michael Caine. And, although he wouldn't direct another film until *Salvador* in 1986, Oliver Stone was no longer content to just write screenplays for hire. He would do them, but there had to be an ulterior reason. Take *Year of the Dragon.* Stone only agreed to work on the screenplay for that Michael Cimino thriller if producer Dino DeLaurentiis would help finance *Platoon.* DeLaurentiis agreed, and in October 1984, the *Hollywood Reporter* announced that *Platoon* would begin shooting in the Philippines sometime in January 1985.

There was some talk about shooting the film in Mexico, but after a first location scout to the Philippines, Stone was convinced, especially since he needed Asian extras to play the Vietnamese fighters. Actor John C. McGinley remembers getting a call from Stone to take on the part of Tony (Sgt. Barnes's radio man), a part later given to Ivan Kane. He was all set to fly to Manila when DeLaurentiis suddenly got cold feet and the whole project fell apart.

Not only was DeLaurentiis backing out of financing *Platoon,* he refused to return the rights to the screenplay to Stone. So, Stone had to sue to essentially get his life rights back — which he did when DeLaurentiis eventually backed down. (Note to Dino and any other producer: Don't screw around with a Vietnam combat veteran. He's seen it all and isn't afraid of confrontation.)

Fortunately, Stone had convinced Hemdale, a British company run by John Daly, to finance *Salvador,* another one of Stone's projects that chronicled a journalist's journey to El Salvador during the military takeover in 1980. When Daly visited him on the set in Mexico and offered him some constructive criticism, Stone offered him a look at the *Platoon* script.

"I told Oliver," Daly said, "I want this to be your next picture, it will take three months to get the financing." It ended up taking six. Daly explained that he "shared with Stone a penchant for the underdog, plus a revulsion at the Vietnam exploitation films that were surfacing." To Daly, the *Platoon* script said, "It doesn't matter who the enemy is. Nobody wins."[15]

While Daly was extolling the virtues of Stone's long-dormant script, it had been given to lawyer-turned producer Arnold Kopelson, who had cut his teeth on low-budget horror films (*The Legacy,* 1978), crime thrillers (*Night of the Juggler,* 1980), and raunchy teen comedies (*Porky's,* 1982).

Kopelson read *Platoon* and was blown away. "I could not read the pages fast enough," he related. "My heart was racing and my head throbbed. I was covered with perspiration. When I reached the last page and read Chris Taylor's voice-over, 'I think now, looking back, we did not fight the enemy, we fought ourselves — and the enemy was us,' tears were streaming down my face. Anne [Kopelson, his wife] asked if I was all right. I could barely speak, but through my tears I told her that I had just read the most powerful screenplay I had ever read. It was not like the John Wayne war movies or the surrealism of *Apocalypse Now* and *The Deer Hunter.* The realism was brutal. I could feel and smell death."[16]

As much as Kopelson loved the script, he was unsure whether anyone would want to see such a dark journey, let alone finance the movie. He was also unconvinced that Stone could achieve his vision. He, too, decided to travel to Cuernavaca, Mexico, and watch Stone direct *Salvador,* an experience that proved positive for them both. It turns out that Hemdale wanted to fund *Platoon,* but they also wanted Stone to make cuts in *Salvador,* which he was refusing to do. Kopelson stepped in and got Stone to sign a contract that guaranteed that Hemdale would fund *Platoon* if he would make the required cuts in *Salvador.* Stone signed, Kopelson

Oliver Stone spent ten years trying to get a studio interested in *Platoon*. Hemdale's John Daly, Arnold Kopelson and Orion Pictures finally came to his rescue. (Courtesy of Ixtlan)

brought Orion Pictures in as the distributor and *Platoon* was a go with a relatively small budget of $5.6 million.

Mike Medavoy, Orion's executive vice president told the *Hollywood Reporter*, "I think Oliver has made a war movie that really makes you feel as though you're a part of it. It's reminiscent of *All Quiet on the Western Front* and a monumental piece of work."[17]

McGinley was one of Stone's first calls. Related the actor, "When he called, I was two weeks into rehearsal to play opposite Kevin Kline in *Hamlet,* for Joseph Papp's Public Theater in New York. It was Kevin's first Hamlet and a big deal and everyone in New York wanted to be in it. I was the third guy on the right and it was just like working for Johnny Friendly in *On the Waterfront*. I got into Joe Papp's good graces and no actor in their right mind would sever that connection."[18]

However, Stone was now offering him the fourth lead in the picture — Sgt. O'Neill, a part that actor John Spencer had turned down because he had been offered the part of Dan White in *Execution of Justice,* the Harvey Milk story that was going to Broadway. McGinley went to Papp and got his release.

"If Mr. Papp had said, 'If you go do this, you will never work here again,' I wouldn't have gone. Nobody in their right mind would have gone. Remember, *Platoon* was just a little independent doodad that was going to happen in the Philippines."[19]

So McGinley once again packed his bag, preparing to head to the airport when the phone rang. It was February 25, 1986. Bad news from the Philippines — the "People's Revolution"

Oliver Stone (in all white) and Arnold Kopelson (in a white shirt) pose with the cast of *Platoon*. Forest Whitaker is standing, fourth from right, next to Stone and tech advisor Dale Dye is third from right; the film's star, Charlie Sheen, is standing, fourth from left, next to Kopelson. Kevin Dillon is in the center of the first row; John C. McGinley (cigarette in mouth) is seated on the APC, above Stone; Tom Berenger (helmet) and Willem Dafoe are standing behind Dillon, next to Stone. (Courtesy of Ixtlan)

had broken out and President Ferdinand Marcos was being ousted. The Manila airport was shut down, there were tanks in the street, Marcos was refusing to leave the country and movie-making was impossible. Fortunately, Kopelson was able to make an arrangement with the new government and President Ronald Reagan granted Marcos asylum in Hawaii.

Stone was prepared for the worst. If the military had entered into a civil war, he would have taken his cast and crew to Thailand. In reality, the production only lost a week, and McGinley and the rest of the *Platoon* cast and crew were able to embark for Manila.

In selecting actors, Stone had chosen to go against type. Tom Berenger was known mostly for playing sympathic leads. He had portrayed the young Butch Cassidy in *Butch and Sundance: The Early Days* (1979); he also had played the charismatic actor in *The Big Chill* (1983) and he was an ex-rocker in *Eddie and the Cruisers* (1983). In *Platoon*, he would undergo a physical and emotional transformation as the brutish Sgt. Barnes.

On the other hand, Willem Dafoe, who would play the sympathetic Sgt. Elias, was known mostly for playing villains in such films as *Streets of Fire* (1984) and *To Live and Die in L.A.* (1985).

A 20-year-old Charlie Sheen had starred in *Red Dawn* the previous year for director John Milius. The son of actor Martin Sheen and the brother of actors Emilio and Joe Estevez, he was ideally suited to play Chris Taylor, the fresh-faced volunteer.

"Charlie has an interesting stoicism in his face, " said Stone. "At the same time, he evokes a boy that comes from an upper-middle class strata of America, so it was an interesting mixture for me. I liked Charlie's integrity."[20]

"He has the dark-browed beauty of a young Montgomery Clift in *A Place in the Sun* and *Red River*, part of the throwback to the fifties generation … he moves fluidly with the camera; we're doing a take, and I know I want him to do it again because his body attitude is incorrect, but the moment I think it, he eases into the exact position I want…. Equally astonishing is his gradual shift in personality. He arrived a bit of a nerd from the teen films he'd done — Malibu in his soul, hot wings at Hamburger Hamlet, tightly cut hair, with 100 pounds of provisions his mother sent that he would never use. Over the weeks, [he became] tougher, sharper, a jungle vet who can hump sixty pounds and walk right up to a deer in the bush without being heard. The changes exactly mirror those in his character in the script, though we leave it unsaid between us."[21]

Stone continued, "I almost cast his brother Emilio a few years before when I was trying to make the film. So it was interesting that Charlie, whom I had met when he was 15, came back into it when he was 19. The moment he walked into the room, I knew he was the right one."[22]

Before he left for Manila, Sheen took a look at *Salvador* and was very impressed. Since that film was shot like news footage and Stone had hired on the same director of photographer, Bob Richardson, Sheen told *Los Angeles Times* writer Roderick Mann, "I realized right at the start how graphic our movie was going to be." He also knew what kind of responsibility he was carrying as Chris Taylor.

"I mean, I was playing Oliver, wasn't I?" Sheen asked rhetorically. "I'd do a certain scene and then look over at him and sense that he was right back there in the war. It must have been so tough for him sometimes. I think, for him, the film helped exorcize demons about Vietnam."[23]

How do you turn a group of pampered, fun-loving Hollywood actors into a grim, exhausted, Vietnam combat platoon? First, you start with a director who wouldn't settle for less. In fact, during the casting process, Stone made it clear to actors and their agents that he wasn't interested in hiring anyone who would not be willing to go through two weeks of training as light infantry. A number of New York actors objected to the training, and, guess what? They stayed in New York.

Secondly, Stone was introduced to Captain Dale Dye, a U.S. Marine veteran of Vietnam who had just started Warriors, Inc., a Hollywood-based military consulting service for producers (his first credit was Tobe Hooper's remake of *Invaders from Mars*).

Stone explained to author Michael Singer, "I told Dale Dye that I wanted them to know what a year without sleep feels like. I wanted them to really feel what it was like to live with the smell of the jungle. The actors were really pissed off at me and the world after these three weeks of training, which was exactly what I wanted to get them in the right spirit."[24]

Thus, Dye came on board as the film's technical advisor and designed a no-holds-barred boot camp that would simulate the combat experience to an amazing degree.

As we've seen in films like William Wellman's *Battleground*, movie boot camps have existed since the 1940s. But Dale Dye wasn't just interested in making sure the actors looked and acted like soldiers. On the surface, he wanted to achieve a level of realism in war films that had never been achieved before. However, of equal importance to him was not insulting the memories of the soldiers who had fought and died in Southeast Asia.

Remembered Dye, "I think Oliver discovered, after we met, that we were kindred spirits and that we had a similar dedication to making a definitive Vietnam movie, one that had something for everybody — veterans, non-veterans, the guys who were on the line. We wanted something in this that would make the hair on their arms stand up."[25]

Two weeks before shooting began, he gathered the cast at Camp Castaneda, the training camp for the Philippine Constabulary (local police), in Southern Luzon. With him were Stan White, Dye's chief aide and three young "ringers" — U.S. Marine reservists Robert "Rock" Galotti and Mark Ebenhoch, and a former reconnaissance Marine, Drew Clark, who quickly got the nickname "Recon." The ringers, assigned as squad members, helped train the actors and appeared in the film in small roles.

John C. McGinley was there: "I don't think anybody did much homework, you just had to show up for Dale's two weeks of boot camp. You weren't allowed to call anybody by their civilian name. Everyone lost a lot of weight. We split up into three squads of eight. Tom was Alpha, Willem was Bravo and I was Charlie."[26]

During the 14-day training period, Dye taught a group of 30 actors and bit players how to handle field first-aid and what to do about heat exhaustion and insect bites. He also marched them everywhere with 50 and 60-pound packs on their backs.

"We just humped, humped and humped," he recalled. "I worried about their feet, especially when they were in the blue line — the creeks and jungle streams. We had the squad leaders and the platoon

Capt. Dale Dye, U.S.M.C. (Ret.), who, as technical advisor on *Platoon*, brought a whole new level of realism and detail to American war films. (Courtesy of Capt. Dale Dye, U.S.M.C. [Ret.])

sergeant himself—Tom Berenger—check everybody's feet, to make sure they had foot powder … an infantryman is only as good as his weapons and his feet."[27]

Each man was issued a pile of gear—dog tags, an M-16 rifle with a 20-round magazine, a bayonet, bandage pouches, ponchos, poncho liners, flashlights with red filters for night use and four canteens per man. Actor Paul Sanchez, who played Doc, was issued a Unit One medical kit, plus an M-16.

On one of the first field drills, the actors were told to dig two-man foxholes before sundown. As night fell, BLAM, a simulated mortar round exploded nearby, followed by a number of other Dale Dye surprises, including distant flares and additional blasts. After a dinner of MRE's or Meal, Ready-to-Eat Individual (canned Vietnam-era C-rations were in short supply and were saved for actual filming), Dye began his first lesson in Vietnam combat training. With total seriousness, he explained that enemy movement is expected and everyone should be on 50 percent alert, two hours on, two off. In each foxhole, one man stayed awake and on guard for two hours, while the other slept. Then, they traded off.

He gave the password and counter sign—Blue … Lagoon. Then he and White, his deputy, took four men a few hundred meters out past the edge of their night-defensive position and established two-man listening posts. Each man was issued five rounds of blank ammo.

One listening post was manned by Willem Dafoe and Drew Clark, the "ringer." The other was occupied by Charlie Sheen and Kevin Dillon. At two o'clock in the morning, Clark got on his radio and reported movement to his front. It was Dye and White hassling the kids. After a flurry of blank rounds were fired, Dye ordered the listening post units back to the staging area.

On succeeding days, Dye instructed on the use of the M-16 and he taught a class on squad radios and radio procedure, the art of camouflage and dozens of other fine details that were designed to make those hairs stand up on veteran's arms. One of the actors wondered whether the civilians would get all the references to LPs, klicks, bloopers and LZs? Dye replied swiftly, "A) It doesn't matter; B) The script is constructed to cover that and 3) Remember, gentlemen, there were 3.5 million guys who served in Vietnam and they each got five bucks to see this movie."[28]

In addition to combat training, the actors were also put through a rigorous physical training regimen, which included "the Stomp," a brutally fast run-in-place, two-man wrestling matches and the constant "humping." In one case, the men were led on a grueling 12 klick uphill-downhill monster hike with full pack (a "klick" is the slang reference for one kilometer or a little over six-tenths of a mile).

At night, after dinner, Dye would sit down with the men and tell them to open their scripts (for example, to Page 9, Scene 14, exterior platoon CP) and they would become actors again, learning the story dynamics and details.

After one final night action, showing the new-found competence of the "soldiers," dawn broke on Graduation Day, with awards for Best and Worst Grunts, followed by a beer bust that night. However, there was no return to soft hotel room beds and hot showers. Stone and Dye shrewdly wanted to take advantage of the fact that their men were hot, tired and miserable. Thus, the following day, the actors reported for work in the local rain forest. Filming had begun.

Commenting on the experience of Dale Dye's training course, actor Willem Dafoe would later tell the *New York Times*'s Nina Darnton, "There were no usual Hollywood perks, no 'honey wagons' [dressing rooms] for the actors to relax in, no good food. We sat in foxholes and ate rations and never slept more than two hours at a time. So a real camaraderie developed.

Oliver had a story to tell and the training was a kind of initiation that made us somehow worthy to tell the story. I'm not saying we really suffered and I'm not saying we know war, but we did something difficult that helped us get into it. It became very important to all of us to get the respect of Captain Dye and to respect what he had done, regardless of how we felt politically about the war."[29]

For the first two months of shooting, the crew was based in a hotel complex in Puerto Azul, a veritable oasis, about two hours from Manila. President Marcos had originally built the resort for visiting friends. It had all the amenities, including a full golf course. But it was surrounded by atrocious poverty. U.S. President Reagan had closed Clark Field, the big U.S. Air Force Base, as well as the naval base at Subic Bay, so without those military installations generating revenue, the local economy had plummeted.

Actor Tom Berenger often had the earliest call because of the makeup effects that were applied to establish Barnes's scarred face. Makeup artist Gordon Smith was using an interesting new technique for 1986 — a glue-like prosthetic appliance that took an hour to put on. By the end of the production, Smith had reduced the time to a half-hour. As Stone relates, it did have a tightening and deleterious effect on Berenger's skin. To give the actor's skin a break, Stone would occasionally shoot Barnes from the right hand side, with the scarred side of his face off-camera — so that Smith could leave the appliance off.

When Charlie Sheen was cast as Chris Taylor, the film's star and narrator, he was literally following in his father's footsteps. Ten years earlier, Martin Sheen had portrayed the lead and the narrator in *Apocalypse Now*, also shot in the Philippines. The younger Sheen had visited that set, when he was ten. He helped with the extras' makeup, ran errands and saw the sights. Now he was essentially playing Oliver Stone and all eyes were on him.

Filming conditions on *Platoon* were, at times, unbearable. The thermometer would hit 115°, sometimes by 8:30 in the morning. It was wet, humid, jungle heat.

Kopelson commented, "Once we had the camera on a hill, which slowly began to move. It was actually the home of thousands of giant red ants. We had snakes, king cobras and vipers, every possible variation of insect. Spiders the size of my hand and hordes of mosquitoes. The heat was so intense that when I took a towel and dipped it into the tub of ice that was cooling our sodas and waters, it was warm within ten minutes of wrapping it around my neck. So to think that the actors were wearing full military gear with 60 pound packs on their backs and helmets — it certainly made for the authenticity of the film."[30]

Stone hated the mosquitoes the most: "There were serious mosquitoes over there and you got bitten to death. They're so bad that you want to cover up completely and hide from them under a towel or anything. At the same time, you had to keep your eyes open. And in Vietnam we'd have to sit motionless for hours. Movies, of course, go much faster so you had the problem of reality versus movie time. You end up giving it a compressed reflection of the truth."[31]

With a resourceful production team behind him, Stone turned the jungle into a palpable character — a frighteningly hellish world where nothing is benign and comfortable and everything is filled with the smell of misery and death. Are the actors acting? At times, it was probably hard to tell, especially in those first scenes of Chris hacking through the jungle, sweat pouring down his body and an I'm-going-to-collapse-at-any-moment look on his face. When he sees the corpse of a rotting enemy soldier seemingly melded to a decaying jungle tree, you know this isn't the war picture of your father's generation. Compared to *Platoon,* the teeming jungles of *The Bridge on the River Kwai* look like the jungle cruise at Disneyland.

One of the most terrifying sequences in the film is the first night, when Chris is on guard duty in the rain. He's trying to stay dry under his poncho, so only his eyes are visible. And through those eyes, we get our first look at the enemy. Three North Vietnamese regulars emerge out of the rain and mist like ghosts — soundless, camouflaged, nearly invisible. It is clear that these are not ordinary soldiers.

Stone based the sequence on an actual ambush in which his platoon blew their claymore mines and shot three NVA soldiers. However, they only found one body and one long blood trail. The third soldier had simply vanished. Said Stone, "We began to believe that they were an amazing, supernatural type of soldier. They had a tremendous resistance to death and were very tenacious."[32]

Shooting the sequence was no picnic for Stone's director of photography, Bob Richardson, who came over from *Salvador*, along with production designer Bruno Rubeo, film editor Claire Simpson, composer Georges Delerue and special-effects supervisor Yves De Bono. The ambush sequence alone took four nights to shoot. There was rain, real mosquitoes and limited equipment. Stone wanted to maintain a sense of mystery in the jungle — he didn't want to show too much — and he succeeded.

After the ambush sequence, Chris is treated and sent back to his base, where Stone introduces the rest of the platoon, including a number of African American soldiers who have their own unique behind-the-lines lifestyle.

Stone explained, "Most of the people who were in the military in Vietnam were from the lower economic classes, mostly draftees. There were very few middle-class kids or upper-class kids who went, because they were shielded by a crazy set of laws that provided that if you went to college or you had a psychiatric deferment, you could get out of the war. As a result, it never really became a democratic war in that sense. It was more of a class war, and the pressure to end it did not come from the parents of those middle-class people who could have gone. Because if they had gone and started to die in any great numbers, I believe that their parents would have ended that war much faster."[33]

The marijuana-scented world of the dopers is well represented in *Platoon*. King introduces Chris to an underground nightclub where his fellow soldiers — the blacks and the stoners — smoke their Vietnamese-grade weed in great quantities. Once again, it was all based on Stone's own experiences. It was here in this alternative lifestyle that Stone was introduced to cool music like black jazz, Motown, The Doors and Jefferson Airplane.

However, not every grunt was a doper. In another hooch, we meet the rednecks and the good old boys. Their intoxicant of choice is booze, their game is poker, their music is country and their decorations include the Confederate flag. Here, Barnes, Bunny and O'Neill rule the roost.

In a movie with many strong, unforgettable sequences, the toughest to watch is when the platoon moves into a Vietnamese village. Their friend Manny (Corkey Ford) has been captured, tortured and his throat has been slit. They have reason to suspect that the village is sympathetic to the enemy and a series of events escalate into nearly a My Lai incident. Bunny takes the butt of his rifle and bashes in the face of a retarded Vietnamese teenager; Barnes shoots the wife of the village elder in the head and is about to shoot a child when Elias arrives to restore order by clipping Barnes with his gun butt. Lt. Wolfe breaks up a vicious fight between the two sergeants, but it's clear he has little authority or motivation to court martial his top sergeant. Even as the platoon torches the village and evacuates the remaining villagers, Chris comes across some of the rednecks raping some young village girls, a despicable act that he stops. It's clear that Chris has reached the end of his rope. And now, with Elias going to the Colonel to explain what happened in the village, it's also clear that a full-on civil war has divided the platoon into two warring halves.

As John C. McGinley remembered, "The scene where Kevin Dillon does the number on the Vietnamese kid really did a number on Dale Dye. He had to walk away."[34]

Dye agreed: "This was one of the most difficult sequences in the whole film for Oliver and I to do, not only because of what happens here story-wise, but because we were working with real Vietnamese. At one point, I remember Oliver and I had to walk off the set because it brought back so many nervous, chilled feelings. I remember pondering at this point and thinking … if it can make Oliver and I antsy, if it can really get to us, if it can call back those emotions after 20 to 25 years, we have something special here, we've got something that's going to touch some people, maybe break some of that ice, some of that we-don't-want-to-face-it, let's-ignore–Vietnam, maybe-it-will-go-away attitude on the part of the public and a part of many veterans."[35]

Stone had actually grabbed some affluent Vietnamese tourists to play the key villagers. The mother whom Barnes kills was actually an upper-class Vietnamese who had never acted, but she understood English and handled the job perfectly.

Stone told author Michael Singer, "Kevin Dillon, with his very strong Irish-American features, brought a real coldness and cruelty to the role that was true for the character. There was nothing more dangerous in Vietnam than a 19-year-old American with a shotgun."[36]

Dye, at first, objected to the rape sequence, claiming that it was too over-the-top in a section of the film that was already too brutal. He was also concerned that viewers might think atrocities were common every time combat troops entered a village. Stone understood Dye's concerns, but he also wanted to make a comment that Chris Taylor still had his sense of right and wrong intact. In hindsight, Dye agreed with Stone.

Since Stone was shooting *Platoon* almost entirely in continuity, when actors "died" in battle, they left the production, until there was only a small core left for the last battle sequence. There was no money to house actors who had finished, no extra food allowance, no extra per-diem, when you were done, you got shipped home, just like a real soldier.

McGinley remembered, "O'Neill doesn't die, so Charlie and me and Francesco Quinn [Anthony Quinn's son] and a couple of other guys were still there in the end. The longer you stayed in the Philippines, the more you heard rumors that the Army was taking over Aquino's government and there would be a counter-revolution. And all you're thinking about is getting out of there, you've got to get out of there. So that played with the story we were telling."[37]

The weather, the insects, the snakes and an unidentified fever bug was also whittling down the crew. At one point in the last two weeks of shooting, half of Stone's crew was out sick. Somehow, they scratched and clawed their way through the final shooting days.

The final battle in *Platoon*, when a North Vietnamese regiment launches a massive attack on the American perimeter, was based on a real attack that occurred on the night of New Year's Day 1968.

"They hit us bad," remembered Stone. "January was when they were moving towards Saigon for Tet. Surprisingly, they took us on. We were along the Cambodian border — the 25th and First Divisions and a lot of us were draftees. The press fell for the feint that all the action was at Khe Sanh. The North Vietnamese knew that Saigon was the key to the country, so they feinted with their left and attacked with their right — targeting Saigon for the Tet Offensive and us."[38]

It would be a challenging sequence, particularly for Bob Richardson, who had limited lighting availability.

Recalled Richardson, "Jim Fitzpatrick, the gaffer, and I came up with the idea to use real flares as our principal light and some bare bulbs mounted on cords strung around the camp for balance. We also used the glare from explosions both on and off frame as source light."[39]

Dale Dye also recommended that tracer rounds be used in the final battle. He explained, "The finger of light, at night, from tracers, incoming or outgoing, is a frightening thing. You feel like it's coming right at you."[40]

For the hand-to-hand combat scenes, Dye worked closely with the sound mixer. For instance, to create the sound of a bayonet penetrating a chest, Dye stabbed a watermelon with a real bayonet.

Dye was also playing the company commander, Captain Harris, who takes over the perimeter defense when his commanding officer (played by Oliver Stone) is taken out by an infiltrating Vietnamese suicide bomber. Playing a part in *Platoon*, Dye admits, was one of the most intimidating moments of his life.

"But the guys were just wonderful to me," he remembered fondly. "I had put them through hell at this point and they had their opportunity to put me through hell right here and they didn't do it. 'Just be Captain Dye and that'll be fine.' I can't say it was brilliant, I hope I didn't embarrass anybody, but I'm certainly proud to have had that opportunity."[41]

Stone officially wrapped *Platoon,* after 54 shooting days, in May 1986. By keeping his shooting schedule relatively short and working six-day weeks, he had avoided the disaster that befell Francis Ford Coppola's crew on the endless shoot for *Apocalypse Now. Platoon* was in the can.

"I don't want to party with the cast and crew," Stone said at the time. "They're having too good a time and I don't want to bring my director's consciousness to bear on them — so I ride home alone with the driver as the light comes up over the paddies and the water buffalo and the peasants come out as they always do to work in fields in that first pink light of an Asia dawn. It is just another late spring day in the World (as we called it in Vietnam) and nobody cares that we just finished this little 'thing in the jungle.' Why should they? Yet, as I press my face against the window of the silently moving car, in my soul there is a moment there and I know that it will last me forever — because it is the sweetest moment I've had since the day I left Vietnam."[42]

Unlike previous foreign location shoots, it took a while before some of the actors could return to normal. Forest Whitaker, who portrayed gentle Big Harold, related, "I definitely experienced a strange culture shock. I didn't fit in for a moment there ... it was the weirdest thing. I took quite a while to accept being really back home. Why? I guess because the project was so submerging ... it wasn't that easy to just let it go. We were so far into the characters and what was going on.

"I had a cousin," he continued, "who went to Vietnam and came back a different person. He was my favorite relative. He slept in my room and I watched him crawl the walls at night. I used to ask why. Now I know the answer."[43]

McGinley found himself restless, edgy: "So I just got on my motorbike and went out to Newark to some batting cages. And I just hit balls until my hands were red."[44]

McGinley was concerned when he found out that the film had a Christmas release date.

"I thought, oh great, this is really a heart-warming tale to bring out at Christmas," he remembered. "People are really going to spring out to see this."[45]

But McGinley was wrong. *Platoon* became a true phenomenon that winter of 1986 and when the Oscars rolled around the following spring, the film won Best Picture, Oliver Stone won Best Director, Claire Simpson won Best Editing and the film took home an additional Oscar for Best Sound. Unfortunately, Stone was denied a double win when Woody Allen's

Hannah and Her Sisters beat him out for Best Screenplay; and cinematographer Robert Richardson lost to Chris Menges for *The Mission*.

But, more important than a gold-plated statuette, *Platoon* achieved its own mission of winning over the very public that had shunned the soldiers when they returned from Vietnam. Oliver Stone had achieved something that no other filmmaker had — he had humanized the Vietnam War and won the veterans over to his side. They could, perhaps, get at least one good night's sleep, secure in the knowledge that the "man in the street" finally had a sense of what they had endured.

After *Platoon,* war movies stuck to that level of realism.

CHAPTER TWELVE

Gettysburg

The Vietnam War wasn't the only American conflict to receive short shrift in the movies. The Civil War, certainly the most dramatic and deadly war in American history, has generated a feeble number of films, most of which have nothing to do with the historical record. Those that have been produced run the gamut from pure soap opera (*Gone with the Wind, Raintree County, Cold Mountain*) to fast and loose fiction (*Rocky Mountain, The Good, the Bad and the Ugly*).

Prior to 1993, only a few films shed a keen light on the actual experience of fighting in the Civil War. These included John Huston's under-appreciated 1951 adaptation of Stephen Crane's seminal novel, *The Red Badge of Courage* (with Audie Murphy portraying the main character) and *Glory*, director Edward Zwick's powerful 1989 study of the African American experience in Civil War combat, which won newcomer Denzel Washington the Oscar for Best Supporting Actor that year.

And then there was *Gettysburg*. Conceived originally as a mini-series for Ted Turner's fledgling TNT television network, then turned into a modest theatrical release for New Line Cinema (which Turner had just purchased), *Gettysburg* was a true film event, the culmination of 15 years of inspired work on the part of writer/director Ronald F. Maxwell.

When I interviewed Maxwell in February of 2010, one of my first questions to him was: Why are there so few memorable Civil War combat films?

"I have some theories about it," he began. "I've seen how hard it is at first hand. But it's not just about an historical event like the American Revolution or the War of 1812 or even the Spanish American War where it's simply the good guys versus the bad guys. The Civil War is connected to the race issue, which is still so much in our political consciousness that it immediately arouses a response in people.

"So when you go to the Civil War," he continued, "it's like you're making a movie about contemporary politics. Everybody has an opinion, everybody gets their back up and everybody has a vested interest in the outcome and a point of view. Whether you're writing a book or producing a movie, you're stepping into a meat grinder at every level. Just on the military level, people think this is how it happened and how dare you say it happened any other way."[1]

To quote William Faulkner, who is referenced by Civil War historian James McPherson on the commentary tracks for the *Gettysburg* DVD, 'The past is not dead, it's not even past."[2]

Maxwell also points out that to produce a Civil War film requires an enormous logistical commitment. There are no low-budget Civil War films — if you're going to make one, you have to commit to an epic scale of filmmaking.

Like John Sturges on *The Great Escape* and Oliver Stone on *Platoon,* Maxwell undertook an incredibly long and difficult journey to get his film made. Only enormous passion and infinite patience allowed him to survive such an undertaking.

Gettysburg was based on *The Killer Angels,* author Michael Shaara's Pulitzer Prize–winning historical novel, which was published in 1974 by David McKay, after 15 rejections by other publishers. Shaara was the great-grandson of a member of the Fourth Georgia Infantry, who had been injured at Gettysburg and who later wrote letters that described his war experience.

Shaara was a character in his own right. An ex-prize fighter, Marine combat veteran, author and college professor (of Shakespeare and creative writing), Shaara was inspired by the family letters to take an historical trip to the Gettysburg battlefield in 1966 to learn more. The result was a unique historical novel that narrowed down the huge scope of the epic battle to a few critical characters who fought on both sides of the conflict.

Representing the North was college professor Joshua Lawrence Chamberlain, the inspired abolitionist, who left the lecture halls of Maine's Bowdoin College to join the Union Army, going on to command a regiment of the 20th Maine infantry and defend Little Round Top. Also representing the North was General John Buford, the veteran Union cavalry officer, whose quick thinking on the first day of the battle prevented the rebel forces from taking the high ground.

On the Southern side, there was General James Longstreet, the capable but cautious Virginia corps commander who stubbornly tried to convince his commanding officer, General Robert E. Lee, to abandon a frontal assault on the federal positions. And then there was Lee himself, who was determined to achieve one final and decisive victory over the North.

Explained McPherson, "Shaara's motivation for writing *The Killer Angels* was to do something for American history similar to what Shakespeare had done for English history, with his history plays. And he looked around and realized that Gettysburg was the ideal venue. And if you look at the structure of that novel, which gets reflected in the film as well, it's structured more like a three-act play than a typical novel — with Day One, Day Two and Day Three."[3]

Ronald F. Maxwell's girlfriend presented the young director with a copy of the Shaara book in 1978. Maxwell, a history enthusiast, had produced and directed the World War II–era *Verna USO Girl* for Public Television. His work was recognized by agents, producers and actors (including Barbra Streisand) on the West Coast, and he was invited to be flown there for a meeting. At the time, Maxwell had a mortal fear of flying. Traveling instead by train, he had plenty of time to crack open Shaara's book. By the time he arrived in Los Angeles, he was so profoundly affected by the experience of reading the book that he was determined to immediately acquire the film rights and produce and direct the movie version.

Explained Maxwell:

I'm interested in people who find themselves in conflict either because they're caught up in it through reasons they don't understand, or, like the characters in *The Killer Angels,* they make a conscious decision to do something. Whether its pure patriotism, states rights, the abolition of slavery or the preservation of the Union, they've made a decision, and this was particularly true in the early years of the Civil War because these were, for the most part, volunteer armies. These are not the sadists and born killers, there's something else going on here and that's what I was interested in exploring.

Because of the world we live in today, it's very easy to slide into judgments, especially with the Confederate characters. What could they possibly be fighting for? How could they even dare defend a country that has such a heinous institution at its center? There is a French term that refers to the shiny side of a medal, but if you turn it over, there is a side of the medal that never sees the light of the day, which is the dark side. A filmmaker has to look at both sides without judgment, without preconception, and without taking the smallest step towards propaganda.[4]

Maxwell was also fascinated by the events that led to the clash at Gettysburg, how neither army really knew where the other was, that despite the cavalry patrols and spies, their lack of information was incredible. Here was a battle that was going to determine the future of the United States of America and it was being decided by two huge armies who stumble blindly into one another at an unknown crossroads town called Gettysburg. What amazing drama!

Explained Maxwell: "One of the most unique things about Michael Shaara's book and the movie we made from it is that you're rooting for everybody. Usually, you're either rooting for the guys in blue or the guys in gray, but here there are no bad guys. When you're with the Yankees, you know the Confederates are going to attack their left flank, but they don't know it yet. You think, quick, get up there because the Confederates are coming. When you're with the Confederates and they're talking about attacking the middle of the Federal line, you say, 'My God, the Yankees are reinforcing their middle, it'll be suicide.' So you're sympathizing with the obstacles facing both sides. I loved that aspect of the story."[5]

When his train came to a stop in Los Angeles, the enormously inspired Maxwell ran to a phone booth to call his agents and ask if the rights to *The Killer Angels* were available. To his delight, they were, and his agents, Jeff Berg and Dan Ostroff at ICM, told him that Shaara wanted to meet him.

"I had been working in Public Television," recalled Maxwell, "and I certainly didn't have any money for options. I was a single father at the time, my kids were little and going to school in New York so, for the time being, I was bi-coastal. I was in survival mode and I was going out to L.A. to try and get started."[6]

Somehow, Maxwell was able to raise a $10,000 down payment on a $40,000 option that was due in full in three years. With the option in hand, Maxwell began work on the screenplay for *The Killer Angels.* Curious as to why Shaara would put his trust in a virtually unknown director, Maxwell later found out from Shaara that he impressed the author with his sincerity and dedication. It also didn't hurt that Shaara's mother's maiden name was Maxwell.

With the option in hand, Maxwell was clear to begin the screenplay. Fortunately, he was determined to keep Shaara's unique dramatic structure intact — it made for a natural storyline. Unlike some book-to-film transformations where the original source material is eviscerated, Maxwell was only too happy to stay as faithful to the book as possible. The result is one of the most authentic adaptations ever made. He explained:

It's an extremely cinematic book. You could almost put scene numbers on the page. It's like you're reading a book and watching the film at the same time. I thought the characterizations were mesmerizing, the dialogue was jumping off the page, it was colloquial, it belonged to the people and the time, the action was riveting and the suspense was there.

That's not to say it was easy. It took me many drafts over many years to whip it into shape because it was unwieldy and huge and filled with detail. But at the end of the day, it's an extremely faithful adaptation.

Now having said that, there were a couple of areas where I wanted the story to breathe a little more. And those areas had to do with the relationship between Confederate General Lewis Armistead and Union General Winfield Scott Hancock, which to me was the archetype of the brothers torn asunder — which is a universal theme going right back to Greek literature. There are whole scenes with Hancock and Armistead that are not in the novel. I think that's the only place where I took a kind of poetic license.[7]

Maxwell was also very impressed with the amount of research Shaara had done.

The Killer Angels is so meticulously researched that you think you're reading history. It won the Pulitzer Prize for fiction, and when you have a book chock full of characterization and people thinking things and dialogue, you're in the world of fiction. You're not in history anymore. However, even when I started to do my own research, I discovered that Shaara was well grounded. He didn't get any big things wrong, no historian has come out and attacked the book or our film and said we got something terribly wrong. And the reason why is that we just did our homework. I surrounded myself from the beginning with experts on the Battle of Gettysburg and on the characters who fought there. I made it my business to find the people who had written books and I met them, talked to them, got to know them and brought them in as historical consultants in the earliest stages of the film.

I was more well-versed in Civil War history than the average citizen, which isn't saying much. But I was always an avid reader of American history, even back in grammar school and junior high. When it came to studying historical events like the American Revolution and the Civil War, I can even remember my teacher turning over the class to me. I would get up and teach.

We grew up in New Jersey, so we were far from the Civil War battlefields, but my dad took us to the battlefields of the American Revolution, the French and Indian War, all over New Jersey, Pennsylvania and upstate New York, places like Fort Ticonderoga, Fort William Henry. So I had a working knowledge of history, but I was certainly not an expert on the Battle of Gettysburg when I started the script.

I wanted to use Shaara's title of *The Killer Angels,* not only because of its literary pedigree, but because it sums up in a title the whole paradox of the war, the whole contradiction of the war, that all of these people were angels and killers at the same time. Ted Turner wanted to call it *Gettysburg,* and in hindsight I can't argue with his decision. But *The Killer Angels* sums up all of these characters who were prepared to die for their country.[8]

Maxwell had bitten off quite a challenge when he started to shop the finished screenplay around. He was immediately up against what became known as the "Post Vietnam Syndrome," which meant that nobody wanted to make war pictures — Oliver Stone included. This was the era when science fiction and fantasy started becoming the genre of choice for studio epics. *Star Wars* had been released in the summer of 1977 making money hand over fist and inspiring, over the next five years, a huge influx of epic science fiction and fantasy films including *Superman, Close Encounters of the Third Kind, E.T., Raiders of the Lost Ark, Poltergeist* and *Ghostbusters* — all big moneymakers, and having nothing to do with history or war.

Maxwell had other challenges. Nobody wanted to make a film involving American history and nobody wanted to make a film without female cast members. The days of *Lawrence of Arabia, The Great Escape* and *The Longest Day* were long gone.

"There were people who encouraged me to put women in the story, which, of course, would have been ludicrous," said Maxwell. "Every time someone would mention that, I would just cringe. I told them it was a story about men in combat. It is a love story, but it's a love story of men in combat."[9]

Actor Hal Holbrook turned out to be one of Maxwell's first resources. Maxwell had directed Holbrook when the latter hosted a Public Television series called *Theater in America.* Knowing that the actor was a history buff (he was renowned for touring in an inspired one-man show as Mark Twain), Maxwell mentioned the script to him. Holbrook, in turn, mentioned that he had been narrating a series on Turner Broadcasting and had discovered how much media mogul Ted Turner loved the Civil War. He offered to show the script to Turner, and Maxwell was delighted.

Unfortunately, in the early 1980s, Turner was in no position to finance a $15 million Civil War combat film. He was too busy running a television network and making a play to acquire MGM. Maxwell got him on the telephone and Turner raved about the script, but he lamented the fact that he was not producing feature films. Six months later, Maxwell was in Georgia, scouting locations for his film, *The Night the Lights Went Out in Georgia*, when he met a young actress and future CNN anchor named Liz Wickersham. It turned out she was a good friend of Ted Turner and Turner called him to get Liz a part. Maxwell called her in for an audition, but he later signed actress Sunny Johnson for the role that Liz coveted. Ten years would pass before Maxwell and Turner would speak again.

In 1983, Maxwell decided to have a reading of the massive script. He wanted to hear actors speaking the dialogue, so he assembled a cast of 30 actors in Los Angeles at the Mark Taper Forum and they read from six o'clock in the evening until midnight. One of those actors was Maxwell's good friend, Richard Jordan, who read the pivotal role of Confederate Brigadier General Lewis Armistead (a role he would play in the finished film).

Maxwell had met Jordan in New York in the early 1970s through Jordan's wife, actress Kathleen Widdoes. Jordan was a rising star in New York and he almost immediately began to offer Maxwell advice on *The Killer Angels*. The role of Armistead was molded to Jordan from the beginning.

"Richard Jordan, could have had the career of a Robert DeNiro, he had that kind of heat on him," related Maxwell. "He certainly had the star quality, the talent and the intellect. He was as talented as DeNiro, but he just never reached that level of stardom."[10]

In addition to Jordan, Maxwell brought in Hal Holbrook to play Robert E. Lee during the reading. A third actor read all the scene descriptions so that Maxwell could listen and make his notes.

"I had gotten to the point where the script was huge, over 250 pages and I didn't know where to cut it," remembered Maxwell. "I didn't want to make a mini-series, so we had this reading and it was one of the most important moments in the life of the project. And it turned out to be a stunning evening. We read for two and half hours, took a dinner break, then read until midnight. Nobody left, nobody went home until we were done. There was a great feeling of satisfaction. I knew that night, even more, that I had to make the movie."[11]

Despite his renewed enthusiasm, progress on *The Killer Angels* remained slow. Continuing to prune the script and search for possible financiers, Maxwell concentrated on getting directing work, and, in the wake of the success of *Little Darlings*, he became

Richard Jordan, who played Confederate General Lewis Armistead, represents a high point of *Gettysburg*.

the kid picture go-to guy, working on *Kidco* for Fox and *The Parent Trap 2* for Disney. He was thrilled to be working, but his assignments were about as far from the bloody battlefields of the Civil War as you could get.

Two epiphanies came to him in the mid–1980s. The first was a realization that if he kept taking teen movie assignments, he would never get his picture off the ground. It was time for him to go for broke. The second was determining that the only way to make the film was to shoot it inexpensively in Eastern Europe.

Thus, in the summer of 1988, he visited Hungary, Poland and Yugoslavia, making production contacts, working up budgets and schedules and figuring out ways to hire the Red Army to fill out the ranks of the North and South.

"This was just prior to the time when the reenactor movement in the U.S expanded," Maxwell explained. "There were a few thousand people scattered all over the country, but nothing as organized as it would be later."[12]

No sooner did Maxwell return to the United States to take advantage of what he learned than ominous tidings came back from Eastern Europe. The old map of communist Europe was crumbling and by 1989, the Berlin Wall had come tumbling down and that map was being redrawn all across the now-former Iron Curtain countries. The once-thriving film business in those countries was in total chaos, with established filmmakers driving cabs and shining shoes to make a living. There was no way Maxwell was going to make *The Killer Angels* in a region that no longer (politically) existed.

Fortunately, a key event had taken place that would greatly influence the future of Maxwell's pet project. In the summer of 1988, thousands of reenactors gathered in Gettysburg to celebrate the 125th Anniversary of the battle. It was the largest assemblage of Civil War reenactors in history and Maxwell was there, marveling at their numbers and their amazing attention to detail. Not only did they look like Civil War–era combat soldiers, but they drilled like them, saluted like them, and each man was a virtual walking history lesson.

Maxwell quickly abandoned the (by now misbegotten) idea of shooting overseas and focused on budgeting the film to utilize a sizable reenactor contingent in the States. Maxwell realized how much money the production could save by not having to create their own costumes, rifles, pistols, cannon and rolling stock. He reasoned that he would have to create costumes and weaponry for his 100 main characters, but reenactors would provide the bulk of everything he needed.

During his summer trip to Gettysburg, he also realized that he could film part of the movie right where it took place, within the grounds of the huge historical park. The whole movie could not be shot there because of the number of huge monuments that now sat on places like Cemetery Ridge, Little Round Top and the site of Pickett's Charge. Plus, a huge observation dome had been constructed in the park, further hampering the sight lines of his movie cameras. That said, there were still great open spaces available to stage the two armies. And what an unprecedented coup it would be, to recreate the Battle of Gettysburg on the ground where it was fought.

Now possessing an impressive network of historians and Civil War buffs, Maxwell was aware of many different Civil War–related events that would take place in and around the country. On one of these occasions, he was invited to the East Side Armory in New York City where a Civil War Roundtable group was presenting a few minutes of a new documentary series that was about to debut on Public Broadcasting. The documentary filmmaker was a young man named Ken Burns and the documentary was *The Civil War*. Ironically, Burns showed a section of the documentary series that focused on Joshua Chamberlain and the fight on Little Round Top. He later confessed to Maxwell that the Chamberlain incident was part of the reason he had conceived the documentary series in the first place. Burns told Maxwell that he would help him in any way he could.

What happened next is a typical scenario in Hollywood. Every studio and network had pretty much rejected the project for the same reasons — We don't like American history, we don't like films without women, and we don't like the politics of the Civil War. And then Ken Burns's documentary ran on PBS.

Suddenly, everybody wanted a Civil War picture, particularly the broadcast TV networks. They were impressed with the fact that between 30 and 40 million people had seen the documentary series. Seemingly overnight, Ken Burns had made the Civil War a cool subject again. With his authentic Matthew Brady photographs and the inspired narration of David McCullough, he had taken the conflict to another level, intriguing multiple generations of viewers, from school kids to grandparents — all of whom were fascinated.

When the series debuted on PBS, Maxwell was in the panhandle of Alaska scouting locations for a film called *Raven Warrior.* His new producing partners, Moctezuma Esparza and Robert Katz, called him and told him about the phenomena that Burns's *The Civil War* was fast becoming, and that it was imperative that he return to California for pitch meetings.

No sooner had Maxwell returned to Los Angeles than it was announced in one of the trade papers that CBS was going to develop a mini-series on the Battle of Gettysburg. And they didn't want to hear from Maxwell or see his script. Adding insult to injury, they were partnering with a prominent producer of situation comedies.

"It was a nightmare," he remembered. "I'm twelve years into this project, everyone is interested in the Civil War again, and they're going to make some other guy's Gettysburg movie? How could that happen?"[13]

It was clear that Maxwell, Esparza and Katz had to get their project done first. It was going to be a race. Rejecting a sudden overture from CBS for him to step down as director and sell them his script, Maxwell and company went to producer Bob Rehme, whose protégé, Jon Feltheimer, was running New World Films and Television at that time and could deficit finance the picture. In other words, they would bear any costs of production that went beyond what a broadcast network would pay to license the film for premiere. Rehme called Feltheimer who jumped on board immediately, and he, in turn, called Alan Sabinson, head of movies and mini-series at ABC.

Recalled Maxwell, "Alan Sabinson was a very smart, sophisticated and well-educated guy, with what some people call 'uptown tastes.' And he just loved the project and said, 'Let's do it.' And it didn't bother him that CBS had announced their Gettysburg project, it got him on fire. So suddenly we went from 'oh, we're going to get beat by another network' to 'we're going to beat them to it.'"[14]

Maxwell made the deal with New World and was in the midst of closing the deal with ABC when Alan Sabinson got fired. It was right after the network had produced the big mini-series, *Son of the Morning Star,* about Custer's Last Stand. Sabinson was now out and so was *The Killer Angels.*

It was then, in early 1991, that Maxwell received a call from Ken Burns. It seemed that Burns was going to get an award from the Producers Guild for Best Documentary Film for his *The Civil War.* And, he had been told, the man who was going to present the award was none other than Ted Turner. Burns invited Maxwell to sit at his table and he offered to make the introduction to Turner.

Maxwell arrived at the Producers Guild dinner on crutches (he had recently broken his leg) and he sat at Burns's table, listening to Turner talk for what seemed like 15 minutes on why Hollywood was not making movies about the Civil War. In extolling Burns's film, Turner identified it as living proof that when somebody does a good job, the entire American public wants to see it. He couldn't understand what was wrong with Hollywood and why more people weren't exploring the rich history of our country. Maxwell sat there, elated and dumbfounded. He couldn't believe what Turner had just said to all the power elite of Hollywood.

Immediately after the presentation, Burns introduced Maxwell to Turner. Said Turner, "Oh you're Ron, I remember reading that script ten years ago. I bet I was the first one who said it was a great script. I want to do it. You have your people call my people. I want to do this."[15]

Maxwell shook hands with Turner and couldn't believe that events had turned so dramatically in his favor. It seemed like he was finally coming out of the clouds after so many years of futility.

"So the word had come down to TNT, the new Turner Network Television entity, from Ted Turner to do the deal," Maxwell remembered. "So we're gonna do the deal as a miniseries. I'm on a roller coaster ride. We get the lawyers and the agents to start negotiating and we've got momentum behind us. The movie had been prepped, we knew where we were going to shoot it, we knew all the reenactors, the historians, the whole Civil War community, and the script had been honed to a knife's edge. And then, suddenly, the production head of TNT, Linda Berman, says we need a rewrite. I had this frozen smile on my face. But what I wanted to say was, 'You *&^%$ idiot, what are you doing in that job, who put you there?' I'm sitting there talking to this complete and utter lightweight, who is telling me this crap after I've lived with this project for 12 years. I was seething."[16]

Esparza and Katz took Maxwell aside and told him to go along with it. They said another writer would be brought in and he would have to share writing credit, but they could get the movie made. Maxwell, however, thought the whole exercise was a colossal waste of time, especially since they were in a race to beat CBS to the air. However, Maxwell didn't know Turner well enough to pick up the phone and tell him what was going on, so a deal was struck and another writer was brought in.

So instead of going into pre-production, *The Killer Angels* went into development, which is one of the ugliest words in the Hollywood lexicon. Instead of walking the real Little Round Top in Gettysburg, Maxwell was forced to sit across from the new writer and listen to his notes.

"And I'm hearing the biggest gobbledygook of my life," Maxwell remembered. "Places I would never go, things I would never consider doing. To add insult to injury, they haven't paid me a penny. I've sacrificed 12 years of my life to get this project moving and this guy gets a $100,000 writing fee. I'm still struggling, trying to figure out how to pay my rent, meanwhile, we're eating up the entire fall of 1991."[17]

Finally, Maxwell saw the new script and it made him heartsick. He had basically thrown out Maxwell's entire draft and started from scratch. As Maxwell put it, although it was competently written, it was radically different and not the movie he wanted to make. At the same time, fortunately, they discovered that the CBS project had stalled on budget issues. A first pass at the budget apparently had projected a $150 million cost for the project — which was impossible for a TV mini-series at that time.

Maxwell was digging in his heels, determined to avoid using the new script at all costs, when the incredible happened. Linda Berman was suddenly fired and replaced by … Alan Sabinson. Sabinson came on board, took one look at the new draft, threw it out immediately, and put Maxwell's draft back in. He was authorized to go into pre-production immediately. *The Killer Angels* was back on track.

Now entitled *Gettysburg* (Turner had wanted to call it that, for good reasons), Maxwell's epic was greenlit with a $15 million budget and a start date of June 1992. He was also given only four months to prep one of the biggest television movies in history. Because of the number of daytime exteriors, and the need to shoot as late as possible into the day, filming needed to commence by early summer.

However, this was where Maxwell's enormous amount of prep work paid off. He knew every location, he had established relationships with the reenactors, he had established budgets and schedules. At the first production meeting, the topic of where to shoot came up and locations as diverse as Canada, Australia and Georgia were suggested. Maxwell looked at the people at the table and said simply, "There is only one place to do this picture and that's right at Gettysburg."[18] And, because he knew exactly what he needed to do, he convinced everyone at the table to do just that.

The casting of *Gettysburg* began immediately. There was initial pressure to back the $15 million budget with some solid star talent. For TNT, this was a huge outlay back in 1992.

When the movie was being sold as a theatrical feature, Maxwell had meetings with Kevin Costner to co-produce and to portray Joshua Lawrence Chamberlain, but that never progressed beyond the talking stage and Costner would never have signed on to do a television miniseries. Maxwell had also shown the project to Robert Duvall, who was the perfect age to play Robert E. Lee (he was even a direct descendent of Lee). However, when casting began in early 1992, Duvall was unavailable for a summer shoot. Hal Holbrook's name came up as a capable Lee, but the network felt he was too much of a character actor and not enough of a marquee name.

"Lee is a very demanding role to cast," explained Maxwell, "because you need a terrific actor who can deliver authority and an imposing quality and keep it real. Some actors, no matter how good they are, they can't pull off that kind of gravitas. If gravitas is part of your tool kit that's great, but if it's not, you can't pretend it. We were also hampered by the fact that we needed a 'name.'"[19]

Chamberlain was similarly complicated to cast. He needed to project the inner intellectual life of a college professor, based on literature, language and religion, and yet be a natural born leader. It was a rare combination of qualities — a bookish, almost reclusive academic who was also an extroverted man's man. And, it had to be a name!

Maxwell was commuting between L.A., Gettysburg and New York City, where casting was underway. During the four months of preparation for the film, he estimated that he saw over 1,000 actors. One of the actors he found in New York was crusty Kevin Conway, who was quickly given the role of Union Sergeant "Buster" Kilrain, who would play Colonel Joshua Lawrence Chamberlain's top sergeant. Years later, he would turn down the roll of Theoden, King of Rohan in *The Lord of the Rings: The Two Towers*, to reprise the role of Kilrain in Maxwell's prequel to *Gettysburg*, *Gods and Generals*.

But who was going to play Chamberlain? A friend of Maxwell's called up one day and mentioned that there was a new actor in Los Angeles from New Zealand who had not done any American pictures but had done some local films in his native country. Maxwell invited him to come out to his home in Hidden Hills, outside Los Angeles, asked him to do a cold reading of the character and was thrilled with the result. Related Maxwell:

> So nobody knows this guy, he hasn't done any American work and I knew Sabinson wanted a star name. I asked him if he would learn a couple of the big Chamberlain speeches and come back. I told him I'd get him a Civil War uniform and I went to a costume house. He came back a week

later and I put him on tape. I thought I had my Chamberlain. I told him I wasn't the final decision maker, and he understood.

I then went into Alan Sabinson's office and showed him the tape and Sabinson complimented
the performance and told me they weren't hiring him. I told him I wasn't going to find anybody
better — he fulfills my vision of the role. It was as if somebody walked into my house and became
the incarnation of the character I had written ten years earlier. Why should we waste any more
time, we'll put names around him. No one will care. This is like discovering Peter O'Toole in
Lawrence of Arabia. I made all these arguments and Alan Sabinson said no.[20]

The actor was Russell Crowe.

Once again, Maxwell thought about calling Ted Turner and once again he decided not
to. He knew what it meant to hopscotch over executives and you can make enemies very
quickly by doing things like that. Maxwell also knew that Sabinson had been a fan of the
project from the first time he saw it and was responsible for getting it greenlit so quickly at
TNT. Maxwell did try to build his case, seeking and getting the support of Esparza and Katz
and Bob Rehme. It did no good. Finally, Sabinson looked Maxwell square in the eye and told
him that if he mentioned Crowe's name one more time, the picture would be shelved.

Casting continued. Western veteran Sam Elliott came aboard as Union cavalry Brigadier
General John Buford, which was a huge plus for the picture. Elliott was, indeed, a man's man
and was perfectly cast as the stalwart horse soldier who leads two brigades of Union cavalry
against the advance guard of Lee's entire army. By holding his ground in Gettysburg on the
first day, Buford bought time for General John Reynolds' infantry to arrive and secure the
high ground at Cemetery Ridge and Little Round Top. (Nine years later, Elliott would play
a similar stand-up guy — this time as an infantry sergeant — in director Randall Wallace's Vietnam War combat film, *We Were Soldiers*.)

One of the first actors to come in and meet with Maxwell was *Platoon* veteran Tom
Berenger. Within five minutes, Berenger talked about how enthusiastic he was about the
script, how much he knew the characters, the Shaara book and Civil War history. And, as a
result, without having to read a single line, he won the part of Confederate Lieutenant General
James Longstreet.

Focusing on the part of Robert E. Lee, the casting director, Joy Todd, suggested Martin
Sheen to Maxwell. Sheen was the right age, he had the required gravitas and he was a name.
More importantly, he was available and he was approved enthusiastically by Sabinson. (It was
hard to believe that the actor who would portray this white-bearded, wrinkled-browed Con-
federate military genius, was the same youthful infantry officer who tracked down Marlon
Brando 14 years earlier in Francis Ford Coppola's *Apocalypse Now*.)

Maxwell was running out of time. Filming would begin soon and he still didn't have his
Chamberlain. In a movie like *Gettysburg*, you couldn't just show up to work, you had to be
outfitted, you had to have your facial hair styled (and no movie in the history of movies had
more facial hair than *Gettysburg*) and, for Chamberlain, an enormous amount of dialogue
(much of it in long monologues) had to be learned. Plus, there were two weeks of scheduled
rehearsals.

Actor Jeff Daniels's name came up shortly after the idea of Russell Crowe was jettisoned.
Everyone was excited about it. He was considered a terrific actor, he was a recognizable name
like Martin Sheen and Tom Berenger and he had a terrific body of work — from Oscar-winning
dramas *(Terms of Endearment)* to Woody Allen comedies (*The Purple Rose of Cairo, Radio
Days*) to horror-thrillers (*Arachnophobia*).

However, Maxwell didn't want to sign Daniels until they had a talk first. A conditional offer was thus sent to his agent, pending a meeting. What came back was a similar request — Daniels was interested, but he also wanted to meet Maxwell before he signed.

The meeting took place in Ann Arbor, Michigan where Daniels was running The Purple Rose Theater Company. After a play performance, Maxwell and Daniels segued to a local bar where Maxwell started the talking: "Jeff, I'm privileged that you want to play this part. You've done some amazing work, but in all that work, I see the professor, I see the gentleman, the humorous man, the intellectual — a lot of the qualities that Joshua Lawrence Chamberlain should have. But nothing in your work demonstrates a man who can say 'Fix bayonets and charge' and is willing to kill other people for something he believes in. So I have to ask you the question, because I don't want to be on the set, two and half weeks from now and not believe that you at least believe you can do it. Can you deliver the steel?"

Daniels fixed his eyes on Maxwell and said, "Oh, I'll show you the steel, but can you show me the steel when you're on the set? Will you go to the mat for this script? Will you make this movie and not succumb to the pressure that I know is going to come down on you when they say it's too talky, or it's too historical? Are you going to shoot this script as written?"

"And I said yes," related Maxwell, "and we had a male-bonding moment, committing to one another that we would go the distance and live up to the high expectations we both felt about making a movie about the Battle of Gettysburg. I think Jeff Daniels did one of the great portrayals in the movies. It's right up there with Gary Cooper as Sergeant York."[21]

Maxwell found his George Pickett in New York City when he went to see actor Billy Campbell (*Rocket Man*) about the part of Jeb Stuart. Campbell was appearing as Laertes in a local stage production of *Hamlet*. Playing opposite him, as the title character, was Stephen Lang. They had been discussing Maxwell's visit and when the director introduced himself, Lang shook hands and said, "Hi, I'm George Pickett." And according to Maxwell, he was right. Campbell was given the role of Stuart, but close to the start of production, he suddenly lobbied Maxwell to switch him to the tiny role of Union Lt. Pitzer, who gives Chamberlain the word that he's relieved and that his shattered regiment should report to the safest place on the battlefield — the Union center. Maxwell acquiesced, and casting was finished.

"Everyone threw themselves into the film with a ferocity I've never seen," said Maxwell.[22]

Complementing the 100 speaking parts that were cast would be over 5,000 reenactors who arrived in Gettysburg that June — like holy pilgrims headed for Bethlehem or Mecca. They came in full Civil War uniform — rebel gray or yankee blue — and they carried their own muskets, cartridge belts, canteens, packs and bayonets. They arrived with cavalry horses, cannons, caissons, tents, and cooking gear.

They were divided into two basic groups: the majority came with 20th century tents, coolers, electric fans, radios and food; the smaller group lived exactly like the Civil War soldiers of the 1860s: eating hardtack and nothing out of a can. They lived in lean-tos and pup tents or out in the open. Billy Campbell actually chose to forgo his air-conditioned hotel room to live with the hard-core reenactors.

While casting was going on and the reenactors were given their marching orders, Maxwell had been huddled with his director of photography, Dutchman Kees Van Oostrum. Van Oostrum had previously served as the director of photography on two major television event films, *Son of the Morning Star* (the Custer bio-pic that had been Alan Sabinson's swan song at ABC) and *Day One* (a well-made historical film about the Manhattan Project).

In Los Angeles, moving from lot to lot, Maxwell and Van Oostrum screened a number of epic war films from such filmmakers as Akiro Kurosawa, Sergei Bondarchuk and John Huston. The director and DP weren't looking at how the Civil War was portrayed as much as how the classic filmmakers had filmed large groups of men in combat, where cameras had been placed, what kind of coverage was featured. They learned, for instance, that long-lens shots tended to pull the audience out of the time frame and give it a modern feel. In many of the epic films of the late 1960s and early 1970s, long lenses were utilized and many close-ups and tracking shots were far from the actors.

They also learned the value of moving large bodies of men in broken terrain, something that director Akira Kurosawa was known for. Gettysburg, with its rocky hills, townscapes, vales, forests, roads and wheat fields, was thus perfect for deploying Civil War–era armies for the movie cameras.

If Maxwell and Van Oostrum had known up front that the film would debut in theaters, they would have shot the film in a wide-screen format. If the movie was shot purely for television, they could have shot it full-frame. To compromise, because they didn't know how the film would debut, they shot the movie in the 1:85 aspect ratio, which meant you could go either way. And that's what they did. For the theaters, they blew up the negative to 70mm widescreen; for television they debuted in standard Academy full frame.

Maxwell's elaborate advance planning and all of the connections he had made in the historical community didn't help him when final plans were being made to film on the Gettysburg battlefield itself. When the park rangers objected to the film company disrupting tourist visits at the height of the season, Maxwell turned to his producing partner, Moctezuma Esparza, who, fortunately, had a personal relationship with Henry Cisneros, who would soon become the Secretary for Housing and Urban Development in the Clinton Administration.

Confederate Soldiers: (Back row from left): Col. Freemantle (James Lancaster), Gen. Jim Kemper (Royce Applegate), Veneable Marshall (Tim Ruddy), General Lewis Armistead (Richard Jordan), T. J. Goree (Ivan Kane), Gen. James Longstreet (Tom Berenger), Moxley Sorrell (Kieran Mulroney), Harrison the Actor/Spy (Cooper Huckabee). (Sitting, Front Row, from left): Gen. George Pickett (Stephen Lang), Gen. Robert E. Lee (Martin Sheen); and Maj. Walter Taylor (Bo Brinkman).

With Cisneros's help, Maxwell was allowed to bring his enormous undertaking to Gettysburg — with certain caveats. For safety reasons, he was told that he could not film sequences involving opposing fire. In other words, in the same shot, he couldn't have two people, two groups or two armies shooting at one another. Maxwell was also not allowed to disrupt tourist visits to the park. He could stop them during takes, but he could not prevent the hundreds of thousands of tourists from seeing one of the most revered historical parks in the United States, at the height of tourist season. Even with these restrictions and the presence of scores of monuments that restricted his camera angles and moves, Maxwell claims that 60 percent of the film was shot on the actual battlefield.

But key sequences had to be filmed elsewhere. The Battle of Little Round Top, for instance, was filmed on private hill property west of Gettysburg. There was no way it could be filmed on the actual Little Round Top, which was now covered with commemorative monuments. It would also be difficult to build rocky fortifications for the defending Union troops since the park officials were adamant about any changes to the topography, even if the rocks would be removed at the end of filming. Similarly, Pickett's Charge was filmed on private land, also west of the battlefield, between the town and the Eisenhower farm. Fortunately, its proximity to the battlefield meant that the topography and foliage were identical to the real location.

Thus, in the summer of 1992, a little over 14 years after he first read *The Killer Angels*, Ronald Maxwell, now surrounded by an enormous film crew and thousands of reenactors, was ready to direct *Gettysburg*.

Did the incredible journey leave its scars on Maxwell? He claimed that he was probably being tested. He explained:

> The test was how badly do you want to tell this story and do you deserve to tell this story? And I thought, well, yeah, it needed to take all these years before I was on the set with cameras. Because I was going to tell the story of people who sacrificed so much more.
>
> Maybe I was ready intellectually and physically at 30, but maybe I hadn't lived enough, maybe I didn't have enough life mileage to tell the story. I had never been in combat, but I don't think a director has to be a combat veteran to portray this any more than you have to murder somebody to do a murder mystery.
>
> You have to be empathetic to the people who fought there. You have to try and understand the participants, you have to some extent respect them, you have get to the paradoxes and complexities of the human condition and that takes humility. I don't believe you can sit as a judge. You end up making propaganda and people intuitively know it and they reject the film for those reasons.
>
> The films that hold up over the years — Jean Renoir's *Rules of the Game* or Stanley Kubrick's *Paths of Glory* or Lewis Milestone's *All Quiet on the Western Front*—they don't have that attitude, their attitude is one of humility. They're more determined to get to that "heart of darkness," to find the truth of these men who are caught in this horrible, demanding situation and that's why we want to see these movies. There is a tremendous variety of war movies, but the good ones share a profound empathy for the soldiers and they're devoid of judgment.[23]

In dramatizing Shaara's novel, Maxwell remained faithful to the book, which does not dramatize every aspect of the Battle of Gettysburg. There is no battle in the peach orchard or the wheat field. You see no assault up Culp's Hill. Like Shaara, Maxwell focused on the three crucial events that took place on the three days of Gettysburg: Buford's delaying action; Chamberlain's defense of Little Round Top and Pickett's Charge. However, significant time is spent with Robert E. Lee and James Longstreet as they discuss the Confederate strategy for the battle; Maxwell expands upon the relationship between two old friends, Confederate General Armistead and Union General Hancock; and literally dozens of other officers on both sides are introduced and included in the order of battle.

Maxwell's depiction of Chamberlain's defense of Little Round Top is certainly the centerpiece of *Gettysburg* and the most realistic Civil War battle ever staged for film. Little did Colonel Joshua Lawrence Chamberlain, commander of the 20th Maine Regiment, know that when his unit arrived in Gettysburg on July 2, 1863, after an exhausting, excruciatingly hot, forced march, that they would end up altering the course of the most important battle of the Civil War. If Confederate General John Bell Hood's rebels had turned the flank on Chamberlain, there is the possibility that the Confederates would have completely rolled up the Union left flank, and, given his reputation for exploiting a devastating flanking attack, Lee might have won the Battle of Gettysburg. Those were the stakes facing Chamberlain as he and his men climbed Little Round Top and prepared to face a massive frontal assault.

Four miles west of Gettysburg, Maxwell was able to find a hill with the same degree of incline as the real Little Round Top, the same trees, the same basic topography. Walking over that ground, Maxwell and cinematographer Kees Van Oostrum decided to cover the battle sequence with a constantly moving camera. So Van Oostrum went to the key grip and explained that he wanted to dolly up and down the hill for three days. The grip looked at him and said, "Are you out of your mind?" Two person camera dollies weigh around 700 pounds. To maneuver the camera up and down that hill, the grip came up with a unique solution — designing a "pendulum dolly." Two tracks were laid, one for the main camera dolly and a second for another equally weighted dolly, linked by a rope and a block. The result: a weightless scenario in which the camera dollies could move up and down the hill effortlessly.

For tracking dolly shots, where the camera moves past a line of Union infantrymen, firing their muskets point blank into the lens, Maxwell's grip team protected the camera lens with a Plexiglas shielding plate. At that distance, even blank ammunition could have killed the camera operators. Meanwhile, the art department helped build the rocky barriers behind which the Union sharpshooters fired.

Maxwell determined to shoot the sequence with a full second-unit crew headed by Steve Boyum. While Maxwell worked with the principal actors Jeff Daniels, C. Thomas Howell (as Chamberlain's brother, Tom) and Kevin Conway, Boyum would be responsible for shooting the stuntmen and reenactors as they crouched, ran, loaded, reloaded, and engaged in hand-to-hand combat. He also staged the Confederate charge on a separate hill, so as not to interfere with Maxwell's main unit shooting. Whenever the camera is behind the Union line, shooting the Confederates with the Chamberlain brothers and Kilrain in the foreground frame, that is the main Maxwell unit.

Maxwell was well prepared for this critical battle sequence — he had story-boarded every angle. He explained: "You can't wing a picture like this. When you have 5,000 extras and 200 principals, and horses, cannons, explosions, you can't improvise. You have to get the work done so there are a lot of production meetings, story boards, shot lists and then when you come to a situation with real cannons, muskets, bayonets, if you're not careful and if every single person doesn't know what they're doing on every single setup, you could kill somebody."[24]

Maxwell's vigorous depiction of the Battle of Little Round Top was unprecedented. Although there are battle sequences in the few worthwhile Civil War films that have been made over the years, no filmmaker had ever decided to recreate a famous battle with the amount of detail and care that Maxwell devoted. With the number of reenactors available, a first-class stunt-and-effects team and the time to do their work properly, he pulled it off. He also benefited from the outstanding work of sound mixer J. Stanley Johnson, a direct descendent of Confederate General Joseph Johnston.

Johnston would go out with a microphone and record musket fire at 50 feet, 100 feet, 300 feet and so forth, building a kaleidoscope of musket sound effects that would be invaluable in the final mix. Maxwell would hire him again for *Gettysburg's* prequel, *Gods and Generals*.

Outnumbered, running out of ammunition and in danger of being overrun and flanked, Chamberlain decides at a critical juncture to fix bayonets and charge down the hill, an act of incredible bravery and spontaneity for which he was awarded the Congressional Medal of Honor.

"When they're fixing bayonets, those are all real bayonets," Maxwell explained. "But when their charging down the hill, only the front rank of soldiers had real ones. We gave rubber bayonets to the soldiers that followed. The last thing we wanted was someone to trip and fall holding a real bayonet."[25]

Additional safety precautions were applied to the camera crews who wore padding and had visors over their face. Maxwell's effects team was utilizing real black powder in the musket blanks, so if you stood in front of a firing blank musket you could be killed or possibly blinded by the discharge.

Commenting on the finished sequence in a special documentary that was featured on the film's DVD release, American Civil War historian James McPherson said of Maxwell's depiction of Little Round Top, "I think it's the best part of the movie ... the fight at Little Round Top is quite accurately portrayed as being crucial to the ability of the Union Army to prevent the Confederates from rolling up their flank.... It's a good choice to portray that fighting and a good way to symbolize the failure of the Confederates attack to achieve any kind of a break-through or a successful flanking attack on the second day of the battle."[26]

McPherson, by the way, pointed out that, although Longstreet had ordered the attack on the Union right flank at 11 o'clock in the morning of July 2 (when Little Round Top was still unoccupied), the attack couldn't be coordinated until 4:00 in the afternoon. By then, Chamberlain's 20th Maine had time to deploy and defend the hill.

While Little Round Top was the centerpiece of *Gettysburg*, Maxwell's depiction of Pickett's Charge on the final day, was the film's *pièce de résistance*, deploying every possible resource he had, and then some.

Shooting Pickett's Charge in the dead of summer in Pennsylvania presented Maxwell with some of the same challenges that had faced General Robert E. Lee 129 years earlier. During the six days during which the final charge was filmed, local ambulances were running an hourly shuttle between the battlefield and the local hospital. Standing in 90–100-degree heat in historically accurate Civil War–era woolen uniforms was a virtual nightmare, and although the sweat pouring down the soldier's faces was real and usefully accurate to history, the experience was extremely uncomfortable for the reenactors.

Maxwell's craft service crew, which supplied snacks and drinks to the crew, was delivering case after case of Gatorade to the reenactors. If a reenactor dropped from heat exhaustion, he was immediately stabilized and hydrated. The medical personnel assigned to the crew knew that you just couldn't throw a heat exhaustion victim in an ambulance — they could die.

Unfortunately, one Confederate reenactor collapsed during the middle of Pickett's Charge, was taken to a hospital, and died of a massive heart attack. In a mystical sense, he was the last casualty of the Battle of Gettysburg. Maxwell later led a memorial service for the family.

Filming with thousands of extras presented challenges to Maxwell and his cinematographer, Kees Van Oostrum. To cover as much of the battlefield as possible, Van Oostrum deployed a number of stationary cameras, plus a miniature helicopter camera, which filmed above the troops. At first, the mini-helicopter camera was a blessing, but in reality, it only had a 200-yard range. Even when the controller was put in a car and drove under the moving mini-copter, the shot wasn't as graceful as it could be. Fortunately, nobody seemed to mind.

But it wasn't only the numbers that impressed those that were present for the climactic charge. The sound was incredible. Summoning every reenactor artillery unit they could find, Maxwell's ordnance specialists assembled 60 Civil War replica cannons. Even with blank shot, the tremendous sound of 60 cannons firing was estimated to be the loudest sound heard in Pennsylvania since the Civil War.

The colorful deployment of Pickett's division is perhaps augmented by the sequences that preceded the actual charge. One of the film's most resonant sequences was not featured in Shaara's book, and served to give the attack even more meaning for audiences. That sequence, which takes place in the woods before Pickett's division deploys is between Confederate Brigadier General Armistead, played so well by Maxwell's good friend and comrade, Richard Jordon, and actor James Lancaster who portrays British soldier and observer, Lt. Colonel Arthur Fremantle of the Coldstream Guards.

Observing the naiveté of Fremantle as to the identities of the advancing Confederates, Armistead fills in that background, introducing relatives of such famous Americans as Patrick Henry and President John Tyler. He also claimed that all Virginia was represented there for what could be their last charge. It is a beautifully poetic way of introducing the bloodbath that Pickett's Charge would soon become.

As the Confederate cannonade continues to rock the Union center, Maxwell and Van Oostrum designed a shot that starts low on the ground, comes up over a cannon, just before the cannon fires and then goes right over the muzzle, as Longstreet arrives to get a status report from Artillery Officer Porter Alexander. The scene was rehearsed very carefully with the reenactor cannoneers who had their clear order to pull the lanyard and fire the cannon at a specific moment. The camera itself was being pulled on a crane by a grip, working alongside the camera operator and a camera focus puller who adjusts focus onto Longstreet.

Maxwell rehearsed the sequence five times because, if something went wrong around that firing cannon, someone could get killed. His crew was outfitted with visors, and big heavy coats, and the camera once again had a Plexiglas shield in front of it.

The director explained, "Today, you wouldn't have an operator near that situation, you'd have the camera there and the worst case scenario is that you would lose the camera, but you wouldn't put anybody at risk."[27]

Unfortunately, due to budget constraints, Maxwell didn't have a sophisticated crane and remote-control system; he had the older equipment that you had to move with grips and assistants. After a number of rehearsals, it was assumed that everyone knew their position and responsibility. Unfortunately, the cannoneer froze and forgot to open fire on time. When he did finally pull the lanyard and the muzzle exploded, the camera crew was within two seconds of being right in front of it. That proved to be the closest call they had on the set of *Gettysburg*.

"When the sun was high enough in the sky and it looked like the middle of the day on July 3, 1863, the final day at Gettysburg," related the director, "when we were blessed with the same kind of blue sky day and I said, 'Action,' and the Confederate drums rolled out the cadence of the attack and the bugle sounded and the explosives that were pre-planned started to explode and the Confederates moved off with their flags flapping in the breeze, I can tell you it was absolutely one of the most emotional experiences I had ever known on a movie set, and I don't think it's an exaggeration to say that everyone else there felt the same way."[28]

One reenactor who felt that way was 26-year-old Matt McNabb, an assistant manager of the Disney Store at Main Place Mall in Santa Ana, California. In October 1993, he described the experience of participating in Pickett's Charge to a reporter for the *Orange County Register*: "Incredible doesn't even begin to describe something like that. You're standing with 3,000 guys, you're screaming at the top of your lungs. You're standing where someone died. It's like you're replacing someone who was there."[29]

McNabb's buddy, Cliff Cramp, a 31-year-old historical illustrator and graduate student at California State University, Fullerton, also shared his feelings with the *Orange County Register*: "Cannons are firing and shells are bursting all over the place. It made you realize that those soldiers had to have a lot of nerve to walk out of the woods, just to be decimated."[30]

Almost from the beginning, Ted Turner had let Ron Maxwell know that he wanted to be in the picture. It's not every day that a studio head requests a cameo, but *Gettysburg* was the inaugural film for the "Mouth from the South's" new Turner Pictures, and he wasn't going to pass up an opportunity to play a combat soldier in the immortal Pickett's Charge.

"We went looking for a character for Ted," explained Maxwell, "and we found Colonel Waller Tazewell Patton, of the Seventh Virginia Infantry, who was mortally wounded while taking part in Pickett's Charge. We researched his uniform which was tailored to Turner's frame and we gave him basically one line, 'Let's go, boys.'"[31]

At a party for cast and crew the night before Turner's sequence would be shot, Maxwell went up to Turner and said, "Ted, we can shoot your scene one of two ways. I can shoot you against the sky with the camera mounted low and we can put five or ten soldiers around you; or, since we have 4,000 soldiers on the set anyway, we can just lift up the camera and shoot you with 4,000 soldiers behind you. It's your choice — we can go either way."[32]

Turner opted for the big shot, with Maxwell putting together two setups for the man who had turned Maxwell's dream project into living color. In one tracking shot, Patton leaps forward between explosions and massed musket fire and you can't miss him. The second setup was a fixed shot where he says his line, "Let's go, boys" and then gets shot. For the latter sequence, Maxwell's effects team placed exploding blood squibs on Turner. The shot was completed in two takes. Afterwards, Turner looked at Maxwell and said, "Just call me Two-Take Ted."[33]

Maxwell's friend, Ken Burns, also requested a cameo in the picture and Maxwell was happy to oblige. Burns was given the part of the young Union officer who, during Pickett's Charge, pleads with Union General Hancock to get down from his horse and take cover, to which Hancock responded, "There are times when the life of a corps commander doesn't count."[34]

Playing host to studio moguls like Turner and friends of the production like Burns was fun for Maxwell, but Turner had even more dramatic news to share with him. After he sent back the first batch of daily footage (the "dailies"), Maxwell learned that Turner wanted to release the film theatrically before it came to Turner Network Television. *Gettysburg* was going to be seen on the big screen, after all.

Meanwhile, Maxwell was knee-deep in the Union sequences of the picture and one day he had a problem with one of the Chamberlain speeches delivered by Jeff Daniels. It was at the end of the day and it was a key sequence where Chamberlain addresses the mutineers from the Second Maine. Losing the light, Maxwell wrapped the crew, figuring he could reshoot the following day. However, the Turner executives in charge of the shoot wanted to wait and see what the dailies looked like before ordering a reshoot. Maxwell explained that he didn't need the dailies to know that the scene wasn't working — after all, he was right there shooting it.

But he was forced to wait, and when the executives said the dailies looked fine, they refused to pay for a reshoot, Maxwell was forced to insist. The reply came back that if Maxwell was going to insist on a re-shoot, they were going to cut out all the sequences between Chamberlain and his brother, Tom Chamberlain (C. Thomas Howell) to make up for the time lost. Maxwell was astonished. He sought fellow producer Bob Rehme's advice and Rehme told him to go for it and he would back him up.

Maxwell thanked Rehme, then he brought in some reinforcements of his own — namely actors Jeff Daniels, C. Thomas Howell and Kevin Conway. He walked into Daniels's trailer and explained what he needed. Daniels looked at Maxwell and said to him, 'Remember that conversation we had in Ann Arbor?'"

"Sure I do," Maxwell replied.

"Well, tell those executives from L.A. to get their asses here in the morning, I want to talk with them," Daniels said.[35]

Maxwell had an inkling of what Daniels was about to do, but he went along with it. When the Turner "suits" arrived, Daniels placed the *Gettysburg* script on the coffee table and said, "Here's the deal. I have a contract to shoot this script, not a word less, not a letter less, not a scene less, and if you guys think you're going to pull these scenes out of the movie, I'm on a plane tomorrow morning at nine and—" he gestured to Conway and Howell, "so are these gentlemen. We're on a plane, you've breached the contract and we're done." And then he walked out with Conway and Howell. It was not a bluff, and the Turner execs knew it.[36]

But it worked, and Maxwell got his reshoot, plus a lot of screaming and "you put them up to this" tirades from the suits. Maxwell and Daniels had lived up to the commitments they had made in Ann Arbor. Daniels had delivered "the steel," and so had Maxwell.

And then there were the beards. When I interviewed Ron Maxwell for this chapter, I debated whether to even bring it up. *Gettysburg* is so important as a document of those incredible events of July 1863, I thought it would be insulting to mention the criticism that the beards received. However, I brought it up gently and Maxwell was only too happy to discuss something that has always bothered him. As he puts it, "It will probably still be bothering me when I'm dead and buried in my grave."[37]

Most of the criticism was leveled at the beard of Tom Berenger's James Longstreet character, who was referred to, disparagingly, as either looking like an "Amish elder" or one of the Smith Brothers, the bearded gentleman on the cough drop boxes.

Maxwell freely admits that, because of their budget restraints, they didn't hire the hair team that wins Oscars. It was unfortunate because, as he points out, at no time in human history has there been more complicated facial hair than in the middle of the 19th century.

Explained the director, "You've got to get it exactly right, there's no room for error with face hair when you have big close-ups. Initially, the one that hits you like a ton of bricks is Longstreet's. And we paid the price because we couldn't afford to bring the hair and makeup team in two weeks earlier for tests. I was only allowed a few days of hair prep and, under those conditions, you have no time to fix things. Once you start shooting it's too late. And that was a battle I lost.

"By the time we did the visual tests, they said that they looked good on film — nobody would dare tell me that today, I'd fire them on the spot. I had finally gotten my movie financed, I was 44 years old and I was already on the set, and you can go just so far. So by the time we did the tests, it was the Saturday before we started shooting. To be preoccupied with beards, after 14 years of trying to make the movie, I was, to say the least, very unhappy."[38]

It wasn't nitpicking on Maxwell's part, it was a legitimate problem and it could have been fixed with $100,000, but the budget was fixed and immutable. When the first days shooting came back, and Maxwell saw what he terms "that big bush on Longstreet," he immediately called for the beard to be cut back.

"So I ordered them to thin it out," he related, "and so the worst scene for him is the one we shot on the first day when he's walking with Lee along a rail and Bonnie Blue Flag is playing in the background. In no other scene does it look that bad because we trimmed it."[39]

Unfortunately, it needed additional trimming and Berenger was adamantly against it. He showed Maxwell a photograph and pointed to the General's long beard as evidence that beards were much fuller in the 1860s than they are today.

"It was the first two days of shooting," recalled Maxwell, "and I thought if I push this guy anymore, he's not going to be able to act. I'll be at war with one of our leads. Of course, at some point, you can't change it, otherwise you'll have continuity problems. So we did the best we could with what we had and, in reality, the worst of it was on those first two days of shooting."[40]

Having learned the lesson the hard way, on his prequel to *Gettysburg*, *Gods and Generals*, Maxwell hired Manlio Rocchetti, perhaps the greatest hair and makeup artist in the movies.

Ronald F. Maxwell's *Gettysburg* was released in theaters by New Line Cinema in November 1993. Its per screen average was so high that the studio had to scramble to quadruple the number of theaters where it would play.

In the summer of 1994, the film ran as a two-night mini-series on Turner Network Television (TNT), breaking all Nielsen records for a cable TV broadcast, reaching more than 36 million viewers.[41]

SECTION IV

WAR FILMS IN THE 21ST CENTURY

It was once explained to me that the reason we see very few westerns today is because the filmmakers who specialized in the western genre are all gone. Now, I don't believe that westerns are entirely dead. The Coen Brothers' *True Grit* (2011) was a hit, but there was a time when you couldn't name all the westerns being filmed. Of course, there was also a time when television was rife with westerns.

War films aren't as invisible as westerns, but some of the same criteria applies. The directors who made the classic war films — John Sturges, Robert Aldrich, Sam Fuller, Stanley Kubrick, Stanley Kramer, Henry Hathaway, Mark Robson, Robert Wise, Don Siegel, David Lean — are gone, as well as all the writers whose craft was forged in the drama of Pearl Harbor and the Bulge.

Today, studios, for the most part, make movies for teenagers. That's why we see so many films based on comic books, graphic novels, popular TV shows and Disneyland rides. To mount a project based on war, you have to have a name like Steven Spielberg, Clint Eastwood or Oliver Stone.

The Vietnam War soured mainstream America on war films. And, in many ways, the genre has never recovered from that. And although America supports the military and its continuing war against international terrorism, the country hasn't really supported a U.S. military mission since the Second World War. And if the military mission isn't universally supported, as it has not been in Vietnam, Iraq and Afghanistan, people

Michael Bay walks Cuba Gooding, Jr., through his paces during the filming of *Pearl Harbor*.

will not be standing in line to see a movie about it. It's that simple.

I would also maintain that the studios, and, hence, the filmmakers who sell to them today are less interested in history and more interested in fantasy and the capabilities of special effects. Whether you like it or not, the studios are in the "tent pole" business. No longer run by single individuals like Louis B. Mayer and Jack Warner, they're corporations that are usually part of bigger corporations, with hundreds of executives, huge marketing and distributions staffs and a mission statement to generate huge sums of money to support the overhead. Nothing is left to chance anymore. Formulas are the rule, and if history says that a *Godzilla* sequel is guaranteed at least $200 million in revenue around the world, then, by golly, a *Godzilla*

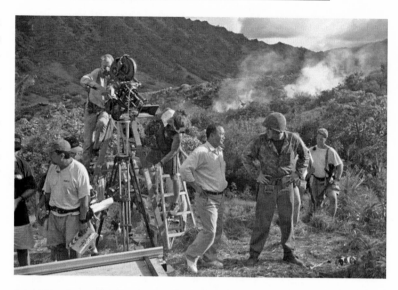

John Woo (center) goes over a scene with Nicolas Cage (right) during the filming of *Windtalkers*.

Bruce Willis (center) and Colin Farrell (right) flank director Gregory Hoblit during filming on *Hart's War*.

sequel will be put into production, whether the public likes it or not.

When a huge special-effects-saturated movie is put into production, the budget numbers are staggering. I remember when everyone was giving James Cameron grief over his $100 million budget for *Titanic*. Today, it seems like every studio tent pole costs a minimum of $100 million, or $150 million, or $200 million. Whether it's Disney's *Pirates of the Caribbean*, Fox's *X-Men*, Sony's *Spider Man*, Warner's *Harry Potter*, MGM's *James Bond* or whatever, these movies not only soak up all of the money available to make movies, they also absorb the attention of executives who are no longer free to speculate on potential dramatic films that don't have franchise possibilities.

If producer Buddy Adler went to Sony and pitched *From Here to Eternity* today he would probably have been rejected by a lower-tier development executive, who would have to explain that the studio was only interested in franchise titles. I can just hear the conversation. "We love Burt Lancaster and Montgomery Clift, but we don't see McDonald's selling a lot of burgers and soda with their pictures on drink cups."

Getting back to Messrs. Spielberg, East-

With the advent of digital special effects, filmmakers can now take live-action battle sequences like this one in *Lord of the Rings* and turn 100 soldiers into 10,000. These epic fantasies have appealed to a new generation of war film fans.

wood and Stone, war movies can be sold if the right ingredients are present. It usually takes a major filmmaker. But the results can be mixed.

Director Michael Bay had major clout in Hollywood when he did the $140 million *Pearl Harbor* in 2001. His previous three films, *Bad Boys* (1995), *The Rock* (1996) and *Armageddon* (1998), were all big money makers.

Director John Woo was coming off the success of *Face/Off* (1997) and *Mission Impossible II* (2000) when he was given the opportunity to helm *Windtalkers* in 2002.

Although he wasn't in the same mega-class as Bay and Woo, director Gregory Hoblit's grosses on *Primal Fear* (1996) and *Frequency* (2000) were respectable enough to get him *Hart's War* (2002). None of these films were really much about history. They were pitched as good dramatic entertainment, and that's probably why they were greenlit.

The attention to detail that Steven Spielberg paid to *Saving Private Ryan*, Clint Eastwood paid to *Flags of Our Fathers* and *Letters from Iwo Jima*, and Oliver Stone paid to *Platoon*, were the exceptions and not the rule. And, yet, those films were done and done well. Combined with the huge success of the HBO mini-series *Band of Brothers* (2001), the war film genre is still breathing.

However, I would maintain that today more effort is put into animating droid armies (*Star Wars: The Phantom Menace*), orcs and trolls (*The Lord of the Rings: The Return of the King*) and mutants (*X-Men*) than is spent on amassing tanks, planes and artillery for contemporary war films. Thus, the fantasy adventure films of today have taken a page from the epic quality of past war films and have adapted it as their own. It is no surprise that producer George Lucas, in developing his plan to shoot the first *Star Wars* film back in the mid–1970s, screened old World War II aviation films like *633 Squadron* and *The Dam Busters* as a blueprint for his futuristic action sequences. The drama was already there. All he had to do was update it.

CHAPTER THIRTEEN

Saving Private Ryan

And then came *Saving Private Ryan.*

The summer 1998 release of director Steven Spielberg's mammoth World War II drama was not only a colossal international hit with critics and audiences alike, but it signaled a dramatic paradigm shift in the way audiences experienced war films.

Some 23 years earlier, in the summer of 1975, Spielberg had taken his cameras into the calm waters of New England to film a movie based on a bestseller called *Jaws.* For many people, the ocean never looked the same again. Why? Because when someone went into those gentle waters for a swim, the camera was right there with them, with the lapping water, with the easy body strokes, with the pleasant sun glinting off the surf, with the cheerful laughter coming from shore. When a terrifying Great White Shark arrived, it was also right there with you. With his voyeuristic camera, Steven Spielberg had made something as simple as swimming in the ocean the most horrifying of experiences. With *Saving Private Ryan,* he took everything he had learned since then and applied those skills to creating realistic combat action. The result was nothing short of astonishing.

For visceral impact, no one had ever experienced anything like the first 22 minutes of *Saving Private Ryan.* In Spielberg's hands, *you* are on Omaha Beach on the morning of June 6, 1944. As *your* landing craft filled with puking G.I.'s approaches the beach obstacles, *you* are about to walk into a blistering wall of enemy machine gun, mortar and artillery fire. *You* are jumping over the side of your landing craft, before you end up like a bunch of hamburger meat. *You* are struggling in the water, as bullets strike your friends, leaving bright red watery plumes. *You* rise to the surface, unable to hear, your ears clogged by sea water and the shock of battle. *You* wedge yourself against a hedgehog obstacle as enemy fire rakes the beach, killing indiscriminately. Landing craft explode, bodies fly into the air, soldiers cower amongst the obstacles, some are screaming, some are crying, everyone is yelling, "What do we do?" *You* have to take command.

It is in this hellish netherworld of death and chaos that *we* are introduced to Captain John Miller (Tom Hanks), a U.S. Army Ranger, sent ashore to clear a path through the beach obstacles. This is definitely not your father's war film — this doesn't have the wide impersonal vistas of *The Longest Day,* documentary-like as they were. This was up close and personal war — a form of storytelling that is simultaneously horrifying and fascinating — the product of a filmmaker working at the top of his game, fashioning his masterwork. And, although he received the Best Picture Oscar for producing and directing *Schindler's List* in 1993, *Saving*

Irish Army reservists, dressed as World War II era American infantrymen, head for invasion work on Curracloe Beach, Western Ireland. (Courtesy of *Battleground — The Making of Saving Private Ryan in Ireland*, by Tom Moony and Stephen Eustace)

Private Ryan is his masterwork — a film that defines war, not only for a new generation of viewers, but for the surviving veterans who are finally able to answer the question they had been asked continually for nearly 50 years: What was combat *really* like in World War II?

Although the story of the making of *Saving Private Ryan* properly begins with screenwriter Robert Rodat walking through a village square in New Hampshire, where he was inspired by a Civil War-era memorial, in truth, the building blocks of *Saving Private Ryan* were fashioned much earlier than that.

In 1943, Arnold Spielberg, Steven's father, was a radio operator flying B-25 supply missions over Burma. Here Spielberg described that seminal influence:

> He was in charge of a fifty caliber machine gun over his head. He only got in one combat mission — most of the time he was with a group flying supplies between the British and Americans in Burma. He used to have reunions with his friends when I was growing up. They'd all tell war stories, and they were horrifying. I kept wondering, How come movies haven't done it that way, if that's what really happened?
>
> You hear from a veteran what it was like, and then you see Hollywood's version of what it was like, and for many years I believed Hollywood. This war has not really been explored on film except with ulterior motives. During the war itself, it was explored for purposes of bolstering the home front, or encouraging enlistment, or selling War Bonds.... Soldiers die with lovely last words that sound like they were written by poets. The gunfire is never loud enough, the damage is never honest enough — all because the purpose is to do everything about the war except tell you what it was like to be in one.
>
> During the 1960s, in films like *Kelly's Heroes, The Great Escape, Where Eagles Dare,* World War II is simply an excuse for adventure. In my own *Raiders* films, the incidents of Germans in Africa were just a way to give Indiana Jones villains I couldn't be criticized for killing.[1]

Arnold Spielberg's World War II memories would forever inspire his son, who started to make short films about the war when he was a teenager. It's well known that he borrowed his father's movie camera and started making films in the desert when the family lived in Arizona. What most people don't know is that those first movies were World War II movies. One of his first was a 40-minute 8mm color silent picture called *Escape to Nowhere*, about a battle in North Africa. It won first prize in a statewide amateur film contest.

Arnold Spielberg recalled his son's first war movie experiences: "They'd dye shirts dark and light, so they could be Nazis and Americans and they played warfare out in the desert in Phoenix. First, he wanted to use real explosives, but I wouldn't go to the drug store and buy gunpowder to make explosives, so we used this mud trick and it worked pretty good. We'd take a stick and bury one end of the stick in the mud and it pivoted on a stone; the kid who was acting as a soldier and was supposed to get blown up, would run up, step on the stick and flip the mud up in the air, which would look like an explosion and he'd fall on his face and contort and roll over and all kinds of stuff like that."[2]

"We didn't have any special-effects expertise," Steven Spielberg admitted. "I didn't read any books. It was just, 'How do you make this come to life?' I'm in *Escape to Nowhere*, I'm the guy driving the jeep, scrunched down so he looks real small.

"*Fighter Squadron* was a movie I made around the same age I made *Escape to Nowhere*.... It was the first time I made an actual black and white movie, because I had seen all the documentaries of World War II and they were all in black and white in those days.

"I went out to the Sky Harbor Airport in Phoenix, and they had a bunch of old World War II airplanes in mothballs. P-40s, Thunderbolts, F6F Hellcats. They were all kind of lined up and my dad got us permission to let us sit in the cockpits of a couple of these airplanes. My dad actually did all the costumes for me, because I used the actual outfit he brought back from Burma to makes these movies with. So if I had nine kids flying these airplanes, I actually had only one airplane and one leather helmet with one set of goggles — we kept trading them off. In those days, when 8mm was all the rage, the camera shops also sold documentaries from World War II, so I intercut a 14 year old in my dad's leather hat, flying these airplanes with actual gun camera footage."[3]

Steven Spielberg would never lose his fascination with the war. "Clearly half of my films take place in the 1930s and '40s," he admitted. "When you look at the *Raiders* films, *Empire of the Sun*, *1941* (my comedy), even *Schindler's List,* which I don't consider a war film — the Holocaust is in a category all its own — I've had windows into war in many films that I've directed, but I don't think I've done anything like this movie."[4]

Prior to *Saving Private Ryan*, Spielberg always put something extra into his World War II–era films. There was a level of respect, almost reverence, given to the veterans, their mission, the times in which they lived, even their equipment — whether it was the planes they flew, the ships they served on or the tanks they were riding.

As early as *Jaws* (1975), this approach is clearly evident in the way the character of U.S. Navy veteran, Quint (Robert Shaw) is depicted, when he relates the story of the sinking of his ship, the USS *Indianapolis*. It's commonly known that writer John Milius was brought in to write that one sequence, one of the best scenes in the film and one of the most atmospheric veteran's stories ever presented. It's just a drunken Quint sitting there in the main cabin of the little fishing boat, telling Brody (Roy Scheider) and Hooper (Richard Dreyfuss) how the *Indianapolis* was on its way to Leyte in the Philippines, having dropped off the A-bomb on Tinian when it was attacked and sunk by a Japanese submarine.

"Eleven hundred men went into the water, vessel went down in twelve minutes. Didn't see the first shark for half an hour, tiger, thirteen footer ... what we didn't know was our bomb mission had been so secret no distress signal had been sent. They didn't even list us as overdue for a week...."

In many ways, Quint became a high school history teacher for a few minutes, telling us about a U.S. Navy disaster we probably had never heard of, and in gruesome detail.

"Very first light, Chief, sharks come cruising. So we formed ourselves into tight groups, kind of like all square in a battle, like you see on a calendar, like the Battle of Waterloo. And the idea was that a shark comes to the nearest man he starts pounding, hollering, screaming, sometimes the shark go away, sometimes he wouldn't go away."[5]

I don't think it was a coincidence that Brody kills the shark while firing Quint's World War II–era M-1 rifle.

Two years after the release of *Jaws*, Steven Spielberg directed *Close Encounters of the Third Kind*, a science-fiction thriller that begins with the discovery of five vintage World War II U.S. Navy Avenger torpedo bombers in the middle of the Mexican desert — the mysterious Flight 5 that disappeared off the coast of Florida in December 1945. There was just something about the way he presented those pristine warplanes that, once again, showed his respect for the war effort and the storied planes that helped win it.

When one of the mission control leaders says "Welcome back Navy" to the returning World War II veteran pilot at the end of the film, you almost wish Spielberg had spent more time with these veteran pilots, telling us where they'd been for 32 years.

Two years later, he gave us *1941*. Granted, it's the wildest and wackiest World War II comedy ever presented, but Spielberg still had enormous respect for the period and the efforts of the military to keep the peace in a Los Angeles, which is all aflutter with war jitters. The film is filled with details.

While other filmmakers were content in subbing modern Patton battle tanks in World War II scenarios, Spielberg not only gave motor pool maintenance Sergeant Frank Tree (Dan Aykroyd) a beautiful and vintage M-3 Lee tank, but he named it *Lulu Belle*, which was an affectionate homage to the M-3 Grant tank that Humphrey Bogart commanded in *Sahara* (1943). The film is filled with original, spot-on accurate equipment, including John Belushi's gorgeous P-40 "Tigershark" fighter, a B-17 parked at LAX, Army staff cars, motorcycles with sidecars, sky-sweeping anti-aircraft guns, searchlights, proper helmets, web gear and more.

In 1981, Steven Spielberg directed *Raiders of the Lost Ark*, a wonderful homage to the edge-of-your-seat serials that had been so popular in the 1930s. Spielberg has indicated that one of the reasons the film features Nazis is that you can kill as many as you want and nobody writes you a protest letter. However, there is no question that placing Indiana Jones (Harrison Ford) in Nepal and Egypt, circa 1936, and putting him up against plundering Nazis who are seeking religious objects for supernaturally obsessed Adolf Hitler, is pretty cool story material.

Once again, satisfying his fascination with World War II story elements and equipment, Spielberg filled the movie with vintage props, vehicles and aircraft. A centerpiece of the action is a celebrated and bruising fistfight between Jones and a German mechanic who battle while a small, two-man, German Flying Wing begins moving on its own power.

In 1987, Spielberg directed *Empire of the Sun*, a truly epic story of Jim, a pampered young English school boy who is separated from his parents and spends most of World War II in a Japanese internment camp, outside Shanghai, China. When I originally saw this film, I didn't particularly care for the boy (a young Christian Bale), but I was totally blown away by the ferocity of the P-51 attack on the nearby Japanese airfield. In subsequent viewings, however, this has become one of my favorite Spielberg films, again, because of his respect for the period and the enormous amount of period detail devoted to this unusual setting for a World War II picture. And the imagery — it's nothing less than stunning.

In one frenetic sequence, a famished young Jim wanders through a surreal and unfriendly downtown Shanghai where a movie theater sports a huge advertisement for *Gone with the Wind*. In another sequence, Jim is attending a holiday costume party when he runs into the huge backyard to fly his glider, only to discover a battalion of Japanese infantry having their lunch. It's one of those great Spielberg crane shots in which the camera follows Jim as he walks up a little berm and then we're treated to the sight of all of these soldiers.

Once again, a Spielberg film is filled with inspired references and images of World War II, particularly aircraft. Jim is introduced as a huge fan of the Japanese Zero; he later explores the wreck of a downed fighter plane, almost as though he is visiting a religious tomb. When Shanghai is bombed, he loses his mother's grasp when he stoops to pick up the toy Zero he dropped, and all the while the sky is filled with enemy aircraft. When Jim arrives in the internment camp, he discovers that his fellow Brits are being used as slave labor to construct a Japanese airfield; he bows his head to a parked Zero when he first arrives. He's introduced to American planes by the American prisoner, Basie (John Malkovich), who asks him if he saw a Mustang, to which Jim replies, "The Cadillac of the Sky," a term he obviously learned from the Americans. He witnesses a distant B-29 attack on the Shanghai docks and sees the slow deterioration of the Japanese fighter strip and their Zeros and then views their utter destruction by a seemingly unstoppable and murderous flight of sleek new P-51 Mustangs.

All of these images — all of his inspirations and fascinations — plus the tremendous attention to detail made all of these films standout from the thousands of World War II movies that preceded them. You just got the impression that no one had treated the war with this much respect, ever.

And then came *Saving Private Ryan*.

For screenwriter Robert Rodat, it began with a crying baby. The year was 1994, the 50th anniversary of D-Day, and Rodat was the proud father of a newborn son, who, like every other baby on the planet, liked to wake up before dawn and start wailing. To let the rest of the family sleep, Rodat would gather up his son and take him for a long walk through his sleepy New Hampshire hometown of Keene.

> We would often walk through the graveyard which was always shrouded in morning mist, and pass a monument that has the names of the men from the village who had died in combat, from the Revolution up through Vietnam. And on each side of the monument, from each conflict, there are repeated last names. Brothers, cousins, fathers, sons. There's one family that has five dead from the Civil War and three from the Revolutionary War. And so, with this infant son in my arms and another sleeping in the house, the idea of losing a son to combat was painful beyond description. The idea of losing more than one was inconceivable. That's where the first seed of *Saving Private Ryan* came from.
>
> My wife had given me a bunch of books that had come out about the Normandy landing, one of which was Stephen Ambrose's *D-Day*. My dad had been in World War II and had been injured on the second-to-last day of the war when an 88-shell exploded next to a halftrack. So I wanted to write something about his generation. I was reading all these books and thinking about all of this around the time my second son was born.[6]

Melding his visit to the monument with his newfound interest in the Normandy invasion, Rodat began researching families that had lost multiple sons in the war. The most notable and tragic was the five Sullivan brothers who were killed when their light cruiser, USS *Juneau*, was sunk during the Naval Battle of Guadalcanal in 1942. He also found out about the Niland brothers, two of whom were killed in the assault on Normandy, while a third — an officer in the Air Corps — was reported missing in action in the Pacific. The fourth brother was informed that, in keeping with the edict by President Franklin D. Roosevelt that no family should suffer the loss of more than two sons, he was being ordered home. Edward, the Air Corps officer, was later found alive, having escaped from a Japanese prison camp.

These stories were definitely noted by Rodat, but his plan was to keep things purely fictional — *Saving Private Ryan* would be anchored in the true events of Normandy in June of 1944, but it would not be a true story.

Rodat was trying to sell a Jack the Ripper script when he met producer Mark Gordon in Los Angeles in 1995. Gordon was an established producer who had just scored with *Speed*, the Keanu Reeves thriller which had introduced Sandra Bullock to the mass audience. Gordon really liked Rodat's script and invited him to pitch some more ideas. In fact, he even invited the writer to come to his office for weekly brainstorming sessions.

"I think we had two meetings," recalled Gordon. "We had some things we were playing around with, but nothing was really jumping out at either of us. And on the third or fourth meeting, he came to me and said, 'I have this idea, I don't know if you're going to like it or not,' and he pitched me the trailer for *Saving Private Ryan*. He explains that it's D-Day and a general has just been given word that three brothers have died in combat, two on Omaha Beach and one in the Pacific. The general says that's a terrible story, and they say it gets worse, there's a fourth brother, he's behind enemy lines somewhere in France, nobody knows where he is, and the general looks at the guy and says, 'Wherever he is, we're going to get him.' And Rodat told me it was loosely based on a true story.

"And I looked at him and said, 'Wow, that's the most incredible story I've ever heard. And he said, 'You think?' And I said, 'Yeah, I really do, I think it's amazing.' And he said, 'Do you think anybody will buy it?' And I said, 'We got to get this thing going; this is the most wonderful story I've heard in a long, long, long time.'"[7]

Gordon and Rodat polished the pitch and started to take it to studio executives. They received passes from everyone they met.

"They told us you can't make a World War II movie," Gordon explained. "No one wants to see a World War II movie. It's typical of our business, where we're so pre-disposed to say no. For example, any time somebody comes in and says, 'I want to make a film about the entertainment industry,' the response is, 'no one is interested and nobody will buy it.' And the same thing happened to us when it came to making a World War II movie."[8]

As an example of how the script was received by most of Hollywood, here is the comment one studio reader gave the Rodat draft in May 1996:

> This is a professionally written but rather dated war story, the likes of which we haven't seen made in probably forty years. It's not often you find a script filled with such good old-fashioned heroism and larger-than-life daring-do [sic]. It's well done, for what it is, but it also seems jarringly out of synch with the times…. The dialogue is often snappy, but aside from the profanity, it still sounds like an old-fashioned war flick. In short, the writing is competent, but anachronistic. It's a respectable script, but it's also a good thirty years too late. Pass.[9]

According to Mark Gordon, "The last place we went was Paramount [where Gordon had originally developed *Speed*, until it was dumped and Fox bought it]. And we ended up pitching to Don Grainger and he absolutely loved it."[10]

Unbeknownst to Gordon, Grainger, who admired films like *The Guns of Navarone* and *Destination Tokyo*, was looking for a World War II film and believed that, contrary to popular opinion in the "suit" community, they had not gone out of style.

Grainger turned around and pitched the idea to his boss, John Goldwyn, who enthusiastically approved development money for the script. Gordon explained:

> Rodat and I made an agreement. Because we knew this was going to be a difficult movie to sell. Number one, Rodat was going to write the film and structure it in such a way that it wasn't going to cost a fortune (because at this point, we had no idea it was going to be Steven Spielberg and Tom Hanks). So as you know, there was a battle at the beginning and a battle at the end and there was some skirmishing in the middle that wasn't expensive. So we conceived of the thing to be made for a reasonable price.
>
> Secondly, we agreed that we would not show the script until we both believed it was a movie. We didn't want to typically submit a draft, get some notes, submit another draft, etc. We ended up probably having 15 drafts before we even showed it to anyone. We had a draft where we found Ryan on Page 30 and the story was getting him back. We had a draft where we found Ryan on Page 60 and we had a draft where we found Ryan on Page 90. We even had a draft where we never found Ryan at all. There were so many different versions of this story and we kept working on it. In terms of collaboration, it was one of the great experiences.[11]

Unfortunately, Paramount didn't flip for it. "And I was shocked and disappointed," recalled Gordon, "and all the things you are when people don't think what you think is good is as good as you think it is."[12]

Gordon was also informed that there were two other World War II films suddenly in consideration at the studio. One was a feature film version of the ABC television series *Combat!* which had Bruce Willis on board to play the Sergeant Saunders part immortalized by actor Vic Morrow; and *On Wings of Eagles,* a World War II drama that had Arnold Schwarzenegger attached to play a good German officer. The studio was basically saying that the first producer to get his film up and running would get the greenlight. Gordon went to work and quickly outdistanced the other films.

A number of things happened in the winter of 1997, and they happened quickly. Gordon sent the script to a young CAA agent named Karen Sage, who fell in love with it. So much so that she enthusiastically pitched the concept to Steven Spielberg when the director came in to meet a conference room full of agents who wanted to pitch him material.

Simultaneously, Gordon called actor Tom Hanks, who once shared a building with Gordon at 20th Century–Fox. "It was just a small building," said Gordon, "that was later torn down and replaced with a bunch of standing satellite dishes. He had the upstairs, I had the downstairs. And I called him up and said, 'Hey, I have this script, I think you'll really love it. It's called *Saving Private Ryan*. Why don't you read it?' And he said he would. I also spoke to his agent, Richard Lovett, also at CAA, and I told him he should read it too.

"I also spoke to other agencies, giving them a list of directors I was interested in and asked them to read it. So I get a call from one agent who says his client is very interested. And he shall remain nameless. Let's just say he could get my movie made. And we had dinner with Don Grainger and Rodat and it all went very well. Then I had lunch with Tom Hanks and we talked about the movie. And he said, 'What do you think about Spielberg directing?' And I said, 'Well, that's a great idea, I'd love it.' And Tom explained that he and Steven had wanted to do a movie together, blah, blah, blah."[13]

In this initial meeting, Hanks also indicated that, although he thought the premise of the film was fascinating, he thought the character of Captain John Miller, with his Medal of Honor, his cigar and his tendency to say things like, "Come on, you sons of bitches," was drawn as too standard a war hero for his taste. He indicated that, if he was to play him, he would have to be redrawn and softened, and Miller would have to be reborn through his experience of rescuing Private Ryan.[14]

A couple of days later I get a call from Richard Lovett and the call goes something like this: "Look, Tom Hanks and Steven Spielberg want to do this movie. But you can't tell anybody at Paramount because I need to take care of some business first, so you just have to keep it quiet." I later found out that Karen Sage had pitched the project to Spielberg who also later heard from Hanks.

So that was four in the afternoon and by six I'm like giddy with enthusiasm. I then get a call from John Goldwyn at Paramount, informing me that he had great news, this other director wants to do the movie and the studio was ready to make the deal. And I said, "You can't do that." And he said, "Why?" And I said, "I can't tell you. Just trust me that I have something better." I couldn't say anything, I had promised Lovett and, of course, Goldwyn wants to know everything.

I told him, "I can't tell you, I have been asked not to tell you. You're just going to have to trust me to put the brakes on this thing for a minute. Because you cannot make a deal with this other director." And he just blurts out, "Tell me who it is." And I told, "John, I can't tell you." And I didn't.

Finally, Lovett calls and tells me it's okay, the deal is done. It's going to be Steven Spielberg directing, Tom Hanks starring, we're going to do the deal with Dreamworks financing and Paramount distributing. Jeffrey Katzenberg then called me and I had known him for years (because I had done two movies at Disney) and he was all excited because Dreamworks had just started. He said it was a great script. And I was on Cloud Nine, as you can imagine. Then Sherry Lansing, the chairman of Paramount, called me at eleven o'clock that night and starting screaming with excitement. It was so cute. It's Sherry Lansing, the chairman of the studio calling me and saying she couldn't believe it, she was so excited. And that's how the whole thing came together.[15]

The first time Gordon spoke to Spielberg was over a video conference line to his home in the Hamptons in New York. Spielberg told Gordon that "people are going to feel like they've been at D-Day when they see this thing."[16] Truer words were never spoken.

Although Rodat would join the production briefly in Europe to do some re-writing, a series of writers now stepped in to take the ball from Rodat and create a new shooting draft. These included Frank Darabont (*The Shawshank Redemption*), Scott Frank (*Get Shorty*) and Steve Zaillian (*Schindler's List*).

Hanks's character, Captain John Miller, was redrawn to fit the actor's requirements. New characters were added, including the Jewish soldier, Mellish (Adam Goldberg) and the tough Italian kid, Caparzo (Vin Diesel).

"Steven was making his choices," Rodat recalled. "It was his choice to be very lean on back story. My preference was to add more back story regarding secondary characters. To Steven, however, the back stories seemed unnecessary. Here were these kids hitting the beach — what difference did it make what they did for a living or where they came from? That was Steven's point of view."[17]

For example, in Rodat's early drafts, Reiben (the character that would be played by Ed Burns) had much more to say about his previous work in a woman's lingerie shop. After cutting the back story, Reiben is left with one humorous anecdote that takes place in Ramelle, before the final battle.

While work on the script continued, Spielberg telephoned Dale Dye, who, 12 years after *Platoon*, had not only become the top military technical advisor in Hollywood, but had carved out a niche as a character actor. Spielberg had previously cast him in *Always*, in which he played the captain of the aerial firefighters. Dye recalled:

Steven was a big fan of my voice and my carriage as a ground commander in *Platoon*. So he cast me in *Always* and I began to act for him and get involved in scenes and I was willing to do anything — jump out of airplanes, run through fire, I didn't care.

Steven and I got to be much more personally acquainted and I discovered at that point his

Steven Spielberg (left) points Tom Hanks in the right direction on Curracloe Beach, Ireland, for the incredibly realistic and bloody opening of *Saving Private Ryan*.

interest in World War II and the military in general. He believed, as I do, and this was a moment where we really got simpatico — that war is man's greatest adventure. Hemingway was right. Now you can like that, or lump it, but there's a reason that movie makers and novelists and storytellers keep going back to the combat genre. And that is because every human emotion that's imaginable from the absolutely atrocious to the absolutely most honorable and heroic is on display in a brief period of time in a firefight and that's what's called drama. And he said, "You're right." And we had conversations like that so I knew he was interested in these things. I had no idea that he would take a shot at making one but he did.

I'll never forget. I was down on Ventura Boulevard, shopping or doing something and my cell phone rings and it's Steven, personally. He said, "Dale, we're going to do this World War II movie and I need you. What are you doing?" And I said, "I'm doing whatever you tell me to do." And that began it.[18]

Although Robert Rodat and Mark Gordon had determined to develop a World War II combat picture at a reasonable budget, *Saving Private Ryan* was no simple picture to produce. It had been over 20 years since director Richard Attenborough had put together *A Bridge Too Far*, and no filmmaker had attempted an epic combat film since.

Spielberg hired production designer Tom Sanders to begin recreating World War II. Sanders had just recreated England and Scotland of the Middle Ages in Paramount's *Braveheart*. This time, pikes and broadswords would be replaced by B.A.R.s and Tiger Tanks.

As June 1997 was penciled is as the starting date, the first determination was where to shoot the film. Although some effort was made to shoot the film in Normandy, new tax incentives made Ireland a more practical location. When Tom Sanders had worked on *Braveheart*, the Irish government had supplied the production with 1,000 reservists who donned medieval garb and played soldiers. For *Saving Private Ryan*, the same offer was made and the availability of these military extras to play combat troops on Omaha Beach helped seal the deal.

The site of the landings would be Curracloe Beach, a long sandy beach in County Wexford, near the villages of Curracloe and Blackwater. Said Dye, "It's in southeast Ireland and it's an Atlantic beach so it had shale and it had the high ground at its rear. It looked a lot like Omaha Beach, but on a smaller scale."[19]

To this barren beach, Sanders would bring in a major crew to plant beach obstacles, which included steel hedgehogs that were manufactured in Ireland, and "Belgian gates" (logs supported on two legs that were designed to flip over landing craft). On the bluffs above the beach, Sanders designed an enormous blockhouse, which is festooned with enemy machine guns. It was constructed by using a mild concrete into which bullet squibs could be placed. Behind the blockhouse, a maze of concrete communication trenches were also built (and through which Captain Miller leads his men once they break out from the beach).

But Spielberg needed more than a beach for *Saving Private Ryan*. The script required the crew to shoot in a number of ruined and bombed-out villages, all of which had to be recreated by Sanders on a protected "backlot."

That backlot turned out to be a former aerospace factory site in Hatfield, England, about 30 minutes northwest of London. It had huge hangars, workshops and enough open space to build the rubble-strewn town of Ramelle, where the climactic battle would take place. Sanders designed the town with some additional angles that would allow Spielberg to use it as the first French town Miller's unit reaches — where, in the rain, they meet a paratrooper unit, as well as a German sniper who kills Pvt. Caparzo (Vin Diesel).

What was Dale Dye's initial mission when he arrived in England in early 1997? Said Dye:

Steven wanted me out there early to work with his department heads — wardrobe, special effects, the armorers, because he wanted my input on those things. And, because I was carrying Spielberg's imprimatur, I became a pivotal source — everybody had to check something with me before they did it.

The producers had hired good folks — Brits — and all of them knew that they were about to work on a Spielberg epic. The big problem was that because they were Brits, their impression of World War II was a British impression, or what they'd read in some research book. A lot of my work was to kind of un–Brit them and get them looking at World War II from an American perspective. For instance, the British looked at the Germans differently. There was, within the wardrobe and props departments, a tendency to make the Germans look cookie-cutter — like some bad 1930s movie where all Germans wore leather trench coats.

The Germans who fought in Normandy were all solid fighters, but they were not cookie-cutter Germans. They individualized their uniforms and equipment and did things just like all soldiers do. So I pushed for that look. They also tended to look at Omaha Beach from what they knew of the British landings on Sword and Gold, which were entirely different.[20]

One of line producer Ian Bryce's initial challenges was to find workable landing craft for the beach landings. Of all places, Bryce found ten LCVPs (aka Higgins Boats), stored in the desert in Palm Springs, California. They were transported to St. Austell, Cornwall, England, where they were overhauled by Robin Davies of Square Sail, a marine shipyard which owns and maintains a fleet of square-rigged tall ships, as well as providing marine services to filmmakers on such projects as the amazingly detailed *Hornblower* mini-series. Davies's marine unit would refurbish the landing craft, as well as organize all the support and safety boats and serve as marine tech advisors on the Irish shoot.

Walking around the Hatfield facility was an experience for Dale Dye, who marveled at the ingenuity of the British craftsmen. On one stage, a group of retired aviation enthusiasts, some in their 70s and 80s, were putting the finishing touches on some full-scale prop Waco

Behind the scenes on Curracloe Beach in Ireland, filling in for Omaha Beach on D-Day.

gliders. These would be used as crashed gliders in the sequence in which Miller's squad desperately tries to find Private Ryan's dog tag amongst a bunch of paratrooper casualties.

While the craftsmen were dealing with *Saving Private Ryan*'s marine and air wings, another unit was figuring out the peculiarities of German armor. The key question: Where was production going to find Tiger Tanks? Recalled Dye:

> One thing we knew that was going to be crucial was the fact that Rodat had written and Spielberg was in love with the concept of Tiger 1 tanks. They weren't the King Tigers, but they were the Mark 6 Tigers and he wanted those. I got to talking to Steve Lamonby, the picture vehicle coordinator, and we tried to figure out what the hell we were going to do, because there are no running Tigers that we could find anywhere.
>
> So we hit on the idea that the best chassis would be a Soviet T-55. If we could find some running T-55s, we could bring them in and rebuild the entire hull to look exactly like a Tiger. Lo and behold, we found two running T-55s in Northern England, which we bought and the art department went to work on them. It was pure magic.
>
> The only thing we never beat — and the freeze-frame fanatics got us on that — were the interleaved road wheels, which were standard on a Tiger, that we couldn't recreate. The Germans felt that these type of wheels added stability and strength to the chassis. Other than that, our Tigers were smack on.[21]

There is no question that Spielberg and his crew were determined to give *Saving Private Ryan* the ultimate level of realism, but this did not only extend to Higgins Boats, Waco Gliders and Tiger Tanks, even the soldiers' dialogue referred to details that had never been featured in a World War II movie.

In previous war films, American troops attacked enemy machine gun nests. In *Saving Private Ryan,* American troops take out German MG-42s. In previous films, soldiers are killed; in *Saving Private Ryan* they are KIA. Infantry squads also refer to enfilade and defilade tactics. The Rodat script was filled with technical terminology that gave the finished product an unusually high level of realism.

Dye wasn't concerned that audiences might be confused with unfamiliar terms. "That's how real soldiers talk," he declared, "and the audiences gets it. We're a media-saturated society and we hear this terminology. Look at how much soldier talk has found its way into civilian conversation. People will get this and Steven absolutely wanted it. He loved the term 'defilade.'"[22]

The term "defilade" comes into play when Private Jackson (Barry Pepper), the sharpshooter, ducks under the German machine gun nests that are guarding the beach exits on Omaha. Dye explained what the term means: "Defilade is a term that refers to the angle of the weapon and its beaten zone. There is a point at which the weapon cannot be depressed any more without exposing the fire crew to incoming fire. The space between that beaten zone and its maximum angle of depression and the actual position of the gun is what's called a defilade position. It means that you can't be hit. Everybody tries to get into the 'defilade position' of a weapon that is firing at you."[23] Which Jackson achieves, allowing him to knock out the German beach gunners.

When *Saving Private Ryan* was released, Dye took a lot of flack for putting Captain John Miller's captain's rank on his helmet. "All the freeze-frame-button counters went nuts over that," said Dye.

> I researched this thoroughly, not just in books, but with guys who were there. We had a challenge in the picture to make sure that the audience could always recognize our main characters. In working with the prop guys, the weapons guys, the webbing guys and the uniform guys, we always gave each of the characters a little different look to their equipment.
>
> We wanted to make sure that Tom was seen in the chaos of the beach, so we decided to put the

rank on his helmet. Even within the staff, I had people screaming and yelling that that wasn't a good idea. It turns out that it was an individual regimental call. Some regimental commanders absolutely wanted all of their officers to be seen at all times by their men. Other said, "Nah, I'm just asking you to get killed." It depended on the unit. And that's entirely historically support-able. But it was the controversy that would not die.[24]

It is arguable that *Saving Private Ryan* has one of the greatest casts ever assembled for a war film, at least since *The Longest Day* and *The Great Escape*. Once Tom Hanks and Steven Spielberg signed on, it wasn't difficult to pick and choose the faces that would take on the likes of Sgt Mike Horvath, Corporal Timothy P. Upham, Private Richard Reiben, Private Adrian Caparzo, Private Daniel Jackson, T-5 Medic Irwin Wade, Private Stanley Mellish and Private James Francis Ryan.

Tom Sizemore's casting experience was a bit nerve-wracking for the young actor who won his spurs in such action classics as *True Romance, Natural Born Killers* and *Heat*.

Recalled Sizemore:

When I first came to the movie, only Tom was cast. I was very flattered to be asked at all. Steven was directing *Amistad* with Matt McConaughey and Morgan Freeman and they had just come back from the East Coast, Boston I believe, and they were on the lot at Universal. I had a two o'clock meeting with Spielberg and I couldn't be one second late. So I got there at 1:30. Bonnie Curtis, who was Steven's longtime assistant, met me and took me to a secluded area. At two o'clock on the button he walks in. Although he's a very intimidating guy in my mind, I had never met him. I had seen *Jaws* and *Close Encounters of the Third Kind* when I was a kid and I loved those movies. And here he is, probably the most powerful man in the history of this town. The most successful director ever, no on can touch him.

I was very nervous. I couldn't talk for a minute. When he's comfortable, he thinks everyone's like him. I looked at him and said I usually read, I hadn't done just an interview before, so I asked him what he wanted to know. And Steven said, "I'm looking for you." And I told him, "You're not going to find me today, I'm too nervous, I'm nowhere to be found. Please, Mr. Spielberg, go back and direct your movie, I'll come back tomorrow as me." And he started to laugh. And I said, "What do you want me to do?" And he said, "Be my quarterback." And I said, "I don't know how to be him yet, you wouldn't let me have a script." I knew nothing other than the fact that I would be playing Tom's sergeant — a by-the-book sergeant who has his eye on his Captain and is, at times, overwhelmed. That's all I was told.

"Can I read the script?" and they said, "No." I'm at CAA, Steven's at CAA, I told my agent, Fred Spektor, "I'm going to call Ovitz," and he said, "If you call Ovitz, I'm going to shoot you." Mike Ovitz and I were friendly so I called him anyway and even he couldn't get the script, it wasn't done. Spielberg is always tweaking his scripts.

Steven explained that the script had been written by a young writer named Robert Rodat, Frank Darabont was doing a rewrite, and right now the script is all over the place. He then said, "Here's the story. I know you've been cast in *The Thin Red Line*. Do you like Terry Malick?" I said, "So far, so good." Spielberg then says, "So you like him, huh. Well I like him fine." And I said, "Is that a trick question?" And Spielberg says, "No, no. But would you like to go to Great Britain and Ireland with Tom and me or do you want to go to Australia with Terry and Sean [Penn]?"

I said, "I'd rather go to Great Britain and Ireland with you and Tom." And he said, "That's a very good choice. Because I'm going to cast you in this movie. Do you want to be in it? It's a half-million dollars across the board, favored nations. Tom makes different money than anyone else."

And I looked at him and said, "Can I call my mom?" And he laughed and said, "Call your mom. That's the closer. Bonnie, come in here, he wants to call his mother." So I called my mom and told her, "Mom, you're not going to believe this, I am going to be in *Saving Private Ryan* for Steven Spielberg." So Steven asked to be on the phone and said, "Mrs. Sizemore, this is Steven Spielberg, I just cast your son in my movie," and he gave me the phone back.

Having fought their way off Omaha Beach, Tom Hanks (captain's helmet) and company receive new instructions from their Eisenhower — director Steven Spielberg.

So after that, he told me that I had to drop out of *The Thin Red Line* today. "Do Terry a favor and let him recast your part. This is a pay-or-play offer and I'll have Bonnie make the call to Fred Spektor. I'll see you — I've got to go finish my movie, *Amistad*." And I asked him, "Is McConaughy going to be a star?" And he said, "You actors are all the same," and he said, "yes." And he left.

I was in shock. I had never been cast in a movie in a room without reading in my career. This was a big jump up for me.[25]

After Sizemore, other actors fell into the formation. Giovanni Ribisi was hired to play Wade, the medic. Hanks had directed and liked him in *That Thing You Do!* (1996). Edgy Adam Goldberg had been doing mostly television when he was cast to play the Jewish soldier, Mellish. Goldberg had just written, directed and starred in an independent film entitled *Scotch and Milk*, which co-starred Ribisi.

Goldberg wasn't the only filmmaker in the bunch. Edward Burns had already written, directed and starred in three critically acclaimed independent films (*The Brothers McMullen, She's the One, No Looking Back*) when he was cast to play wisecracking Private Reiben.

Vin Diesel, on the cusp of stardom (*The Fast and Furious* was three years away), had been spotted by Spielberg in a short film entitled *Multi-Facial*, which the actor had also written and directed. He was hired to play Caparzo, a soldier who becomes the film's first casualty.

Like Goldberg, Barry Pepper had been doing mostly television before *Saving Private Ryan*. But he was deemed perfect for the pivotal role of Jackson, the bible-spouting Southern sharpshooter.

For the part of mild-mannered Upham, the typist-turned-combat soldier and interpreter,

Spielberg chose Jeremy Davies, who had previously appeared in a small part as a tornado chaser in Amblin's *Twister*. Davies has one of the most wrenching moments in the film, when, frozen in fear, he's unable to come to the aid of a desperate Mellish, locked in a fatal knife fight with a German soldier.

The final piece of the casting puzzle concerned who was going to play the film's title character, Private Ryan. Matt Damon, at 27, had just shared a screenwriting Oscar with Ben Affleck for their *Good Will Hunting*. He had been knocking around Hollywood for 10 years, appearing in a number of films, including *School Ties* (1992), *Geronimo: An American Legend* (1993), *Courage Under Fire* (1996), *Chasing Amy* (1997) and John Grisham's *The Rainmaker* (1997). Spielberg sensed that, in addition to having that boyish look, Damon had serious acting chops. He was hired.

Filling out the cast were some top American character actors in unusual roles. Chicago actor Dennis Farina, best known for his comic gangster and cop roles in films like *Midnight Run* and *Get Shorty*, plays Captain Miller's no-nonsense commanding officer, who gives him his orders to find Ryan. Paul Giamatti plays an embattled paratrooper sergeant who helps Miller's unit try to find Ryan's outfit. And TV comedy veteran Ted Danson shows up as a paratrooper captain whose unit saves Miller's men when they blow away a German squad after a wall collapses in the small French town.

It had been 12 years since Captain Dale Dye had taken a group of Hollywood actors and turned them into Oliver Stone's rock-hard Vietnam combat platoon. Now, under Steven Spielberg's command, Dye was no less committed to Captain Miller's squad.

As always there were challenges. Said Dye:

> They were a disparate group, from different schools, different training and different background. My task was not only to acquaint them with what soldier's went through — the philosophies and psychologies of the day, and the military technical stuff — but they needed to understand what we were there to do.
>
> Originally, when I got them, they were doing what actors do, they were thinking, "I've got to develop my character here and I've got to add this nuance and that nuance." I immediately told them, "Bullshit. Just stop. You can't go anywhere unless you understanding soldiering and that's what we're here to do. Then you can use what you've learned, taking these insights and developing your character. So stop worrying about that crap." The good thing about the training was that it was miserable, cold, horrible English weather and it rained all the time and we were in mud. And I was running them four and five miles every morning.[26]

As the actors arrived from the States, they were blindfolded and driven out to a dark forest (not far from the Hatfield production compound) where they could take their blindfolds off. Tom Sizemore remembered how spooky it was:

> It was cold and dark and Dye said, "Get out, gear up, bivouac." I remember thinking, I wanna go home, this is stupid. Why can't we pretend we're in boot camp and they can show us what to do.
>
> We had to make tents, and I know how to make a tent, but my fingers were so cold. Barry Pepper was far more adept at this stuff than anyone else because he had grown up outside. He knew everything — this knot, that knot — so his tent goes up faster than anyone. Ed Burns didn't take anything seriously. He was a real New York guy.
>
> We got one blanket. If you put it on top of you, the ground would suck all the heat out of your body and you'd freeze. If you put the blanket under you, you'd be warm momentarily, but you'd be freezing on top — so there wasn't really much sleeping going on. So that first night was terrible and he had us up at five to do a five-mile run. It was called "PT" — physical training.
>
> I had been cast in the movie about three and half months prior to boot camp and I could not run five miles when I was cast. I was in fairly decent condition, but I went up to San Ysidro

Ranch and I stayed there for seven weeks with my wife and I worked with a trainer. I researched the role of Sergeant Horvath and I later told Steven that a lot of these guys were not ripped-up pieces of steel. These guys went over there and they looked like normal guys, a lot of them were thick. I think Horvath is a strong man — he's a plow horse. That's how I saw him and Steven liked that. He's 33 years old and he's softened up a little bit, because he doesn't exercise. But he's a big man and, even in this war, he's maintained his size. So I was lifting weights and running, but the big thing was to get my wind up. I got up to three and a half miles and I could run it without a problem. But I couldn't run five miles. I finally got up to four, but that was murder. So we went on this five-mile run with Dye and I got close to four and dropped out. Now, at that point, two or three guys had already dropped out. I ended up throwing up. I think Tom, Burns and Pepper finished it and the rest of us didn't.[27]

Sizemore had some experience playing a soldier on the *China Beach* television series. He had an uncle who died in Vietnam and a grandfather who served in the 82nd Airborne Division in World War II.

"My grandfather said one thing to me," remembered Sizemore. "The people who died in combat, they didn't get up and walk back to their trailer. Dead is forever. He was over in Europe for three and a half years. Americans were different then, especially with the level of sacrifice that people were willing to make. If I was called up, A) I'd go; B) I would fight; C) I would fight with courage; D) I would fight for the guy next to me; and E) I would come home, but if I didn't, that's the way it goes. People die in war and we're a free country because of the wars. They defined us. We had to take Omaha Beach, we had to win World War II."[28]

If the actors began to whine and threaten mutiny, it was Tom Hanks who kept them on track.

Said Dye, "Tom just stood up and said, 'I don't know what you're whining about, we're going to get one shot in our lives to do this. Let's not screw it up.' And after a brief call to Spielberg where people could vent, I said we were going to continue on.

"Tom is a techno geek. He wants to know how everything works. He wants to know things I didn't really think I had time to teach him. I only had about five days in the forest with these guys. Barry Pepper was terrific. He's an old-school Canadian hunter/fisherman from way back. He's left-handed and he wanted to know whether he should shift to his right hand and I told him to stay with his left because there were left-handed snipers. Eddie Burns was terrific with that Browning Automatic Rifle [B.A.R.]. He understood how it worked and he cared how it worked."[29]

"By the time we were done," recalled Hanks, "we were exhausted, miserable, tired, achy, hungry and we wanted to go home. And we were playing guys who were exhausted, miserable, tired, achy, hungry and wanted to go home. It was perfect."[30]

"The only thing we couldn't do was go to the bathroom in the woods," Hanks continued. "The nature conservancy in Hatfield wouldn't allow us to do that, so we had to use an outhouse which was not a pleasant place. Even finding it was a challenge. You have a brand of pitch blackness in England that I've never quite experienced."[31]

Actor Giovanni Ribisi thought the K-rations tasted like cat food. He also recalled that, as in *Platoon*, the actors were not allowed to use their real names during the training. "By the fourth day, you start to lose all sense of self," says Ribisi. "Tom was the best student, the star student. He remembered everything better than anyone else."[32]

Just like in *Platoon*, the actors literally went from training to shooting, reporting for duty on Curracloe Beach in Ireland.

Before Spielberg shot the opening 22-minute sequence on Omaha Beach, Dye recalled discussing the carnage level with him:

We had several conversations. The one I remember most significantly was when Steven related a story. Ian Bryce was there. Steven had either spoken to someone or read a story about a guy in the First Infantry Division who had his arm blown off, and he picked up his own arm and walked back toward the surf. Steven said it was such an extraordinary image and somebody said, "Jeez, I don't know how much of that we can show, we're already looking at an R-rating and we don't want to go X."

Steven just said, "Look, war is brutal and I think we need to take an unblinking look at it, because if we don't take an unblinking look at it, we're going to do a disservice to the people who were actually on that beach. And I'm not here to do that." Of course, I chimed right in and said, "Hallelujah."[33]

When Spielberg arrived in England to direct *Saving Private Ryan*, he landed in his private jet at Luton Airport and was greeted by a huge reception committee, which included Dye, standing in the back, in uniform. Spielberg saw him and took him aside immediately.

"I told him everything was going well," recalled Dye, "and he says to me, 'I'm not really sure how to do this, but you are, so let's do this — You stage the war and I'll shoot it.' And in the military, we call those mission-type orders, and you can't ask for anything better than that. He was telling me that I was his compatriot, his fellow filmmaker, not just an advisor at his shoulder and, man, that motivated the hell out of me. I was now ready to do whatever needed to be done, I was going to go all out."[34]

Curracloe Beach was ready. Cinematographer Janusz Kaminski's camera crews were in position. Nearly a thousand Irish Army reservists, all dressed in U.S. Army uniforms, were ready to fight their way onto Omaha Beach. At least 100 of them, those closest to the camera, were equipped with weapons that could fire blank cartridges — and those men were also supplied with extra clips of ammunition.

Tom Hanks, seen here in Curracloe, plays the part of Captain Miller in *Saving Private Ryan*.

Dale Dye was standing on top of the German blockhouse, looking through his binoculars, while on the radio, his three NCOs — John Barnett, Brian Maynard and Laird Macintosh — were receiving last-minute instructions. Dye wanted to make sure everyone had their ammunition and were ready to go. In front of Dye were landing craft in the distance bobbing on the choppy Irish Sea, 14 armored vehicles ready to roll into the sand. Part of the NCOs' mission was to stay in contact with the tank drivers and make sure they didn't run anyone over.

Dye recalled, "The weather wasn't bad that day. It was a little windy and it was an offshore wind, making the boats bob pretty seriously, but we thought that offshore wind was going to be good for us. We had kind of a hazy sunshine, so it wasn't really hot or blazing.

"What I remember is that it was quiet just before we were ready to go. My NCOs were down there making everybody pay attention and get focused. I looked at the Germans — we had about 25 — and they had their weapons at their shoulder and they were waiting for the 'unlock' signal. I heard engines idling offshore and I could hear the surf hitting and I could hear very quiet conversations amongst the film crew. And I remember thinking that this was going to be the last time for at least ten minutes that we're going to hear anything silent."[35]

In the main blockhouse, Dye had deployed three MG-42 machine gun crews, two on the flanks and one in the center.

"We wanted to see the muzzle flashes," Dye explained. "Nothing does it better than actually firing a weapon, and everybody knew that. The problem with the MG-42s — they were called "Hitler's Zippers" — was that they fired 1,000–1,200 rounds a minute, so the guys we had in the blockhouse had to be handy with loading ammo. The key was that they had to keep firing because Spielberg's individual camera operators were constantly looking for things to shoot, and you never knew when they had the blockhouse in their sights. It wasn't like we could arbitrarily shoot only when cameras were pointed at us."[36]

And then Steven Spielberg called action, Dye ordered the soldiers to unlock their weapons and Omaha Beach came to life. Once it got started, there was no way to stop it.

"It was noisy," said Dye. "When those kids hit the beach and the first rounds cracked, it was like we were in Pickett's Charge. I was constantly talking to my guys on the beach, the guys in the boats and everybody else I was supposed to be communicating with. What I began to do was find parts of the beach, which were lagging. I would say, 'Macintosh, pull it up, pull it up, push them harder through.'"[37]

"When I was a kid," said Hanks, "and saw movies like *The Dirty Dozen* and *The Great Escape*, we immediately went outside and played our versions of the same movie. I don't think many kids are going to go out and play *Saving Private Ryan....* We've all seen amphibious landings in the movies before. A young Richard Jaeckle or Marty Milner is standing on the

Curracloe Beach, Ireland, gets a makeover for its transformation into Omaha Beach on D-Day.

Director Steven Spielberg wades into the water of Curracloe Beach, Ireland, as his camera crew prepares another setup on "Omaha Beach." (Courtesy of *Battleground — The Making of Saving Private Ryan in Ireland,* by Tom Moony and Stephen Eustace)

boat. Maybe they're nervous about whether they're going to get killed but none of them are seasick and none of them are throwing up.

"Though we did it in two- or three-minute bursts, it was so loud on that beach. The first time it happened, it was horrifying. We ended up wearing ear protection because otherwise we'd all have severe damage to our ears. There are a lot of weapons going off and while they're blanks, they're full loads, and you've got mortars and the tanks. It was a cacophony. Plus there are moments when hot shells are landing on you, little bits and pieces of the pyrotechnics coming down."[38]

"I can't imagine how frightening the real invasion was," admitted actor Ed Burns, "because it was scary doing some of the things in the movie. Bullets aren't flying but dirt and rocks and stuff are flying in your face. You never thought you were at war but you kind of forget for a second you were on a movie set. Your blood gets pumpin,' you're firin' your gun and you just kind of get amped up. The fact that he shot all handheld exteriors meant we were never sitting around waiting for lighting. There was a lot of room for us to experiment."[39]

"The biggest challenge was to create reality for the viewer," said Janusz Kaminski, who would win an Oscar for Best Cinematography on *Saving Private Ryan.* "We did not want a documentary feel. We wanted it to feel like the viewer is in the battle, with explosions, bullets, physical hardships and immediate danger. As a cinematographer, you are like a painter, and I used a mix of tools after a series of tests and used my knowledge of everything I have done up to *Saving Private Ryan....* Where they hit the beach, and Tom Hanks is stunned by a blast, I wanted to get into Tom's head — the witnessing, the horror, the dying, the danger. We slowed the camera to 12 frames a second and then printed each frame twice. You start getting a staccato movement. The sound becomes different, too, and a hyper-reality is reached — a

Aerial view of Curracloe Beach, Ireland.

very crisp, aware feel and everything is immediate. A hard part was maintaining continuity and style, and not have a sequence that spins off visually from the rest of the movie."[40]

The master shot of the beach landing on Omaha was only done once. Once that huge operation was completed and the men had fought their way to the shale portion of the beach, facing the barbed wire, Spielberg called "Cut." He then started moving into coverage of the key cast members as they rally behind Hanks and fight their way forward.

"We spent 18 consecutive days on Omaha Beach," said Sizemore. "Three six-day weeks. Everyone came through okay. By day three, we knew we were doing something special. Steven turned to the cast and said, 'I've already directed this movie. I've cut it, scored it and I've locked it in my head. I just need you guys to carry out the rules, so let's listen to me because I know what rules need to be made. I'm not saying you can't deviate or look for your spontaneous moments; I want you to do that, but don't stray too far.' I had never heard a director say that."[41]

Once work was completed on the beach sequence, Spielberg brought his crew back to England and nestled into the Hatfield complex, where interior work began. In keeping with a plan to stay within continuity, the director filmed the sequences in which the mission to save Ryan is organized at the highest level.

Although the opening sequence on Omaha Beach is the most memorable scene in the film, the final battle for Ramelle was no less exciting, as Miller's squad finds Private Ryan and then helps a small group of American paratroopers hold off a devastating counterattack by Nazi panzers and panzer grenadiers.

Production designer Tom Sanders's crew of expert British craftsmen had performed a near miracle of engineering on the backlot of the Hatfield facility. Here was Remelle, a devastated French village, with rubble-strewn thoroughfares, a partially destroyed main street and a wrecked church steeple. For fans of the *Combat!* television series, it echoed the old

European village on the MGM studios backlot in Culver City, especially in the scene in which Sanders included a small bridge, which rose over the local river. It was behind this bridge that Captain Miller places his final redoubt — his "Alamo" — the place where the paratroopers and Rangers are instructed to fall back. If they can't hold, their orders are to blow the bridge and prevent the Nazi panzers from breaking through to the beachhead.

Since his command will be badly outnumbered, Captain Miller comes up with a few creative ideas that will augment their defense — like the sticky bombs that his soldiers will stick on the wheels of the advancing tanks with axle grease.

"The sticky bomb came from something Rodat had read in an old Ranger training manual," explained Dye. "I had seen it before and recognized it. The innovation was using it in G.I. socks. Sticky bombs were originally made with a kind of net bag and they had this glutinous substance inside them. And you could take them and slap them against something and they would stick and explode."[42]

Dye came up with the idea of using mortar rounds as hand grenades:

That came from a Medal of Honor citation that I read from Italy. I knew that 60mm mortars had a setback fuse, with a spring inside the round. And we were taught in my early days of training as a mortar man, that if you pull the fuse-arming pin and smack it real hard, that spring opens and you now have a live round. So if you can take that round and throw it, it will detonate if it hits a hard surface.

I remembered that, and some people were saying it would never happen, but in that Medal of Honor citation, one guy kept Germans off a strategic hill by launching 60mm mortar rounds by hand, after he'd set the fuse. Once I had pulled that out of history, everybody said "okay."[43]

A behind-the-scenes view of Ramelle, from the church tower. This amazing set was the creation of production designer Tom Sanders.

Dye and Spielberg did have a spirited discussion about the hand-to-hand combat between Mellish and a German panzer grenadier.

"I didn't like it," Dye admitted. "Steven did, and he felt the scene said something. I said, 'Look, I've been in hand-to-hand fights and all you want is to get it over with in a hurry.' He said that's what the German is trying to do, but I said he shouldn't talk to the guy. We argued and argued. I never did like the sequence, but after I saw it on the big screen, I changed my mind. Steven was right."[44]

Tom Sizemore gets shot twice in the final battle and staggers back to the redoubt across the bridge where Captain Miller has collected the survivors. Screenwriter Scott Frank was working with Spielberg at that time and it was decided that Sizemore needed a line when Miller asks him if he's okay. Remembers Sizemore:

> So I say, "I'm fine, I just got the wind knocked out of me," and the reason you have that line is that if Miller thought there was something wrong with Horvath, if he was in distress or dying, he would not blow the bridge in a timely fashion. Horvath knew this and needed Miller to continue the fight. The whole idea was to do two things — let Ryan do what he wants, which is to fight with the only brothers he has left, and hold the bridge for as long as he can.
>
> The battle was metaphoric for Steven, because it showed how Americans, who were outgunned and outnumbered, were creative and courageous and fought their asses off.
>
> When Tom whispers to Ryan and says, "Earn this," I thought it was one of the greatest moments in the movie. I was right behind the camera when he said that. I didn't even know the line was in the script. It was the right thing for Ryan to hear. Look what we did for him, look what we lost.[45]

Saving Private Ryan, released in the United States and Canada on July 24, 1998, was a huge hit for Steven Spielberg and Dreamworks. The 50th anniversary of D-Day had taken place four years earlier and there was still a great deal of interest in the World War II veterans and their legacy. No one had ever seen a combat film like this, and veterans, critics and audiences everywhere embraced the film, propelling it to a $479 million worldwide gross.

Said producer Mark Gordon, "I saw the completed movie over at Dreamworks Animation in Glendale and it was pretty amazing. The first time you see it, you don't recover from those first 22 minutes. You're so bombarded and shell-shocked from the visual images and the sound, it's almost hard to connect to the rest of it."[46]

Saving Private Ryan would go on to be nominated for 11 Academy Awards, winning the Oscar for director Steven Spielberg, cinematographer Janusz Kaminski, film editor Michael Kahn, sound and sound-effects editing. Shockingly, it lost the Best Picture nod to *Shakespeare in Love*.

CHAPTER FOURTEEN

Black Hawk Down

When "Wild Bill" Wellman directed *Battleground* in 1949, the veteran MGM art department — the same team that had built the Munchkin village of *The Wizard of Oz* and Tara for *Gone with the Wind* — built the Ardennes Forest of Bastogne on a soundstage at MGM in Culver City. Dirt, trees, shrubbery, demolished buildings, destroyed vehicles, and a ton of fake snow was hauled through the cavernous soundstage doors and Hollywood magic was achieved. By late 1940s standards, this was a sizable effort.

How times have changed! Flash forward to early 2001. On a budget approaching $100 million, director Ridley Scott and producer Jerry Bruckheimer joined forces to mount *Black Hawk Down*, a motion picture dramatization of the Battle of Mogadishu, a stirring, amazingly realistic, portrait of modern American men in war. Shot on location in Morocco, this truly epic combat film pulled out all the stops in terms of military cooperation with the Pentagon, overseas location filming, art direction, pyrotechnics and special effects, not to mention the collective work and spirit of an enormously talented and experienced cast and crew. In military jargon, *Black Hawk Down* was the tip of the spear.

Very few civilians understood what was going on in strife-torn Somalia, East Africa, in the winter of 1992. Like most stories that take place in sub–Saharan Africa, this one began with widespread famine, death and corruption. After the death of some 300,000 Somalis, the United Nations organized a humanitarian relief operation and President George H.W. Bush sent in the U.S. Marines to neutralize the Somali warlords and gunmen who were stealing the food and disrupting humanitarian efforts. In effect, the entire country was being held hostage by the warlord-led clans. However, the Marines had too much firepower, and they defeated the gunmen. The country was stabilized and the UN settled into a peacekeeping mission.

The peace lasted only a few months. Then, in June 1993, another brutal warlord, Mohamed Farrah Aidid, leader of the Habr Gidr sub clan, began to take power and men under his command ambushed, murdered then mutilated the bodies of 24 Pakistani peacekeepers. The UN was outraged, and permission was sought to use force. But how do you take action against one criminal warlord who has the entire city of Mogadishu (an urban center of one million people) under his thumb? The UN did organize a military strike in July after receiving intelligence that a major meeting of the Habr Gidr clan was taking place in a specific building in Mogadishu. The UN sent in U.S. Cobra helicopter gunships, which fired their missiles into the requisite building. However, they missed the clan leaders, and amongst the

70 dead were a number of women and children. With that blast, and in the eyes of the people of Somalia, the UN was no longer a peacekeeping entity. They were the enemy.

Eventually, it was determined that the only way to end Aidid's reign of terror was to take out Aidid himself.

To accomplish that goal, newly elected President Bill Clinton authorized a military mission to Somalia, involving the 160th SOAR (Special Operations Aviation Regiment) with its deadly compliment of Black Hawk and Little Bird helicopters, a contingent of U.S. Army Rangers and a detachment of the First Special Forces Detachment — Delta, better known as Delta Force. Under the command of General William F. Garrison, this strike force was set up to either capture or kill Aidid and his fellow clan leaders. With the head of the cobra destroyed, it was felt that the clan body would wither. However supportive of the operation they were, the Clinton Administration left one critical piece of support off the table: armor.

Colonel Tom Matthews, who led the 160th SOAR into Mogadishu, later served as a technical advisor on *Black Hawk Down* (and was portrayed in the movie by Glenn Morshower) explains why a light infantry force was deployed in Mogadishu, rather than a mechanized armored task force:

> The administration (and this is a political comment but it's a fact) did not want a big military footprint in Mogadishu. We were on a UN mission, and it was felt we could manage this in some UN way. If we sent in tanks, then that would be too belligerent, too warlike and not UN-like. Tanks are weapons of war and we were on a peacekeeping/peace enforcement mission. In reality, we were at war with the Somalis.
>
> Had the United States had the armor support, we could have done it differently. Aidid went out publicly twice a week and spoke to the crowds, inciting them against the UN presence. He went to a public location with grandstands. We could have easily followed him to his house in an armored force that would have protected our troops from harm, got on the bullhorn and asked him to come out and it would have all been over.[1]

What did happen on October 3–4, 1993, was a carefully planned mission to extract two of Aidid's lieutenants from another building in Mogadishu, utilizing the best abilities and capabilities under Garrison's command. The 160th SOAR would transport a force of 75 U.S. Rangers and 40 Delta Force soldiers to the target building. The Rangers would "fast rope" down from hovering Black Hawks, while Little Birds carried the Delta Force onto the roof. Simultaneously, an armed Ranger convoy of 12 Humvees and trucks would travel straight down Hawlwadig Road to pick up the prisoners and return them.

The mission duration was planned as one hour or less. Nearly 16 hours later, the last battered elements of Task Force Ranger arrived at their base. In what would be the biggest urban firefight the Army had waged since the end of the Vietnam War 20 years earlier, Garrison's command successfully captured a number of Aidid's lieutenants, but the extraction process was short-circuited when a U.S. Army Black Hawk helicopter was shot down five blocks northeast of the target building. With a Black Hawk down, the mission morphed into a rescue operation, which further morphed into a siege on the order of the Alamo and Rorke's Drift. Aidid's gunmen converged on the crash site, Lt. Colonel Danny McKnight's Humvee and truck convoy was wracked by fire, a second Black Hawk was shot down and nearly one hundred American Rangers and Delta Force irregulars were cut off and engaged in a desperate firefight with hundreds of Aidid's heavily armed followers.

Despite the overwhelming odds against them, Garrison's men relied on their expert training and contingency plans and they affected a successful escape from a cauldron of death. The results: 18 Americans died, 73 were injured and Aidid's forces received huge casualties. But

Aidid's lieutenants were taken, and although Aidid's power was neutralized, the UN decided to abandon its mission and the American presence ended in Somalia.

To an uninformed American public — and the Mogadishu fight was a brief blip on the national news media radar — the events of October 3–4, 1993, were perceived as a military defeat and an early foreign affairs failure of the Clinton administration. To the naïve, the fact that 18 Americans died there was further proof of a military fiasco. Nothing could be further from the truth.

In reality, with the pain of Vietnam but a dim memory, Americans had long forgotten the experience of taking military casualties in a fight and they assumed that death in Mogadishu equaled defeat. Having witnessed the deployment of cruise missiles and remotely guided bombs during the first Gulf War, the public was getting used to an "antiseptic" form of conflict — war as video game.

Fortunately, the Battle of Mogadishu and the bravery and ingenuity of the American fighting force was not forgotten by journalist Mark Bowden, whose seminal book, *Black Hawk Down: A Story of Modern War* (originally based on a series of articles he wrote for the *Philadelphia Inquirer*), was published in 1999. Like military historian S.L.A. Marshall, who had similar motivation with *Pork Chop Hill* nearly 40 years earlier, Bowden wanted to get inside the battle and match feelings and experience to the anonymous soldiers who fought in that ruined city for 16 gut-wrenching hours.

After some initial research, Bowden had an epiphany when he was invited by Jim Smith — the father of Corporal Jamie Smith, a Ranger who was tragically killed in the fight — to a dedication ceremony of a building that was being named in the young man's honor. Bowden then met 12 other Rangers who had fought in Mogadishu with young Smith, and all agreed to be interviewed. This was the beginning of a journey that led Bowden to years of additional research, many interviews and a perilous journey into Somalia in the summer of 1997.

The finished book would eventually catch the attention of Jerry Bruckheimer, who was not only one of Hollywood's most successful producers (with credits including *Flashdance, Top Gun, Beverly Hills Cop, Crimson Tide, Armageddon* and *Pearl Harbor*), but who was — and continues to be — a staunch supporter of the military.

"I read the book before it came out in bookstores and fell in love with it," Bruckheimer remembered. "I've always liked to tell stories that involve brotherhood amongst men, caring about somebody else's life more than you care about your own. And that's what these Rangers, Delta Force soldiers and pilots did. It was more important to get their buddy home alive than it was to save themselves. It's heroism under fire and that's a powerful subject for any film.

"Bowden really did an amazing job with his book and how he took it inside the lives of these young men and what they went through. You know, things happen in 15-second sound bites, so the battle was very quickly forgotten. Hopefully, this movie will honor the lives of the young men who sacrificed so much."[2]

The next step for Bruckheimer was to bring in a director, and all roads led to veteran Brit, Ridley Scott. Bruckheimer was no stranger to the Scott family. He had employed both Ridley and his brother, Tony, as commercial helmers when he was an advertising agency executive, and Tony had become his go-to guy in such action films as *Top Gun, Beverly Hills Cop II, Days of Thunder, Crimson Tide* and *Enemy of the State*. But, at this point, brother Ridley was Bruckheimer's first and only choice for *Black Hawk Down*. The former was coming off of one of his biggest successes ever — *Gladiator* — the huge costume epic that was nominated for 12 Academy Awards in 2000, and won 5, including Best Picture and a Best Actor award for Russell Crowe.

A trained artist and extremely successful commercial director, Scott had started his entertainment career as a production designer in 1960s episodic television in England. After segueing to television directing, he made an auspicious feature directing debut in 1977 with the costume-actioner *The Duellists*, which starred Keith Carradine and Harvey Keitel. But it was his next film, the amazingly atmospheric and iconic science-fiction thriller, *Alien*, that brought him worldwide acclaim and propelled him quickly to the front rank of film directors.

Alien confirmed Ridley Scott's talent as a truly artistic film director with an amazing eye for performance and visual splendor on the screen. In many of the films that followed — the fascinating futuristic epic, *Blade Runner* (1982), the gorgeous fantasy, *Legend* (1985) and the wildly entertaining *Thelma and Louise* (1991) — Scott continued to carefully design his films with a painstaking attention to physical detail. Although *Gladiator* was a huge international hit, Bruckheimer already knew that *Black Hawk Down* needed a craftsman like Ridley Scott to pull it all together.

When Mogadishu was going down in 1993, Scott was in London. "I recall watching BBC News and seeing this tragic sight of what was clearly two bodies that were being seriously mauled," he remembered. "And I realized, my God, those are U.S. troops. I'd already spent 20-odd years in and out of the United States, and I pretty well had a handle on how Americans respond to such things. I knew that it would be a giant shock to the system, seeing that being pushed into the forefront of their lives on the television sets at home.

"Those of us who live in protected societies tend to forget how lucky we are to be born in them. Witnessing the kind of events that occurred in Mogadishu makes one start to grasp what it's like to live in third-world countries. But protected societies also tend to be somewhat isolationist, and they like to close down and shut out the horrors. I think that when you're coming from such a successful society — and America is regarded as the most successful and wealthiest society in the world — there's a cozy comfort zone that one tends to wrap oneself up into.

"The feeling back then was whether it was worth it to send Americans to fight in a part of the world that 90 percent of the people couldn't even identify on the map. But I think that the events of this past year [the 9/11 tragedy] proved that you have to, because if you don't … if you let things slip past you, even though for the moment they apparently have nothing to do with you … they will come back around the other side and bite you."[3]

Working from a solid adaptation of the Bowden book by screenwriter Ken Nolan, who created composites of some of the actual soldiers (much like W.R. Burnett and James Clavell had done for *The Great Escape* nearly 40 years earlier), Scott began to assemble his team. Fortunately, many of the artists who had turned *Gladiator* into an international smash were available.

One of the first to join the party was production designer Arthur Max, who had started his association with Scott on commercials in the 1980s, then joined him on the film front with *G.I. Jane* in 1997, and went on to design the epic *Gladiator*, receiving an Academy Award nomination for his work. (Unfortunately, he lost to Tim Yip, who took home the Oscar for Art Direction on *Crouching Tiger, Hidden Dragon*).

In 1965, when contemplating *The Sand Pebbles,* director Robert Wise and his production designer, Boris Leven, realized that shooting the film in Red China would be impossible. Whether it was the Red Curtain or the Bamboo Curtain, filming a major Hollywood motion picture in a communist country was unthinkable.

Ridley Scott and Arthur Max faced a similar situation in 2000. Seven years after the events depicted in Mark Bowden's book, Mogadishu, Somalia, was still a very dangerous city, overrun with clans and gunmen — perhaps one of the most inhospitable places on earth.

Jordan was considered as a location, but Amman, the capital city, lacked the urban topography needed by the filmmakers. Additionally, it was hilly and land-locked, and although the King of Jordan himself invited the filmmakers to tour the country, the location was rejected.

Morocco was more interesting and appropriate, and Max was very familiar with the country, having just worked there on *Gladiator*. And, although they didn't need the rural villages and desert terrain that are so prevalent around Ouarzazate, they could definitely use the urban environment in the capital city of Rabat.

Through the Minister of Film of Morocco, Scott and Max were given a tour of Rabat, which is a very beautiful city with palaces, embassies and a very "up-market" feeling. However, on the other side of the Bou Regreg River, they discovered the suburb of Sale, a former home of the Barbary Pirates, which was considered one of the worst urban settlements in Morocco.

Max described the architectural look: "It was predominantly a kind of 'no man's land' of un–permitted construction, where people would come out of the desert and build temporary shelters for themselves, and, interestingly, if you had a shelter and a roof over your head, the government would term your dwelling an official building and they would supply you with water and power.

"So there were all of these squatters, a huge longstanding squatters encampment, with lots of rough-and-tumble buildings of breeze block and corrugated tin. We were looking for a town on the sea like Mogadishu and Sale was right on the ocean. It also had working-class neighborhoods with very narrow, congested streets."[4]

Max was also interested in the fact that, like Somalia and its history as an Italian colony, Morocco had the French and Spanish influence, so there was a kind of similarity.

"And when we looked at aerial photos of Mogadishu," he continued, "and compared them with aerial photos of Sale, they were almost identical."[5]

Max tried to do a research trip to Mogadishu, but there was so much security and paranoia about going there that eventually the studio, Columbia-Tri-Star, wouldn't allow him to go.

"We ended up getting a lot of our research through the European news media," Max admitted. "They were covering it very closely when the Americans were present, and there was a lot of news footage and photographs taken by French and Italian news reporters that became useful for our research."[6]

"We had to do this film relatively quickly," said Ridley Scott, "because we started in March and were going to release in December of the same year. It's really about decisions, and how fast you make them. While I was mixing *Hannibal* [the sequel to *Silence of the Lambs*], I asked Branko [Lustig] and Arthur to scout locations; we looked at the photographs they came back with, and went straight in to Morocco. That's how you get a kick start."[7]

In many ways, *Black Hawk Down* was a charmed film. Not only did Sale, Morocco, provide the production with an ideal location that could perfectly match the Mogadishu urban battleground they needed, but the King of Morocco offered to supply military material to the production, which included tanks, Humvees and some support helicopters.

Military cooperation from the U.S. also came quickly and decisively. Secretary of Defense William Cohen was already a big fan of Hollywood, having seen how films like *Top Gun* could aid recruitments and rebuild the image of a military, which had taken a long time to shed the shadows of Vietnam. Cohen had also recently authorized cooperation with producer Jerry Bruckheimer on the latter's World War II epic, *Pearl Harbor*, which was due in theaters in May 2001.

U.S. military cooperation was critical because the production needed a contingent of Black Hawk and Little Bird helicopters, as well as a unit of U.S. Army Rangers. Although it was possible, Max did not want to create Black Hawks and Little Birds by mocking up civilian or obsolete Moroccan military helicopters. He needed the real deal.

In late November 2000, U.S. Army Colonel Tom Matthews was working in operations at the Pentagon for the chairman of the Joint Chiefs of Staff. With 28 years of service under his belt, Matthews was a veteran combat officer with a specialty in helicopters, who had led a unit of the 160th SOAR into battle in Mogadishu in 1993. He was also nearing retirement.

When Ken Nolan's script came to the Pentagon, requesting the U.S. Army Black Hawk and Little Bird helicopters and a Ranger contingent, it was first sent to U.S. Army Special Operations, but since nobody in that division had served in the Somalia campaign, they sent it to Matthews.

"And they said, 'You were there; why don't you take a look at it? We don't know how accurate it is,'" said Matthews. "So I looked at the script and I was thoroughly unimpressed. At that time, according to the script I read, the general was an idiot, the sergeants were insubordinate, nobody said, 'Sir,' the whole attitude and swagger of the narrative was your typical 'This-is-going-to-be-a-shitty movie.' I thought it would look like all the bad movies in which I'd ever said, 'Why'd they do that?' so I wrote all my comments down and sent them to Phil Strub, at the Office of Public Affairs."[8]

In late December 2000, Matthews found himself sitting quietly in a Pentagon conference room in Washington, D.C., meeting with Jerry Bruckheimer, producer Mike Stenson, who was the president of Jerry Bruckheimer Films, and Phil Strub. Towards the end of the meeting, Strub informed Bruckheimer and Stenson that if they had any more questions, they should ask them quickly about Colonel Matthews, since he was retiring in the next couple of weeks and would probably be unavailable after that.

Tipped off, they marched right over to Matthews and offered him the technical advisor job on the film, which he turned down immediately. Shocked by Matthews's response, they asked him why.

"And I told them that I didn't have a very good impression of war movies from Hollywood," Matthews stated.[9] Still, he agreed to think about it.

Matthews went home to his wife, thinking to himself that there was no way he was going off to Morocco for five months to be the technical advisor. What surprised him was how his wife reacted to the offer.

"She told me that I couldn't turn down Mr. Bruckheimer's offer," he said. "We argued back and forth and finally it came down to this. The Battle of Mogadishu was the most significant military operation of my career. They actually shot down five of my helicopters; they killed five of my guys and wounded a number of others. This was going to be the one time in my life where I could ever possibly influence the outcome of a movie, and if I didn't help try to get it right, I would have had to sit there afterward and say to myself, 'Boy, did they screw that up.'"[10]

The Special Operations Aviation Regiment (SOAR) was a tactical aviation unit that the U.S. Army developed in the wake of the 1979 hostage crisis in Iran and the disastrous helicopter rescue operation that followed. After that debacle, the Pentagon determined that a special unit must be developed that can handle a number of wartime and peacetime missions, including the transportation or rescue of armed military personnel in a hostile situation. SOAR's primary birds were either the powerful and versatile Black Hawks or the light, swift and heavily armed Little Birds (their official designation was OH-6 and their official nickname was Cayuse). All military helicopters in the U.S. Army are named after Native American tribes, except for the Cobra.

Having a technical advisor of Tom Matthews's experience was one thing, but even *he* couldn't authorize the use of American military helicopters and Ranger personnel.

"To deploy the troops and helicopters," explained Phil Strub, director of Entertainment Media at the Department of Defense and the government's key military liaison with Hollywood, "a memorandum had to be signed by the Secretary of Defense or his deputy. That memorandum was then sent to the director of the Joint Chiefs of Staff, who created a deployment order, which is a classified message that lays out exactly who is going where and with what. And that memo had to be signed off by every principal in the building, including the general counsel, the controller, the undersecretary for policy, etc. As they do for any deployment, all the senior leadership had to sign off on that memo."[11]

Although it was clear that everyone at the Pentagon was in favor of telling the story of the Mogadishu battle, *Black Hawk Down* was still blessed by the fact that it had key influences in high places. Not only did Secretary of Defense Cohen believe in the importance of telling this important story, but also, for instance, General Hugh Shelton, the chairman of the Joint Chiefs of Staff, was a Special Forces officer in Vietnam, and his son was a helicopter pilot who eventually served in the 160th SOAR. Additionally, the commander of the U.S. Special Operations Command was General Brian "Doug" Brown, a former commander of the 160th SOAR.

Said Matthews, "All the stars were aligned for *Black Hawk Down*. Had this production started after 9/11, you wouldn't have had access to one of those helicopters and you wouldn't have been allowed near any of the Rangers. It was just a very fortuitous window of time with the right people amenable to do this, with the forces available to do it."[12]

Black Hawk Down would get its complement of helicopters, although the studio would pay for the privilege. After three months in Morocco, the total bill for flying eight helicopters, deploying their pilots and about 40 U.S. Rangers, was about $3 million. As Matthews points out, it was a small price to pay for the expertise and realism they were getting in return.

The site of the downed Black Hawk helicopter is an outdoor location set built by production designer Arthur Max in the poor Sale suburb of Rabat, Morocco. (Courtesy of Tom Matthews)

Matthews was only one part of the technical advisory staff. He was joined by former Navy SEAL, Harry Humphries (who was a fixture in Bruckheimer-produced films, including *The Rock, Con Air, Armageddon, Enemy of the State* and *Pearl Harbor*); Major Tom McCollum, a U.S. Army major from the public affairs department of the Special Operational Forces command; and Colonel Lee Van Arsdale, a Special Forces veteran.

Meanwhile, production designer Arthur Max turned his attention to the streets of Sale, Morocco, focusing on the section known as Sidi Moussa and its main drag, Avenue Nasser. His first order of business was to get the neighborhood on his side.

"This was pre–9/11," explained Max, "so there wasn't that much concern about anti–terrorist security. It was more of a question of intruding into neighborhoods, and, in some cases, getting too close to mosques. But we worked very closely with the local community leaders, and the local governors who were excited to hear that we would be employing a large number of locals, especially because unemployment was very high in Sale.

"We also agreed to improve some of their school facilities and repair some of the local mosques that had fallen into disrepair. So it was a very symbiotic relationship in the end — and it took some politics to get to that point."[13]

In addition to placing the proper signage and graffiti on the Sidi Moussa walls, Max had to ensure that the Moroccan streets were properly designed for the camera.

"We built heavily into the Sidi Moussa neighborhood," said Max, "especially where there were gaps. Buildings were very sporadic and there was no town planning, so in between buildings there were vacant grounds where we would build sets that production would later blow up."[14]

The target building, in front of which the Little Bird helicopters deposit their Delta Force troops, who then rush in to capture Aidid's followers, was built from scratch in the heart of Sidi Moussa. Max was able to take over a soccer field, and his construction crew went to work.

"It had all the character surrounding it–narrow streets, two- or three-story buildings, etc. It was built in the style of traditional Arabic buildings, based on some of the structures we saw in the research on Mogadishu — with lots of colonnades and a courtyard, Arabic arches, tiling and a lot more."[15]

The first Black Hawk crash site and several buildings surrounding it (dubbed the "Alamo Complex") was designed and constructed over an unfinished housing development in the Hay Arrahma district of Sale, about two miles from Avenue Nasser in Sidi Moussa. Max used the half-built apartments as a skeleton and added his set pieces onto it. The set pieces included ancient arches, restaurants, shop fronts, beauty salons, and a movie theater, even a communist-inspired fountain as its centerpiece. Since there were four entrances into this area, it truly became a backlot for Ridley Scott, who made use of every possible angle during coverage of the battle.

The prime movers on Max's construction team were Italian artisans from the movie *U-571*, whom Max had met during *Gladiator*, when both crews were working on the island of Malta.

"The Italians had been working in Morocco for years," said Max, "on various biblical television series and other movies for Italian television. Also, a lot of them spoke French, which is the second language of Morocco. It was a new team for me, but they did a great job. We also had Somali refugees who helped us with some of the graffiti that appears on the walls."[16]

In addition to building sets along real streets to maintain a continuous façade, Max needed to dress the streets to look like ravaged Mogadishu, as he explained: "It was pretty grim, to start with. We had a gang of prop men and set dressers who kind of went through the streets and added another layer of ravage. We also put in a load of telephone poles with hanging cables and crisscrossed wires, which was typical of Mogadishu, which didn't have a very sophisticated power system."[17]

As Max continued turning the Sidi Moussa area of Sale into war-ravaged Mogadishu, the casting process had begun in Hollywood. As is the case in most pictures produced by Jerry Bruckheimer or directed by Ridley Scott, there were a huge number of parts to fill.

In adapting Mark Bowden's book, screenwriter Ken Nolan focused the action around a smaller group of characters, and although we get to know nearly 40 people during the course of the battle, most of the critical action concerns young Ranger Sergeant Matt Eversmann, who takes over the command of Chalk Four after its leader has an epileptic seizure the night before the mission. It is Eversmann's Rangers who make it to the downed Black Hawk crash site, which becomes their own personal Alamo. Eversmann's Delta Force counterpart is Sergeant First Class "Hoot" Gibson, who leads his elite team into the target building, helps capture the key gunmen associates of Aidid, and then, when the prisoners are returned to the base, jumps back into a Humvee and helps find the trapped Rangers.

The Rangers, meanwhile, are led by Lt. Colonel Danny McKnight, who is in charge of the Humvee and truck column headed for the crash site; and Captain Mike Steele, who leads another unit that is trying to hook up with Eversmann's advance unit. While the action unfolds on the ground, Nolan's script also featured the tense atmosphere of headquarters, where General Garrison tracks the ebb and flow of the battle, and, in the air, where Colonel Matthews deploys his helicopters and deals with the fate of his downed birds.

For Eversmann, Bruckheimer didn't have to look very far. Josh Hartnett, who had just starred in *Pearl Harbor*, was cast as the gritty Ranger sergeant who is suddenly ordered to take his Chalk Four to the Black Hawk crash site.

Said Bruckheimer, "I think Josh is unique in that while the camera certainly loves him, and he has undeniable 'heartthrob' appeal, he's a young actor of genuine commitment and depth, who completely immerses himself in his work. Handsome as Josh is, there's also a remarkable vulnerability and humanity about him, which was perfect for the role of Matt Eversmann."[18]

"What really sets this movie apart," says Hartnett, who was 22 at the time, "is that it tells a story about something important that most of us don't know all that much about. It's one of those stories that when people watch it, they'll say, 'My God, I can't believe this actually happened.' And, hopefully, it will get people interested in all the other things that are happening around the world."[19]

A 32-year-old Australian newcomer, Eric Bana, who had just scored strongly as the title character in the true crime thriller *Chopper*, was chosen to play Gibson, the arrogant but resourceful Delta Force operative.

Said Bana, "I grew up watching war films, but *Black Hawk Down* is different in the sense that it's about modern urban warfare, which hasn't really been captured on film. I was a little bit angry with myself for not knowing more about the Battle of Mogadishu, but then realized that most people don't, which is a great reason to make this movie. As tragic as aspects of the event are, the heroism of those soldiers is unbelievable."[20]

Bana wasn't the only non–American actor to win a key role as an American combat soldier in *Black Hawk Down*. Scottish actor Ewan McGregor, fresh off a career-making role as the young Obi-Wan Kenobi in *Star Wars Episode 1: The Phantom Menace*, took on the part

During training at Fort Benning, Georgia, Ewan McGregor (right) takes weapons instruction. (Courtesy of U.S. Army Special Operations Command)

of Grimes, the coffee-making Ranger who is a last-minute addition to the combat mission. Brit Orlando Bloom, fresh off a year of working for director Peter Jackson as Legolas the Elf archer in *The Lord of the Rings* trilogy, was cast as Blackburn, the unfortunate Ranger who falls 70 feet out of a Black Hawk during the fast-rope maneuver, yet survives. Bloom didn't hesitate to tell the casting directors that he had broken his back a couple of years earlier. Welsh actor Ioan Gruffudd, who had dazzled television audiences in the U.S. and Great Britain by playing the title character in the lavish *Hornblower* mini–series, took on the role of another Ranger. Gruffudd, who had previously portrayed the lone British officer who, while piloting a lifeboat, searches for survivors in James Cameron's *Titanic,* would soon raise his profile considerably by playing one of the *Fantastic Four.*

Brit Jason Isaacs, who, at 35, was one of the elder statesmen amongst the actors cast as Rangers, had one of the more amusing auditions.

"I'm ashamed to say that I didn't do the appropriate amount of preparation," Isaacs remembered. "I had a copy of the book and a script and I was flicking through the script on the way to the audition. And I caught sight of a couple of fun lines spoken by a guy named Mike Steele.

"So I went in there and Ridley Scott asked me if I had read it. And I said, 'It was fantastic, absolutely gripping, a real page turner, incredibly moving.' I then segued as smoothly as I could into my experience playing a parachute regiment soldier in a British series about the Falklands. I had gone off and trained with the paras for a while, so playing a soldier was comfortable territory for me. Ridley then steered the conversation back to *Black Hawk Down* and

U.S. Army Colonel Tom Matthews (right), a tech advisor on *Black Hawk Down*, goes over radio chatter with Josh Hartnett, who plays Ranger chalk leader Eversmann. (Courtesy of Tom Matthews)

asked me if there was a part that leaped out at me. And I said that I thought Mike Steele was a really interesting guy, not really knowing much about Mike Steele other than I had seen a couple of lines of dialogue. And Ridley said, 'Are you sure? Because he wasn't that popular; he's quite a controversial character.' And I thought, Oh f**k, what have I done? I really should have read this thing more carefully. And I told Ridley, 'That's particularly why I want to play him; I think he's misunderstood.' So the meeting ended.

"They came through with an offer and I then read the book and the script and was enormously relieved to see that everything I said was true. Steele did turn out to be a controversial man, who polarized various members of the Rangers' regiment. Some people hated him, some people were in awe of him, some people thought he did a fantastic job that night and some thought the opposite. It all worked out brilliantly, but it started off with an exercise in bluff and bullshit that could have gone horribly wrong."[21]

One American who was perfectly cast in the roll of Ranger Lt. Colonel Danny McKnight was *Saving Private Ryan* veteran Tom Sizemore. Like Isaacs, Sizemore, at 37, was one of the film's elder statesmen. Said Sizemore, "I wanted to work with Ridley Scott because I think he's one of the finest directors in the world. And Danny McKnight is a kind of American icon, a fighting man who doesn't flinch. He's a real leader, and was already 37 years old — exactly my age — when he fought in the battle."[22]

Sizemore wasn't surprised when he was ordered to report to Ranger military training class at Fort Benning, Georgia. After surviving Dale Dye's regimen on *Saving Private Ryan*, he was ready for anything they threw at him. Military technical advisor Harry Humphries actually divided the cast into three training commands: Rangers went to Benning, Delta Force

Tom Sizemore (left), portraying U.S. Army Ranger Colonel Danny McKnight, gets knot-making instructions at Fort Benning. (Courtesy of U.S. Army Special Operations Command)

went to Fort Bragg, North Carolina, and the helicopter pilots went to Fort Campbell, Kentucky, headquarters for the 160th SOAR.

At Fort Benning, they received instruction from Sergeant James Hardy, the commander of the Ranger training detachment, who had been a team leader in Mogadishu, and had lost several of his men in the battle. Hardy instructed the actors on the Ranger mentality, history and way of life.

Jason Isaacs was a little confused when he arrived at Fort Benning for his Ranger training: "They were amazingly welcoming at Fort Benning, but there was a slight misunderstanding. The instructors somehow felt that the parts we were playing in the film would carry over into our training. So, because I was playing Captain Steele and I was in charge of the men, they basically put me in charge of 30 actors for a week. I tried to explain to them that, in the hierarchy of Hollywood, I wouldn't be in charge of actors like Josh Hartnett and Ewan McGregor, but they wouldn't listen. It turned out to be like a week-long improvisation.

"I was getting people out of bed, telling them when they could stop and have a drink of water, calling people by their character names. And I'm also the 35-year-old guy who had to lead all these 21 and 22 year olds in their physical training, which was all very well conceptually, but fell apart in practice."[23]

"What really got me at training camp was the Ranger Creed," said Sizemore. "I don't think most of us can understand that kind of mutual devotion. It's like having 200 best friends, and every single one of them would die for you ... That's a different type of person ... that's a Ranger."[24]

During training at Fort Benning, Georgia, in early 2001, Jason Isaacs (center), portraying U.S. Army Ranger Captain Michael Steele, takes instruction from a base Ranger officer. (Courtesy of U.S. Army Special Operations Command)

The actors soon realized that part of the makeup of the Battle of Mogadishu was that the American soldiers were not only using their training to fight like wild lions against overwhelming odds, they were unwilling to leave anyone behind — living, wounded or dead. The Ranger mission of getting to the crash site and securing it was, thus, unwavering and their creed of bringing their people back extended to the members of the 160th SOAR.

Recalled Isaacs, "I remember the last night at Fort Benning. We had a very social evening of pizza and beer, the instructors reverted to calling us by our real names, there was a question-and-answer session and we went to bed. The next morning, we woke up and found a note under the door, written by one of the soldiers that had been killed in the Mogadishu battle [it was actually written by one of the living soldiers on the base]. It just listed their name and at the bottom it [read], 'Please tell our story true.' It was an unbelievably moving reminder.

"We had met the families of the people who died and we'd learned from the veterans who were there about what it was like to hold your friends in your arms as they died — yet, somehow, this piece of paper was more powerful and spoke more than any of the human encounters we'd had. It felt like a message from beyond the grave."[25]

Meanwhile, at Fort Bragg, actors Eric Bana, William Fichtner and Danish actor Nikolaj Coster-Waldau were getting their Special Forces training, which included a live simulation at the Urban Terrain site, a cinderblock mock village, where Special Forces soldiers demonstrated movement through a city that poses a threat at every turn. It was Waldau-Coster (as Gordon,

Josh Hartnett (behind and to the right of the instructor) and Jason Isaacs (in front of window, holding helmet) learn the basics of modern urban warfare at a special urban training center at Fort Benning, Georgia. (Courtesy of U.S. Army Special Operations Command)

the Delta Force sniper) who volunteers to help protect the second Black Hawk crash site, and is posthumously awarded the Congressional Medal of Honor.

At Fort Campbell, actors Ron Eldard and Jeremy Piven, both of whom play helicopter jockeys with the 160th SOAR, were getting acquainted with the big Black Hawk birds. They would also get a chance to meet Eldard's real-life counterpart, Chief Warrant Officer Mike Durant, who was flying the second Black Hawk that was downed that day, and who became a prisoner of the Somalis. Piven would be playing Chief Warrant Officer Cliff Wolcott, who was one of the two pilots killed in the first downed Black Hawk.

Recalled Piven, "Every pilot who came up to me during training said, 'Just do Cliff Wolcott proud, because he was the real deal. All we ask is that you all try to keep it real.'

"Flying Black Hawks is incredibly intense," Piven added. "All of one's motor skills are needed at every moment; the controls are so responsive and delicate. We trained in simulators and studied the actual Black Hawks on the ground, and these machines are incredible, the highest level out there. They can maneuver into anything. They can fly at night. They're jet black, they're ominous. You have to be at the top of your game to fly them."[26]

When the actors arrived in Morocco, they were ready to take on the huge challenge of recreating one of the deadliest firefights that has ever involved American troops. Actor Jason Isaacs had learned what it meant to be called Ranger: "Here's the difference between a Ranger and me or you," he explained. "Every army has people who perform every single function — from playing in the brass band to peeling potatoes and working a computer. But every single

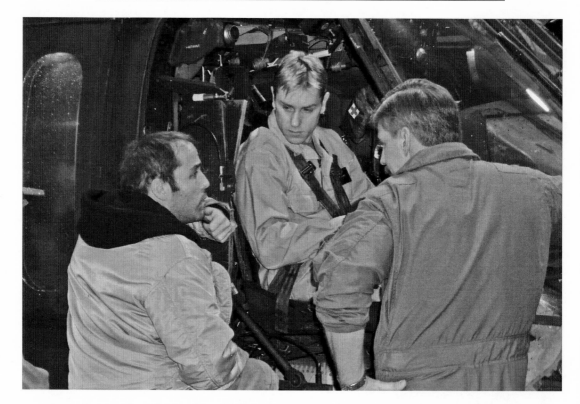

Actors Jeremy Piven (left) and Ron Eldard (center), as Black Hawk helicopter pilots, get their instructions from a flying officer at Fort Campbell, Kentucky. (Courtesy of U.S. Army Special Operations Command)

army needs people who run into dark spaces when bullets are flying at them, and who run at those bullets. The Rangers and the Deltas are the frontline infantrymen, the absolute tip of the spear. They're not there to dig ditches, they're not there to hand out water, and they're not there to win hearts and minds. They're there to kill or be killed in unbelievably and unimaginably hostile situations."[27]

The actors marveled at what Arthur Max had created in the poor urban neighborhoods of Sale, Morocco. Max had been dealing with a series of challenges to keep his enormous "set" intact and to ensure the safety of the thousands of people who surrounded it on a daily basis.

Max had discovered that the helicopter rotors were so powerful on the Black Hawks that their wash could quickly jar loose the laundry lines, television antennas and other bric-a-brac that sat on the roofs of Sale. He, thus, had to keep a crew busy battening everything down with safety cables.

"I remember one rehearsal," Max recalled, "where the Black Hawks were starting to descend and a refrigerator, which we had placed outside a café as set dressing, ending up bounding down the street like a tumbleweed."[28]

Long hair is not permissible in the Ranger book and the actors were forced to get their "high and tight" done before shooting began. Jason Isaacs was snipping around up there and, as Chico Marx of the Marx Brothers once said, "He snipped a little too much."

"So I shaved my head, which was one of the options you had at Benning," Isaacs remembered. "I remember working on the first day and Ridley looked at me, kind of startled and

Jason Isaacs learns basic Ranger tactics at Fort Benning, Georgia. (Courtesy of U.S. Army Special Operations Command)

kind of saying, 'What have you done?' And I said I shaved my head, because a lot of these guys shave their heads. And he asked, 'Was that how you were going to have it?' And I said, 'Well, yeah. We start today. I've got no choice, have I?' And he said, 'No, all right, that will be fine.' When people ask me where I was in the movie, I say, 'I'm the bald guy.'"[29]

The early shots of the Americans getting ready for action at their base of operations were shot at a working Royal Moroccan Air Force field, some 20 miles north of Rabat, in the coastal town of Kenitra. This field was simulating Mogadishu's coastal airfield, from which the real combatants staged the assault.

It is interesting to note how compact this war-torn city of one million residents was. Colonel Tom Matthews explains that you can fly from the air base on the coast to the desert beyond Mogadishu in two minutes. He could fly the full length of the city, from northeast to southwest, in about four minutes.

"Within that small area," recalled Matthews, "were a million people. And in that group of a million people, I would submit to you that every household was armed, because it was just that kind of dangerous place ... and you can imagine the volume of fire we eventually had that day."[30]

Filming on *Black Hawk Down* was a daily spectacle for cast, crew and its enormous audience. Since Ridley Scott was filming in the middle of the city, thousands of people could mill around, watching the actors-turned-soldiers in action. There were no soundstage doors to close, no cones of silence to lower. Filming took place in the open air.

There were complaints from the local citizenry, especially on night-shooting days when the explosions woke up sleeping babies, daytime workers and anyone else who wasn't used to the blast of RPG rockets, the retort of a .50 caliber machine gun or the incessant sound of M-16 or AK-47 rifle fire.

"But they were happy to have us," recalled Max, "because at one time we were the biggest employer in town, and we were there for 16 weeks."[31]

Recalled Jason Isaacs, "It was a pretty grim environment to shoot in. Very uncomfortable, very hot and dry. When we shot, it was very loud and noisy and confusing, and when we were waiting, we were just standing around baking somewhere, but none of us ever got too self-indulgent as to imagine we were even approaching the foothills of real experience. You wouldn't complain as you would on a normal movie because we were constantly aware of the responsibility of recreating this unbelievably traumatic night in the lives of the American soldiers and the Somalis. You were aware of the resonance of that. This wasn't one of those situations where you'd complain that your mint tea was too cold."[32]

Given the level of importance the U.S. military was placing on *Black Hawk Down* and the level of cooperation that was being given the production in Morocco, there were bound to be moments where history and filmmaking would collide and compromises had to be engineered.

At one point, air support advisor Tom Matthews began to think the film would place some blame for the confusion of the battle at the feet of the 160th SOAR, specifically the Command and Control helicopter (C-2), which Matthews flew in during the actual battle.

"It was apparent to me that the answer to the questions, 'Who screwed up?' and, 'How come things were so confusing?' was going to be pinned on the C-2 bird," remembered Matthews. "That sounds a little bit paranoid, but I'm just relating the sense I had of where this was going — that they were going to set this whole thing up that the C-2 bird was screwed up and confused and led to all the misdirection and fatalities. So, they kept asking me how come you couldn't see this and how come you couldn't see that? I said, 'Hold it guys — if you're asking me to sign off on establishing that the C-2 bird was responsible — if that's what you need here — then I'm not signing up for that. So we had a real 'Come to Jesus' meeting.

"They replied, 'Hold on now, wait, don't take it that way — you don't understand.' And the result was that they ended up characterizing the C-2 bird as kind of vanilla — kind of ho-hum, bland, and somewhat forgettable. I think it settled out as neutral, and they focused on all the other confusion in the battle.

"The guy who played me [Glenn Morshower] was a nice guy and a sincere guy and he was very concerned about doing a good job. There was a good sense with almost all the actors that this was a very significant event; people did really die, they were using real names and their families would watch this. And they wanted to get it right — they didn't want to embarrass the memory of the soldiers."[33]

"We did a shot at the Alamo," said actor Josh Hartnett, "that took half a day to set up and maybe about three minutes to shoot, in which I run across one building, grab a strobe on the ground, flick it up on top of another building where Somali militiamen are positioned — who are shooting at me the whole time — and then two American Little Bird helicopters fly over the building and strafe the Somalis. The way Ridley sets up and films the shot, it's continuous action from the beginning to the end of the scene, and it totally affects you.

"You never know what it's going to be like. You have guys on the building, shooting blanks at you, so you hear the noise and gunshots, you hear the RPGs and see the explosions right next to you. It's easy for an actor to suspend his disbelief and feel like he's actually being shot at."[34]

Jason Isaacs related:

In Morocco, we kept up our training regimen. We all became slightly obsessed with keeping fit. We all ran every day. As an actor, [the experience of working on] *Black Hawk Down* was different from anything I ever worked on before or since. Everybody left every morning on buses at the crack of dawn, whether you were working or not. We all went down to base camp and you were given your filthy, disgusting, dusty, bloody old uniform and your weapon and helmet, which you had to hang on to all day. And you were basically left alone until you were suddenly given an order to run down there, blow this up, jump over this, etc. There was an awful lot of running around, jumping and diving through things. Orders and instructions were relayed to you on a walkie-talkie down a chain of four or five people, so you weren't quite sure where the orders were coming from.

It felt like confusion and panic from our point of view, but it probably wasn't at all, or it may have been deliberately orchestrated. But it went like clockwork and nobody was injured.

My first shot of the entire film, I remember Ridley coming up and he's always chomping on a cigar in the middle of this filthy, dusty, fetid environment, and he's always wearing a spotless pair of chinos. And he starts gesturing up the street—[he says,] "Right, Jason, you're going to run up here, you and your men, right, and shit's going to blow up, cars are going to come flying out, the wall's going to come down, people are going to run out, trucks are going to come—you just keep shooting and people are going to duck down around you—you'll get to the end, things are going to be flipping over and people falling out of windows, and you shoot a couple of people and do your lines on the way there. So let's go for it." And I said, "What do you mean, 'let's go for it'? I don't understand." And he interrupted and said, "Let's do one," and I agreed.

So I'm running down the street, there are explosions, the ground opens up in front of me, bodies are dropping, and there's a deafening rattle of machine guns everywhere. Because I'm not battle-hardened and I haven't been in a thousand live-fire environments, I am pretty sure I'm wincing like an eight-year-old girl. I was constantly ducking and cringing and I get to the end and I get down behind the vehicle, stopping to do my dialogue into the radio, and it's been a huge deal—it probably took a day to set this up. And I realized that the weapon I had been firing with had no magazine, which I had obviously dropped on the way, so I was firing a gun with no bullets. So I ran up to Ridley and told him I didn't have my magazine, and he simply said he'd cover it later. So much for being an experienced Ranger commander.[35]

In between setups, Isaacs did have an interesting question for Ridley Scott. He asked the director, "How do you stop this film from becoming *Zulu*, about a bunch of white people fighting off hordes of black people?"[36]

Scott explained that *Black Hawk Down* was not *Zulu*: "It's a time when American involvement in a foreign conflict was absolutely moral. They'd come there at the behest of the UN and they were doing something that the world had asked them to do and they executed that with remarkable prowess."[37]

CHAPTER FIFTEEN

The Hurt Locker

The Hurt Locker, director Kathryn Bigelow's and writer Mark Boal's soulful and realistic tribute to the U.S. Army's crack Explosive Ordnance Disposal (EOD) teams in Iraq, was the darling of America's film critics in 2009. The film was featured on hundreds of Top 10 lists, and, in March 2010, it was awarded the Best Picture Oscar at the Academy Awards, beating out nine other films, including *Avatar*, which was produced and directed by Bigelow's ex-husband, James Cameron.

Boal was an embedded journalist who spent two weeks in Iraq in 2004, with a real EOD team. It was that nerve-wracking experience on the front lines of the insurgent's war against the United States. That inspired Boal to write *The Hurt Locker.*

Boal wasn't the first newspaper reporter to embed himself with a combat outfit. Some 60 years earlier, war correspondent Ernie Pyle was embedded with U.S. Army combat units fighting in Europe. His fresh-from-the-front-lines-style of reporting appealed to those back in the States who wanted to know what daily life was like for the ordinary G.I. In those days, there was no such thing as national TV news. You either heard about the war by reading Pyle's newspaper columns, or you listened to the radio, or you went to the movies and watched the newsreels. The combat newsreel footage was usually weeks late, black and white, and heavily censored.

The Vietnam War was the first conflict to be featured nightly on television. Baby Boomers clearly remember images of the leading newsmen of the day — Walter Cronkite, Charles Kuralt, Mike Wallace, Dan Rather — reporting from the jungles of Southeast Asia, while their producers cut away to the sound of enemy machine gun fire. And it was that same news coverage that inspired and rallied the anti–war protests that would soon change the country's feeling towards the conflict.

Decades later, a single event forever changed the way people received their war news. On January 17, 1991, U.S. and coalition attack aircraft and ship-launched cruise missiles began the systematic bombing of Baghdad. It signaled the beginning of America's involvement in the Persian Gulf War, the initial step towards Operation Desert Storm, and the end of Iraq's aggressive move into nearby Kuwait. CNN, the relatively new 24-hour news service owned by mogul Ted Turner, hired a number of television-savvy war correspondents and put their boots on the ground. The result: Americans were glued to their television sets, watching night time Baghdad light up like a never-ending Fourth of July fireworks exhibition. The era of instantly accessible, around-the clock, 24/7 news coverage had begun. Suddenly, it seemed like there were flat-screen televisions everywhere, especially in bars and restaurants where every drinker and diner had a birds-eye view of the news.

CNN led the way, but people began to get their news instantly from new sources like the Internet, and later, even their own cell phones. You didn't even have to turn on the television anymore. Like the news reporters who set up their satellite dishes in the middle of the desert and began broadcasting their reports, an average citizen could flip open their laptop or cell phone and be instantly connected to the world. The reality of that world was everywhere. And it wasn't just affecting news reporting. Television entertainment glided into reality, too.

Scripted television series were squeezed out by ever-popular reality television shows like *Survivor, American Idol, Who Wants to Be a Millionaire?, The Apprentice, Big Brother, The Great Race, America's Biggest Loser* and hundreds of other shows that introduced people's problems, challenges and lifestyles to the obsessed masses with moving cameras, natural soundtracks and voice-overs. Combine that reality phenomenon with the reach of radio talk show hosts like Rush Limbaugh and Howard Stern and television hosts like Oprah Winfrey, Dr. Phil and Ellen Degeneres, and you can begin to see how people have become obsessively interested in news, gossip, sports and sex, in all of its facets.

So how does this affect a filmmaker who is about to direct a war picture in the early 21st century? For Kathryn Bigelow, there was no question in her mind that the only way to present the story of *The Hurt Locker* was to make it as immediate and realistic as possible.

"Mark [Boal] had come back from Iraq with these incredible observations," she said. "A real first-person look at a day in the life of a bomb tech. So I kept thinking, 'How can I preserve the reportorial quality the script has?' His script really read like you were there ... so I wanted to protect that feeling and give the audience that opportunity to be on an embed with a bomb squad."[1]

Boal had chosen a dramatic time to be embedded in Baghdad, as he described, "It was eye-opening to see the tidal wave of bombs erupting all over the city and the everyday courage and professionalism of the people trying to deal with it. The IED [Improvised Explosive Device] had become the central tactic of the insurgency. it was an incredibly lethal, unpredictable environment, between the bombs and the gunfire. Not to mention the kidnappings and executions. Journalists were a high-value target for propaganda reasons. It was difficult to quantify the threat when you don't speak the language and the enemy is not wearing a uniform or engaging in traditional warfare, but using hit-and-run ambush tactics. I tried to capture all of this in *The Hurt Locker*."[2]

Boal decided to fictionalize one EOD unit, led by Sergeant First Class William James, a maverick demolitions expert who plays by his own rules, much to the consternation of the other two men in his unit, Sergeant JT Sanborn and Specialist Owen Eldridge. Through the eyes of these three men, the audience is introduced to what it was like on the ground in Baghdad in 2004.

Boal put his journalistic skill to work as he described the detailed, agonizing work of a modern EOD team. It is a story about men working with their hands, de-activating explosive devices that can turn a tanker trailer truck into a skeletal pile of molten-steel remains or reduce human beings to dust. It is an urban war story in which civilians are watching from balconies, rooftops or storefronts, where something as simple as a cell phone can detonate a device and blow an EOD team to hell and gone. There are no enemy soldiers in uniform; in fact, there isn't an enemy in sight. But the threat is sitting right there in the dirt — a half-buried 155mm artillery shell, attached to an intricate pattern of wires that can explode at any moment. What James, Sanborn and Eldridge can do to prevent that device from exploding is what makes great cinema.

Before James even arrived in the outfit, the first sequence in *The Hurt Locker* involved another demolitions sergeant who works with Sanborn and Eldridge. This sergeant first deploys a robot to deactivate an IED buried next to a Baghdad street. Boal described how the robot worked, how it deployed its video cameras which are hooked up to monitors in the unit's Humvee—how it is designed to work in place of a human. And he described how it malfunctioned, forcing the sergeant to put on a heavy, sophisticated bomb suit, and approach the IED himself. And Boal described it all in a professional, let's-get-down-to-business view. There are no ticking clocks, phony heroics, bad guys twisting their mustaches or conversations about the girls back home—this is real urban war in the 21st century.

However, artistic vision alone wasn't going to get *The Hurt Locker* made. Bigelow and Boal were fighting an industry-wide slump in military pictures about the Iraq and Afghanistan wars. Once again, the theory arose that audiences who were getting their daily dose of war news on the television weren't interested in film stories, no matter how compelling they might be.

The only film that had broken through and done decent business was writer/director David O. Russell's serio-comic 1999 film, *Three Kings*, which was closer in tone to a modern *Kelly's Heroes*, as opposed to a serious commentary on the first Gulf War. *Black Hawk Down* had grossed over $150 million worldwide in 2001–02, but it was not a political film, either.

The filmmakers also had to deal with the same factors that had bedeviled Oliver Stone in the 1980s—selling a movie project about another unpopular war. As much as American audiences supported the troops—which was the major difference between the Vietnam and Iraq eras—the Bush administration's arguments for continuing the deadly conflict in the Middle East were wearing thin.

American soldiers were dying in the desert every week, and civilians were beginning to question their deployment. Could America really build a democracy on the bones of Saddam Hussein's dictatorship? Politicians and news commentators were knee-deep in that question, but the average American didn't have a clue, and probably didn't care. Gradually, they were convinced that the troops should come home, and soon.

Bigelow and Boal realized that, to get their movie made, they would have to raise the money independently—no studio was going to touch the subject matter, that was a given. Fortunately, in the late summer of 2006, they aligned themselves with Nicholas Chartier, a producer with strong film financing connections through his newly formed company, Voltage Pictures. At a lunch with Kathryn Bigelow at the Chateau Marmont Hotel in West Hollywood, Chartier agreed to take on *The Hurt Locker* as a client.

The first thing that Chartier did was cut the projected budget of the film. Bigelow felt she needed $20 million to do the picture justice, but Chartier cut the number to $13 million. It still took nine months to piece together the financing package. At one point, Chartier agreed to mortgage his house to get the last bit of financing in place—it was a risk he was willing to take. A start date in July 2007 was then locked in place. The filming location: Amman, Jordan.

It was Boal's idea to scout locations in Jordan. Like the king of Morocco, who supplied Ridley Scott's *Black Hawk Down* team in 2001, the royal family of Jordan offered to equip the smaller crew of *The Hurt Locker* with military equipment, including U.S.-built Humvees and trucks, locations, and military experts. Still, Jordan was a bit of a wild card as a location. Unlike Morocco, which was in a relatively peaceful part of North Africa, Jordan was wedged between Israel and Iraq. Some of the locations chosen for filming were only a few miles from the Iraqi border. Prior to shooting, terrorists had targeted the very hotels that were chosen to house the crew. This was definitely a hot zone.

"The Hyatt had a very strange lobby," Boal recalled. "It's really big and there are concrete barriers in the front. I asked, 'Why is the lobby designed this way?' and they responded, 'That's because if there is an explosion on the ground floor, we set the building back so the first and second floors wouldn't be affected.'"[3]

Special-effects expert Richard Stutsman was hired to handle all of the explosives in the film — no small task — and he immediately decided to check out the location where they would be filming.

"I got on the Internet and looked up Jordan and did my homework on how dangerous it was," he remembered. "I kind of call Jordan the Switzerland of the Middle East. They don't have any oil; nobody's trying to invade them. They're stable, western-friendly, they have peace treaties with Israel and Egypt and they have an American as their queen.

"When I got over there, it worked out [as] they love Americans. You get in every taxi, I was all prepared to say I was from Canada because no one hates the Canadians, but, boy, every taxi driver said they love America and Americans and they have many friends there."[4]

The first major challenge Bigelow faced was choosing a cast.

"I knew that we needed relatively unfamiliar faces," she explained. "These are actors that are known within the industry, but probably not to the public at large. Jeremy Renner, Anthony Mackie and Brian Geraghty ... created a nice ensemble. At the same time, because they are somewhat unfamiliar, the audience can't project onto them a sense of vulnerability or invulnerability, like you can with someone who is more well-known.

"I had seen Jeremy in a small independent movie called *Dahmer* [2002], and he played a serial killer. I suppose my feeling is that if you are capable of that, you are capable of virtually anything. And Anthony Mackie just really leapt off the screen in *Half-Nelson* [2006], even though it was a fairly small part, he was so charismatic and larger than life. And Brian Geraghty gave an extraordinary performance in *Jarhead* [2005]."[5]

Said Mackie, "I originally met with Kathryn to play Eldridge, but after reading the script I was so blown away by the way Mark Boal had written Sanborn, I kind of gave her my pitch on why I should play him. Within two weeks, I knew that she wanted me to play that role."[6]

Given her reputation as a gifted filmmaker and because of the relationships she had developed in the 25 years since she had made her feature directing debut on the motorcycle film, *The Loveless* (1982), Bigelow was able to bring in some talented name actors for interesting cameo roles.

Two-time Academy Award nominee Ralph Fiennes (*Schindler's List, The English Patient*) was cast as the Contractor Team Leader, whose unit is caught in an Iraqi ambush with James' EOD unit. Fiennes had previously starred in Bigelow's 1995 crime drama, *Strange Days*. In *The Hurt Locker*, his character is taken out by a sniper's bullet. Character actor David Morse (*The Green Mile, Disturbia*), flew into Amman for a one day part as Colonel Reed, who is absolutely fascinated with James's record in bomb disposal.

Bigelow had always wanted to work with actor Guy Pearce, and the feeling was mutual. They got their chance when Pearce agreed to come on board as Staff Sergeant Matt Thompson, James's predecessor, who is killed in the movie's first thrilling scene.

While Bigelow assembled her cast, Richard Stutsman began his own battle to get customs to clear his pyrotechnic supplies. Veteran British special effects man David Harris (*Indiana Jones and the Temple of Doom*), who, in the spring of 2007 had worked on the Iraq war film, *Redacted*, which was also shot in Jordan, told Stutsman to bring his own detonators.

Special-effects chief Richard Stutsman detonates an explosion, simulating an Improvised Explosive Device (IED) in an Amman, Jordan, street, in the first bomb sequence in *The Hurt Locker.* (Courtesy of Richard Stutsman)

Stutsman took his advice and went out and bought $10,000 worth of detonation equipment and supplies, including bullet hits (which are very expensive, coming in at $15 a hit). They were loaded onto a Federal Express plane and, when they arrived in Amman, they got stuck in customs.

"It was absolutely horrible," Stutsman remembered. "Up until the day before shooting started, I didn't know if I was going to have stuff to work with. Finally, we got a customs official to come and we got our first batch of material cleared."[7]

Meanwhile, Stutsman and his second in command, New Zealander Blair Foord, set up an FX shop in an old Mazda dealership outside Amman.

One of the first things you notice about the bomb-disposal sequences in *The Hurt Locker* is that there is no artifice in filming them. No musical score suddenly swells up with drama; no soldier suddenly starts calling out his girlfriend's name and no clock is ticking at the bottom of the screen. From the first frame of the film, Bigelow and her cinematographer, Barry Ackroyd, deployed four separate camera units and made sure they covered the action in a naturalistic style that plants the audience right in the middle of the action.

Said Bigelow, "The idea was not to impose an aesthetic, but to let the material reveal itself ... we worked without marks. I blocked with the actors without Barry for the first take, so Barry would discover it as the actors discovered it, in tandem with each other. And then we would move the cameras after each take and the actors wouldn't anticipate where any lens might be or not be."[9]

A wardrobe assistant (right) helps Guy Pearce with his bomb suit. Even before he puts the helmet on, the actor is drenched with sweat. (Courtesy of Richard Stutsman)

"I kind of necessarily wanted to get out of the way of the inherent drama and tension of what these guys do every single day," Bigelow added. "How do you present this information? Well, you let it speak for itself—that tension is just inherent in what they do—you're in a 24/7 threat environment. "I also wanted to avoid imposing certain conventions that would make the audience more comfortable. Once you take those conventions away, suddenly, as you see from the opening sequence, all bets are off."[10]

Watching Sgt. Thompson approach the IED in a bomb suit at the beginning of *The Hurt Locker* makes you wonder whether you've stumbled into the right movie or not—it could be a science-fiction film set in a post–apocalyptic world.

In reality, the bomb suit is very much a part of the EOD specialist's wardrobe. In a scene reminiscent of those deep-sea diver movie moments when the deck crew helps the diver affix his big bubble-top helmet to his suit, Sgt. Thompson gets his helmet in place and then approaches the buried IED on a slow, agonizing walk to the target. Renner would later don the same suit for a couple of his own missions. His prep work included instruction from EOD specialists and an official EOD test.

"It weighed about 80–100 pounds, depending on how much gear you had on you," he explained. "And, you know, they kept telling me how awful the suit was, so ... I put this thing on and I said, 'This is no problem; I can do jumping jacks in this thing! What do you want?' Then they said, 'Okay, there's a stack of paper clips on the ground, there are 50 of them; just bend down and pick one up and then go ten feet over and put it on the ground.' And they asked me to do that ten times. By the tenth time, I was fogging up and I was dying. I was already asking about how to pop the helmet off.

"Then in the last 15 minutes of the test, you take the helmet off and all your gear and you go to a chalkboard and they ask you what is 49 divided by 7? All I could think of was, 'I like cookies.'"[11]

Interestingly, Bigelow found him to be a difficult actor to double.

"I think I went through 10–15 people trying to replicate Jeremy's walk," she explained. "It was such a signature of his character, the kind of lift to his gait and the cadence of the walk was absolutely Jeremy Renner, so even in the wide shots, that's him."[12]

For the site of the film's first bomb disposal sequence (the one that involved Guy Pearce), Bigelow chose an active railway line that ran alongside a busy street in the Mataban district of East Amman, which accommodated 250,000 cars a day. "It was a great one to pick," she said, "because it actually looks a lot like Baghdad. Baghdad has many of these wide boulevards and the texture and tone of the buildings is similar to what it looks like there, too. So, it was perfect aesthetically; it's just that the mayor of Amman didn't quite see it that way. But we were able to get a call from the U.S. ambassador to the mayor's office, at the last possible moment, to get this location approved."[13]

"I was very nervous about damaging windows in those apartment buildings," said FX maestro Richard Stutsman. "But the locals said they didn't care. They said, 'Go ahead and break the windows—we'll just fix them.' That's not the way we do it here. So I admit I was conservative on the blast. Everybody liked it, it looked good, but, from my perspective, I wished I had taken another mortar and pointed it at Guy Pearce and buried him in the dust. To my eye—and I have a very jaded view of it—the explosion is a little too far away from him. But the effect of the ground rising was real, shot with a high-speed camera."[14]

Bigelow was also eager to please the actual bomb techs, who complained about HMEs— Hollywood Movie Explosions—which always featured a predominance of gasoline to give the explosions that bright orange plume which had become a Hollywood signature. What Bigelow wanted to achieve was a recreation of what Boal had seen firsthand in Baghdad—a dense, dark gray cloud of particulant matter.

An IED takes out Staff Sergeant Matt Thompson (Guy Pearce) at the beginning of *The Hurt Locker*.

"That first explosion," she explained, "in downtown Amman was about four stories high and we had several cameras covering it. It was fairly remarkable and a fairly accurate recreation of the explosions Mark saw in Iraq."[15]

"The opening sequence is a learning curve for the audience," Bigelow continued. "This is bomb disarmament and this is what happens if the bomb disarmament doesn't go as you anticipated or hoped. It also sets the tone that there is no margin for error — the margin of error is zero. So it was important to emphasize that and make it palpable and you carry that information with you for the rest of the film, consciously or subconsciously."[16]

Although the IED that takes out Guy Pearce's Sgt. Thompson is the first explosion featured in the film, the first sequence shot by Bigelow was the sniper scene in the desert, which featured Ralph Fiennes as the Contractor Team Leader.

"The day before we shot that sequence," remembered Stutsman, "I had received a 50-pound box of black powder from the Jordanian military. It was labeled Hercules Powder Company, from the U.S., and the date of manufacture was 1967. They took me to the bunkers on the mountainside and there were hundreds, if not thousands, of these cases, so I took a box.

"However, on the day before shooting when we wrapped some of the black powder into bombs that were simulating incoming mortar rounds, all we got were puffs of white smoke. So I sent drivers out with cash to every store in Amman that sold Chinese fireworks. We bought hundreds and hundreds of dollars' worth and started tearing them open and collecting all the black powder. We had four gallon baggies full and I was hoping that would be enough."[17] Stutsman and his associate, Blair Foord, placed the black powder bombs in a cardboard tube attached to an electric match, and then taped them together with strong electrical tape. And they worked just fine. However, this was one location that was particularly hard on the actors

In Jordan, Kathryn Bigelow works along the old Turkish railway line that was once destroyed by Arab armies working for Lawrence of Arabia.

While Kathryn Bigelow hunkers down with her portable monitor, her team prepares another shot, this one focusing on the American soldiers under sniper attack in the desert. (Courtesy of Richard Stutsman)

and crew. First of all, there were no trailers, no Winnebagos, no Honey Wagons. The only shelter from the sun was provided by Bedouin tents that were erected on site.

"There were no movie trailers available in Jordan," said Bigelow, "so we created these tents and all the actors and crew housed themselves in there if they were not on camera. That created another sense of a barracks ... there was no escape. There's no decompression — you are there on point 24/7 just like in Baghdad. There is no time off. That contributed a lot to the sense of immersion."[18]

"I remember going into one of the tents," said Boal, "and seeing our guys and they were hot and they're sitting on these little cots, and I just felt bad for them. Anthony, Brian and Jeremy in their military uniforms. It's a big old canvas tent on some poles in the middle of the desert and there's no air conditioning. We had ice water and then it melted."[19]

Bigelow would take a week to shoot the complicated ambush sequence that was shot near the actual narrow-gauge railway line that had been targeted by Lawrence of Arabia's Arab irregulars in World War I.

"It was us laying in the desert on our bellies for a week in 150-degree heat," recalled actor Anthony Mackie, "trying not to be bitten by scorpions and waving off flies. That week kind of put the war in perspective for me and opened my eyes as to what these soldiers were going through."[20]

Mackie and some of the other crew members were also concerned with their proximity

Another view of the old Turkish railway line used as a location in *The Hurt Locker*. (Courtesy of Richard Stutsman)

to the Iraqi border. "We were in the middle of the desert, in the middle of nowhere," he remembered. "If something happens, if someone decides they're going to take over the film, there's nothing anyone can do. A lot of the fear you saw in that scene was actual fear. We were two miles from the Iraqi border, about three miles off the main highway."[21]

In keeping the film as realistic as possible, Bigelow designed her shots with an eye towards a typical bomb-disarmament scenario, which called for a 300-yard containment area. Thus, her outdoor urban locations in Amman were enormous. She would then place her four camera crews, but she wouldn't necessarily tell the actors where they were. Former documentarian Barry Ackroyd placed his cameras on rooftops, in building windows, in crevices, below ground, above ground, wherever he could get a unique shot of the soldiers.

Said Mackie, "In many ways, with the camera set up that Kathryn designed, it was like doing a play. You knew that whatever you did, as long as you did it correctly, it would get caught on film. We weren't worried about our good side or our bad side or where the light was coming from. Kathryn and Barry worked very well together in that regard.

"The thing about it is that Kathryn never really got in the way of the characters we were trying to create, the things we were trying to do. She really allowed us to push it as hard as we wanted to. And she tried to craft the story around that, which was unique and, at the same, very liberating. She really helped us and talked to us and never got in the way of the bond we created. She never felt insecure that we were talking to one another and not talking to the director. It was really great that before every shot, she would come to us and explain what she was doing, how it fit into the film and why she was shooting it. Most directors don't do that. She was a tour de force."[22]

"Kathryn had obviously done her homework," said Stutsman. "She and Mark both had been over this over and over and they had a pretty good feel as to what the movie would look like. And I saw the original script, and they stuck to it. When I first saw the movie, they didn't deviate much at all. Usually, the first draft is nothing like what ends up on the screen. Barry has a very documentary-type style. He had shot *United 93*. I went back and watched that and it has the same feeling as *The Hurt Locker*. The camera is always moving and it's in the crowd of people."[23]

But it wasn't Barry Ackroyd's camera work alone that makes *The Hurt Locker* a fascinating movie experience; it was the work of the cast, particularly Jeremy Renner, who makes Sgt. James one of the most compelling combat heroes since the days when Steve McQueen and William Holden ruled the Hollywood roost. McQueen had made a career of playing brash and cocky heroes who marched to their own drummers. Renner was definitely cut from the same cloth.

Said Boal, "James was a fictionalization, but there really were a lot of guys in 2004 who were making the rules up as they went, because the military was taken a little bit by surprise by the tidal wave of IEDs, and there was no strict handbook on how to deal with them. Some

Crew members help Jeremy Renner with his bomb suit, while co-star Anthony Mackie (center) takes a break. (Courtesy of Richard Stutsman)

guys work quite cautious, more along the lines of the first team leader that you see; some were like James, who developed their own way of doing things."[24]

In regards to how he created the character of Sgt. James, Renner admitted, "I didn't base it off anyone or anything. I based it off of circumstances and, I guess, instinctual things. Some things I found in the day ... like the bomb parts were such a throwaway little thing, but I laced them throughout the entire movie because it was a big informing thing for me for this character.

"I had the ultimate respect for the guy. The love for the craft ... makes him a sane person and not some junkie. It's so obvious that this guy could be a thrill junkie, this guy's bravado and all — that's just one note that I did everything in my power to not play — that is part of him, absolutely, but I just focused on all of the things — the bomb part, the love for his craft, the respect for his job, the relationship with the child that really was an important aspect to the character — those things informed me."[25]

The "child" that Renner refers to is Beckham, a likable (though foul-mouthed) Iraqi youth who tries to sell Sergeant James a batch of pirated DVDs in a Baghdad marketplace.

The role was not cast until executive producer Tony Mark, special-effects chief Richard Stutsman and some other crew members were lounging on their day off in the lobby of a Dead Sea hotel.

Recalled Stutsman, "We were ready to go home when we heard this beautiful piano music coming out of the bar, so we wandered over and here was this kid playing piano at the bar. And Tony looked at him and said, 'You know what, there's our Beckham.' It turned out that his father was an American Marine veteran of Jordanian descent, who was now an international arms trader. Tony started talking to him and the kid [Christopher Sayegh] was cast."[26]

Later in the story, James is leading his bomb squad through an abandoned and ruined factory that has become a temporary bomb-making facility, when he comes across the corpse of a young boy whose body was being implanted with a bomb. Now, when I saw the film, I thought the body on the table was Beckham and, apparently, James thought so, too.

Explained Boal, "The kid on the table is *not* Beckham, although it looks like him. Sanborn and Eldridge knows its not the same kid, but they don't realize how much its affecting James. We see Beckham alive and well later."[27]

It does affect James deeply, and in a fierce rage, he takes an Iraqi trader hostage at gunpoint and ventures into the city to find out what happened to Beckham. But the trader doesn't know anything, and James has to beat it back to base, where he's nearly killed at the checkpoint.

Kathryn Bigelow was thrilled with the location chosen for the moody, atmospheric sequence during which James finds the child's body.

"It was an old chocolate factory," she revealed. "And our production designer, Karl Júlíusson, preserved and accentuated all that texture and raw degradation. I remember, when we scouted it, we found camels inside. There was a mosque on one side and a church on the other, so you would have the call to prayer and church bells going off all day long."[28]

Said Stutsman, "Barrie Rice, our security tech, was pulling out a lot of techniques the insurgents would use for a scene like that. For instance, when James leads the squad in, they step on some broken glass. It's not apparent to most people, but insurgents would put glass on the ground as a warning, so that if they were in the bomb factory, they would hear it and know somebody was coming.

"They'd also put an old *Playboy* magazine down on the ground with a trip wire underneath it. Because they know that American soldiers will always grab a *Playboy* and check it out ... They are no dummies."[29]

Kathryn Bigelow (center) works with young Christopher Sayegh, who portrays Beckham, the DVD hawker. Crew members on the left and right are unidentified.

Another one of James's signature moments in *The Hurt Locker* was to remove his bomb suit while disarming a slew of artillery shells that he finds in the trunk of a car.

"It's really a great movie moment when Jeremy takes off the suit," said Boal, "because you really get to learn a lot about his character in this moment, and his bravado and hubris. It was based on a true incident that an EOD guy told me actually happened in Israel. It makes sense when you think about it. From a practical standpoint, there are so many explosives in the back of that car, that wearing the suit doesn't matter, so why not take it off? But it certainly takes a certain type to have that thought process. In that moment, 99% of the population would keep the suit on."[30]

One of the challenges facing screenwriter Mark Boal was to come up with a sequence that gave closure to the relationship between James and Sanborn, but didn't appear overly melodramatic. The sequence he chose to write, in which James tries to save an Iraqi suicide bomber who has second thoughts, is incredibly tense and terrifying.

"It really felt like you needed something towards the end of the movie that encapsulates where we are in the story," said Boal, "and that, finally, James and Sanborn are about to have their real reckoning and a real kind of understanding of each other. At the same time, you want to finally show, in a way that's fairly uncontroversial, the real tragedy of the war and the fundamental logistical impossibility of disarming all of these IEDs. And, here is it, in a very sort of over–the–top symbolic sense — there's literally not enough time to do something as simple as breaking through the locks [holding the explosives in place]. It's not about some-body's heroism. It's the simple time-space puzzle that can't be solved."[31]

Members of an elite U.S. Army Explosive Ordnance Disposal (EOD) unit, detonate explosives in the desert. (Courtesy of Richard Stutsman)

On the day the suicide-bomber sequence was shot, there was a great deal of emotion on the set, and not just that expressed by Jeremy Renner's character. The crew hung around quietly and was in no hurry to break down the equipment and head for home. They were spent.

And what actually is The Hurt Locker? Special effects maestro Richard Stutsman answered that question: "Mark [Boal] explained it to me. He had heard it from bomb techs over there — that it's a place in your brain where you lock up all those horrible things you see. You see your buddy get blown up, the only way you're going to survive is to take all those feelings and emotions and lock them up some place and go on with your life. That's 'The Hurt Locker.'"[32]

Released with limited fanfare in the United States, in the summer of 2009, *The Hurt Locker* was a smash critical hit wherever it played. Because it was about a subject Americans stayed away from, however, the film was never a huge box-office success. With all the attention that was given the movie, it is very telling that the film grossed only $15.7 million in the U.S. And that's with nine Academy Award nominations, including wins for Best Picture, Best Director, Best Original Screenplay, Best Editing, Best Sound and Best Sound Editing.

Still, because of ancillary sales to home video, pay-per-view and television, *The Hurt Locker* was seen by more Americans, by far, than any other movie produced about the conflict in Iraq.

Director Kathryn Bigelow's canny decision to present a realistic story with a strong

Sgt. James (Jeremy Renner, center) tries desperately to use a bolt cutter to break off the locks holding the explosives of a suicide bomber (Suhail Aldabbach), while Sgt. Sanborn (Anthony Mackie, left) guards the street. (Courtesy of Richard Stutsman)

documentary feel, bereft of clichés and phony dramatic moments, was a huge success with everyone who sat down and watched the 131-minute film. Like Ridley Scott's *Black Hawk Down* and Oliver Stone's earlier *Platoon*, it gave audiences the ultimate visceral experience of being beside our troops in the most desperate situations imaginable. Bigelow's desire to put "boots on the ground" worked, and her film's six Oscars will guarantee *The Hurt Locker*'s lasting place in the pantheon of memorable and realistic war films.

Chapter Notes

Chapter One

1. Brown, Harry, Letter to author Steven Jay Rubin, November 2, 1975.
2. Ibid.
3. Ibid.
4. *A Walk in the Sun*, 20th Century–Fox, 1946.
5. Brown, Harry, Letter to author Steven Jay Rubin, November 2, 1975.
6. Lewis Milestone papers, Academy of Motion Picture Arts and Sciences.
7. Ibid.
8. Brown, Harry, *A Walk in the Sun*, University of Nebraska Press, 1998, p. 11.
9. *New York Times*, January 13, 1946.
10. *Citizen's News*, April 19, 1945.
11. Ibid.
12. Ibid.
13. Ibid.
14. Ibid.
15. Ibid.
16. Ibid.
17. Ibid.
18. *Cue Magazine*, January 12, 1946.
19. *Los Angeles Times*, June 26, 1946.
20. *Daily Variety*, November 28, 1945.

Chapter Two

1. *Los Angeles Times*, November 11, 1949.
2. Interview with Robert Pirosh by the author, January 1974.
3. Ibid.
4. Ibid.
5. Ibid.
6. Ibid.
7. *New York Times*, October 23, 1949.
8. Interview with Robert Pirosh by the author, January 1974.
9. Ibid.

Chapter Three

1. Interview with Beirne Lay, Jr., by the author, June 1974.
2. Ibid.
3. Ibid.

4. Interview with Sy Bartlett by the author, August 1974.
5. Interview with Beirne Lay, Jr., by the author, June 1974.
6. Interview with Sy Bartlett by the author, August 1974.
7. Interview with Beirne Lay, Jr., by the author, June 1974.
8. Ibid.
9. Interview with Sy Bartlett by the author, August 1974.
10. Ibid.
11. Interview with Henry King by the author, September 1974.
12. Ibid.
13. *Twelve O'Clock High*, 20th Century–Fox, 1949.

Chapter Four

1. Pierre Boulle, *My Own River Kwai* (Jackson, TN: Vanguard Press, 1967).
2. Interview with Carl Foreman by the author, June 1974.
3. Ibid.
4. Ibid.
5. Ibid.
6. *The Bridge on the River Kwai*, press notes, 1957.
7. Interview with Carl Foreman by the author, June 1974.
8. Ibid.
9. Ibid.
10. Letter from Michael Wilson to the author, May 9, 1975.
11. *The Bridge on the River Kwai*, press notes, 1957.

Chapter Five

1. S. L. A. Marshall, *Pork Chop Hill* (New York: Caliber Books, 2000), 2–4.
2. Interview with Joseph Clemons by the author, March 2010.
3. Ibid.
4. Interview with Walter Russell by the author, May 2010.
5. Ibid.
6. Ibid.
7. Interview with Joseph Clemons by the author, March 2010.
8. Ibid.
9. Gregory Peck Special Collection of the Library of the Academy of Motion Picture Arts and Sciences.
10. *Pork Chop Hill*, United Artists, 1959.
11. Gregory Peck Special Collection of the Library of the Academy of Motion Picture Arts and Sciences.
12. Interview with Joseph Clemons by the author, March 2010.
13. Gregory Peck Special Collection of the Library of the Academy of Motion Picture Arts and Sciences.
14. Ibid.
15. Gregory Peck Special Collection of the Library of the Academy of Motion Picture Arts and Sciences.
16. *Pork Chop Hill*, United Artists, 1959.
17. Interview with Hal Needham by the author, March 2010.
18. Letter, dated April 11, 1958 from Geoffrey M. Shurlock, vice-president and director, Production Code Administration, Motion Picture Association of America to Marvin B. Meyer, Melville Productions.
19. Letter, dated June 13, 1958, from screenwriter James R. Webb to Mr. Hiram W. Kwan, Attorney at Law, Chairman, Citizens Rights Committee for the Chinese American Citizens Alliance.
20. Interview with Hal Needham by the author, March 2010.
21. Ibid.
22. Interview with Joseph Clemons by the author, March 2010.
23. Interview with William Wellman, Jr., by the author, March 2010.
24. Ibid.
25. *Pork Chop Hill*, United Artists, 1959.
26. Letter from actor Viraj Amonsin to Gregory Peck, dated November 24, 1958, *Pork Chop Hill* files, Gregory Peck Special Collection of the Library of the Academy of Motion Picture Arts and Sciences.
27. *Pork Chop Hill*, United Artists, 1959.
28. Letter from Gregory Peck to United Artists' Arnold Picker, dated June 12, 1959, *Pork Chop Hill* files, Gregory Peck Special Collection of the Library of the Academy of Motion Picture Arts and Sciences.
29. Letter from Arnold Picker, United Artists, to Gregory Peck, dated June 16, 1959, *Pork Chop Hill* files, Gregory Peck Special Collection of the Library of the Academy of Motion Picture Arts and Sciences.

30. Letter from Arnold Picker, United Artists, to Gregory Peck, dated June 23, 1959, *Pork Chop Hill* files, Gregory Peck Special Collection of the Library of the Academy of Motion Picture Arts and Sciences.

Chapter Six

1. *Look* magazine, June 10, 1969.
2. Ibid.
3. Ibid.
4. Ibid.
5. Ibid.
6. Ibid.
7. *Variety* (Weekly Edition), June 8, 1960.
8. *Film Daily*, December 5, 1960.
9. Ibid.
10. Interview with Frank McCarthy by the author, October 1974.
11. Interview with Gerd Oswald by the author, November 1974.
12. Interview with Elmo Williams by the author, December 1974.
13. Mel Gussow, *Don't Say Yes Until I Finish Talking: A Biography of Darryl F. Zanuck* (Garden City, NY: Doubleday, 1971), 216.
14. *Life* magazine, October 12, 1962.
15. Ibid.
16. Gussow, 222.
17. Interview with Gerd Oswald by the author, November 1974.
18. Ibid.
19. Interview with Elmo Williams by the author, December 1974.
20. Interview with Frank McCarthy by the author, October 1974.
21. Gussow, 220.
22. *The Longest Day*, 20th Century–Fox, 1962.
23. *Daily Variety*, October 3, 1961.
24. Ibid.
25. Interview with Elmo Williams by the author, December 1974.
26. Ibid.
27. Interview with Gerd Oswald by the author, November 1974.
28. Interview with Elmo Williams by the author, December 1974.
29. Interview with Gerd Oswald by the author, November 1974
30. Interview with Elmo Williams by the author, December 1974.
31. Gussow, 228.
32. *Variety* (Weekly Edition), October 24, 1961.
33. Gussow, 233–234.
34. *The Longest Day*, 20th Century–Fox, 1962.

Chapter Seven

1. Interview with Robert Pirosh by the author, January 1975.
2. Ibid.
3. Ibid.
4. Ibid.
5. Ibid.
6. Ibid.
7. Ibid.
8. Interview with Don Siegel by the author, February 1975.
9. Interview with Robert Pirosh by the author, January 1975.
10. Interview with Richard Carr by the author, January 1975.
11. Interview with Robert Pirosh by the author, January 1975.
12. Interview with Don Siegel by the author, February 1975.
13. Ibid.
14. Interview with Richard Carr by the author, January 1975.
15. Ibid.
16. Interview with Don Siegel by the author, February 1975.
17. Ibid.

18. Interview with Robert Pirosh by the author, January 1975.
19. Ibid.
20. Ibid.
21. Interview with Richard Carr by the author, January 1975.
22. Ibid.
23. Interview with Don Siegel by the author, February 1975.
24. Ibid.

Chapter Eight

1. Paul Brickhill, *The Great Escape* (Greenwich, CT: Crest Books, 1961), 28.
2. Ibid., 209–210.
3. Interview with John Sturges by the author, June 1974.
4. Ibid.
5. Ibid.
6. Ibid.
7. Interview with William Roberts by the author, August 1974.
8. Interview with John Sturges by the author, June 1974.
9. Interview with W.R. Burnett by the author, November 1974.
10. Interview with Robert Relyea by the author, March 1993.
11. Interview with John Sturges by the author, June 1974.
12. Interview with Bud Ekins by the author, April 1974.
13. Interview with Jud Taylor by the author, May 1974.
14. Interview with Robert Relyea by the author, March 1993.
15. Ibid.
16. *Films and Filming* magazine, February 1974.
17. Interview with James Garner by the author, July 1993.
18. Interview with W.R. Burnett by the author, November 1974.
19. Interview with Robert Relyea by the author, March 1993.
20. Interview with Bud Ekins by the author, April 1974.
21. Ibid.
22. Interview with John Sturges by the author, June 1974.
23. Interview with Robert Relyea by the author, March 1993.
24. Ibid.
25. Interview with Bud Ekins by the author, April 1974.
26. Interview with Robert Relyea by the author, March 1993.
27. Interview with John Sturges by the author, June 1974.
28. Interview with Robert Relyea by the author, March 1993.
29. Ibid.
30. Ibid.

Chapter Nine

1. *The Sand Pebbles* DVD Commentary, 20th Century–Fox, 2007.
2. Interview with Robert Liu by the author, February 2010.
3. Interview with Richard Attenborough by Michael Thomas, 2004.
4. *The Sand Pebbles* DVD Commentary, 20th Century–Fox, 2007.
5. Ibid.
6. *Los Angeles Times*, December 22, 1965.
7. *The Sand Pebbles* DVD Commentary, 20th Century–Fox, 2007.
8. Interview with Richard Attenborough by Michael Thomas, 2004.
9. *The Sand Pebbles* DVD Commentary, 20th Century–Fox, 2007.
10. Ibid.
11. Ibid.
12. Ibid.
13. Ibid.
14. Interview with Robert Liu by the author, January 2010.
15. *The Sand Pebbles* DVD Commentary, 20th Century–Fox, 2007.
16. Ibid.
17. Ibid.
18. Ibid.

Chapter Ten

1. Interview with Frank McCarthy by the author, February 1975.
2. *Patton* production files, Academy of Motion Picture Arts and Sciences.
3. Interview with Frank McCarthy by the author, February 1975.
4. *Patton*, 20th Century–Fox, 1970.
5. Ibid.
6. Ibid.
7. Ibid.
8. *Patton*, Francis Ford Coppola screenplay draft, 1966.
9. Interview with Frank McCarthy by the author, February 1975.
10. Ibid.
11. Ibid.
12. Ibid.
13. Ibid.

Chapter Eleven

1. Interview with Oliver Stone by the author, March 2010.
2. Ibid.
3. Ibid.
4. Ibid.
5. Ibid.
6. Ibid.
7. Ibid.
8. *American Film Magazine*, January/February 1987.
9. Interview with Oliver Stone by the author, March 2010.
10. Ibid.
11. Ibid.
12. Ibid.
13. *Rolling Stone*, January 29, 1987.
14. Interview with Oliver Stone by author, March 2010.
15. *Los Angeles Times*, March 29, 1987.
16. Arnold Kopelson, *My Platoon Experience,* 2003, a short essay on Mr. Kopelson's experience during the making of *Platoon.*
17. *The Hollywood Reporter*, September 10, 1985.
18. Interview with actor John C. McGinley by the author, March 2010.
19. Ibid.
20. *Platoon*, DVD Audio Commentary, 2006.
21. *American Film Magazine*, January/February 1987.
22. *Platoon*, DVD Audio Commentary, 2006.
23. *Los Angeles Times*, December 28, 1986.
24. Michael Singer, *Platoon*, April 20, 2002.
25. *Platoon*, DVD Audio Commentary, 2006.
26. Interview with actor John C. McGinley by the author, March 2010.
27. *Platoon*, DVD Audio Commentary, 2006.
28. Ibid.
29. *New York Times*, January 1987.
30. *Screen International*, March 14, 1987.
31. *Platoon*, DVD Audio Commentary, 2006.
32. Ibid.
33. Michael Singer, *Platoon*, April 20, 2002.
34. Interview with actor John C. McGinley by the author, March 2010.
35. *Platoon*, DVD Audio Commentary, 2006.
36. Michael Singer, *Platoon*, April 20, 2002.
37. Interview with actor John C. McGinley by the author, March 2010.
38. Interview with Oliver Stone by the author, March 2010.
39. *Film and Video Production*, June 1987.
40. *Platoon*, DVD Audio Commentary, 2006.
41. Ibid.
42. *American Film Magazine*, January/February 1987.

43. *Los Angeles Times*, February 19, 1988.
44. Interview with actor John C. McGinley by the author, March 2010.
45. Ibid.

Chapter Twelve

1. Interview with Ronald F. Maxwell by the author, January 2010.
2. *Gettysburg* DVD commentary, Turner Pictures, 1993.
3. Ibid.
4. Interview with Ronald F. Maxwell by the author, January 2010.
5. Ibid.
6. Ibid.
7. Ibid.
8. Ibid.
9. Ibid.
10. Ibid.
11. Ibid.
12. Ibid.
13. Ibid.
14. Ibid.
15. Ibid.
16. Ibid.
17. Ibid.
18. Ibid.
19. Ibid.
20. Ibid.
21. Ibid.
22. Ibid.
23. Ibid.
24. Ibid.
25. Ibid.
26. *Gettysburg* DVD Commentary, Turner Pictures, 1993.
27. Interview with Ronald F. Maxwell by the author, January 2010.
28. Ibid.
29. *Orange County Register*, October 13, 1993.
30. Ibid.
31. Interview with Ronald F. Maxwell by the author, January 2010.
32. Ibid.
33. Ibid.
34. *Gettysburg*, Turner Pictures, 1993.
35. Interview with Ronald F. Maxwell by the author, January 2010.
36. Ibid.
37. Ibid.
38. Ibid.
39. Ibid.
40. Ibid.
41. Ibid.

Chapter Thirteen

1. Hendrik Hertzberg, *The New Yorker*, July 27, 1998.
2. Interview with Arnold Spielberg, *Saving Private Ryan* DVD Special Features, 1998.
3. Interview with Steven Spielberg, *Saving Private Ryan* DVD Special Features, 1998.
4. Ibid.
5. *Jaws*, Universal Pictures, 1975.
6. *New York Daily News*, August 2, 1998.
7. Interview with Mark Gordon by the author, May 2010.
8. Ibid.
9. Anonymously written studio coverage, dated May 13, 1996.
10. Interview with Mark Gordon by the author May 2010.

11. Ibid.
12. Ibid.
13. Ibid.
14. *Detour magazine*, March 1999.
15. Interview with Mark Gordon by the author May 2010.
16. Ibid.
17. *Detour magazine*, March 1999.
18. Interview with Dale Dye by the author, May 2010.
19. Ibid.
20. Ibid.
21. Ibid.
22. Ibid.
23. Ibid.
24. Ibid.
25. Interview with Tom Sizemore by the author, February 2010.
26. Interview with Dale Dye by the author, May 2010.
27. Interview with Tom Sizemore by the author, February 2010.
28. Ibid.
29. Interview with Dale Dye by the author, May 2010.
30. *Rave*, July 24, 1998.
31. *Times of London*, August 19, 1998.
32. *L.A. Daily News*, Marilyn Beck and Stacy Jenel Smith, August 26, 1997.
33. Interview with Dale Dye by the author, May 2010.
34. Ibid.
35. Ibid.
36. Ibid.
37. Ibid.
38. *Los Angeles Times*, Sean Mitchell, July 19, 1998.
39. Ibid.
40. *Daily Variety*, February 19, 1999.
41. Interview with Tom Sizemore by the author, February 2010.
42. Interview with Dale Dye by the author, May 2010.
43. Ibid.
44. Interview with Dale Dye by the author, May 2010.
45. Interview with Tom Sizemore by the author, February 2010.
46. Interview with Mark Gordon by the author, May 2010.

Chapter Fourteen

1. Interview with Tom Matthews by the author, May 2010.
2. *Black Hawk Down* Press Kit, 2001.
3. *Black Hawk Down* Press Kit, 2001.
4. Interview with Arthur Max by the author, May 2010.
5. Ibid.
6. Ibid.
7. *Black Hawk Down* Press Kit, 2001.
8. Interview with Tom Matthews by the author, May 2010.
9. Ibid.
10. Ibid.
11. Interview with Phil Strub by the author, May 2010.
12. Interview with Tom Matthews by the author, May 2010.
13. Interview with Arthur Max by the author, May 2010.
14. Ibid.
15. Ibid.
16. Ibid.
17. Ibid.
18. *Black Hawk Down* press kit, 2001.
19. Ibid.
20. Ibid.
21. Interview with Jason Isaacs by the author, May 2010.
22. *Black Hawk Down* press kit, 2001.

23. Interview with Jason Isaacs by the author, May 2010.
24. *Black Hawk Down* press kit, 2001.
25. Interview with Jason Isaacs by the author, May 2010.
26. *Black Hawk Down* press kit, 2001.
27. Interview with Jason Isaacs by the author, May 2010.
28. Interview with Arthur Max by the author, May 2010.
29. Interview with Jason Isaacs by the author, May 2010.
30. Interview with Tom Matthews by the author, May 2010.
31. Interview with Arthur Max by the author, May 2010.
32. Interview with Jason Isaacs by the author, May 2010.
33. Interview with Tom Matthews by the author, May 2010.
34. *Black Hawk Down* press kit, 2001.
35. Interview with Jason Isaacs by the author, May 2010.
36. Ibid.
37. Ibid.

Chapter Fifteen

1. Interview with Kathryn Bigelow by Mali Elfman, *Screen Crave*, June 23, 2009.
2. Interview with Mark Boal, *London Daily Telegraph*, August 25, 2009.
3. *The Hollywood Reporter*, December 13, 2009.
4. Interview with Richard Stutsman by the author, January 2010.
5. *The Hurt Locker* DVD Commentary, Summit Entertainment, 2010.
6. Interview with Anthony Mackie by the author, March 2010.
7. Interview with Richard Stutsman by the author, January 2010.
9. Ibid.
10. Interview with Kathryn Bigelow, *Reel Time on Sirius Radio*, March 2010.
11. Interview with Jeremy Renner by Mali Elfman, *Screen Crave*, June 22, 2009.
12. *The Hurt Locker* DVD Commentary, Summit Entertainment, 2010.
13. Ibid.
14. Interview with Richard Stutsman by the author, January 2010.
15. *The Hurt Locker* DVD Commentary, Summit Entertainment, 2010.
16. Interview with Kathryn Bigelow, *Reel Time on Sirius Radio*, March 2010.
17. Interview with Richard Stutsman by the author, January 2010.
18. Interview with Kathryn Bigelow, *Reel Time on Sirius Radio*, March 2010.
19. Interview with Mark Boal, *Reel Time on Sirius Radio*, March 2010.
20. Interview with Anthony Mackie by the author, March 2010.
21. Ibid.
22. Ibid.
23. Interview with Richard Stutsman by the author, January 2010.
24. *The Hurt Locker* DVD Commentary, Summit Entertainment, 2010.
25. Interview with Jeremy Renner by Mali Elfman, *Screen Crave*, June 22, 2009.
26. Interview with Richard Stutsman by the author, January 2010.
27. *The Hurt Locker* DVD Commentary, Summit Entertainment, 2010.
28. Ibid.
29. Interview with Richard Stutsman by the author, January 2010.
30. *The Hurt Locker* DVD Commentary, Summit Entertainment, 2010.
31. Ibid.
32. Interview with Richard Stutsman by the author, January 2010.

Bibliography

Interviews

Anhalt, Edward, writer, *The Young Lions, In Love and War*, June 1974.
Attenborough, Richard, actor, *The Sand Pebbles* (by Michael Thomas, 2004).
Bartlett, Sy, writer *Twelve O'Clock High*; producer, *Pork Chop Hill*, March 1974.
Blankfort, Michael, writer, *Halls of Montezuma*, November 1973.
Blum, Edward, writer, *Stalag 17*, October 1974.
Burnett, W. R., writer, *The Great Escape*, November 1974.
Carr, Richard, writer, *Hell Is for Heroes*, January 1975.
Clemons, Joseph, technical advisor, *Pork Chop Hill*, March 2010.
Clotheir, William, cinematographer, *Merrill's Marauders*, April 1974.
Daves, Delmer, director, *Destination Tokyo*, May 1974.
Dmytryk, Edward, director, *The Young Lions*, June 1974.
Dye, Dale, technical advisor, *Saving Private Ryan*, May 2010.
Ekins, Bud, stunt coordinator (motorcycles), *The Great Escape*, April 1974.
Foreman, Carl, writer, *The Bridge on the River Kwai*, June 1974.
Foy, Brynie, producer, *PT-109*, June 1974.
Garner, James, actor, *The Great Escape*, July 1993.
Garnett, Tay, director, *Bataan*, June 1974.
Gay, John, writer, *Run Silent, Run Deep*, March 1974.
Goldstone, Richard, writer/director, *No Man Is an Island*, June 1974.
Gordon, Mark, producer, *Saving Private Ryan*, May 2010.
Grainger, Edmund, producer, *Sands of Iwo Jima*, June 1974.
Guffey, Burnett, cinematographer, *From Here to Eternity*, April 1974.
Hathaway, Henry, director, *The Desert Fox*, December 1974.
Isaacs, Jason, actor, *Black Hawk Down*, May 2010.
Johnson, Nunnally, writer/producer, *The Desert Fox*, May 1974.
King, Henry, director, *Twelve O'Clock High*, May 1974.
Kramer, Stanley, producer, *Home of the Brave*, April 1974.
Lay, Beirne, Jr., writer, *Twelve O'Clock High*, March 1974.
Lewin, Robert, writer, *The Bold and the Brave*, January 1974.
Litvak, Anatole, director, *Decision Before Dawn*, March 1974.
Liu, Robert, assistant director, *The Sand Pebbles*, February 2010.
Mackie, Anthony, actor, *The Hurt Locker*, March 2010.
Maltz, Albert, writer, *Destination Tokyo*, February 1974.
Martinson, Leslie, director, *PT 109*, June 1974.
Matthews, Tom, technical advisor, *Black Hawk Down*, May 2010.
Mayes, Wendell, writer, *The Enemy Below*, July 1974.
Max, Arthur, production designer, *Black Hawk Down*, May 2010.
Maxwell, Ronald F., writer/director, *Gettysburg*, January 2010.
McCarthy, Frank, producer, *Patton,* February 1975.
McGinley, John C., actor, *Platoon*, March 2010.

Miller, David, director, *Flying Tigers*, November 1974.
Montaigne, Lawrence, actor, *The Great Escape*, April 1974.
Murphy, Richard, writer, *The Desert Rats*, June 1974.
Needham, Hal, stuntman, *Pork Chop Hill*, March 2010.
Nolan, Lloyd, actor, *Manila Calling, Guadalcanal Diary*, June 1974.
North, Edmund, writer, *Patton*, December 1973.
Oswald, Gerd, director, *The Longest Day,* November 1974.
Pirosh, Robert, writer, *Battleground, Hell Is for Heroes*, January 1974, January 1975.
Relyea, Robert, assistant to the director, *The Great Escape*, March 1993.
Roberts, William, writer (uncredited), *The Great Escape*, August 1974.
Rosenberg, Aaron, producer, *To Hell and Back*, October 1974.
Russell, Walter, Korean War veteran, *Pork Chop Hill*, May 2010.
Schaffner, Franklin, director, *Patton*, September 1974.
Seaton, George, director, *36 Hours*, February 1974.
Shaw, Irwin, author, *The Young Lions*, August 1974.
Sherdeman, Ted, writer, *Hell to Eternity*, July 1974.
Siegel, Don, director, *Hell Is for Heroes*, February 1975.
Sizemore, Tom, actor, *Saving Private Ryan*, February 2010.
Sperling, Milton, producer, *Battle of the Bulge*, October 1974.
Stone, Oliver, director, *Platoon*, March 2010.
Strub, Phil, Director of Entertainment Media, Department of Defense, *Black Hawk Down*, May 2010.
Sturges, John, director, *The Great Escape*, June 1974.
Stutsman, Richard, special effects supervisor, *The Hurt Locker*, January 2010.
Taradash, Daniel, writer, *From Here to Eternity*, March 1974.
Taylor, Jud, actor, *The Great Escape*, May 1974.
Thompson, J. Lee, director, *The Guns of Navarone*, December 1974.
Trivers, Barry, writer, *Flying Tigers*, June 1974.
Viertel, Peter, writer, *Decision Before Dawn*, August 1974.
Wellman, William, Jr., Actor, *Pork Chop Hill*, March 2010.
Williams, Elmo, coordinator of battle scenes, *The Longest Day*, December 1974.
Wise, Robert, director, *The Desert Rats, The Sand Pebbles*, November 1974.
Zinnemann, Fred, director, *From Here to Eternity*, August 1974.

Letters

Amonsin, Viraj. Letter from actor Viraj Amonsin to Gregory Peck, dated November 24, 1958, *Pork Chop Hill* files, Gregory Peck Special Collection of the Library of the Academy of Motion Picture Arts and Sciences.
Brown, Harry. Letter to author Steven Jay Rubin, November 2, 1975 (*A Walk in the Sun*).
Peck, Gregory. Letter from Gregory Peck to United Artists' Arnold Picker, dated June 12, 1959, *Pork Chop Hill* files, Gregory Peck Special Collection of the Library of the Academy of Motion Picture Arts and Sciences.
Picker, Arnold. Letter from Arnold Picker, United Artists, to Gregory Peck, dated June 16, 1959, *Pork Chop Hill* files, Gregory Peck Special Collection of the Library of the Academy of Motion Picture Arts and Sciences.
_____. Letter from Arnold Picker, United Artists, to Gregory Peck, dated June 23, 1959, *Pork Chop Hill* files, Gregory Peck Special Collection of the Library of the Academy of Motion Picture Arts and Sciences.
Shurlock, Geoffrey M. Letter, dated April 11, 1958 from Geoffrey M. Shurlock, vice-president and director, Production Code Administration, Motion Picture Association of America to Marvin B. Meyer, Melville Productions (*Pork Chop Hill*).
Webb, James R. Letter, dated June 13, 1958, from screenwriter James R. Webb to Mr. Hiram W. Kwan, attorney at law, chairman, Citizens Rights Committee for the Chinese American Citizens Alliance (*Pork Chop Hill*).
Wilson, Michael. Letter to author Steven Jay Rubin, May 9, 1975 (*The Bridge on the River Kwai*).

Books

Boulle, Pierre. *My Own River Kwai*. Jackson, TN: Vanguard Press, 1967.
Brickhill, Paul, *The Great Escape*, Crest Books, March 1961 (first published by W.W. Norton, 1950).
Brown, Harry. *A Walk in the Sun*. Lincoln: University of Nebraska Press, 1998 (first published by Alfred Knopf, 1944).
Gussow, Mel. *Don't Say Yes Until I Finish Talking: A Biography of Darryl F. Zanuck*. Garden City, NY: Doubleday, 1971.
Marshall, S. L. A. *Pork Chop Hill*. New York: Caliber Books, 2000 (first published by William Morrow, 1956).

Articles

American Film Magazine, January/February 1987 (*Platoon*).
Citizen's News, April 19, 1945 (*A Walk in the Sun*).
Cue Magazine, January 12, 1946 (*A Walk in the Sun*).
Daily Variety, October 3, 1961 (*The Longest Day*).
Daily Variety, November 28, 1945 (*A Walk in the Sun*).
Daily Variety, February 19, 1999 (*Saving Private Ryan*).
Detour Magazine, March 1999 (*Saving Private Ryan*).
Film Daily, December 5, 1960 (*The Longest Day*).
Films and Filming Magazine, February 1974 (The Great Escape).
Film and Video Production, June 1987 (*Platoon*).
Hollywood Reporter, September 10, 1985 (*Platoon*).
Hollywood Reporter, December 13, 2009 (*The Hurt Locker*).
Life Magazine, October 12, 1962 (*The Longest Day*).
London Daily Telegraph, August 25, 2009 (*The Hurt Locker*).
Look Magazine, June 10, 1969 (*The Longest Day*).
Los Angeles Daily News, Celebrities Column by Marilyn Beck and Stacy Jenel Smith, August 26, 1997 (*Saving Private Ryan*).
Los Angeles Times, June 26, 1946 (*A Walk in the Sun*).
Los Angeles Times, November 20, 1949 (*Battleground*).
Los Angeles Times, December 22, 1965 (*The Sand Pebbles*).
Los Angeles Times, December 28, 1986 (*Platoon*).
Los Angeles Times, March 29, 1987 (*Platoon*).
Los Angeles Times, February 19, 1988 (*Platoon*).
Los Angeles Times, July 19, 1998 (*Saving Private Ryan*).
New York Daily News, August 2, 1998 (*Saving Private Ryan*).
The New Yorker, July 27, 1998 (*Saving Private Ryan*).
New York Times, January 13, 1946 (*A Walk in the Sun*).
New York Times, October 23, 1949 (*Battleground*).
New York Times, January 1987 (*Platoon*).
Orange County Register, October 13, 1993 (*Gettysburg*).
Rave Magazine, July 24, 1998 (*Saving Private Ryan*).
Rolling Stone Magazine, January 29, 1987 (*Platoon*).
Screen Crave, June 22, 2009 (*The Hurt Locker*).
Screen Crave, June 23, 2009 (*The Hurt Locker*).
Screen International, March 14, 1987 (*Platoon*).
The Times of London, August 19, 1998 (*Saving Private Ryan*).
Variety, Weekly Edition, June 8, 1960 (*The Longest Day*).
Variety, Weekly Edition, October 24, 1961 (*The Longest Day*).

Papers

Gallo, Lew. Gregory Peck Special Collection of the Academy of Motion Picture Arts and Sciences.
Kopelson, Arnold. *My Platoon Experience*, 2003.
Milestone, Lewis. Academy of Motion Picture Arts and Sciences, Los Angeles.
Singer, Michael. *Platoon* papers, April 20, 2002.

Radio Interviews

Reel Time, Sirius Radio, March 2010 (*The Hurt Locker*).

DVD Commentary Tracks

Gettysburg, Turner Pictures.
The Hurt Locker, Summit Entertainment.
Platoon, Orion Pictures.
The Sand Pebbles, 20th Century–Fox.
Saving Private Ryan, DreamWorks/Paramount Pictures.

Index

Page numbers in *bold italics* indicate illustrations.